Better Homes and Gardens®

BIGGEST BOOK OF
SOUPS
& STEWS

Meredith® Books
Des Moines, Iowa

BIGGEST BOOK OF SOUPS & STEWS

Project Editor: Shelli McConnell
Contributing Editors: Janet Figg; Linda J. Henry; Kristi Thomas, R.D.; Mary Williams
Writer: Lisa Kingsley
Contributing Designer: Joyce DeWitt
Cover Designer: Daniel Pelavin
Copy Chief: Terri Fredrickson
Publishing Operations Manager: Karen Schirm
Senior Editor, Asset and Information Manager: Phillip Morgan
Edit and Design Production Coordinator: Mary Lee Gavin
Editorial Assistant: Cheryl Eckert
Book Production Managers: Pam Kvitne, Marjorie J. Schenkelberg, Rick von Holdt, Mark Weaver
Contributing Copy Editor: Michelle Bolton King
Contributing Proofreaders: Gretchen Kauffman, Susan J. Kling, Diane Penningroth
Indexer: Kathleen Poole
Test Kitchen Director: Lynn Blanchard
Test Kitchen Product Supervisor: Marilyn Cornelius
Test Kitchen Home Economists: Paige Boyle; Marilyn Cornelius; Juliana Hale; Laura Harms, R.D.; Jennifer Kalinowski, R.D.;
    Maryellyn Krantz; Jill Moberly; Dianna Nolin; Colleen Weeden; Lori Wilson; Charles Worthington

Meredith® Books
Executive Director, Editorial: Gregory H. Kayko
Executive Director, Design: Matt Strelecki
Senior Editor/Group Manager: Jan Miller
Marketing Product Managers: Gina Rickert

Publisher and Editor in Chief: James D. Blume
Editorial Director: Linda Raglan Cunningham
Executive Director, New Business Development: Todd M. Davis
Executive Director, Sales: Ken Zagor
Director, Operations: George A. Susral
Director, Production: Douglas M. Johnston
Director, Marketing: Amy Nichols
Business Director: Jim Leonard

Vice President and General Manager: Douglas J. Guendel

Better Homes and Gardens® Magazine
Editor in Chief: Karol DeWulf Nickell
Deputy Editor, Food and Entertaining: Nancy Hopkins

Meredith Publishing Group
President: Jack Griffin
Executive Vice President: Bob Mate

Meredith Corporation
Chairman and Chief Executive Officer: William T. Kerr
President and Chief Operating Officer: Stephen M. Lacy

In Memoriam: E. T. Meredith III (1933-2003)

Our Better Homes and Gardens® Test Kitchen seal on the back cover of this book assures you that every recipe in *Biggest Book of Soups & Stews* has been tested in the Better Homes and Gardens® Test Kitchen. This means that each recipe is practical and reliable, and meets our high standards of taste appeal. We guarantee your satisfaction with this book for as long as you own it.

Copyright © 2005 by Meredith Corporation, Des Moines, Iowa. First Edition. All rights reserved. Printed in the China.
Library of Congress Control Number: 2005921395
ISBN: 0-696-22580-8

All of us at Meredith® Books are dedicated to providing you with the information and ideas you need to create delicious foods. We welcome your comments and suggestions. Write to us at: Meredith Books, Cookbook Editorial Department, 1716 Locust St., Des Moines, IA 50309-3023.

If you would like to purchase any of our cooking, crafts, gardening, home improvement, or home decorating and design books, check wherever quality books are sold. Or visit us at: **meredithbooks.com**

Pictured on front cover:
Fireside Beef Stew, page 334; Champion Chili with the Works, page 247; Vegetable & Orzo Soup with Pistou, page 161

TABLE OF CONTENTS

INTRODUCTION

It's no wonder the Mock Turtle from *Alice's Adventures in Wonderland* enthuses, *"Beautiful Soup, so rich and green, waiting in a hot tureen! Who for such dainties would not stoop? Soup of the evening, beautiful soup!"*

Simply put, soup is good-mood food: If you're not in one, eat some and you will be. Soup is also one of the world's most versatile and perfect foods. There are hot soup for cold days and cold soup for hot days, simple soup to start a meal, and hearty stew that is a meal. Soup can be creamy and rich or brothy and light. And you can't beat it for convenience. Make a big pot of soup and enjoy leftovers the rest of the week or put it in the freezer for a future date.

With more than 350 recipes, *Biggest Book of Soups & Stews* has a bowl for every taste and every situation—long-simmering soups for special occasions and weeknight soups that will satisfy the troops in 30 minutes or less. Whether you prefer chowder or chili, hot or cold, soup or stew, there's something in this book for you. In addition to the recipes for soups and stews, the chapter of recipes for salads and breads will help you make your soup a meal. The Soup Basics section tells you how to make a great bowl of soup from start to finish—from broth to toppers.

So get stirring: It's always a good time for soup!

SOUP BASICS

D0903795

SOUP TALK

When does a soup become a stew—
and what's the difference between a
stew and a ragoût? In general, these
are the categories of soups and stews:

• **Soup:** Any combination of meat,
poultry, fish, and vegetables cooked in
liquid. There are broth-based soups
and cream soups.

• **Stew:** A long-simmered combination
of meat, poultry, fish, and vegetables
cooked in a stewing liquid such as
broth or stock and the natural juices
from the ingredients. Stews have less
liquid than soups, are usually chunkier,
and are often thickened with flour or
some other starch.

• **Ragoût:** A highly seasoned stew
made primarily of meat, poultry, or fish.

• **Bisque:** A velvety soup that's usually
made of pureed seafood, such as lobster
or shrimp, and cream.

• **Chowder:** Any thick, chunky soup
(think of corn chowder), but seafood
chowders usually come to mind when
the word is mentioned. New England-
style chowder has milk or cream in it;
Manhattan-style chowder is made
with tomatoes.

MAKING SOUP

Equipment needs (not much!)

One of the most beautiful things about soup
is that it requires no fancy equipment; you
probably have everything necessary to make
most soups in your kitchen right now.

All you really need for many soups are a
4- to 6-quart Dutch oven, a good chef's knife
and a small paring knife, a cutting board,
measuring spoons and cups, a couple of
wooden spoons, ladles in a few different sizes,
and a medium-mesh strainer for straining
pureed soups if the recipe calls for it.

Stocks and broths

All soups and stews are cooked in liquid
—most often a stock or broth, although
sometimes wine is added too. Generally,
there are four types of stocks or broths:
poultry (chicken or turkey); meat (beef or
veal); vegetable; and seafood. Stocks and
broths are generally interchangeable. Broths
tend to be lighter than stocks, which are
usually more intensely flavored.

Soups always taste best made with
homemade broths or stocks, but life today
doesn't always lend itself to spending a few
hours stirring up broth for the freezer.
When it doesn't, canned broth is perfectly
fine. Try the low-sodium version of canned
broth; it is less salty and has more flavor of
the key ingredient, whether chicken, beef,
or vegetables.

Roast first

One way to get additional flavor into homemade chicken or beef broth is to roast the meat before you combine it with water and any other flavorings, such as vegetables. Roasting concentrates the flavor of the bones and—later—adds to the flavor of your broth. Spread the meat pieces—usually chicken wings, backs, and/or necks, or beef short ribs or shank crosscut bones—in a roasting pan and roast at 450°F about 30 minutes or until well browned. Before transferring the bones to the Dutch oven, drain and reserve any liquid they give off.

Straining broth

The easiest way to separate the solids from the liquid when a homemade broth is made is to strain it through 2 layers of 100-percent-cotton cheesecloth. Line a large colander or sieve with the cheesecloth, then set the colander in a large heatproof bowl. Carefully pour the broth mixture into the lined colander. The solids can then be wrapped up into the cheesecloth and discarded.

Clarifying broth

For an especially clear broth, return strained broth (see "Straining broth," above) to the Dutch oven. Combine 1/4 cup cold water and 1 beaten egg white. Stir the water mixture into the broth and bring to boiling. Remove from heat and let stand for 5 minutes. Strain as directed in "Straining broth," above.

Skimming the fat

If you want to make your homemade broth a bit healthier, you can remove some of the fat. Simply use a large metal spoon and skim off the fat that rises to the top. A more thorough way to remove fat—if you have the time—is to refrigerate the broth for 6 to 8 hours. The fat will solidify on the surface and can easily be removed with a spoon.

Browning meats

Recipes for stews often call for browning cubes of meat in oil—sometimes after coating them with flour—before combining them with the rest of the ingredients. This preparation accomplishes a couple of things: It gives the meat a beautiful mahogany color and toothsome crust that cooking in liquid alone doesn't; it also creates drippings in the bottom of the pan that contribute great flavor to your stew. Any flour used to coat the cubes of meat before browning also helps to thicken the stew.

Chop, chop!

One thing that all soups and stews have in common is that they are made with ingredients that are cut into smaller pieces than the hunk of meat, the onion, or the potato with which you started. How you cut those ingredients affects how the soup will look and taste. A large chunk of garlic, for instance, tastes entirely different from a tiny mince of it—even if its flavor does mellow when it's cooked. Here are some common cuts:

Slice: Thin pieces of vegetables, meat, or fruit. You can usually still detect the shape of the original ingredient, such as rounds of carrot, onion, or zucchini.

Cube: Large pieces—usually of meat or potatoes—cut in rough squares. Cubes are usually between 1/2 and 1 inch in size.

Dice: Small cubes, usually between 1/4 and 1/2 inch in size.

Mince: The tiniest, finest cut of all. Minced garlic, herbs, or citrus peel, for instance, has the consistency of fine confetti.

Chop: Pieces are not uniform in size. They're bigger than a mince but smaller than a cube. You can chop with a knife, a chopper, or in a food processor.

Julienne: Thin, fine sticks of vegetables or fruit that are usually 2 or 3 inches long and about 1/8 inch square.

Adding herbs

Herbs are wonderful for flavoring soup. Whether you are using fresh or dried herbs determines when you add them to the kettle. Dried herbs are usually added at the beginning of cooking so they have time to rehydrate and release their flavor. Fresh herbs, on the other hand, are usually added right before serving so they retain their flavor and color. Fresh herbs should appear fresh and green— not wilted and gray.

Perfectly pureed

Creamy soups—whether they have cream in them or not—get that way by being pureed. Bisques employ this technique across the board. Many bean soups are at least partially pureed with some of the liquid to give the soup body and a smooth texture. Soups can be pureed in a couple of different ways:

Using a blender or food processor: Ladle the soup into the blender or food processor until the vessel is no more than one-third full. If you're using a blender, make sure the lid is on—although you might want to remove the round plastic piece in the center of the lid to let steam escape and avoid getting burned. Hold a towel around the seal of the lid and always use slow speed. Transfer the pureed soup to a bowl. Repeat the process, then pour all of the pureed soup back into the soup kettle.

Using an immersion blender: You can put this handheld blender directly in the soup kettle to puree the soup. If you make a lot of creamy soups, it's a great idea to invest in one of these handy gadgets. They make the job of pureeing soups much easier, safer, and less messy than with a blender or food processor.

SERVING SOUP
Temperature matters
Serving cold soup in a chilled bowl and hot soup in a warm bowl enhances the experience of eating. It will keep your soup appropriately cold or hot longer than if you don't do it, and it requires very little effort:

To warm bowls: Turn your oven to its lowest setting to preheat, then turn it off. Place the bowls in the oven for 5 or 10 minutes before serving time.

To chill bowls: Place bowls in the refrigerator 10 to 15 minutes before serving time.

Top it off

A garnish or topper is the icing on the cake, so to speak, of a bowl of soup or stew. Toppers add flavor, freshness, texture, color, and visual appeal to all kinds of soups.

Some recipes may call for a specific garnish; others can be improvised based on the ingredients or the flavor profile of the dish—and what you have in your refrigerator or pantry. (Consider salsa, for instance, on a Mexican-style soup or sliced scallions for an Asian-style soup.) Offering soup toppers is a simple step toward a great presentation.

Think about any of the following, purchased or homemade:

Croutons
Crispy fried wonton strips
Fried or toasted tortilla strips
Interesting crackers
Toast points
Squares or triangles of baked puff pastry
Gremolata
Pesto
Tapenade
Chopped or sliced olives
Edible flowers
Fresh herbs, sprigs or chopped
Scallions
Sliced or diced fruit; whole berries
Citrus peel
Slices of lemon, orange, or lime
Smoked paprika
Chopped pistachios
Toasted pine nuts
Sliced toasted almonds
Very thin slices of fresh chile pepper
Salsa
Splash of extra-virgin olive oil
Caviar
Crumbled crisp-cooked bacon
Crumbled or diced hard-cooked eggs
Grated cheese
Sour cream, crème fraîche, or yogurt
Slice of flavored butter *(herbed, chile pepper, garlic, sun-dried tomato)*

Tuck in: beds for stews

The bottom of the bowl can be as interesting as the top. Stews can be eaten with or without a "bed," that is, a starchy base on which to ladle this thicker, heartier version of soup. As with toppers, a recipe may call for a specific type of accompaniment, but other options almost always exist. Consider the following and choose based on the ethnic origin or flavor profile of the stew:

Couscous
Mashed potatoes
Pasta or buttered noodles
Rice
Soft-cooked polenta
Toasted bread or crostini

STORING SOUPS & STEWS

Soup, by nature, is usually made in fairly large quantities. So unless you're hosting a big dinner party or feeding the neighborhood, you're almost assured of some leftovers. (Sometimes you may intentionally make a double batch.) Whether they're intentional or not, soup leftovers are always welcome.

For short-term storage, ladle the cooled soup into a covered container and store in the refrigerator for up to 4 days. For long-term storage, ladle the cooled soup into an airtight container and freeze for up to 3 months. Always defrost in the refrigerator, not at room temperature.

Use this basic broth as the base for many soups.

CHICKEN BROTH

3	pounds bony chicken pieces (wings, backs, and/or necks)
3	stalks celery with leaves, cut up
2	carrots, cut up
1	large onion, unpeeled and cut up
1	teaspoon salt
1	teaspoon dried thyme, sage, or basil, crushed
1/2	teaspoon whole black peppercorns or 1/4 teaspoon black pepper
4	fresh parsley sprigs
2	bay leaves
2	garlic cloves, unpeeled and halved
6	cups cold water

PREP:
25 minutes
COOK:
2 1/2 hours
MAKES:
about 6 cups broth

1 If using wings, cut each wing at joints into 3 pieces. Place chicken pieces in a 6-quart Dutch oven. Add celery, carrots, onion, salt, thyme, parsley, peppercorns, bay leaves, and garlic. Add water. Bring to boiling; reduce heat. Simmer, covered, for 2 1/2 hours. Remove chicken pieces from broth.

2 Strain broth. Discard vegetables and seasonings. If desired, clarify broth. If using the broth while hot, skim off fat. Or chill broth; lift off fat.

3 If desired, when bones are cool enough to handle, remove meat; reserve for another use. Discard bones. Store broth and reserved meat in separate containers. Cover and chill for up to 3 days or freeze for up to 6 months.

Nutrition Facts per cup broth: 30 cal., 2 g total fat (1 g sat. fat), 5 mg chol., 435 mg sodium, 1 g carbo., 0 g fiber, 2 g pro.

Roasting the soup bones first develops their rich flavor.

BEEF BROTH

PREP:

30 minutes

ROAST:

30 minutes

COOK:

3¹/₂ hours

OVEN:

450°F

MAKES:

8 to 9 cups broth

4	pounds meaty beef soup bones (beef shank cross cuts or short ribs)
10½	cups water
3	carrots, cut up
2	medium onions, unpeeled and cut up
2	stalks celery with leaves, cut up
1	tablespoon dried basil or thyme, crushed
1½	teaspoons salt
10	whole black peppercorns
8	fresh parsley sprigs
4	bay leaves
2	cloves garlic, unpeeled and halved

1 Place soup bones in a large shallow roasting pan. Roast in a 450° oven about 30 minutes or until well browned, turning once. Transfer soup bones to a large kettle. Pour ¹/₂ cup of the water into the roasting pan and scrape up browned bits; add water mixture to kettle. Stir in carrots, onions, celery, basil, salt, peppercorns, parsley, bay leaves, and garlic. Add the remaining 10 cups water. Bring to boiling; reduce heat. Simmer, covered, for 3¹/₂ hours. Remove soup bones.

2 Strain broth. Discard vegetables and seasonings. If desired, clarify broth. If using the broth while hot, skim off fat. Or chill broth; lift off fat.

3 If desired, when bones are cool enough to handle, remove meat; reserve for another use. Discard bones. Store broth and reserved meat in separate containers. Cover and chill for up to 3 days or freeze for up to 6 months.

Nutrition Facts per cup broth: 38 cal., 3 g total fat (1 g sat. fat), 5 mg chol., 598 mg sodium, 1 g carbo., 0 g fiber, 1 g pro.

Stir-frying the vegetables helps caramelize their natural sugars and mellows the flavors.

VEGETABLE BROTH

1	tablespoon olive oil
4	medium yellow onions, unpeeled and cut into wedges
4	medium carrots, cut into 2-inch pieces
3	medium potatoes, cut into 2-inch pieces
2	medium parsnips, turnips, or rutabagas, cut into 2-inch pieces
1	small head cabbage, cut into 2-inch pieces
8	cups water
1	teaspoon salt
½	teaspoon dried dill, basil, rosemary, or marjoram, crushed
¼	teaspoon black pepper

1 In a 6-quart Dutch oven heat oil. Add onions, carrots, potatoes, parsnips, and cabbage; cook and stir over medium heat about 10 minutes or until vegetables start to brown. Stir in water, salt, dill, and pepper. Bring to boiling; reduce heat. Simmer, covered, for 2 hours.

2 Strain broth. Discard vegetables and seasonings. If desired, clarify broth. If using the broth while hot, skim off fat. Or chill broth; lift off fat. Cover and chill for up to 3 days or freeze for up to 6 months.

Nutrition Facts per cup broth: 36 cal., 2 g total fat (0 g sat. fat), 0 mg chol., 347 mg sodium, 4 g carbo., 0 g fiber, 1 g pro.

PREP:

30 minutes

COOK:

2 hours

MAKES:

about 7 cups broth

For a sensational meatless soup, cook wild rice and vegetables in this all-vegetable stock.

ROASTED MUSHROOM BROTH

PREP:

20 minutes

ROAST:

30 minutes

COOK:

2 hours

OVEN:

450°F

MAKES:

about 4 cups broth

4   medium onions, unpeeled and quartered

4   stalks celery with leaves, cut up

2   carrots, cut up

6   cloves garlic, halved

1   teaspoon salt

¼   teaspoon whole black peppercorns

2   pounds fresh button or other mushrooms, halved

4   cups cold water

2   fresh thyme sprigs or 2 teaspoons dried thyme, crushed

2   fresh marjoram sprigs or 2 teaspoons dried marjoram, crushed

2   fresh parsley sprigs

1 Place onions, celery, carrots, and garlic into a shallow roasting pan. Sprinkle with salt and peppercorns. Roast, uncovered, in a 450° oven for 15 minutes. Stir in mushrooms; roast for 15 minutes more.

2 Transfer vegetable mixture to a 6- to 8-quart Dutch oven. Stir in water. Bring to boiling over high heat; reduce heat. Simmer, covered, for 1½ hours. Stir in thyme, marjoram, and parsley. Simmer, covered, for 30 minutes more.

3 Strain broth. Discard vegetables and seasonings. If desired, clarify broth. Cover and chill for up to 3 days or freeze for up to 6 months.

Nutrition Facts per cup broth: 30 cal., 1 g total fat (0 g sat. fat), 0 mg chol., 603 mg sodium, 5 g carbo., 0 g fiber, 2 g pro.

COLD & HOT SIDE-DISH SOUPS

1

Perfectly ripe avocados are firm but yield to gentle pressure. To ripen avocados, place them in a brown paper bag on the countertop for 2 to 4 days. Store ripe avocados in the refrigerator for a few days to keep them at their prime.

CHILLED AVOCADO SOUP

PREP:

15 minutes

CHILL:

3 hours

MAKES:

6 servings

3	ripe avocados, halved, seeded, and peeled
1	cup chicken broth
¼	cup water
1	cup half-and-half or light cream
¼	teaspoon salt
⅛	teaspoon onion powder
	Dash white pepper
1	tablespoon lemon juice
	Lemon slices (optional)

1 Place avocados in a blender or food processor. Add broth and water; cover and blend or process until smooth. Add half-and-half, salt, onion powder, and white pepper. Cover and blend or process until combined.

2 Transfer to a glass bowl. Stir in lemon juice. Cover and chill for at least 3 hours or up to 24 hours. Stir before serving. If desired, garnish with lemon slices.

Nutrition Facts per serving: 167 cal., 15 g total fat (5 g sat. fat), 15 mg chol., 287 mg sodium, 7 g carbo., 3 g fiber, 3 g pro.

Serve this chilled soup in small bowls nestled in bowls of ice or in mugs garnished with celery sticks.

GAZPACHO

6	medium Roma tomatoes, quartered
1½	cups vegetable or tomato juice
3	tablespoons red or white wine vinegar
3	tablespoons olive oil
½	teaspoon Worcestershire sauce
1	clove garlic, halved
1¾	cups chopped, seeded cucumber
1	cup chopped cauliflower
¾	cup chopped green sweet pepper
½	cup chopped onion
¼	cup snipped fresh parsley
3	tablespoons snipped fresh chives
1	tablespoon snipped fresh thyme
½	teaspoon salt
½	teaspoon black pepper

PREP:
30 minutes
CHILL:
4 hours
MAKES:
8 to 10 servings

1 In a blender or food processor combine tomatoes, vegetable juice, vinegar, oil, Worcestershire sauce, and garlic. Cover and blend or process until smooth.

2 Transfer tomato mixture into a large glass bowl. Stir in cucumber, cauliflower, sweet pepper, onion, parsley, chives, thyme, salt, and black pepper. Cover and chill for 4 to 24 hours. Stir before serving.

Nutrition Facts per serving: 81 cal., 5 g total fat (1 g sat. fat), 0 mg chol., 281 mg sodium, 8 g carbo., 2 g fiber, 2 g pro.

This make-ahead chilled soup is a colorful blend of tomatoes, tomatillos, cucumber, shrimp, and cilantro—it's as refreshing as it is easy. (Recipe pictured on page 97.)

RED & GREEN GAZPACHO

PREP:

30 minutes

CHILL:

1 hour

MAKES:

6 servings

3	cups chopped red and/or partially green tomatoes
½	cup chopped tomatillo
1	16-ounce can tomato juice (2 cups)
½	cup chopped, seeded cucumber
1	tablespoon seeded and finely chopped fresh jalapeño chile pepper*
¼	cup finely chopped green onions
¼	cup finely snipped fresh cilantro
1	clove garlic, minced
1	tablespoon olive oil
1	tablespoon lime juice
¼	teaspoon bottled green pepper sauce
	Dairy sour cream (optional)
6	ounces peeled, cooked medium shrimp (12 to 15)

1 In a glass bowl combine tomatoes, tomatillo, tomato juice, cucumber, jalapeño pepper, green onions, cilantro, garlic, oil, lime juice, and pepper sauce. Cover and chill at least 1 hour.

2 To serve, reserve six shrimp. Coarsely chop remaining shrimp. Stir chopped shrimp into gazpacho. Spoon gazpacho into chilled bowls. If desired, top each serving with a spoonful of sour cream and a reserved whole shrimp.

***NOTE:** When working with chile peppers, wear plastic or rubber gloves. If your bare hands do touch the chile peppers, wash your hands well with soap and water.*

Nutrition Facts per serving: 90 cal., 3 g total fat (0 g sat. fat), 55 mg chol., 371 mg sodium, 10 g carbo., 2 g fiber, 8 g pro.

With lots of lobster and crunchy fresh vegetables, this pleasingly herbed soup is the perfect starter anytime.

LOBSTER GAZPACHO

2	6-ounce fresh or frozen lobster tails
2	cups chopped, peeled tomatoes
1/2	cup chopped, seeded cucumber
1/2	cup chopped green, red, or yellow sweet pepper
3/4	cup vegetable juice cocktail
2	tablespoons sliced green onion
2	tablespoons red wine vinegar
1	tablespoon olive oil
1	tablespoon snipped fresh cilantro or Italian (flat-leaf) parsley
2	teaspoons snipped fresh basil
1	small clove garlic, minced
1/4	teaspoon ground cumin
	Fresh basil sprigs (optional)

PREP:
45 minutes
CHILL:
4 hours
MAKES:
6 servings

1 Thaw lobster tails, if frozen; rinse under cold running water. In a large saucepan cook lobster tails, uncovered, in enough boiling salted water to cover for 7 to 8 minutes or until shells turn bright red and meat is just tender; drain. Hold under cold running tap water. When cool enough to handle, remove and discard shells. Coarsely chop meat (you should have about 1 1/2 cups). Cover and chill until ready to use.

2 In a large glass bowl combine tomatoes, cucumber, sweet pepper, vegetable juice, green onion, vinegar, oil, cilantro, basil, garlic, and cumin. Gently stir in lobster. Cover and chill for 4 to 8 hours to allow flavors to blend. If desired, garnish with basil sprigs.

Nutrition Facts per serving: 102 cal., 3 g total fat (0 g sat. fat), 54 mg chol., 259 mg sodium, 7 g carbo., 2 g fiber, 12 g pro.

Soymilk, an increasingly popular alternative to milk, is now available at most grocery stores.

SMOOTH & CHUNKY MELON SOUP

PREP:

15 minutes

CHILL:

3 hours

MAKES:

8 servings

6	cups cubed cantaloupe
1½	cups mango nectar
1	teaspoon freshly ground dried whole green or black peppercorns
1½	cups vanilla-enriched soy-based beverage (soymilk) or 1½ cups plain yogurt
2	cups cubed cantaloupe and/or honeydew melon (optional)
	Peppered Yogurt (optional)
	Prosciutto Gremolata (optional)

1 In a blender or food processor combine 3 cups of the cantaloupe, half of the nectar, and ½ teaspoon of the pepper. Cover and blend or process until smooth. Transfer to a bowl. Repeat with remaining 3 cups cantaloupe, nectar, and pepper.

2 Stir soymilk into cantaloupe mixture in bowl. Cover and chill for 3 hours or until serving.

3 Ladle soup into bowls and, if desired, add some of the remaining melon cubes in the center of each bowl. If desired, garnish with Peppered Yogurt and Prosciutto Gremolata.

Nutrition Facts per serving: 99 cal., 1 g total fat (0 g sat. fat), 0 mg chol., 38 mg sodium, 21 g carbo., 1 g fiber, 2 g pro.

PEPPERED YOGURT: In a small bowl stir ½ teaspoon freshly cracked dried whole green or black peppercorns into ½ cup plain yogurt. Store in refrigerator.

PROSCIUTTO GREMOLATA: In a small bowl combine 2 ounces chopped prosciutto, 1½ teaspoons snipped fresh parsley, and 1 teaspoon finely shredded lemon peel.

This tangy soup is the perfect way to start a spring or summer brunch.

STRAWBERRY-MELON SOUP

1   small cantaloupe
½   of a small honeydew melon
½   cup unsweetened pineapple juice
⅓   cup sugar
1   tablespoon grated fresh ginger
4   cups fresh or frozen unsweetened strawberries
1   8-ounce carton vanilla yogurt
1   8-ounce carton dairy sour cream
2   cups milk

PREP:
30 minutes
COOK:
5 minutes
CHILL:
overnight
MAKES:
8 to 10 servings

1 Using a small melon baller, scoop cantaloupe and honeydew into balls or use a knife to cut melons into cubes. (You should have about 4 cups cantaloupe and 2 cups honeydew.) Set melon aside.

2 In a small saucepan combine pineapple juice, sugar, and ginger. Bring to boiling, stirring until sugar dissolves; reduce heat. Simmer, uncovered, over medium heat for 5 to 7 minutes or until mixture is the consistency of a thin syrup. Remove from heat; cool. Transfer syrup to a storage container. Add 2 cups of the cantaloupe pieces and all of the honeydew pieces. Cover and chill overnight.

3 Meanwhile, place strawberries in a blender or food processor. Cover and blend or process until smooth; remove and set aside. Cover and blend or process remaining 2 cups cantaloupe pieces until smooth. In a large glass bowl stir together yogurt and sour cream. Add pureed strawberries, pureed melon, and milk; stir until combined. Cover and chill overnight.

4 To serve, drain melon balls, reserving syrup. Stir reserved syrup into chilled soup. Ladle soup into chilled bowls; top with melon balls.

Nutrition Facts per serving: 220 cal., 8 g total fat (5 g sat. fat), 19 mg chol., 77 mg sodium, 34 g carbo., 3 g fiber, 6 g pro.

On a sweltering summer day, nothing refreshes like watermelon. This light soup provides a delightful new way to chill out.

WATERMELON SOUP WITH VEGETABLES

PREP:

25 minutes

CHILL:

4 hours

MAKES:

6 servings

1   5- to 6-pound seedless watermelon
Sugar (optional)

¾ cup thin strips of carrot, zucchini, and/or
yellow summer squash

1   tablespoon balsamic vinegar

1 Halve melon; scoop out pulp. Process in batches in a blender or food processor. Line a large colander with a double thickness of 100-percent-cotton cheesecloth. Strain pulp through cheesecloth, pressing out as much juice as possible. Discard pulp. Measure 6 cups of the juice (save remaining for another use or add water if necessary to make 6 cups).

2 If desired, add sugar to taste to the 6 cups juice. Chill until ready to serve.

3 Meanwhile, cook vegetables in a small amount of boiling lightly salted water for 2 minutes. Drain and transfer to a bowl of ice water to cool. Drain and wrap in plastic wrap; chill 4 hours or until ready to serve.

4 Stir vinegar into juice mixture. Ladle into soup bowls. Float vegetables on top.

Nutrition Facts per serving: 69 cal., 0 g total fat (0 g sat. fat), 0 mg chol., 13 mg sodium, 17 g carbo., 1 g fiber, 1 g pro.

This refreshing chilled fruit soup is the perfect curtain-raiser for a springtime brunch.

TROPICAL FRUIT SOUP

2   cups cubed, peeled mango, papaya, and/or cantaloupe

¾   cup passion fruit nectar

2   teaspoons snipped fresh mint

1½   cups cubed pineapple

¾   cup papaya, mango, or guava nectar

    Sliced strawberries (optional)

    Fresh mint leaves (optional)

1 In a blender or food processor combine mango, passion fruit nectar, and mint. Cover and blend or process until nearly smooth; transfer to a large glass bowl.

2 In the same blender or food processor combine pineapple and papaya nectar. Cover and blend or process until nearly smooth; add to mango mixture in bowl, stirring to combine. Cover and chill for 4 to 24 hours. If desired, garnish with strawberries and mint.

Nutrition Facts per serving: 121 cal., 1 g total fat (0 g sat. fat), 0 mg chol., 4 mg sodium, 31 g carbo., 3 g fiber, 1 g pro.

PREP:
20 minutes
CHILL:
4 hours
MAKES:
4 to 6 servings

Using a high oven temperature concentrates the mulled-fruit flavor of the pear, plums, cranberries, and apple in this gently spiced dessert soup.

ROASTED FRUIT SOUP

PREP:

10 minutes

ROAST:

35 minutes

OVEN:

450°F

MAKES:

6 servings

1   cup cranberries

½   cup packed brown sugar

1   medium pear, cored and cut into thin wedges

1   medium cooking apple (such as Rome Beauty, Jonathan, or Fuji), cored and cut into wedges

3   plums, halved and pitted

3   cups cranberry-apple juice

1   tablespoon lemon juice

2   3-inch pieces stick cinnamon

1 In a 3-quart rectangular baking dish stir together cranberries and brown sugar. Add pear and apple wedges. Roast, uncovered, in a 450° oven about 20 minutes or just until fruit is tender. Add plum halves. Roast, uncovered, for 15 minutes more or until fruit is tender and edges of fruit begin to brown or curl. Stir gently to combine.

2 Meanwhile, in a large saucepan combine cranberry-apple juice, lemon juice, and cinnamon sticks. Bring to boiling; reduce heat. Simmer, uncovered, for 10 minutes. Remove and discard cinnamon sticks. Gently stir fruits and their juices into cooked mixture in saucepan.

Nutrition Facts per serving: 185 cal., 0 g total fat (0 g sat. fat), 0 mg chol., 7 mg sodium, 47 g carbo., 3 g fiber, 1 g pro.

Roasting the vegetables takes only a little more time than cooking them in water and pays big flavor returns.

ROASTED ASPARAGUS SOUP

2	bunches green onions
1½	pounds asparagus, trimmed and cut in 2- to 3-inch pieces
1	medium onion, cut into thin wedges
2	tablespoons olive oil
2	14-ounce cans reduced-sodium chicken broth or 3½ cups homemade chicken broth
¼	teaspoon salt
¼	teaspoon black pepper
½	cup half-and-half, light cream, or milk
1	tablespoon snipped fresh dill
	Fresh dill sprigs (optional)

PREP:
15 minutes
ROAST:
15 minutes
OVEN:
450°F
MAKES:
5 or 6 servings

1 Trim root ends from green onions. Cut white parts into 1-inch lengths. Cut green tops into 1-inch lengths and reserve. Place the white onion parts, asparagus, and onion wedges in an even layer in a shallow large roasting pan. Drizzle vegetables with olive oil. Roast, uncovered, in a 450° oven for 15 to 20 minutes or until vegetables are charred and tender, stirring once.

2 Transfer half of the roasted vegetables to a blender or food processor. Add half a can of broth. Cover and blend or process until smooth. Transfer to a large saucepan. Repeat with remaining roasted vegetables, and half a can of broth. Stir in remaining can of broth, salt, and pepper. Heat through. Stir in half-and-half and snipped fresh dill. Top with reserved green sections of onions and, if desired, dill sprigs.

Nutrition Facts per serving: 128 cal., 8 g total fat (3 g sat. fat), 9 mg chol., 598 mg sodium, 10 g carbo., 3 g fiber, 6 g pro.

Wrap the unused half of the vanilla bean in plastic wrap, place in an airtight jar, and store in the refrigerator for up to 6 months. (Recipe pictured on page 99.)

GREEN BEAN SOUP

PREP:

25 minutes

COOK:

15 minutes

MAKES:

6 to 8 servings

2   14-ounce cans vegetable broth or 3½ cups homemade vegetable broth

½   cup chopped onion

½   of a vanilla bean, split lengthwise

3   tablespoons butter or margarine, softened

3   tablespoons all-purpose flour

1   pound green beans, trimmed and cut into bite-size pieces (3 to 3½ cups)

1   recipe Herbed Sourdough Breadsticks (optional)

1 In a large saucepan bring broth, onion, and vanilla bean to boiling; reduce heat. Simmer, covered, for 10 minutes or until onion is tender. Discard vanilla bean.

2 In a small bowl stir together butter and flour. Whisk into broth mixture. Cook and stir until slightly thickened and bubbly.

3 Add beans to broth mixture. Return to boiling; reduce heat. Simmer, covered, for 5 to 7 minutes more or until beans are crisp-tender. If desired, serve with Herbed Sourdough Breadsticks.

Nutrition Facts per serving: 94 cal., 7 g total fat (4 g sat. fat), 16 mg chol., 607 mg sodium, 11 g carbo., 3 g fiber, 2 g pro.

HERBED SOURDOUGH BREADSTICKS: Cut half of a 12-inch sourdough baguette lengthwise into ½-inch slices. Cut the slices into 1-inch-wide sticks. Brush cut surfaces with 2 tablespoons olive oil and sprinkle with 1 teaspoon snipped fresh thyme. Place on baking sheet. Bake in a 375°F oven about 16 minutes or until golden, turning once.

It takes just five ingredients to capture the old-world feeling of this traditional soup. (Recipe pictured on page 99.)

BEET SOUP

1¾   pounds small beets

1   tablespoon olive oil

1   or 2 cloves garlic, minced

1½   cups diced, peeled russet potato

2   14-ounce cans chicken broth or 3½ cups
     homemade chicken broth

     Salt

     Black pepper

     Crème Fraîche or dairy sour cream (optional)

PREP:
15 minutes
COOK:
1 hour
MAKES:
6 servings

1 Cut off all but 1 inch of beet stems and roots; wash beets. Do not peel. In a large covered saucepan cook beets in boiling salted water for 35 to 45 minutes or until tender. Drain and cool slightly. Slip skins off beets, discarding stems and roots. Dice beets.

2 In the saucepan heat oil. Add garlic; cook over medium heat about 1 minute. Add potato; cook and stir for 5 minutes. Add beets and broth. Bring to boiling; reduce heat. Simmer, covered, for 20 minutes.

3 Transfer half of the mixture to a blender or food processor. Cover and blend or process until smooth. Repeat with remaining mixture. Return all beet mixture to the saucepan; heat through. Season to taste with salt and pepper. If desired, top with Crème Fraîche.

Nutrition Facts per serving: 124 cal., 4 g total fat (1 g sat. fat), 0 mg chol., 700 mg sodium, 20 g carbo., 3 g fiber, 4 g pro.

CRÈME FRAÎCHE: In a medium bowl whisk together ½ cup dairy sour cream and ½ cup whipping cream (not ultra-pasteurized). Cover with plastic wrap. Let stand at room temperature for 5 to 8 hours or until mixture thickens. When thickened, cover and chill until serving time or up to 48 hours. Stir before serving.

The earthy, fresh flavor of mushrooms complements the beets.

BORSCHT

PREP:
20 minutes

COOK:
50 minutes

STAND:
20 minutes

MAKES:
8 servings

3	cups boiling water
¾	to 1 ounce dried mushrooms
2	teaspoons cooking oil
1	cup chopped onion
2	cups peeled and chopped beets (about 12 ounces)
½	cup chopped carrot
½	cup chopped celery
1	14-ounce can beef broth or 1¾ cups homemade beef broth
1	medium onion, peeled but left whole
2	bay leaves
1	tablespoon tomato paste
1	teaspoon lemon juice
½	teaspoon black pepper
¼	teaspoon salt
1	cup chopped cabbage
½	cup dairy sour cream

1 In a medium bowl pour the boiling water over dried mushrooms; let stand for 20 minutes. Drain mushrooms in a strainer, reserving liquid. Rinse mushrooms well under running water. Drain mushrooms; cut up large pieces. Line a strainer with 100-percent-cotton cheesecloth. Pour reserved mushroom liquid through cheesecloth-lined strainer to remove any grit. Measure mushroom liquid; add enough water to equal 3 cups total liquid. Set aside.

2 In a large saucepan heat oil. Add chopped onion; cook over medium heat for 4 minutes. Add beets, carrot, and celery; cook for 5 minutes more, stirring occasionally. Carefully add mushroom liquid, beef broth, the whole onion, bay leaves, tomato paste, lemon juice, pepper, and salt. Bring to boiling; reduce heat. Simmer, covered, for 20 minutes. Remove and discard the whole onion and bay leaves. Stir in cabbage; simmer, covered, for 20 minutes more. Stir in mushrooms; heat through. Top with sour cream.

Nutrition Facts per serving: 83 cal., 4 g total fat (2 g sat. fat), 5 mg chol., 291 mg sodium, 11 g carbo., 2 g fiber, 2 g pro.

Make extra Curry Croutons to sprinkle over salads.

CREAMY CARROT & NUTMEG SOUP

2	tablespoons butter or margarine
1	tablespoon cooking oil
½	cup chopped onion
3	cups chopped carrots
⅓	cup peeled and chopped turnip
2	14-ounce cans chicken or vegetable broth or 3½ cups homemade chicken or vegetable broth
½	teaspoon ground nutmeg
½	teaspoon salt
¼	teaspoon black pepper
1	recipe Curry Croutons
	Snipped fresh parsley (optional)

PREP:

40 minutes

COOK:

40 minutes

MAKES:

4 servings

1 In a large saucepan heat butter and oil. Add onion; cook and stir over medium heat about 3 minutes or until tender. Add carrots and turnip; cook and stir for 5 minutes.

2 Add broth, nutmeg, salt, and pepper. Bring to boiling; reduce heat. Simmer, covered, for 30 to 35 minutes or until carrots and turnip are tender.

3 Remove soup from heat; cool slightly. Transfer half of the mixture to a blender or food processor. Cover and blend or process until smooth. Return all mixture to the saucepan; heat through. Top with Curry Croutons and, if desired, snipped parsley.

CURRY CROUTONS: Cut 3 slices wheat bread into ¾-inch cubes; set aside. In a large skillet melt 2 tablespoons butter over low heat. Remove skillet from heat. Stir 1 teaspoon curry powder and dash salt into melted butter. Add bread cubes; stir to coat with butter mixture. In a shallow baking pan spread bread cubes in a single layer. Bake in a 300°F oven for 10 minutes; stir. Bake about 10 minutes more or until bread cubes are dry and crisp. Cool before using.

Nutrition Facts per serving: 271 cal., 18 g total fat (9 g sat. fat), 33 mg chol., 1,453 mg sodium, 24 g carbo., 6 g fiber, 6 g pro.

You'll find haricots verts, tiny French green beans, in the specialty section of the produce department.

SPRING CARROT SOUP

START TO FINISH:

25 minutes

MAKES:

4 to 6 servings

1   14-ounce can vegetable broth or 1¾ cups homemade vegetable broth

8   to 10 small carrots with tops, trimmed, scrubbed, halved lengthwise, and then cut in half crosswise (4 ounces)

½   cup trimmed haricots verts or baby green beans

6   ounces peeled and deveined medium shrimp

1   12-ounce can carrot juice

¼   teaspoon bottled hot pepper sauce

Salt

Black pepper

1 In a large saucepan bring vegetable broth to boiling. Add carrots.* Return to boiling; reduce heat. Simmer, covered, for 4 minutes. Add haricots verts and shrimp. Bring to boiling; reduce heat. Simmer, covered, for 3 minutes. Add carrot juice and bottled hot pepper sauce; heat through (do not boil). Season to taste with salt and pepper.

*NOTE: If you prefer the green beans to be more than crisp-tender, add them with the carrots.

Nutrition Facts per serving: 104 cal., 1 g total fat (0 g sat. fat), 65 mg chol., 586 mg sodium, 13 g carbo., 2 g fiber, 11 g pro.

Lemon thyme and fresh lemon slices add a double dose of refreshing flavor to this low-fat soup.

LEMON-ON-LEMON CARROT SOUP

5	cups chicken broth
4	cups carrots sliced ½ inch thick
1	cup sliced leeks (white parts only)
1	bay leaf
3	tablespoons lemon juice
2	to 3 tablespoons snipped fresh lemon thyme or thyme, or 2 to 3 teaspoons dried thyme, crushed
1	teaspoon snipped fresh summer savory (optional)
	Black pepper
1	lemon, thinly sliced
	Fresh lemon thyme or thyme sprigs (optional)

START TO FINISH:

45 minutes

MAKES:

8 to 10 servings

1 In a large saucepan combine broth, carrots, leeks, and bay leaf. Bring to boiling; reduce heat. Simmer, covered, for 20 minutes. Add lemon juice, snipped thyme, savory, if desired, and pepper. Simmer, covered, about 5 minutes more or until carrots are tender. Cool slightly.

2 Remove and discard bay leaf. Transfer half of the carrot mixture to a blender or food processor. Cover and blend or process until smooth. Repeat with remaining mixture. Return all mixture to saucepan; heat through. Garnish with lemon slices and, if desired, lemon thyme.

Nutrition Facts per serving: 69 cal., 1 g total fat (0 g sat. fat), 0 mg chol., 511 mg sodium, 11 g carbo., 2 g fiber, 4 g pro.

Since the first Thanksgiving, corn has had an honored place on American tables. Here it adds golden goodness to creamy crab chowder.

CORN & CRAB CHOWDER

PREP:

30 minutes

COOK:

20 minutes

MAKES:

8 servings

3	fresh ears sweet corn or 1 cup frozen whole kernel corn
1	cup chicken broth
$\frac{1}{2}$	cup sliced green onions
$\frac{1}{2}$	cup chopped green sweet pepper
$1\frac{1}{2}$	teaspoons dried fines herbes, crushed, or $\frac{3}{4}$ teaspoon dried basil, crushed
$\frac{1}{2}$	teaspoon white pepper
3	cups milk
3	tablespoons cornstarch
1	6- or 6$\frac{1}{2}$-ounce can crabmeat, drained, flaked, and cartilage removed, or meat from 1$\frac{1}{2}$ pounds cooked crab legs
$1\frac{1}{2}$	cups shredded process Swiss cheese or process Gruyère cheese (6 ounces)

1 Cut kernels from ears of corn; scrape ears to remove milky portion to total about 1$\frac{1}{2}$ cups.

2 In a large saucepan combine corn, broth, green onions, sweet pepper, fines herbes, and white pepper. Bring to boiling; reduce heat. Simmer, covered, for 5 minutes.

3 Stir together milk and cornstarch. Stir into hot mixture. Cook and stir until thickened and bubbly. Stir in crabmeat and cheese; heat and stir until cheese melts.

Nutrition Facts per serving: 182 cal., 8 g total fat (4 g sat. fat), 53 mg chol., 550 mg sodium, 15 g carbo., 1 g fiber, 14 g pro.

CORN & HAM CHOWDER: Prepare Corn & Crab Chowder as above, except substitute 1 cup diced cooked ham for the crabmeat.

Nutrition Facts per serving: 191 cal., 9 g total fat (5 g sat. fat), 35 mg chol., 684 mg sodium, 16 g carbo., 1 g fiber, 13 g pro.

Roasting the eggplant and garlic adds a toasty depth of flavor to this creamy soup. Top it with a swirl of red sweet pepper cream.

ROASTED EGGPLANT SOUP

1	head garlic
	Olive oil
2	1½-pound eggplants
¼	cup olive oil
⅓	cup finely chopped onion
½	cup tomato puree
	Dash cayenne pepper
6	cups chicken broth or homemade chicken broth
1	cup half-and-half or light cream
2	teaspoons Worcestershire sauce
	Salt and black pepper
1	15-ounce jar roasted red sweet peppers, drained
¾	cup half-and-half or light cream
	Snipped fresh basil

PREP:
40 minutes
COOK:
35 minutes
ROAST:
30 minutes
OVEN:
350°F
MAKES:
8 servings

1 Peel away dry outer layers of skin from garlic. Cut off pointed top portion of garlic head, leaving the bulb intact but exposing cloves. Rub garlic well with olive oil. Prick eggplants with a fork. Place eggplants and garlic head in a baking pan. Roast in a 350° oven for 30 to 40 minutes or until eggplants are tender. Set aside until cool enough to handle. Squeeze garlic paste from cloves. Remove and discard eggplant skins; quarter eggplants. Set garlic paste and eggplants aside.

2 In a 4-quart Dutch oven heat the ¼ cup oil. Add onion; cook over medium heat about 5 minutes or until tender. Stir in tomato puree, cayenne pepper, garlic paste, and eggplants. Cook and stir for 2 minutes; add broth. Bring to boiling; reduce heat. Simmer, covered, for 30 minutes.

3 Using a slotted spoon, transfer vegetables in batches to a blender or food processor. Cover and blend or process until smooth. Return all mixture to Dutch oven. Add 1 cup half-and-half and Worcestershire sauce. Season to taste with salt and black pepper; heat through.

4 Meanwhile, for red pepper cream, wash blender or food processor. Add red sweet peppers and the ¾ cup half-and-half. Cover and blend or process until smooth. Season to taste with salt and black pepper. Transfer pepper mixture to a small saucepan and heat through.

5 Drizzle red pepper cream over bowls of soup. Sprinkle with basil.

Nutrition Facts per serving: 196 cal., 14 g total fat (5 g sat. fat), 21 mg chol., 817 mg sodium, 16 g carbo., 6 g fiber, 5 g pro.

Elegant homemade soup made of fresh mushrooms is surprisingly easy to prepare. This one uses shiitake or white button and oyster mushrooms.

FRESH MUSHROOM SOUP

PREP:

10 minutes

COOK:

10 minutes

MAKES:

6 servings

8 ounces fresh shiitake or button mushrooms

6 ounces small fresh oyster mushrooms

2 tablespoons butter or margarine, melted

$\frac{1}{3}$ cup chopped shallots

2 tablespoons all-purpose flour

$\frac{1}{2}$ teaspoon salt

$\frac{1}{4}$ teaspoon coarsely ground black pepper

1 14-ounce can vegetable or chicken broth or $1\frac{3}{4}$ cups homemade vegetable or chicken broth

2 cups half-and-half or light cream

$\frac{1}{8}$ teaspoon ground saffron or saffron threads

1 Remove any tough or woody stems from mushrooms. Cut large shiitake mushrooms in half; set aside. Chop remaining shiitake mushrooms. Cut oyster mushrooms into large pieces.

2 In a large saucepan melt butter over medium heat. Add mushrooms and shallots; cook, uncovered, over medium-high heat for 4 to 5 minutes or until tender, stirring occasionally. Stir in flour, salt, and pepper. Add broth. Cook and stir over medium heat until slightly thickened and bubbly. Cook and stir for 1 minute more. Stir in half-and-half and saffron; heat through.

TO MAKE AHEAD: Prepare soup as above; remove from heat and cool. Transfer to an airtight container. Store in the refrigerator for up to 2 days or seal, label, and freeze for up to 2 months. To reheat, transfer frozen soup to a large saucepan. Cook, covered, over medium heat about 20 minutes or until heated through, stirring occasionally.

Nutrition Facts per serving: 193 cal., 14 g total fat (8 g sat. fat), 40 mg chol., 565 mg sodium, 15 g carbo., 2 g fiber, 5 g pro.

To rinse wild rice, place it in a pan of warm water, stir, and remove particles that float to the top. Drain and repeat rinsing; drain before using.

WILD RICE-MUSHROOM SOUP

3	cups chicken broth or homemade chicken broth
1/3	cup uncooked wild rice, rinsed and drained
1/2	cup thinly sliced green onions
1	cup half-and-half or light cream
2	tablespoons all-purpose flour
1	teaspoon snipped fresh thyme or 1/4 teaspoon dried thyme, crushed
1/8	teaspoon black pepper
1 1/2	cups sliced fresh mushrooms
1	tablespoon dry sherry

PREP:
15 minutes
COOK:
50 minutes
MAKES:
4 servings

1 In a medium saucepan combine broth and wild rice. Bring to boiling; reduce heat. Simmer, covered, for 40 minutes. Stir in green onions; cook for 5 to 10 minutes more or until rice is tender.

2 In a small bowl combine half-and-half, flour, thyme, and pepper; stir into rice mixture along with mushrooms. Cook and stir over medium heat until thickened and bubbly. Cook and stir for 1 minute more. Stir in sherry; heat through.

Nutrition Facts per serving: 182 cal., 9 g total fat (5 g sat. fat), 22 mg chol., 779 mg sodium, 19 g carbo., 2 g fiber, 7 g pro.

Dress up onion soup mix with fresh mushrooms and onion for a soup that tastes like it came from a French bistro. While the soup simmers, you'll have time to heat garlic bread in the oven.

PRONTO BEEFY MUSHROOM SOUP

START TO FINISH:

15 minutes

MAKES:

4 servings

2	tablespoons butter or margarine
8	ounces sliced fresh mushrooms
½	cup thinly sliced red or yellow onion
1	14-ounce can beef broth or 1¾ cups homemade beef broth
1½	cups water
1	envelope onion-mushroom soup mix or beefy onion soup mix
1	to 2 tablespoons dry sherry (optional)

1 In a medium saucepan melt butter over medium heat. Add mushrooms and onion; cook over medium heat for 5 minutes, stirring frequently. Stir in broth, water, and dry soup mix. Cook and stir over medium-high heat until bubbly; reduce heat. Simmer, uncovered, for 5 minutes. If desired, stir in sherry.

Nutrition Facts per serving: 104 cal., 8 g total fat (4 g sat. fat), 16 mg chol., 861 mg sodium, 7 g carbo., 1 g fiber, 3 g pro.

Don't be tempted to shave off time when cooking the onions; the long, slow simmering makes them mild, sweet, and tender.

FRENCH ONION SOUP

2	tablespoons butter or margarine
1	tablespoon olive oil
2½	pounds onions, thinly sliced
4	14-ounce cans beef broth or 7 cups homemade beef broth
1	bay leaf
1	large sprig fresh thyme
1	sprig fresh parsley
2	tablespoons Madeira or dry sherry
	Salt
	Black pepper
8	¾-inch-thick slices French bread
2	cups finely shredded Gruyère cheese (8 ounces)

PREP:

30 minutes

BAKE:

15 minutes

COOK:

45 minutes

OVEN:

400°F

MAKES:

8 servings

1 In a 4-quart Dutch oven heat butter and oil. Add onions; cook over medium heat about 35 minutes or until softened and translucent, stirring frequently. Increase heat to high. Add ½ cup of the broth, stirring until most of the broth has evaporated. Continue adding broth, ½ cup at a time, stirring until nearly evaporated, until you have used 2 cups of the broth. Stir in remaining broth.

2 Wrap bay leaf, thyme, and parsley in 100-percent-cotton cheesecloth. Tie closed with clean kitchen string. Add to soup; reduce heat to low. Simmer, covered, for 10 to 15 minutes. Remove and discard herbs in cheesecloth. Stir in Madeira. Add salt and pepper to taste.

3 Place bread on a baking sheet; toast in a 400° oven about 5 minutes or until golden. Divide the soup among eight 12- to 16-ounce ovenproof bowls. Sprinkle 2 tablespoons of the cheese over each slice of bread; top each bowl of soup with a bread slice and 2 tablespoons additional cheese. Place bowls in a shallow baking pan. Bake about 10 minutes or until cheese melts.

Nutrition Facts per serving: 297 cal., 16 g total fat (8 g sat. fat), 39 mg chol., 978 mg sodium, 25 g carbo., 3 g fiber, 14 g pro.

Complement the natural sweetness of parsnips by topping with crisp-cooked bacon or broken bagel chips.

CREAM OF PARSNIP SOUP

PREP:

30 minutes

COOK:

50 minutes

MAKES:

6 servings

2 tablespoons butter or margarine

1 cup chopped onion

½ cup chopped celery

2 cloves garlic, minced

5 cups chicken broth

2 cups peeled and cubed parsnips, turnips, or rutabagas

½ teaspoon salt

½ teaspoon black pepper

1 bay leaf

¼ cup whipping cream

1 tablespoon snipped fresh chives

1 In a large saucepan melt butter. Add onion, celery, and garlic; cook and stir over medium heat for 3 to 5 minutes or until tender. Stir in broth, parsnips, salt, pepper, and bay leaf. Bring to boiling; reduce heat. Simmer, covered, for 25 to 30 minutes or until parsnips are very tender. Remove from heat. Cool slightly (do not drain). Remove and discard bay leaf.

2 Transfer half of the parsnip mixture to a blender or food processor. Cover and blend or process until nearly smooth. Repeat with remaining parsnip mixture. Return all mixture to saucepan. Stir in whipping cream. Cook and stir for 4 to 5 minutes or until heated through. Garnish with chives.

Nutrition Facts per serving: 142 cal., 10 g total fat (5 g sat. fat), 25 mg chol., 1,084 mg sodium, 12 g carbo., 3 g fiber, 3 g pro.

The avocado toast is the crowning touch on this elegant soup and is also a great topper for other soups and salads.

CHUNKY RED PEPPER SOUP

4	large red sweet peppers, halved
1	teaspoon olive oil
½	cup chopped onion
2	cups peeled, seeded, and chopped Roma tomatoes
4	cups reduced-sodium chicken broth or vegetable broth
1	tablespoon balsamic vinegar
⅛	teaspoon salt
⅛	teaspoon black pepper
1	recipe Avocado Toast

PREP:
35 minutes
COOK:
15 minutes
ROAST:
20 minutes
OVEN:
425°F
MAKES:
6 servings

1 Remove stems, seeds, and membranes from sweet peppers. Place sweet peppers, cut sides down, on a lightly greased baking sheet. (If desired, brush peppers lightly with cooking oil.) Roast in a 425° oven for 20 to 25 minutes or until skins char and blister. Remove from oven. Wrap peppers in foil; let stand about 15 minutes or until cool. Peel skins off peppers. (If desired, cover and refrigerate peppers for up to 3 days before using.)

2 In a large saucepan heat oil. Add onion; cook and stir over medium heat about 2 minutes or until tender. Add sweet peppers, tomatoes, broth, vinegar, salt, and black pepper. Bring to boiling; reduce heat. Simmer, uncovered, for 10 minutes, stirring occasionally. Cool slightly.

3 Transfer half of the sweet pepper mixture to a blender or food processor. Cover and blend or process until smooth. Repeat with remaining pepper mixture. Return all mixture to saucepan and stir well; heat through. Top with Avocado Toast.

AVOCADO TOAST: Bias-cut six ¼-inch-thick slices from a baguette-style French bread loaf. Place slices on a baking sheet. Broil about 2 minutes or until light brown, turning once. Remove from oven. Spread each piece of toast with about ½ teaspoon Roasted Garlic Paste; set aside. Halve, seed, peel, and slice 1 avocado. Sprinkle avocado slices with ⅛ teaspoon salt; toss with 1 tablespoon lime juice. Arrange several avocado slices and a fresh basil leaf on each baguette toast.

Nutrition Facts per serving: 158 cal., 6 g total fat (0 g sat. fat), 0 mg chol., 614 mg sodium, 22 g carbo., 5 g fiber, 6 g pro.

ROASTED GARLIC PASTE: Peel away dry outer layers of skin from 1 medium head garlic. Cut off the pointed top portion, leaving bulb intact but exposing cloves. Place garlic head, cut side up, in a custard cup. Drizzle with a little olive oil. Roast in a 425°F oven for 25 to 35 minutes or until cloves feel soft when pressed. Set aside until cool enough to handle. Squeeze garlic paste from cloves. Store in an airtight container in the refrigerator up to 1 week.

Yellow sweet peppers are milder and sweeter in flavor than their green cousins. Paired with fennel and cardamom, they make a summer-fresh first course. (Recipe pictured on page 98.)

YELLOW PEPPER SOUP

PREP:

25 minutes

COOK:

20 minutes

MAKES:

4 servings

1   cup plain or low-fat yogurt (do not use nonfat)

1   teaspoon fennel seeds, crushed

2   tablespoons olive oil

5   cups coarsely chopped yellow sweet peppers

¼   cup chopped shallots

¾   teaspoon ground cardamom

1   14-ounce can reduced-sodium chicken broth or 1¾ cups homemade chicken broth

1   cup water

2   tablespoons cider vinegar

¼   cup coarsely chopped cucumber

Black or white pepper

1 In a small bowl stir together yogurt and fennel seeds. Cover and let stand at room temperature for 30 minutes.

2 Meanwhile, in a large saucepan heat oil. Add sweet peppers, shallots, and cardamom; cook over medium heat about 15 minutes or until peppers are just beginning to soften, stirring occasionally. Add broth, water, and vinegar. Bring to boiling; reduce heat. Simmer, covered, for 5 minutes more. Remove from heat and allow to cool slightly.

3 Transfer half of the sweet pepper mixture to a blender or food processor. Cover and blend or process until smooth. Repeat with remaining pepper mixture. Return all mixture to saucepan. Cook and stir over medium heat until heated through.

4 Top with yogurt, cucumber, and black pepper. Serve warm or chilled.

Nutrition Facts per serving: 154 cal., 9 g total fat (2 g sat. fat), 8 mg chol., 306 mg sodium, 15 g carbo., 2 g fiber, 5 g pro.

A generous infusion of garlic complements this golden carrot-potato combination.

POTATO-CARROT SOUP

2   medium heads garlic (about 16 cloves)

3   cups diced, peeled potatoes

1½ cups sliced carrots

4   14-ounce cans reduced-sodium chicken broth or 7 cups homemade chicken broth

⅓   cup whipping cream

    Salt

    Black pepper

PREP:
15 minutes
COOK:
25 minutes
MAKES:
6 servings

1 Separate garlic heads into cloves and peel. In a large saucepan combine potatoes, carrots, garlic, and broth. Bring to boiling; reduce heat. Simmer, covered, for 20 to 25 minutes or until vegetables are very tender. Cool slightly.

2 Transfer one-third of the potato mixture to a blender or food processor. Cover and blend or process until smooth. Repeat with remaining potato mixture. Return all mixture to saucepan. Stir in cream. Season to taste with salt and pepper. Heat through.

Nutrition Facts per serving: 163 cal., 7 g total fat (4 g sat. fat), 18 mg chol., 1,172 mg sodium, 21 g carbo., 2 g fiber, 5 g pro.

This European-style soup is thickened by cooking the vegetables, pureeing a portion of them, and recombining with the soup. This easy trick gives a more intense flavor than thickening with flour or cornstarch.

RICE & POTATO SOUP

PREP:

25 minutes

COOK:

40 minutes

MAKES:

6 to 8 servings

2	tablespoons olive oil
⅓	cup chopped onion
1	cup diced, peeled potatoes
½	cup sliced celery
⅓	cup sliced leek (white part only)
2	cloves garlic, minced
3	cups water
2	14-ounce cans chicken broth or 3½ cups homemade chicken broth
½	cup uncooked long grain rice
1	cup shelled fresh peas or frozen green peas (optional)
	Black pepper
	Grated Parmesan cheese (optional)

1 In a large saucepan heat oil. Add onion; cook and stir over medium heat about 5 minutes or until tender. Stir in potatoes, celery, leek, and garlic. Stir in the water and broth. Bring to boiling; reduce heat. Simmer, covered, for 20 to 25 minutes or until potato is tender. Cool slightly.

2 Transfer half of the onion mixture to a blender or food processor. Cover and blend or process until smooth. Repeat with remaining onion mixture. Return all mixture to saucepan. Bring to boiling. Stir in rice and, if desired, peas. Return to boiling; reduce heat. Simmer, covered, about 15 minutes or until rice is tender. Season to taste with pepper. If desired, sprinkle with Parmesan cheese.

Nutrition Facts per serving: 114 cal., 3 g total fat (0 g sat. fat), 1 mg chol., 554 mg sodium, 20 g carbo., 1 g fiber, 3 g pro.

Use the white part of the leek plus just a little of the green top to lend a hint of color.
Serve this soup hot or chilled.

COUNTRY POTATO SOUP

START TO FINISH:
20 minutes
MAKES:
6 servings

1½ cups refrigerated diced red-skinned potatoes or new potatoes, skinned and quartered

½ cup chopped leek (white part only)

1 clove garlic, minced

2 14-ounce cans reduced-sodium chicken broth or 3½ cups homemade chicken broth

6 fresh chives, cut into 1-inch pieces

⅛ teaspoon white pepper

1 cup half-and-half, light cream, or milk

Snipped fresh chives

1 recipe Garlic Olive Oil or purchased garlic olive oil

1 In a large saucepan combine potatoes, leek, garlic, and 1 cup of the broth. Bring to boiling; reduce heat. Simmer, covered, for 5 minutes (10 minutes for new potatoes, if using) or until leeks are tender.

2 Transfer half of the potato mixture to a blender or food processor. Cover and blend or process until nearly smooth, adding additional broth, if necessary. Repeat with remaining potato mixture. Return all mixture to saucepan. Add cut chives and white pepper. Whisk in remaining broth and half-and-half. Heat through.

3 Ladle soup into bowls. Top with snipped chives and a few drops of Garlic Olive Oil.

GARLIC OLIVE OIL: In a small skillet heat 2 tablespoons olive oil. Add 1 clove minced garlic; cook over medium heat until garlic begins to brown. Strain to remove garlic. Discard any unused oil (do not store).

Nutrition Facts per serving: 96 cal., 5 g total fat (3 g sat. fat), 15 mg chol., 424 mg sodium, 10 g carbo., 1 g fiber, 4 g pro.

*When making this chilled soup, it's important to pick the proper potatoes. Starchy potatoes—
typical baking potatoes—work better than waxy potatoes that have smooth, thin skin.
Plan on making the soup at least 8 hours before serving to give it time to chill.*

VICHYSSOISE WITH CHIVE OIL

PREP:

30 minutes

COOK:

30 minutes

COOL:

20 minutes

CHILL:

8 hours

MAKES:

6 servings

4	medium leeks
1	tablespoon olive oil
1½	pounds russet or Yukon gold potatoes, peeled and cut into 2-inch pieces (about 5 medium potatoes)
4	cups chicken broth
¼	teaspoon salt
⅛	teaspoon black pepper
⅓	cup milk
3	tablespoons finely snipped fresh chives
2	tablespoons finely snipped fresh thyme
1	recipe Chive Oil
	Fresh chives

1 Trim leeks, separating the dark green stems from the white leek. Discard green section. Cut the white part of the leek in half lengthwise and clean out the dirt from between the layers. Cut leek into 2-inch pieces.

2 In a 4-quart Dutch oven heat oil. Add leeks; cook, covered, over medium-low heat for 10 minutes, stirring occasionally. Stir in potatoes; cook 2 minutes. Increase heat to high and add broth, salt, and pepper. Bring to boiling; reduce heat to medium-low. Simmer, covered, for 15 minutes or until potatoes are tender. Remove from heat; let cool slightly.

3 Transfer one-third of the leek mixture to a blender or food processor. Cover and blend or process until smooth. Repeat with remaining leek mixture. Place all mixture in a large bowl; stir in milk and snipped herbs. Cover and chill at least 8 hours or until cold.

4 About 20 minutes before serving, prepare Chive Oil. Serve chilled vichyssoise in small glasses or bowls. Drizzle with Chive Oil and top with chives.

CHIVE OIL: In a small saucepan combine ¼ cup very finely chopped fresh chives and ¼ cup olive oil. Place over low heat for 5 minutes, stirring occasionally. Remove from heat. Add ⅛ teaspoon coarse sea salt and a dash black pepper; let cool 20 minutes. Use immediately. Discard any remaining oil (do not store).

Nutrition Facts per serving: 232 cal., 13 g total fat (2 g sat. fat), 1 mg chol., 821 mg sodium, 25 g carbo., 3 g fiber, 5 g pro.

With no fat and no cholesterol, this soup is a great, heart-healthy way to savor a bumper crop of summer tomatoes. Try it hot or chilled.

FRESH TOMATO SOUP

3	medium tomatoes, peeled and quartered
1½	cups water
½	cup chopped onion
½	cup chopped celery
½	of a 6-ounce can (⅓ cup) tomato paste
2	tablespoons snipped fresh cilantro or basil
2	teaspoons instant chicken bouillon granules
1	teaspoon sugar
	Few dashes bottled hot pepper sauce
	Snipped fresh cilantro or basil (optional)

PREP:
20 minutes
COOK:
20 minutes
COOL:
10 minutes
MAKES:
4 servings

1 If desired, seed tomatoes. In a large saucepan combine tomatoes, water, onion, celery, tomato paste, 2 tablespoons cilantro, bouillon granules, sugar, and hot pepper sauce. Bring to boiling; reduce heat. Simmer, covered, about 20 minutes or until celery and onion are very tender. Remove from heat and cool for 10 minutes.

2 Transfer half of the tomato mixture to a blender or food processor. Cover and blend or process until smooth. Repeat with remaining tomato mixture. Return all mixture to the saucepan; heat through. If desired, garnish with additional cilantro.

CHILLED FRESH TOMATO SOUP: Prepare as above, except after blending or processing, cover and chill soup for up to 24 hours. If desired, top with dairy sour cream.

Nutrition Facts per serving: 54 cal., 0 g total fat (0 g sat. fat), 0 mg chol., 744 mg sodium, 12 g carbo., 3 g fiber, 2 g pro.

Hot or cold, this savory soup is one of the finest ways to enjoy garden-fresh tomatoes.

SUMMERTIME TOMATO-BASIL SOUP

PREP:

20 minutes

COOK:

20 minutes

MAKES:

4 to 5 servings

2	tablespoons butter or margarine
1/2	cup finely chopped onion
1	clove garlic, minced
1	pound ripe tomatoes, peeled, seeded, and quartered, or one 14 1/2-ounce can diced tomatoes, undrained
2 1/2	cups tomato juice
1	bay leaf
1/2	of a 8-ounce package cream cheese, softened
1/8	teaspoon salt
1/8	teaspoon black pepper
1/4	cup snipped fresh basil

1 In a large saucepan melt butter over medium heat. Add onion and garlic; cook and stir about 5 minutes or until onion is tender. Add tomatoes, tomato juice, and bay leaf. Bring to boiling; reduce heat. Simmer, uncovered, for 20 minutes, stirring occasionally. Remove from heat; cool slightly. Remove and discard bay leaf.

2 Transfer half of the tomato mixture to a blender or food processor; add half of the cream cheese. Cover and blend or process until smooth. Repeat with remaining tomato mixture and remaining cream cheese. Return all mixture to saucepan if soup is to be served hot.

3 Add salt, if using fresh tomatoes, and the pepper. Heat through (do not boil). Stir in basil. If desired, season to taste with additional salt and pepper.

4 For chilled soup, transfer to a bowl after processing. Stir in the salt, if using fresh tomatoes, and the pepper. Cover and chill for 4 to 24 hours. Stir in basil before serving. If desired, season to taste with additional salt and pepper.

Nutrition Facts per serving: 210 cal., 16 g total fat (9 g sat. fat), 47 mg chol., 617 mg sodium, 14 g carbo., 2 g fiber, 5 g pro.

Dainty basil-flavored dumplings set this delicious soup apart from any tomato soup you've sampled before. (Recipe pictured on page 100.)

CHUNKY TOMATO SOUP

2	tablespoons olive oil
1	cup coarsely chopped onion
2	tablespoons chopped shallot
2	cloves garlic, minced
1	14-ounce can reduced-sodium chicken broth or 1¾ cups homemade chicken broth
½	cup coarsely chopped carrot
½	cup coarsely chopped celery
½	cup coarsely chopped red sweet pepper
1	tablespoon lemon juice
½	teaspoon sugar
1	14½-ounce can diced tomatoes, undrained
	Dash cayenne pepper
1	recipe Basil Dumplings
	Salt and black pepper

PREP:
30 minutes
COOK:
40 minutes
MAKES:
6 servings

1 In a large saucepan heat oil. Add onion, shallot, and garlic; cook and stir over medium heat about 5 minutes or until onion is tender. Add next 6 ingredients. Bring to boiling; reduce heat. Simmer, covered, for 20 to 25 minutes or until vegetables are very tender. Cool slightly (do not drain).

2 Transfer half of onion mixture to a blender. Cover and blend until smooth. Repeat with remaining mixture. Return all mixture to saucepan. Stir in undrained tomatoes and cayenne pepper. Cook, uncovered, over low heat about 10 minutes or until heated through, stirring often.

3 Meanwhile, fill a Dutch oven half-full with water; bring to boiling. Drop Basil Dumplings dough from a slightly rounded ½ teaspoon measuring spoon into boiling water. Cook for 4 to 5 minutes (start timing when dough rises to surface) or until dumplings are cooked through, turning once. Remove dumplings; drain in a colander. Rinse dumplings under cold running water; drain again. Add half of the dumplings to soup; heat through. Season to taste with salt and pepper. Ladle into bowls. Top with remaining dumplings. If desired, garnish with *fresh basil leaves.*

BASIL DUMPLINGS: In a small bowl combine ⅓ cup all-purpose flour, 1 tablespoon snipped fresh basil, ¼ teaspoon baking powder, and ½ teaspoon salt. In a small bowl stir together 1 beaten egg and 2 teaspoons cooking oil; pour all at once into flour mixture. Using a wooden spoon, beat until a soft, sticky dough forms.

Nutrition Facts per serving: 141 cal., 8 g total fat (1 g sat. fat), 35 mg chol., 817 mg sodium, 15 g carbo., 2 g fiber, 3 g pro.

For the fresh tomatoes in this recipe, use the ripest available. If homegrown or farm-fresh tomatoes are available, they'll make the best soup.

TWO-TOMATO SOUP

PREP:

45 minutes

COOK:

65 minutes

MAKES:

8 servings

1	3-ounce package dried tomatoes (not oil packed)
1	tablespoon olive oil or cooking oil
½	cup chopped onion
¼	teaspoon coarsely ground black pepper
4	cups chopped fresh tomatoes
4	cups water
1	teaspoon salt
1	cup whipping cream

1 Place dried tomatoes in a small bowl. Add enough *boiling water* to cover. Soak for 30 minutes. Drain and rinse. Coarsely chop tomatoes.

2 In a 4-quart Dutch oven heat oil. Add rehydrated tomatoes, onion, and pepper; cook and stir about 5 minutes or until onion is tender.

3 Reserve ¾ cup chopped fresh tomatoes; set aside. Add remaining fresh tomatoes to rehydrated tomato mixture. Cook, covered, over low heat about 20 minutes or until tomatoes are soft. Add water and salt. Cook, uncovered, over low heat for 40 minutes more, stirring often.

4 Transfer one-fourth of the tomato mixture to a blender or food processor bowl. Cover and blend or process until smooth. Repeat with remaining tomato mixture. Return all mixture to Dutch oven. Heat to simmering (do not boil). Stir in cream. Return just to simmering; remove from heat.

5 Ladle soup into bowls. Spoon some of the reserved fresh chopped tomatoes into each bowl.

TO MAKE AHEAD: **Prepare soup as directed up to stirring in the cream. Cool soup. Transfer to an airtight container. Seal, label, and freeze for up to 2 months. To reheat, transfer frozen soup to a saucepan. Cook, covered, over medium heat for 15 to 20 minutes, stirring occasionally. Stir in cream. Cook and stir for 5 to 10 minutes more or until heated through.**

Nutrition Facts per serving: 176 cal., 14 g total fat (7 g sat. fat), 41 mg chol., 540 mg sodium, 13 g carbo., 3 g fiber, 3 g pro.

This mushroom-packed soup can serve as the side-dish accompaniment to sandwiches. Or for a first course, ladle it over toasted slices of French bread in large shallow bowls.

TOMATO-MUSHROOM SOUP

1	tablespoon butter or margarine
1	tablespoon olive oil or cooking oil
½	cup thinly sliced halved onion
1	clove garlic, minced
4	cups sliced fresh mushrooms
1	10½-ounce can condensed chicken broth
1¼	cups water
¼	cup sweet vermouth or dry sherry
¼	cup tomato paste
¼	teaspoon black pepper
¼	cup finely shredded or grated Parmesan cheese (1 ounce)
2	tablespoons snipped fresh parsley or fresh basil

PREP:
20 minutes
COOK:
30 minutes
MAKES:
4 servings

1 In a large saucepan heat butter and oil over medium heat. Add onion and garlic; cook and stir about 5 minutes or until onion is tender. Add mushrooms. Cook, covered, about 5 minutes or until mushrooms are tender.

2 Stir in broth, water, vermouth, tomato paste, and pepper. Bring soup to boiling; reduce heat. Simmer, covered, for 20 minutes. Top with Parmesan cheese and parsley.

Nutrition Facts per serving: 168 cal., 11 g total fat (4 g sat. fat), 16 mg chol., 605 mg sodium, 10 g carbo., 2 g fiber, 8 g pro.

This isn't your grandmother's tomato soup. Southwestern-style seasonings give canned soup character and punch. If you wish, pass additional snipped cilantro to sprinkle on top.

SOUTHWESTERN-STYLE TOMATO SOUP

START TO FINISH:

10 minutes

MAKES:

5 or 6 servings

1   32-ounce jar ready-to-serve tomato soup

1   14½-ounce can Mexican-style chopped tomatoes, undrained

⅛   teaspoon ground cumin

    Dash cayenne pepper or several dashes bottled
    hot pepper sauce

2   tablespoons snipped fresh cilantro

¼   cup dairy sour cream

1 In a large saucepan combine tomato soup, undrained tomatoes, cumin, and cayenne pepper. Cook, covered, over medium heat until heated through, stirring occasionally. Stir in cilantro. Top with sour cream.

Nutrition Facts per serving: 125 cal., 2 g total fat (1 g sat. fat), 7 mg chol., 788 mg sodium, 23 g carbo., 2 g fiber, 3 g pro.

From Mexico—with flavor! Try this colorful soup, featuring the slightly apple-like flavor of tomatillos, as a starter to your next Mexican dinner party. Or simply serve alongside tacos.

ROASTED GARLIC & TOMATILLO SOUP

1	head garlic
	Cooking oil
1	pound tomatillos
3	14-ounce cans chicken broth or 5¼ cups homemade chicken broth
¼	teaspoon black pepper
2	cups chopped, cored tomatoes
1	avocado, halved, seeded, peeled, and chopped
½	cup snipped fresh cilantro
1	cup coarsely crushed tortilla chips
1	cup shredded Chihuahua, queso quesadilla, or Monterey Jack cheese (4 ounces)

PREP:
25 minutes
COOK:
10 minutes
ROAST:
20 minutes
OVEN:
425°F
MAKES:
8 servings

1 Peel away dry outer layers of skin from garlic. Cut off the pointed top portion, leaving the bulb intact but exposing cloves. Rub well with oil; set aside.

2 Remove husks, stems, and cores from tomatillos. Cut tomatillos in half. Place tomatillos, cut sides down, on a foil-lined 15×10×1-inch baking pan. Place garlic on baking pan. Roast in 425° oven for 20 minutes. Set aside until cool enough to handle.

3 Squeeze garlic paste from cloves. In a blender combine half of the tomatillos, the garlic paste, and 1 cup of the broth. Cover and blend until nearly smooth.

4 Transfer blended tomatillo mixture to a large saucepan; add remaining broth and the pepper. Chop remaining tomatillos and add to pan along with chopped tomatoes. Heat through. Top with avocado, cilantro, tortilla chips, and cheese.

Nutrition Facts per serving: 169 cal., 12 g total fat (4 g sat. fat), 15 mg chol., 758 mg sodium, 11 g carbo., 3 g fiber, 6 g pro.

The warm flavor of curry enhances this savory blend of squash, carrots, parsnips, and apple.

SQUASH & PARSNIP SOUP

PREP:
15 minutes

COOK:
20 minutes

MAKES:
4 to 6 servings

4 cups peeled and cut-up butternut squash

2 carrots, peeled and cut into 2-inch pieces

1 to 2 small parsnips, peeled and cut into 2-inch pieces

1 apple, cored, peeled, and cut into wedges

2 14-ounce cans reduced-sodium chicken broth
   or 3½ cups homemade chicken broth

1½ teaspoons curry powder

½ teaspoon salt

   Fresh thyme sprigs

   Dairy sour cream (optional)

1 In a large saucepan or 4-quart Dutch oven combine squash, carrots, parsnips, and apple. Stir in broth, curry, and salt. Bring to boiling; reduce heat. Simmer, covered, for 20 minutes or until vegetables are tender. Cool slightly.

2 Transfer half of the squash mixture to a blender or food processor. Cover and blend or process until smooth. Repeat with remaining squash mixture. Return all mixture to saucepan and heat through. Top with thyme sprigs and, if desired, sour cream.

Nutrition Facts per serving: 110 cal., 0 g total fat (0 g sat. fat), 0 mg chol., 791 mg sodium, 25 g carbo., 5 g fiber, 4 g pro.

This creamy soup mingles fall flavors and makes a great side with sandwiches or a first course for a holiday dinner.

BUTTERNUT SQUASH & APPLE SOUP

1	large butternut squash (about 1¾ pounds)
3	tablespoons olive oil
5	cups chopped, peeled Granny Smith apples
2	cups chopped onions
⅔	cup sliced leeks (white parts only)
4	cups chicken broth
½	teaspoon salt
	Thinly sliced Granny Smith apple (optional)

PREP:

20 minutes

BAKE:

30 minutes

COOK:

20 minutes

OVEN:

400°F

MAKES:

8 servings

1 Cut squash in half lengthwise; remove and discard seeds. Brush squash halves with 1 tablespoon of the oil. Place squash halves, cut sides down, in a baking dish. Bake in a 400° oven about 30 minutes or until tender. Remove squash pulp from shells; set aside.

2 In a covered 4-quart Dutch oven heat remaining 2 tablespoons oil. Add chopped apples, onions, and leeks; cook over medium heat for 10 to 12 minutes or until tender, stirring once or twice. Add squash pulp and 3 cups of the broth. Bring to boiling; reduce heat. Simmer, uncovered, for 5 minutes.

3 Transfer half of the squash mixture to a blender or food processor. Cover and blend or process until smooth. Repeat with remaining squash mixture. Return all mixture to Dutch oven. Stir in remaining 1 cup broth and the salt. Heat through. If desired, garnish with sliced apple.

Nutrition Facts per serving: 172 cal., 7 g total fat (1 g sat. fat), 0 mg chol., 652 mg sodium, 29 g carbo., 3 g fiber, 3 g pro.

Almost like a stew, this recipe makes enough for a casual supper with company. (Recipe pictured on page 100.)

HEARTY SQUASH SOUP

PREP:

30 minutes

COOK:

30 minutes

MAKES:

10 to 12 servings

2	tablespoons butter or margarine
2	teaspoons ground cumin
1	teaspoon ground turmeric
½	teaspoon ground cinnamon
⅔	cup chopped leeks (white parts only)
2½	pounds butternut squash, winter squash, or pie pumpkin, peeled and cut into 1- to 1½-inch pieces (about 9 cups)
4	14-ounce cans chicken broth or 7 cups homemade chicken broth
½	cup uncooked rice
4	cups coarsely chopped green cabbage
	Salt
	Black pepper
1	tablespoon snipped fresh tarragon

1 In a 5½- to 6-quart Dutch oven melt butter over medium heat. Add cumin, turmeric, and cinnamon; cook and stir for 1 minute. Add leeks; cook for 2 minutes, stirring to coat with spices. Add squash pieces and broth. Bring to boiling; reduce heat. Simmer, covered, for 10 minutes.

2 Add rice. Simmer, covered, 10 minutes more. Add cabbage; simmer, covered, for 5 to 10 minutes more or until rice and squash are tender. Season to taste with salt and pepper. Just before serving, add tarragon.

Nutrition Facts per serving: 120 cal., 4 g total fat (2 g sat. fat), 7 mg chol., 760 mg sodium, 18 g carbo., 2 g fiber, 4 g pro.

Velvety smooth and lightly spiced, this soup makes a chicken or turkey sandwich lunch a special occasion.

SWEET POTATO SOUP

2	tablespoons butter or margarine
1	cup chopped onion
1	cup chopped celery
⅓	cup thinly sliced leek (white part only)
1	large clove garlic, minced
5	cups cubed, peeled sweet potatoes
4	cups reduced-sodium chicken broth or homemade chicken broth
1	3-inch cinnamon stick
¼	teaspoon ground nutmeg
1½	cups half-and-half or light cream
2	tablespoons maple syrup

PREP:
25 minutes
COOK:
30 minutes
MAKES:
8 servings

1 In a 4-quart Dutch oven melt butter over medium heat. Add onion, celery, leek, and garlic; cook and stir about 5 minutes or until onion is tender.

2 Add sweet potatoes, broth, cinnamon, and nutmeg. Bring to boiling; reduce heat. Simmer, covered, about 20 minutes or until potato is tender. Remove from heat; cool slightly. Remove and discard cinnamon.

3 Transfer about one-third of sweet potato mixture to a blender or food processor. Cover and blend or process until smooth. Repeat with remaining sweet potato mixture. Return all mixture to Dutch oven. Stir in half-and-half and maple syrup; heat through.

Nutrition Facts per serving: 208 cal., 9 g total fat (5 g sat. fat), 25 mg chol., 381 mg sodium, 29 g carbo., 3 g fiber, 5 g pro.

In colonial times, cooks made much use of pumpkin as a vegetable in robust soups and stews. Try this updated version of savory pumpkin soup.

PUMPKIN SOUP

PREP:

20 minutes

COOK:

20 minutes

MAKES:

8 servings

2	tablespoons butter or margarine
½	cup coarsely chopped onion
3	cups canned pumpkin
2	14-ounce cans chicken broth or 3½ cups homemade chicken broth
2	tablespoons brown sugar
2	bay leaves
¼	teaspoon ground nutmeg
¼	teaspoon black pepper
1	cup whipping cream
1	tablespoon cooking oil
1	cup finely chopped cooked ham

1 In a 4-quart Dutch oven melt butter over medium heat. Add onion; cook and stir about 4 minutes or until tender. Stir in pumpkin, broth, brown sugar, bay leaves, nutmeg, and pepper. Bring mixture to boiling; reduce heat. Simmer, covered, for 10 minutes. Remove from heat. Remove and discard bay leaves. Stir in whipping cream.

2 Transfer about one-third of the pumpkin mixture to a blender or food processor. Cover and blend or process until smooth. Repeat with remaining pumpkin mixture. Return all mixture to the Dutch oven and heat through.

3 Meanwhile, in a medium skillet heat oil over medium heat. Add ham; cook about 10 minutes or until crisp. Drain off oil. Sprinkle ham over soup.

Nutrition Facts per serving: 237 cal., 18 g total fat (10 g sat. fat), 60 mg chol., 637 mg sodium, 12 g carbo., 3 g fiber, 8 g pro.

Calabaza, or West Indian pumpkin, is more like a squash than a Halloween pumpkin. You can find it whole or cut into chunks at a Latin market.

WEST INDIAN PUMPKIN BISQUE

2	pounds calabaza pumpkin or butternut squash, peeled and cut into 1-inch pieces
1	pound sweet potatoes, peeled and cut into 1-inch pieces
1/4	cup butter or margarine, melted
1/2	cup sugar
2	tablespoons olive oil
1	cup chopped onion
1	fresh jalapeño chile pepper, seeded and minced*
6	cloves garlic, minced
1	tablespoon grated fresh ginger
1/4	cup curry powder
2	teaspoons dried thyme, crushed
2	teaspoons finely shredded orange peel
1/4	teaspoon ground nutmeg
1	3-inch cinnamon stick
2	bay leaves
6	to 7 cups chicken broth
1/4	cup whipping cream
1/4	cup purchased unsweetened coconut milk

PREP:
30 minutes
COOK:
25 minutes
ROAST:
1 1/4 hours
OVEN:
350°F
MAKES:
10 to 12 servings

1 In a large roasting pan combine pumpkin, sweet potatoes, butter, sugar, 1 teaspoon *salt,* and 1 teaspoon *black pepper*. Roast, uncovered, in a 350° oven about 1 1/4 hours or until tender, stirring occasionally. Set aside.

2 Meanwhile, in a 5 1/2- to 6-quart Dutch oven heat oil. Add onion; cook and stir over medium heat about 5 minutes or until tender. Stir in chile pepper, garlic, and ginger; cook for 1 minute. Add next 6 ingredients. Cook and stir for 1 minute. Add roasted vegetables and their liquid; stir to combine. Add 6 cups of the broth. Bring to boiling; reduce heat. Simmer, uncovered, for 15 minutes, stirring occasionally. Remove from heat; cool slightly. Discard cinnamon stick and bay leaves.

3 Transfer one-third of the pumpkin mixture to a blender. Cover and blend until smooth. Repeat with remaining pumpkin mixture. Return all mixture to Dutch oven. Stir in cream and coconut milk; heat through. Stir in enough of the remaining 1 cup broth to reach desired consistency.

*NOTE: When working with chile peppers, wear plastic gloves. If your bare hands do touch the chile peppers, wash your hands well with soap and water.

Nutrition Facts per serving: 208 cal., 12 g total fat (5 g sat. fat), 23 mg chol., 867 mg sodium, 25 g carbo., 3 g fiber, 3 g pro.

A medley of fall and winter vegetables, this thick, creamy soup gets a dash of color from the roasted beet topping.

WINTER WHITE VEGETABLE SOUP

PREP:

45 minutes

COOK:

40 minutes

ROAST:

1 hour

OVEN:

400°F

MAKES:

10 servings

1	medium beet, trimmed
1	tablespoon butter or margarine
½	cup chopped onion
4	cups coarsely chopped cauliflower
3	cups turnips peeled and cut into 1-inch pieces
3	cups celeriac peeled and cut into 1-inch pieces
3	cups potatoes peeled and cut into 1-inch pieces
2	cups sliced fennel
1	cup peeled and coarsely chopped parsnips
2	cloves garlic, halved
¼	teaspoon salt
4	cups water
1½	cups milk
	Milk (optional)
1	tablespoon snipped fresh chives (optional)

1 Wrap beet in foil. Roast in 400° oven about 1 hour or until just tender. Cool. Peel and dice or grate; set aside.

2 Meanwhile, in a 4- to 5-quart Dutch oven melt butter over medium heat. Add onion; cook about 5 minutes or until tender, stirring occasionally. Add cauliflower, turnips, celeriac, potatoes, fennel, parsnips, garlic, salt, and water. Bring to boiling; reduce heat. Simmer, covered, for 25 to 30 minutes or until vegetables are very tender. Remove from heat. Stir in the 1½ cups milk. Let cool about 30 minutes.

3 Transfer one-fourth of vegetable mixture to a blender or food processor. Cover and blend or process until smooth. Repeat with remaining vegetable mixture. Return all mixture to Dutch oven. Add additional milk to reach desired consistency. Heat through. Ladle into bowls and sprinkle with beets. If desired, top with snipped chives.

TO MAKE AHEAD: Roast, peel, and dice or grate beet as above. Cover and chill beet for up to 24 hours. Prepare soup through Step 2. After cooling slightly, blend or process as in Step 3. Do not return to Dutch oven as directed. Transfer mixture to a storage container and refrigerate for up to 24 hours. To serve, return mixture to Dutch oven and stir in additional milk to desired consistency. Heat through and serve as above.

Nutrition Facts per serving: 119 cal., 2 g total fat (1 g sat. fat), 6 mg chol., 199 mg sodium, 22 g carbo., 9 g fiber, 4 g pro.

Bread-loving Italian and French cooks have devised wonderful ways to use day-old or older bread. Toasting the bread helps it hold its shape in the soup.

ITALIAN COUNTRY BREAD SOUP

4	cups Italian flatbread (focaccia) cut into ¾-inch cubes
1	tablespoon olive oil
2½	cups chopped zucchini and/or yellow summer squash
¾	cup chopped green sweet pepper
½	cup chopped onion
2	14-ounce cans chicken broth or 3½ cups homemade chicken broth
1	14½-ounce can diced tomatoes with basil, oregano, and garlic, undrained
	Finely shredded Parmesan cheese (optional)

PREP:
10 minutes
BAKE:
10 minutes
COOK:
10 minutes
OVEN:
375°F
MAKES:
6 servings

1 Spread bread cubes in a single layer on an ungreased baking sheet. Bake in a 375° oven for 10 to 15 minutes or until lightly toasted, stirring once or twice.

2 Meanwhile, in a large saucepan heat oil. Add zucchini, sweet pepper, and onion; cook over medium heat for 5 minutes, stirring frequently. Stir in broth and undrained tomatoes. Bring to boiling; reduce heat. Simmer, uncovered, about 5 minutes or until vegetables are just tender.

3 Top each serving with toasted bread cubes and, if desired, Parmesan cheese.

Nutrition Facts per serving: 172 cal., 4 g total fat (1 g sat. fat), 9 mg chol., 526 mg sodium, 27 g carbo., 3 g fiber, 8 g pro.

Roasted tomatoes, eggplant, and leeks take this vegetable soup to a delicious new level.

HARVEST TRIO SOUP

PREP:

1 hour

COOK:

15 minutes

OVEN:

400°F

MAKES:

9 servings

¼ cup olive oil

4 large eggplants, trimmed and halved lengthwise

5 medium tomatoes, cored and halved

2 tablespoons olive oil

1 cup finely chopped leeks (white parts only)

2 teaspoons paprika

2 cloves garlic, minced

¼ to ½ teaspoon cayenne pepper

2 14-ounce cans vegetable broth or 3½ cups homemade vegetable broth

½ cup dry white wine or water

2 tablespoons snipped fresh thyme

2 tablespoons snipped fresh oregano

1 tablespoon balsamic vinegar

¼ teaspoon black pepper

½ cup whipping cream (optional)

Salt (optional)

1 Line two 15×10×1-inch baking pans with foil. Generously grease the foil with the ¼ cup olive oil. Place eggplant and tomato halves, cut sides down, on prepared baking pans. Bake in a 400° oven for 30 to 35 minutes or until eggplant is very soft.

2 Cool eggplant and tomatoes slightly. Scoop out eggplant pulp, discarding peel. Remove and discard skin from tomatoes. Set aside eggplant pulp and tomatoes.

3 Meanwhile, in a 4-quart Dutch oven heat the 2 tablespoons oil. Add leeks; cook and stir over medium heat until tender. Stir in paprika, garlic, and cayenne pepper. Add broth and wine. Stir in eggplant pulp, tomatoes, thyme, and oregano. Bring to boiling; reduce heat. Simmer, uncovered, for 10 minutes. Remove from heat; cool slightly.

4 Transfer one-third of the vegetable mixture to a blender or food processor. Cover and blend or process until smooth. Repeat with remaining vegetable mixture. Return all mixture to Dutch oven.

5 Stir in vinegar and pepper. If desired, stir in whipping cream and season to taste with salt; heat through.

Nutrition Facts per serving: 147 cal., 6 g total fat (1 g sat. fat), 0 mg chol., 406 mg sodium, 22 g carbo., 7 g fiber, 4 g pro.

Baby vegetables have a milder flavor and more tender texture than their full-size counterparts.
Be sure to cook them until just tender for best taste and texture.

BABY VEGETABLE MINESTRONE

2	teaspoons olive oil
½	cup thinly sliced baby fennel
½	cup chopped carrot
2	large cloves garlic, minced
¼	teaspoon lemon-pepper seasoning
2	14-ounce cans reduced-sodium chicken broth or 3½ cups homemade chicken broth
½	cup dried ditalini or other small dried pasta
6	ounces baby zucchini, halved lengthwise
6	ounces baby yellow squash, halved lengthwise
½	cup sliced green onions
¼	cup fresh basil leaves, thinly sliced
6	ounces Parmigiano-Reggiano or Romano cheese, cut into six very thin wedges (optional)

PREP:
20 minutes
COOK:
25 minutes
MAKES:
6 servings

1 In a very large saucepan or 4-quart Dutch oven heat oil. Add fennel, carrot, garlic, and lemon pepper; cook and stir over medium heat for 3 to 4 minutes or until carrot is slightly brown. Carefully stir in broth. Bring to boiling; reduce heat. Simmer, covered, about 8 minutes or until vegetables are just tender.

2 Add pasta. Simmer, covered, for 5 minutes. Add zucchini and yellow squash. Return to boiling; reduce heat. Simmer, covered, about 5 minutes more or until pasta is tender. Stir in green onions and basil.

3 If desired, place a wedge of cheese in each of six warmed bowls. Add hot soup. Let cheese soften slightly before serving.

Nutrition Facts per serving: 83 cal., 2 g total fat (0 g sat. fat), 0 mg chol., 410 mg sodium, 13 g carbo., 4 g fiber, 4 g pro.

Forget mushy little bits of vegetables; this version of vegetable soup boasts a bounty of just-tender chunks of garden-fresh root veggies. (Recipe pictured on page 98.)

FARMER'S VEGETABLE SOUP

START TO FINISH:

45 minutes

MAKES:

4 to 6 servings

2 medium leeks, trimmed and bias-cut into 1- to 2-inch slices (white parts only)

1 medium rutabaga, peeled and cut into 1-inch pieces

1 medium turnip, peeled and cut into 1-inch pieces

$1/3$ cup coarsely chopped parsnip

$1/3$ cup coarsely chopped carrot

3 cups beef broth

3 cups water

$1/2$ cup dry sherry or beef broth

1 4-inch sprig fresh rosemary or $1/2$ teaspoon dried rosemary, crushed

Fresh rosemary sprigs (optional)

1 In a 4-quart Dutch oven combine leeks, rutabaga, turnip, parsnip, carrot, broth, water, sherry, and the 4-inch sprig of rosemary or dried rosemary. Bring to boiling; reduce heat. Simmer, uncovered, for 25 to 30 minutes or until turnip and rutabaga are tender. Remove rosemary sprig. Ladle into bowls. If desired, garnish with additional rosemary sprigs.

Nutrition Facts per serving: 123 cal., 0 g total fat (0 g sat. fat), 0 mg chol., 678 mg sodium, 18 g carbo., 4 g fiber, 3 g pro.

Master just one simple soup-making technique and you can prepare two delicious creamy soups.

CREAM OF VEGETABLE SOUP

	Desired vegetable (see variations below)
1½	cups chicken broth or vegetable broth
1	tablespoon butter or margarine
1	tablespoon all-purpose flour
	Seasoning (see variations below)
¼	teaspoon salt
	Dash black pepper
1	cup milk, half-and-half, or light cream

1 In a large saucepan cook desired vegetable, covered, in a large amount of boiling water according to directions in each variation. Drain well. Set aside 1 cup cooked vegetable.

2 In a blender or food processor combine remaining cooked vegetable and ¾ cup of the broth. Cover and blend or process about 1 minute or until smooth. Set aside.

3 In the same saucepan melt butter over medium heat. Stir in flour, seasoning, salt, and pepper. Add milk all at once. Cook and stir until slightly thickened and bubbly. Cook and stir for 1 minute more.

4 Stir in reserved 1 cup cooked vegetable, blended vegetable mixture, and remaining ¾ cup broth. Cook and stir until heated through. If necessary, stir in additional milk to reach desired consistency. Season to taste with additional salt and pepper.

CREAM OF POTATO SOUP: Cook 5 medium potatoes, peeled and cubed, and ½ cup chopped onion as directed in Step 1 about 15 minutes or until tender. Drain. Reserve 1 cup potato mixture. Blend remaining mixture as directed in Step 2, except use all of the broth. Use ¼ teaspoon dried dill or basil, crushed, in Step 3.

Nutrition Facts per serving: 236 cal., 5 g total fat (3 g sat. fat), 13 mg chol., 509 mg sodium, 40 g carbo., 3 g fiber, 8 g pro.

CREAM OF BROCCOLI SOUP: Cook 4 cups fresh or frozen chopped broccoli as directed in Step 1 for 8 to 10 minutes or until tender. Drain. Reserve 1 cup broccoli. Blend remaining broccoli as directed in Step 2. Use ¼ teaspoon lemon-pepper seasoning in Step 3. Stir in ½ cup shredded American cheese with the blended vegetable mixture in Step 4. If desired, garnish with additional shredded American cheese.

Nutrition Facts per serving: 158 cal., 9 g total fat (6 g sat. fat), 26 mg chol., 729 mg sodium, 10 g carbo., 3 g fiber, 9 g pro.

Two kinds of cheese make this soup creamy and full flavored. Or make one of the easy variations.

CHEESE CHOWDER

START TO FINISH:

30 minutes

MAKES:

6 to 8 servings

1	cup water
½	cup chopped carrot
½	cup sliced celery
½	cup chopped red sweet pepper
¼	cup thinly sliced green onions
3	cups milk
¼	cup all-purpose flour
½	teaspoon instant chicken bouillon granules
¼	teaspoon white pepper
1½	cups shredded sharp cheddar cheese (6 ounces)
1½	cups shredded American cheese (6 ounces)

1 In a large saucepan bring water to boiling. Add carrot, celery, sweet pepper, and green onions; cook, covered, about 5 minutes or until vegetables are tender. Do not drain.

2 In a small bowl gradually stir about 1 cup of the milk into the flour; stir into cooked vegetables in saucepan. Add remaining milk, bouillon granules, and white pepper.

3 Cook and stir over medium heat until thickened and bubbly. Cook and stir for 1 minute more. Add cheddar cheese and American cheese, stirring until melted.

Nutrition Facts per serving: 311 cal., 21 g total fat (13 g sat. fat), 66 mg chol., 748 mg sodium, 13 g carbo., 1 g fiber, 18 g pro.

QUICK CHEESE CHOWDER: Prepare Cheese Chowder as above, except omit celery, sweet pepper, and green onions. In a large saucepan combine the water, carrot, and one 10-ounce package frozen cauliflower or frozen cut broccoli. Bring to boiling; reduce heat. Simmer, covered, about 4 minutes or until vegetables are crisp-tender. Do not drain. Cut up any large pieces of cauliflower or broccoli. Continue as directed in Step 2. Makes 6 to 8 servings.

Nutrition Facts per serving: 311 cal., 21 g total fat (13 g sat. fat), 66 mg chol., 748 mg sodium, 13 g carbo., 1 g fiber, 18 g pro.

BEER-CHEESE CHOWDER: Prepare Cheese Chowder as above, except add ¾ cup beer to the cooked vegetables along with the milk. Makes 6 to 8 servings.

Nutrition Facts per serving: 311 cal., 21 g total fat (13 g sat. fat), 66 mg chol., 748 mg sodium, 13 g carbo., 1 g fiber, 18 g pro.

Pamper your taste buds with this sumptuous soup enriched with whipping cream and dark ale.

CHEESE SOUP

2	tablespoons butter or margarine
½	cup finely chopped onion
½	cup finely chopped carrot
½	cup finely chopped celery
¼	cup thinly sliced green onions
¼	cup all-purpose flour
½	teaspoon dry mustard
4	cups chicken broth or reduced-sodium chicken broth
1	cup dark ale or beer
1	cup whipping cream
1½	cups peeled potatoes cut into ½-inch cubes
1	cup shredded sharp cheddar cheese (4 ounces)
1	cup shredded white cheddar cheese (4 ounces)
¼	cup grated Parmesan or Romano cheese
¼	teaspoon bottled hot pepper sauce
¼	teaspoon Worcestershire sauce

PREP:
30 minutes
COOK:
30 minutes
MAKES:
8 servings

1 In a 4-quart Dutch oven melt butter over medium heat. Add onion, carrot, celery, and green onions; cook and stir for 8 to 10 minutes or until onion is very soft and golden.

2 Stir in flour and mustard; cook and stir for 1 minute. Stir in chicken broth; cook and stir until slightly thickened and bubbly. Stir in ale and whipping cream. Add potatoes. Bring to boiling; reduce heat. Simmer, uncovered, for 10 to 12 minutes or until potatoes are tender.

3 Slowly add cheddar cheeses, whisking until all cheese is melted. Whisk in Parmesan cheese, hot pepper sauce, and Worcestershire sauce.

Nutrition Facts per serving: 341 cal., 26 g total fat (16 g sat. fat), 82 mg chol., 792 mg sodium, 15 g carbo., 1 g fiber, 11 g pro.

Now you don't have to live in New England to enjoy a fine lobster bisque. It's a lavish choice to kick off a special-occasion meal.

LOBSTER BISQUE

START TO FINISH:

1 hour

MAKES:

8 servings

2   8-ounce fresh or frozen lobster tails

1   14-ounce can chicken broth or 1¾ cups homemade chicken broth

½   cup chopped onion

½   cup finely chopped carrot

½   cup dry white wine

2   tablespoons curry powder

1   tablespoon tomato paste

1   bay leaf

3   cups half-and-half, light cream, or whipping cream

¼   cup butter, melted

¼   cup all-purpose flour

3   tablespoons cognac

1   tablespoon snipped fresh parsley

    Salt

    Black pepper

    Snipped fresh chives

1 Thaw lobster tails, if frozen; rinse under cold running water. In a large heavy saucepan combine broth, onion, and carrot; bring to boiling. Add lobster tails. Simmer, covered, for 8 to 12 minutes or until shells turn bright red and lobster meat is tender. Remove lobster tails; cool. Strain broth, discarding vegetables. Return strained broth to saucepan. Stir in wine, curry powder, tomato paste, and bay leaf. Bring to boiling; reduce heat. Simmer, uncovered, for 10 minutes. Meanwhile, remove meat from lobster tails and coarsely chop.

2 Stir half-and-half into broth mixture in saucepan. Stir together melted butter and flour. Stir into cream mixture. Cook and stir until thickened and bubbly; cook for 1 minute more. Stir in lobster meat, cognac, and parsley; heat through. Remove and discard bay leaf.

3 Season to taste with salt and pepper. Garnish with fresh chives.

Nutrition Facts per serving: 440 cal., 40 g total fat (25 g sat. fat), 158 mg chol., 500 mg sodium, 7 g carbo., 1 g fiber, 8 g pro.

For many families, oyster stew is a special treat on Christmas Eve, but it's terrific on any chilly night. Serve it with carrot and celery sticks and, of course, oyster crackers.

OYSTER STEW

2	tablespoons butter or margarine
1½	cups sliced leeks (white parts only)
1	cup finely chopped onion
⅛	teaspoon dried thyme, crushed
2	cups chopped, peeled potatoes
1	pint shucked oysters, undrained
2	cups whipping cream
1	cup milk
2	tablespoons snipped fresh parsley
½	teaspoon salt
¼	teaspoon black pepper

START TO FINISH:

40 minutes

MAKES:

8 servings

1 In a large saucepan melt butter over medium heat. Add leeks, onion, and thyme; cook, covered, over medium-low heat for 15 minutes, stirring occasionally.

2 Meanwhile, in a medium saucepan cook potatoes in a large amount of boiling lightly salted water for 7 to 10 minutes or until tender. Drain.

3 Add undrained oysters to leek mixture. Bring to boiling; reduce heat. Simmer, covered, for 5 to 7 minutes or until oysters curl around edges, stirring occasionally. Add drained potatoes, whipping cream, milk, parsley, salt, and pepper to oyster mixture; heat through.

Nutrition Facts per serving: 331 cal., 27 g total fat (16 g sat. fat), 107 mg chol., 322 mg sodium, 17 g carbo., 1 g fiber, 7 g pro.

You can almost hear a steel drum band in the background as you make this easy soup, originally from Brazil.

SHRIMP & COCONUT SOUP

START TO FINISH:

15 minutes

MAKES:

5 servings

8 ounces fresh or frozen peeled, deveined small shrimp

2 14-ounce cans chicken broth or 3½ cups homemade chicken broth

4 ounces dried angel hair pasta or vermicelli, broken into 2-inch pieces

1 tablespoon curry powder

1 cup purchased unsweetened coconut milk

Sliced green onion or snipped fresh chives

1 Thaw shrimp, if frozen. Rinse shrimp and pat dry. Set aside.

2 In a large saucepan bring broth to boiling. Add pasta and curry powder; return to boiling. Boil gently for 3 minutes. Add shrimp; cook for 2 to 3 minutes or until shrimp turn pink and pasta is tender. Stir in coconut milk; heat through. Sprinkle with green onion.

Nutrition Facts per serving: 268 cal., 14 g total fat (11 g sat. fat), 69 mg chol., 762 mg sodium, 22 g carbo., 2 g fiber, 15 g pro.

HEARTY
SOUPS

2

Can't find a package of frozen succotash? Substitute 1 cup each frozen corn and frozen lima beans.

HAMBURGER-VEGETABLE SOUP

PREP:

20 minutes

COOK:

10 minutes

MAKES:

6 servings

1	pound lean ground beef or pork
½	cup chopped onion
½	cup chopped green sweet pepper
4	cups beef broth
1	14½-ounce can diced tomatoes, undrained
1	10-ounce package frozen succotash
½	cup chopped, peeled potato or ½ cup frozen loose-pack diced hash brown potatoes
½	cup purchased shredded carrot or 1 medium carrot, cut into thin bite-size strips (½ cup)
1	teaspoon dried basil, crushed
1	teaspoon Worcestershire sauce
⅛	teaspoon black pepper

1 In a large saucepan cook ground beef, onion, and sweet pepper over medium-high heat about 5 minutes or until beef is brown and onion is tender; drain off fat. Stir in broth, undrained tomatoes, succotash, potato, carrot, basil, Worcestershire sauce, and pepper. Bring to boiling; reduce heat. Simmer, covered, for 10 to 15 minutes or until vegetables are tender.

Nutrition Facts per serving: 227 cal., 8 g total fat (3 g sat. fat), 48 mg chol., 613 mg sodium, 19 g carbo., 3 g fiber, 20 g pro.

Orzo is a small, rice-shape pasta. If orzo is not available, substitute dried spaghetti or linguine, broken into $1/4$- to $1/2$-inch-long pieces.

BEEFY ORZO & ESCAROLE SOUP

12	ounces lean ground beef
$2/3$	cup chopped fennel
$1/2$	cup chopped onion
2	cloves garlic, minced
4	cups beef broth
2	cups water
1	teaspoon dried oregano, crushed
2	bay leaves
$1/4$	teaspoon coarsely cracked black pepper
$1/2$	cup dried orzo
4	cups shredded escarole, curly endive, and/or fresh spinach
3	ounces Parmesan cheese with rind, cut into 4 wedges (optional)

PREP:

5 minutes

COOK:

25 minutes

MAKES:

4 servings

1 In a large saucepan cook ground beef, fennel, onion, and garlic over medium-high heat about 5 minutes or until beef is brown and vegetables are nearly tender; drain off fat, if necessary.

2 Add broth, water, oregano, bay leaves, and pepper. Bring to boiling; reduce heat. Simmer, covered, for 10 minutes. Remove and discard bay leaves.

3 Add orzo. Return to boiling; reduce heat to medium. Boil gently, uncovered, about 10 minutes or until orzo is just tender, stirring occasionally. Remove from heat; stir in escarole. If desired, serve with wedges of Parmesan cheese.

Nutrition Facts per serving: 262 cal., 10 g total fat (4 g sat. fat), 54 mg chol., 873 mg sodium, 22 g carbo., 7 g fiber, 21 g pro.

The condiments suggested to stir into your soup will thrill most guests and give picky diners some control over their meal.

MEATBALL SOUP

PREP:

35 minutes

BAKE:

15 minutes

COOK:

20 minutes

OVEN:

375°F

MAKES:

6 servings

1	slightly beaten egg
1	cup soft bread crumbs
¼	cup milk
1	tablespoon yellow mustard
¼	teaspoon salt
1	pound lean ground beef
6	cups water
2	cups tomato juice
2	tablespoons instant beef bouillon granules
1½	cups thinly sliced carrots
1	cup dried tiny bow ties
⅓	cup thinly sliced green onions
2	tablespoons snipped fresh parsley
2	medium tomatoes, chopped
6	slices bacon, crisp-cooked, drained, and crumbled
1	cup sliced fresh mushrooms
1	cup shredded mozzarella cheese (4 ounces)
½	cup finely shredded Parmesan cheese (2 ounces)
½	cup croutons

1 For meatballs, in a large bowl combine egg, bread crumbs, milk, mustard, and salt. Add ground beef; mix well. Shape meat mixture into forty-eight ¾-inch meatballs. Place meatballs in a shallow baking pan. Bake in a 375° oven about 15 minutes or until no pink remains. Drain well.

2 Meanwhile, in a 4½- to 5-quart Dutch oven combine water, tomato juice, and bouillon granules. Bring to boiling over medium-high heat. Add meatballs, carrots, and pasta. Return to boiling; reduce heat. Cook, uncovered, about 10 minutes or until pasta is tender. Stir in green onions and parsley.

3 Top each serving with tomatoes, bacon, mushrooms, mozzarella cheese, Parmesan cheese, and croutons.

Nutrition Facts per serving: 414 cal., 19 g total fat (8 g sat. fat), 108 mg chol., 1,782 mg sodium, 30 g carbo., 3 g fiber, 31 g pro.

This family-pleasing soup is as easy to make as it is hearty. (Recipe pictured on page 110.)

QUICK & EASY ITALIAN MEATBALL SOUP

(Recipe pictured on page 110.)

1   14½-ounce can diced tomatoes with onion and garlic, undrained

1   14-ounce can reduced-sodium beef broth or 1¾ cups homemade beef broth

1½ cups water

½   teaspoon dried Italian seasoning, crushed

½   of a 16-ounce package (8) Italian-style frozen cooked meatballs

1   cup frozen mixed vegetables

½   cup small dried pasta (such as ditalini or orzo)

1   tablespoon shredded or grated Parmesan cheese (optional)

START TO FINISH:
25 minutes
MAKES:
4 servings

1 In a large saucepan combine undrained tomatoes, broth, water, and Italian seasoning. Bring to boiling. Add meatballs, frozen vegetables, and pasta. Return to boiling; reduce heat. Simmer, covered, about 10 minutes or until vegetables and pasta are tender. If desired, sprinkle each serving with Parmesan cheese.

Nutrition Facts per serving: 290 cal., 14 g total fat (7 g sat. fat), 38 mg chol., 1,302 mg sodium, 26 g carbo., 4 g fiber, 15 g pro.

Try this tasty recipe for supper with a salad and garlic bread.

SOUPER SPAGHETTI

PREP:

20 minutes

COOK:

25 minutes

MAKES:

6 servings

1	pound lean ground beef
½	cup chopped onion
½	cup chopped green sweet pepper
½	cup chopped celery
½	cup chopped carrot
2	cloves garlic, minced
2½	cups water
2	14½-ounce cans diced tomatoes, undrained
1	13- to 15-ounce jar spaghetti sauce
1	tablespoon sugar
½	teaspoon dried Italian seasoning, crushed
½	teaspoon salt
¼	teaspoon black pepper
	Dash crushed red pepper
2	ounces dried spaghetti, broken into 2-inch pieces

1 In a large saucepan or 4-quart Dutch oven cook ground beef, onion, sweet pepper, celery, carrot, and garlic over medium-high heat about 5 minutes or until beef is brown and vegetables are tender. Drain off fat.

2 Add water, undrained tomatoes, spaghetti sauce, sugar, Italian seasoning, salt, black pepper, and crushed red pepper. Bring to boiling; add pasta. Return to boiling; reduce heat. Boil gently, uncovered, for 12 to 15 minutes or until pasta is tender.

Nutrition Facts per serving: 263 cal., 9 g total fat (3 g sat. fat), 48 mg chol., 960 mg sodium, 28 g carbo., 5 g fiber, 17 g pro.

Corn muffins make the perfect accompaniment to this Southwestern-flavored soup.

TACO SOUP

<table>
<tr><td>1</td><td>pound lean ground beef</td></tr>
<tr><td>1</td><td>15½-ounce can black-eyed peas, undrained</td></tr>
<tr><td>1</td><td>15-ounce can black beans, undrained</td></tr>
<tr><td>1</td><td>15-ounce can chili beans with chili gravy, undrained</td></tr>
<tr><td>1</td><td>15-ounce can garbanzo beans (chickpeas), undrained</td></tr>
<tr><td>1</td><td>14½-ounce can Mexican-style stewed tomatoes, undrained</td></tr>
<tr><td>1</td><td>11-ounce can whole kernel corn with
sweet peppers (Mexi-corn), undrained</td></tr>
<tr><td>1</td><td>1.25-ounce package taco seasoning mix</td></tr>
<tr><td></td><td>Dairy sour cream (optional)</td></tr>
<tr><td></td><td>Bottled salsa (optional)</td></tr>
<tr><td></td><td>Broken tortilla chips (optional)</td></tr>
</table>

PREP:
15 minutes
COOK:
1 hour
MAKES:
8 servings

1 In a 4-quart Dutch oven cook ground beef over medium-high heat until brown; drain off fat. Stir in undrained black-eyed peas, undrained black beans, undrained chili beans, undrained garbanzo beans, undrained tomatoes, and undrained corn. Stir in taco seasoning mix.

2 Bring to boiling; reduce heat. Simmer, covered, for 1 to 2 hours, stirring occasionally. If desired, top each serving with sour cream, salsa, and tortilla chips.

Nutrition Facts per serving: 409 cal., 13 g total fat (5 g sat. fat), 41 mg chol., 1,423 mg sodium, 52 g carbo., 12 g fiber, 26 g pro.

Just as similar soups are served in Vietnamese noodle shops, pass the condiments for this soup at the table so diners can add their own.

VIETNAMESE BEEF-NOODLE SOUP

PREP:

15 minutes

COOK:

4 minutes

STAND:

30 minutes

MAKES:

4 servings

4   ounces rice sticks

8   ounces boneless beef top round steak

6   cups water

3   14-ounce cans beef broth or 5¼ cups homemade beef broth

3   green onions, thinly sliced

2   tablespoons snipped fresh cilantro
    Bottled hot pepper sauce (optional)
    Bottled oyster sauce (optional)
    Snipped fresh basil (optional)
    Lime juice (optional)

1 Soak rice sticks in enough cold water to cover for 30 minutes; drain.

2 Meanwhile, if desired, partially freeze beef for easier slicing. Thinly slice beef across the grain into bite-size strips. Set beef aside.

3 In a large saucepan bring the 6 cups water to boiling. Add drained rice sticks. Boil for 3 to 5 minutes or until tender. (To avoid overcooking, test every minute beginning when rice sticks have cooked 3 minutes.) Drain in a colander; rinse with cold water. Drain again. Divide the cooked rice sticks among 4 large soup bowls.

4 Meanwhile, in a medium saucepan bring beef broth just to boiling. Add beef strips. Cook about 1 minute or just until meat is cooked. Ladle hot broth and cooked beef strips over noodles in soup bowls. Sprinkle each serving with green onions and cilantro. If desired, serve with hot pepper sauce, oyster sauce, basil, and/or lime juice.

Nutrition Facts per serving: 212 cal., 4 g total fat (2 g sat. fat), 31 mg chol., 1,101 mg sodium, 26 g carbo., 1 g fiber, 17 g pro.

Although many families have a skillet concoction they call goulash, this is the real thing. Gulyás originated in Hungary, where it's seasoned with aromatic Hungarian paprika.

GOULASH

2	tablespoons cooking oil
1	pound boneless beef top round steak, cut into ½-inch cubes
½	cup chopped onion
2	tablespoons all-purpose flour
1	tablespoon Hungarian paprika
2	cloves garlic, minced
3	14-ounce cans chicken broth or 5¼ cups homemade chicken broth
1	14½-ounce can diced tomatoes, undrained
1½	cups sliced carrots
2	tablespoons tomato paste
1	bay leaf
½	teaspoon dried marjoram, crushed
½	teaspoon caraway seeds, crushed
½	teaspoon black pepper
2	cups cubed, peeled potatoes
	Dairy sour cream (optional)

PREP:
25 minutes
COOK:
1¼ hours
MAKES:
6 to 8 servings

1 In a 4- to 5-quart Dutch oven heat oil. Add beef and onion; cook and stir over medium-high heat about 5 minutes or until beef is brown and onion is tender.

2 Add flour, paprika, and garlic. Cook, stirring constantly, for 3 minutes. Stir in broth, undrained tomatoes, carrots, tomato paste, bay leaf, marjoram, caraway seeds, and pepper. Bring to boiling; reduce heat. Simmer, covered, for 50 minutes, stirring occasionally. Add potatoes. Simmer, covered, for 25 to 30 minutes more or until potatoes and beef are tender. Remove and discard bay leaf. If desired, top each serving with sour cream.

Nutrition Facts per serving: 244 cal., 9 g total fat (2 g sat. fat), 42 mg chol., 996 mg sodium, 19 g carbo., 3 g fiber, 21 g pro.

If desired, substitute ½ cup regular barley for quick-cooking barley; add it with the water.

BARLEY-BEEF SOUP

PREP:
25 minutes

COOK:
1¼ hours

MAKES:
6 servings

1   tablespoon cooking oil

12   ounces beef or lamb stew meat, cut into 1-inch cubes

4   cups water

1   cup chopped onion

½   cup chopped celery

2   teaspoons instant beef bouillon granules

1   teaspoon dried oregano or basil, crushed

¼   teaspoon black pepper

2   cloves garlic, minced

1   bay leaf

1   cup frozen mixed vegetables

1   14½-ounce can diced tomatoes, undrained

1   cup sliced, peeled parsnips or cubed, peeled potatoes

½   cup quick-cooking barley

1 In a large saucepan heat oil. Add meat; cook and stir over medium-high heat about 5 minutes or until brown. Stir in water, onion, celery, bouillon granules, oregano, pepper, garlic, and bay leaf. Bring to boiling; reduce heat. Simmer, covered, for 1 hour for beef (45 minutes for lamb).

2 Stir in frozen vegetables, undrained tomatoes, parsnips, and barley. Return to boiling; reduce heat. Simmer, covered, about 15 minutes more or until meat and vegetables are tender. Remove and discard bay leaf.

Nutrition Facts per serving: 210 cal., 6 g total fat (1 g sat. fat), 27 mg chol., 515 mg sodium, 23 g carbo., 4 g fiber, 16 g pro.

Mirin and saké are well-known Japanese rice wines. A daikon is a large Asian radish available in large supermarkets and Asian grocery stores.

FIVE-SPICE BEEF SOUP

2	tablespoons cooking oil
1½	pounds beef stew meat, cut into 1-inch cubes
¼	cup sliced green onions
1	1-inch piece fresh ginger
½	teaspoon crushed red pepper
4	cloves garlic, minced
1½	cups chopped tomatoes
1⅓	cups mirin (Japanese sweet rice wine)
1	cup water
1	cup chopped daikon
1	cup chopped carrots
3	tablespoons soy sauce
1	teaspoon five-spice powder
4	cups hot cooked rice

PREP:
25 minutes
COOK:
1¼ hours
MAKES:
6 servings

1 In a 4-quart Dutch oven heat oil. Add half of the beef cubes; cook and stir over medium-high heat about 5 minutes or until beef is brown. Repeat with remaining beef. Drain beef, reserving drippings. Cook and stir green onions, ginger, crushed red pepper, and garlic in reserved drippings for 1 minute.

2 Return beef to Dutch oven. Add tomatoes, mirin, water, daikon, carrots, soy sauce, and five-spice powder. Bring to boiling; reduce heat. Simmer, covered, for 1¼ hours or until meat and vegetables are tender. Skim off fat. Remove and discard fresh ginger. Serve over rice.

Nutrition Facts per serving: 500 cal., 9 g total fat (2 g sat. fat), 67 mg chol., 622 mg sodium, 73 g carbo., 3 g fiber, 29 g pro.

This favorite soup is one you'll turn to time and again for a satisfying family supper.

CLASSIC VEGETABLE~BEEF SOUP

PREP:

30 minutes

COOK:

45 minutes

MAKES:

6 to 8 servings

5½	cups beef broth
2	cups chopped cooked beef
1½	cups cubed, peeled potatoes
1½	cups sliced celery
1½	cups sliced carrots
1½	cups chopped onions
1	cup frozen succotash
½	cup regular barley
¼	teaspoon dried rosemary, crushed
¼	teaspoon dried oregano, crushed
¼	teaspoon dried thyme, crushed
1	14½-ounce can diced tomatoes, undrained
¼	teaspoon salt
	Salt
	Black pepper

1 In a 4½-quart Dutch oven combine broth, beef, potatoes, celery, carrots, onions, succotash, barley, rosemary, oregano, and thyme. Bring to boiling; reduce heat. Simmer, covered, for 30 minutes. Stir in undrained tomatoes and the ¼ teaspoon salt. Simmer, covered, for 15 to 20 minutes more or until vegetables and barley are tender. Season to taste with additional salt and pepper.

Nutrition Facts per serving: 266 cal., 6 g total fat (2 g sat. fat), 41 mg chol., 643 mg sodium, 35 g carbo., 7 g fiber, 19 g pro.

A long simmer on the stove makes this a great Sunday soup. Serve with thick slices of crusty bread, rubbed with olive oil and garlic, to sop up every last bit. (Recipe pictured on page 106.)

BEEF & CABBAGE SOUP

1	pound finely chopped country or smoked bacon or 8 ounces prosciutto
1½	to 2 pounds beef shank cross cuts
6	cups water
1½	pounds tiny new potatoes, quartered
1	cup coarsely chopped onion
4	medium carrots, quartered crosswise
2	turnips, peeled and quartered
1	15- to 19-ounce can navy beans or white kidney beans (cannellini), undrained
4	cloves garlic, minced
1	recipe Herb Bag
4	cups coarsely chopped cabbage
	Kosher salt or salt
8	thick slices hearty country bread, toasted and rubbed with olive oil and garlic

PREP: *50 minutes*
COOK: *2 hours*
MAKES: *8 servings*

1 In a 10- to 12-quart Dutch oven cook bacon over medium heat until crisp. Remove bacon, reserving 2 tablespoons drippings in Dutch oven. Drain bacon on paper towels. (If using prosciutto, add cooking oil to drippings to equal 2 tablespoons.) Set bacon aside.

2 Brown beef shanks on both sides in reserved drippings. Add water, potatoes, onion, carrots, turnips, undrained beans, garlic, and Herb Bag. Bring to boiling; reduce heat. Simmer, covered, for 1½ hours. Add cabbage. Simmer, covered, about 30 minutes more or until meat is tender.

3 Remove and discard Herb Bag. Remove beef shanks from Dutch oven. When cool enough to handle, remove meat from bones. Discard bones. Shred meat. Skim fat from broth. Return meat to Dutch oven; heat through. Stir in bacon. Season to taste with salt.

4 To serve, place a slice of bread in the bottom of each soup plate; ladle soup over bread.

HERB BAG: Cut a 10-inch square of 100-percent-cotton cheesecloth. Place 2 bay leaves, 8 sprigs fresh parsley, 4 or 5 sprigs fresh thyme, 4 or 5 sprigs fresh marjoram, and 12 lightly crushed whole black peppercorns on cheesecloth. Bring up corners and tie closed with clean string.

Nutrition Facts per serving: 504 cal., 18 g total fat (7 g sat. fat), 49 mg chol., 983 mg sodium, 48 g carbo., 8 g fiber, 27 g pro.

Using both beef and pork gives the broth for this Italian-style bean soup double the flavor.
Add dried herbs before simmering to intensify their flavor; if you prefer fresh herbs,
stir them in at the last minute.

TUSCAN BEAN SOUP WITH SPINACH

PREP:

1¹/₂ hours

COOK:

2 hours

MAKES:

8 to 10 servings

8	ounces dry white kidney beans (cannellini)
1	pound beef shank cross cuts
1	tablespoon olive oil
1¹/₂	cups chopped onions
1¹/₂	cups chopped carrots
1	cup chopped fennel or celery
4	cloves garlic, minced
12	ounces meaty smoked pork hocks
1	tablespoon instant beef bouillon granules
1	bay leaf
2	teaspoons snipped fresh thyme or ¹/₂ teaspoon dried thyme, crushed
2	teaspoons snipped fresh rosemary or ¹/₂ teaspoon dried rosemary, crushed
1	14¹/₂-ounce can diced tomatoes, undrained
4	cups torn fresh spinach

1 Rinse beans. In a 4¹/₂- to 5-quart Dutch oven combine beans and 6 cups *water*. Bring to boiling; reduce heat. Simmer for 2 minutes. Remove from heat. Cover and let stand for 1 hour. (Or place beans in water in Dutch oven. Cover and let soak in a cool place for 6 to 8 hours or overnight.) Drain and rinse beans.

2 Sprinkle beef shanks with ¹/₄ teaspoon *salt* and ¹/₄ teaspoon *black pepper*. In a 4¹/₂- to 6-quart Dutch oven heat oil. Add beef shanks; brown on both sides. Remove beef shanks, reserving drippings. Set beef shanks aside.

3 Add onions, carrots, fennel, and garlic to reserved drippings in Dutch oven. Cook, covered, about 10 minutes or until vegetables are tender, stirring occasionally. Return beef shanks to Dutch oven. Add 6 cups fresh *water*, pork hocks, bouillon granules, bay leaf, dried thyme and dried rosemary (if using), and ¹/₂ teaspoon *salt*. Bring to boiling; reduce heat. Simmer, covered, for 1¹/₂ hours. Stir in undrained tomatoes. Return to boiling; reduce heat. Simmer, covered, about 30 minutes more or until beans and meats are tender.

4 Remove beef shanks and pork hocks from Dutch oven. When cool enough to handle, remove meat from bones. Discard bones. Cut meat into bite-size pieces. Skim fat from broth. Remove and discard bay leaf. Return meat to Dutch oven. Add fresh thyme and fresh rosemary (if using) and spinach; heat through.

Nutrition Facts per serving: 231 cal., 6 g total fat (2 g sat. fat), 21 mg chol., 803 mg sodium, 27 g carbo., 11 g fiber, 17 g pro.

Asian cooks have long known that the peppery, slightly sweet taste of ginger perfectly complements mild-flavored pork. Here the combination is even better joined with a bit of fresh mint.

GINGERED PORK & CABBAGE SOUP

6	cups vegetable or chicken broth
1	tablespoon cooking oil
8	ounces lean boneless pork, cut into ½-inch pieces
1	cup chopped onion
2	teaspoons grated fresh ginger
4	cloves garlic, minced
1	cup chopped tomatoes
1	cup chopped carrots
½	cup dried ring macaroni
4	cups thinly sliced Napa cabbage
¼	cup snipped fresh mint
	Napa cabbage leaves (optional)

START TO FINISH:

40 minutes

MAKES:

6 servings

1 In a medium saucepan bring broth to boiling. Meanwhile, in a large saucepan heat oil. Add pork, onion, ginger, and garlic; cook and stir until pork is brown.

2 Carefully add hot broth to saucepan. Bring to boiling. Stir in tomatoes and carrots. Return to boiling; reduce heat. Simmer, covered, for 15 minutes.

3 Stir in pasta. Cook for 6 to 8 minutes more or until pasta is tender but still firm. Stir in cabbage and mint. If desired, garnish each serving with cabbage leaves.

Nutrition Facts per serving: 171 cal., 5 g total fat (1 g sat. fat), 24 mg chol., 1,013 mg sodium, 20 g carbo., 3 g fiber, 11 g pro.

Paella (pi-AY-yuh) is a traditional Spanish rice dish. This soup shares its ingredients and spirit and is sure to satisfy the healthiest appetites.

PAELLA SOUP

START TO FINISH:

35 minutes

MAKES:

4 servings

8   ounces fresh or frozen peeled and deveined shrimp

1   teaspoon cooking oil

½   cup thinly sliced green onions

⅓   cup chopped red sweet pepper

1   clove garlic, minced

1   14-ounce can reduced-sodium chicken broth or 1¾ cups homemade chicken broth

½   cup uncooked long grain rice

1   bay leaf

¼   teaspoon salt

⅛   teaspoon cayenne pepper

⅛   teaspoon ground turmeric

8   ounces cooked pork, cut into ¾-inch cubes

1   cup frozen peas

2   teaspoons snipped fresh oregano

1 Thaw shrimp, if frozen; set aside. In a large saucepan heat oil. Add green onions, sweet pepper, and garlic; cook and stir over medium heat for 2 minutes.

2 Stir in broth, rice, bay leaf, salt, cayenne pepper, and turmeric. Bring to boiling; reduce heat. Simmer, covered, for 15 minutes. Stir in shrimp, pork, and peas. Simmer, covered, for 3 to 5 minutes more or until shrimp turn opaque. Remove and discard bay leaf. Stir in oregano.

Nutrition Facts per serving: 316 cal., 8 g total fat (2 g sat. fat), 132 mg chol., 529 mg sodium, 26 g carbo., 2 g fiber, 32 g pro.

Serve crusty rolls and creamy coleslaw to complement this quick, meaty soup.

QUICK PORK & BEAN SOUP

2	tablespoons cooking oil
12	ounces lean boneless pork, cut into thin bite-size strips
1	cup chopped onion
2	cups water
1½	cups sliced carrots
1	11½-ounce can condensed bean with bacon soup
1	teaspoon Worcestershire sauce
¼	teaspoon dry mustard

PREP:
15 minutes

COOK:
15 minutes

MAKES:
4 servings

1 In a large skillet heat oil. Add pork and onion; cook and stir over medium-high heat for 3 to 4 minutes or until pork is brown. Stir in water, carrots, soup, Worcestershire sauce, and dry mustard. Bring to boiling; reduce heat. Simmer, covered, for 15 minutes.

Nutrition Facts per serving: 312 cal., 13 g total fat (3 g sat. fat), 52 mg chol., 678 mg sodium, 23 g carbo., 6 g fiber, 24 g pro.

Tender barbecued pork spareribs stand amidst a robust assembly of diced veggies and plump navy beans.

NAVY BEAN SOUP WITH PORK RIBS

PREP:

10 minutes

BAKE:

50 minutes

COOK:

1¼ hours

OVEN:

350°F

MAKES:

6 servings

2   pounds meaty pork spareribs or pork loin back ribs

1   tablespoon cooking oil

1   cup chopped onion

1   cup chopped celery

¾   cup chopped carrot

2   teaspoons dried sage, crushed

½   teaspoon black pepper

2   15-ounce cans navy beans, rinsed and drained

2   14-ounce cans chicken broth or 3½ cups homemade chicken broth

¼   cup bottled barbecue sauce

1 Trim fat from ribs. Cut ribs into six two-rib portions. In a 4-quart Dutch oven heat oil. Add ribs, onion, celery, carrot, sage, and pepper; cook, uncovered, over medium heat for 5 minutes.

2 Add beans and broth. Bring to boiling; reduce heat. Cook, covered, for 20 minutes, stirring often. Remove ribs from Dutch oven. Reduce heat. Cook, covered, for 50 minutes more, stirring occasionally.

3 Meanwhile, line a shallow roasting pan with a double thickness of foil. Place ribs, meaty sides down, in pan. Brush with half of the barbecue sauce. Bake in a 350° oven for 25 minutes. Turn ribs; brush with remaining barbecue sauce. Bake about 25 minutes more or until ribs are tender.

4 To serve, place one two-rib portion in the bottom of each soup plate. Slightly mash beans in soup; ladle soup over ribs.

Nutrition Facts per serving: 443 cal., 19 g total fat (7 g sat. fat), 65 mg chol., 1,199 mg sodium, 36 g carbo., 8 g fiber, 31 g pro.

New potatoes are young, very thin-skinned, and waxy fleshed. They are low in starch and hold their shape better than other types of potatoes.

CREAMY HAM & NEW POTATO SOUP

12	ounces tiny new potatoes, quartered (2 cups)
1	cup water
1	cup chopped carrots
1/2	cup chopped onion
1/2	cup chopped celery
1/4	teaspoon dried thyme or basil, crushed, or dried dill
1/4	teaspoon white or black pepper
1 1/2	cups half-and-half, light cream, or milk
1	10 3/4-ounce can reduced-fat and reduced-sodium condensed cream of celery or cream of mushroom soup
1	cup cubed cooked ham
3/4	cup shredded American cheese (3 ounces)
	Snipped fresh parsley (optional)
	Coarsely cracked black pepper (optional)
	Shredded American cheese (optional)

START TO FINISH:
30 minutes

MAKES:
4 servings

1 In a large saucepan combine potatoes, water, carrots, onion, celery, thyme, and pepper. Bring to boiling; reduce heat. Simmer, covered, for 10 to 15 minutes or until potatoes are tender.

2 Stir in half-and-half, soup, and ham; heat through. Do not boil. Reduce heat to low. Add cheese, stirring until melted. If desired, garnish each serving with parsley, cracked pepper, and/or additional American cheese.

Nutrition Facts per serving: 382 cal., 21 g total fat (12 g sat. fat), 76 mg chol., 1,098 mg sodium, 32 g carbo., 4 g fiber, 16 g pro.

Ham and bean soup started out as a thrifty way to use leftover ham bones.
This old faithful features parsnips, carrots, and spinach. (Recipe pictured on page 106.)

HAM & BEAN SOUP WITH VEGETABLES

PREP:

1 1/2 hours

COOK:

2 hours

MAKES:

6 servings

1	cup dry navy beans
12	cups water
1 1/4	to 1 1/2 pounds meaty smoked pork hocks or one 1- to 1 1/2-pound meaty ham bone
1	cup chopped onion
1/2	cup sliced celery
1	tablespoon snipped fresh thyme or 1 teaspoon dried thyme, crushed
1	teaspoon instant chicken bouillon granules
1/4	teaspoon black pepper
2	cups chopped, peeled parsnips or rutabaga
1	cup sliced carrots
1/2	of a 10-ounce package frozen chopped spinach, thawed and well drained

1 Rinse beans. In a 4-quart Dutch oven combine beans and 5 cups of the water. Bring to boiling; reduce heat. Simmer for 2 minutes. Remove from heat. Cover and let stand for 1 hour. (Or place beans in water in Dutch oven. Cover and let soak in a cool place for 6 to 8 hours or overnight.) Drain and rinse beans.

2 Return beans to Dutch oven. Add the remaining 7 cups water, pork hocks, onion, celery, thyme, bouillon granules, and pepper. Bring to boiling; reduce heat. Simmer, covered, for 1 3/4 hours. Remove pork hocks from Dutch oven. Skim fat from broth.

3 Stir parsnips and carrots into Dutch oven. Return to boiling; reduce heat. Simmer, covered, about 15 minutes or until vegetables are tender.

4 When cool enough to handle, remove meat from bones. Discard bones. Coarsely chop meat. Return meat to Dutch oven. Add spinach; heat through.

Nutrition Facts per serving: 224 cal., 4 g total fat (1 g sat. fat), 16 mg chol., 572 mg sodium, 35 g carbo., 12 g fiber, 14 g pro.

An age-old favorite, this soup will satisfy the whole family. (Recipe pictured on page 107.)

PEA SOUP

1 bay leaf

2 whole cloves

1 sprig fresh thyme

¼ cup butter or margarine

1 cup chopped celery

½ cup chopped onion

1 clove garlic, minced

2 14-ounce cans reduced-sodium chicken broth or 3½ cups homemade chicken broth

1 pound meaty smoked pork hocks or meaty ham bone

1 cup dry split peas, rinsed and drained

¼ cup shredded carrot

⅛ teaspoon black pepper

½ cup milk

Few dashes bottled hot pepper sauce

Finely shredded Parmesan cheese (optional)

PREP:
20 minutes
COOK:
45 minutes
MAKES:
4 servings

1 Place bay leaf, cloves, and thyme sprig on a square of 100-percent-cotton cheesecloth. Bring up corners and tie closed with clean string; set aside.

2 In a large saucepan or 4-quart Dutch oven melt butter over medium heat. Add celery, onion, and garlic; cook and stir about 5 minutes or until tender. Add cheesecloth bag, broth, pork hocks, split peas, carrot, and pepper. Bring to boiling; reduce heat. Simmer, covered, for 45 to 55 minutes or until split peas are tender, stirring occasionally.

3 Remove and discard cheesecloth bag. Remove pork hocks from saucepan. When cool enough to handle, remove meat from bones. Discard bones. Chop meat. Return meat to saucepan. Stir in milk and hot pepper sauce; heat through. If desired, sprinkle each serving with Parmesan cheese.

Nutrition Facts per serving: 352 cal., 16 g total fat (9 g sat. fat), 47 mg chol., 987 mg sodium, 35 g carbo., 13 g fiber, 20 g pro.

A subtle touch of tarragon enhances the flavor of this chunky pea soup, which becomes a hearty spring meal when topped with a slice of French bread, prosciutto, and feta cheese. (Recipe pictured on page 103.)

SPRING PEA SOUP

PREP:

25 minutes

COOK:

10 minutes

MAKES:

6 servings

5	cups shelled peas
2	14-ounce cans chicken broth or 3½ cups homemade chicken broth
2	small heads Boston or Bibb lettuce, torn into small pieces
1½	cups sliced green onions
3	tablespoons snipped fresh tarragon
1½	to 2 cups half-and-half, light cream, or milk
	Salt
	Black pepper
6	slices French bread, toasted
2	ounces prosciutto, cut into thin strips
⅓	cup crumbled feta cheese
	Fresh tarragon sprigs (optional)

❶ In a 4-quart Dutch oven combine peas and broth. Bring to boiling; reduce heat. Simmer, covered, for 6 minutes. Add lettuce and green onions. Return to boiling; reduce heat. Simmer, covered, for 4 to 6 minutes more or until peas are tender. If desired, use a slotted spoon to remove ⅓ cup peas; reserve for garnish. Stir in tarragon. Cool slightly.

❷ Transfer one-fourth of the soup to a blender or food processor. Cover and blend or process until nearly smooth. Repeat with remaining soup, blending or processing one-fourth at a time. Return all of the soup to Dutch oven. Stir in half-and-half to reach desired consistency; heat through. Do not boil. Add salt and pepper to taste.

❸ Top each serving with a slice of French bread, some prosciutto, and some feta cheese. If desired, garnish each serving with reserved peas and a tarragon sprig.

Nutrition Facts per serving: 341 cal., 12 g total fat (6 g sat. fat), 36 mg chol., 1,120 mg sodium, 41 g carbo., 9 g fiber, 20 g pro.

Savor the splendor of spring: Small onions, baby carrots, fennel, and tender asparagus join baby lima beans and crisp-cooked pancetta in this rich blend.

FENNEL-ASPARAGUS SOUP

6 cups chicken broth

1 10-ounce package frozen baby lima beans

1 cup small red boiling onions or pearl onions, peeled, or coarsely chopped onion

1 teaspoon fennel seeds, crushed

¼ teaspoon black pepper

1 cup fresh packaged peeled baby carrots

1 medium fennel bulb

12 ounces fresh asparagus spears, cut into 1-inch pieces

4 ounces pancetta, chopped, crisp-cooked, and drained, or 5 slices bacon, crisp-cooked, drained, and crumbled

1 In a 4-quart Dutch oven combine broth, lima beans, onions, fennel seeds, and pepper. Bring to boiling; reduce heat. Simmer, covered, for 10 minutes. Stir in carrots; cook for 5 minutes more.

2 Meanwhile, cut off and discard upper stalks of fennel, reserving some of the feathery tops for garnish. Remove any wilted outer layers and cut a thin slice from the base. Wash and chop fennel.

3 Stir in the chopped fennel, asparagus, and pancetta. Cook about 5 minutes or until vegetables are tender. Garnish each serving with some of the reserved fennel tops.

Nutrition Facts per serving: 276 cal., 11 g total fat (3 g sat. fat), 24 mg chol., 2,071 mg sodium, 33 g carbo., 8 g fiber, 15 g pro.

START TO FINISH:
40 minutes
MAKES:
4 servings

Serve this stick-to-your-ribs soup with thick slices of buttered garlic toast.

HEARTY HODGEPODGE

PREP:

20 minutes

COOK:

2¼ hours

MAKES:

8 servings

6	slices bacon
1	medium onion, thinly sliced
1	pound beef shank cross cuts
12	ounces meaty smoked pork hocks or meaty ham bone
6	cups water
½	teaspoon salt
2	15-ounce cans garbanzo beans (chickpeas), rinsed and drained
3	cups cubed potatoes
1	clove garlic, minced
4	ounces cooked smoked Polish sausage, thinly sliced

1 In a 4- to 6-quart Dutch oven cook bacon over medium heat until crisp. Remove bacon, reserving 2 tablespoons drippings in Dutch oven. Drain bacon on paper towels. Crumble bacon; set aside.

2 Cook onion in reserved drippings until tender. Add beef shanks, pork hocks, water, and salt. Bring to boiling; reduce heat. Simmer, covered, about 1½ hours or until meat is tender. Remove beef shanks and pork hocks from Dutch oven. When cool enough to handle, remove meat from bones. Discard bones. Cut up meat. Skim fat from broth. Return meat to Dutch oven. Add beans, potatoes, and garlic. Return to boiling; reduce heat. Simmer, covered, for 30 minutes. Add Polish sausage. Simmer, covered, for 15 minutes more. Stir in bacon.

Nutrition Facts per serving: 307 cal., 13 g total fat (4 g sat. fat), 36 mg chol., 837 mg sodium, 27 g carbo., 6 g fiber, 19 g pro.

The ingredient list may be long, but this soup is so full of flavor you won't mind a bit. (Recipe pictured on page 102.)

HAM SOUP WITH BLACK-EYED PEAS & HOMINY

2	tablespoons olive oil
1	cup chopped celery
1	cup chopped onion
¾	cup chopped green sweet pepper
2	cloves garlic, minced
1¼	cups diced cooked ham
1	teaspoon paprika
½	teaspoon sugar
½	teaspoon dry mustard
½	teaspoon ground cumin
½	teaspoon dried basil, crushed
½	teaspoon dried oregano, crushed
½	teaspoon dried thyme, crushed
¼	teaspoon ground cloves
¼	teaspoon black pepper
⅛	teaspoon cayenne pepper
1	15½-ounce can black-eyed peas, rinsed and drained
1	14½-ounce can golden hominy, rinsed and drained
1	14½-ounce can diced tomatoes, undrained
1	14-ounce can chicken broth or 1¾ cups homemade chicken broth
1	tablespoon snipped fresh parsley
1	tablespoon mild-flavored molasses

PREP:
20 minutes
COOK:
40 minutes
MAKES:
4 servings

1 In a 4-quart Dutch oven heat oil. Add celery, onion, sweet pepper, and garlic; cook and stir over medium heat for 5 minutes. Stir in ham, paprika, sugar, dry mustard, cumin, basil, oregano, thyme, cloves, black pepper, and cayenne pepper. Cook and stir for 5 minutes more.

2 Stir in black-eyed peas, hominy, undrained tomatoes, broth, parsley, and molasses. Bring to boiling; reduce heat. Simmer, covered, for 30 minutes.

Nutrition Facts per serving: 384 cal., 14 g total fat (3 g sat. fat), 24 mg chol., 1,627 mg sodium, 47 g carbo., 10 g fiber, 17 g pro.

A hearty combination of herbs and spices makes this meatless soup a winter winner.

WINTER YELLOW LENTIL SOUP

PREP:

40 minutes

COOK:

20 minutes

MAKES:

8 servings

6 slices bacon, cut into 1-inch pieces

2 cups chopped onions

3 cups chopped carrots

1 cup chopped celery

¾ cup chopped red sweet pepper

4 cloves garlic, minced

6 cups chicken broth

2 cups yellow or brown lentils, rinsed and drained

1½ cups water

3 bay leaves

2 teaspoons cumin seeds

2 teaspoons dried thyme, crushed, or 2 tablespoons snipped fresh thyme

Black pepper (optional)

Fresh thyme sprigs (optional)

1 In a 4-quart Dutch oven cook bacon over medium heat until crisp. Remove bacon, reserving drippings in Dutch oven. Drain bacon on paper towels; set aside.

2 Cook onions in reserved drippings about 4 minutes or until tender. Add carrots, celery, sweet pepper, and garlic. Cook and stir for 5 to 7 minutes or just until vegetables are tender.

3 Add broth, lentils, water, bay leaves, cumin seeds, and thyme. Bring to boiling; reduce heat. Simmer, covered, for 20 to 30 minutes or until lentils are tender, stirring occasionally.

4 Remove and discard bay leaves. If desired, season with pepper. Sprinkle each serving with cooked bacon. If desired, garnish each serving with thyme sprigs.

Nutrition Facts per serving: 419 cal., 22 g total fat (8 g sat. fat), 22 mg chol., 991 mg sodium, 38 g carbo., 17 g fiber, 19 g pro.

Many cooks prefer kosher salt because of its light, fluffy texture, clean taste, and lower sodium than regular salt. Look for it next to the regular salt in your supermarket. (Recipe pictured on page 105.)

SMOKED SAUSAGE & LENTIL SOUP

1	tablespoon olive oil
4	cloves garlic, minced
½	cup chopped onion
1	cup chopped fennel
1	cup chopped carrots
6	cups water
1¼	cups brown lentils, rinsed and drained
2	teaspoons kosher salt or 1½ teaspoons salt
¼	teaspoon black pepper
6	ounces cooked smoked sausage, cut into ½-inch pieces
3	tablespoons red wine vinegar

PREP:
20 minutes

COOK:
25 minutes

MAKES:
5 to 6 servings

1 In a 4-quart Dutch oven heat oil. Add garlic; cook and stir over medium heat for 1 minute. Add onion. Cook and stir until onion is tender and golden brown. Add fennel and carrots. Cook and stir until tender. Add water, lentils, salt, and pepper. Bring to boiling; reduce heat. Simmer, uncovered, for 25 to 30 minutes or until lentils are tender.

2 Meanwhile, in a large skillet brown sausage; drain on paper towels. Add to Dutch oven along with vinegar; heat through.

Nutrition Facts per serving: 347 cal., 14 g total fat (4 g sat. fat), 23 mg chol., 1,314 mg sodium, 34 g carbo., 20 g fiber, 22 g pro.

Sausage-loving kids will love this soup. The cook in the family will love how easily it comes together—especially using packaged shredded cabbage.

SMOKED TURKEY SAUSAGE & BEAN SOUP

START TO FINISH:

45 minutes

MAKES:

6 servings

2 tablespoons butter or margarine

½ cup finely chopped onion

1 clove garlic, minced

6 cups water

1 pound cooked smoked turkey sausage, sliced

2 cups chopped potatoes

1 15-ounce can red kidney beans, rinsed and drained

1 teaspoon instant beef bouillon granules

2 cups chopped cabbage or packaged shredded cabbage with carrot (coleslaw mix)

¼ cup tomato paste or ketchup

3 tablespoons vinegar

1 In a 4-quart Dutch oven melt butter over medium heat. Add onion and garlic; cook and stir until tender but not brown. Add water, turkey sausage, potatoes, beans, and bouillon granules. Bring to boiling; reduce heat. Simmer, covered, for 15 minutes. Add cabbage, tomato paste, and vinegar. Simmer, covered, for 10 minutes more.

Nutrition Facts per serving: 267 cal., 11 g total fat (4 g sat. fat), 61 mg chol., 955 mg sodium, 27 g carbo., 6 g fiber, 19 g pro.

Fennel seeds are easily crushed using a mortar and pestle. If you don't have one, try cracking them with a wooden spoon against the inside of a bowl.

ITALIAN SAUSAGE SOUP

1	pound Italian sausage (remove casings, if present)
1	cup chopped onion
1	cup chopped carrots
½	cup chopped celery
8	cups chicken broth
1	14½-ounce can diced tomatoes, undrained
1	8-ounce can tomato sauce
1	teaspoon dried oregano, crushed
½	teaspoon dried rosemary, crushed
½	teaspoon dried basil, crushed
¼	teaspoon dried thyme, crushed
¼	teaspoon fennel seeds, crushed
1	clove garlic, minced
1	bay leaf
½	cup dried orzo
	Finely shredded Parmesan cheese (optional)
	Crusty Italian bread (optional)

PREP:
30 minutes
COOK:
1½ hours
MAKES:
8 servings

1 In a 4-quart Dutch oven cook sausage, onion, carrots, and celery over medium heat until sausage is brown; drain well. Add broth, undrained tomatoes, tomato sauce, oregano, rosemary, basil, thyme, fennel seeds, garlic, and bay leaf. Bring to boiling; reduce heat. Simmer, covered, for 1 hour.

2 Add orzo. Return to boiling; reduce heat. Cook, uncovered, for 30 minutes more. Remove and discard bay leaf. If desired, serve with Parmesan cheese and Italian bread.

Nutrition Facts per serving: 293 cal., 19 g total fat (7 g sat. fat), 43 mg chol., 1,413 mg sodium, 13 g carbo., 2 g fiber, 15 g pro.

Instant rice cooks in minutes, retaining its shape and a pleasant firmness in this weeknight soup.

HEARTY RICE & SAUSAGE SOUP

PREP:

20 minutes

COOK:

25 minutes

MAKES:

4 servings

1	pound bulk pork sausage or turkey sausage
½	cup chopped onion
½	cup coarsely chopped green sweet pepper
1	clove garlic, minced
2	cups water
1	14½-ounce can Mexican-style stewed tomatoes, undrained
1	10½-ounce can condensed beef broth
½	of a 6-ounce can (⅓ cup) tomato paste
½	teaspoon chili powder
⅓	cup uncooked instant white rice
1	medium zucchini, halved lengthwise and cut into ¼-inch slices
	Dairy sour cream (optional)
	Broken tortilla chips (optional)

1 In a large saucepan or 4-quart Dutch oven cook sausage, onion, sweet pepper, and garlic over medium heat until sausage is brown; drain off fat.

2 Stir in water, undrained tomatoes, broth, tomato paste, and chili powder. Bring to boiling; reduce heat. Add uncooked rice. Simmer, covered, for 5 minutes. Add zucchini; cook about 5 minutes more or until rice and zucchini are tender. If desired, top each serving with sour cream and tortilla chips.

Nutrition Facts per serving: 499 cal., 33 g total fat (13 g sat. fat), 65 mg chol., 1,499 mg sodium, 24 g carbo., 2 g fiber, 19 g pro.

COLD & HOT SIDE-DISH SOUPS

Red & Green
Gazpacho

page 16

COLD & HOT SIDE-DISH SOUPS

Yellow Pepper Soup

page 38

Farmer's
Vegetable Soup

page 60

COLD & HOT SIDE-DISH SOUPS

Beet Soup

page 25

Green Bean Soup

page 24

COLD & HOT SIDE-DISH SOUPS

Hearty Squash Soup

page 52

Chunky Tomato Soup

page 45

HEARTY SOUPS

**Thai-Style
Shrimp Soup**

page 149

HEARTY SOUPS

New Potato Simmer

page 139

**Ham Soup with
Black-Eyed Peas
& Hominy**

page 91

HEARTY SOUPS

Chicken Soup with Ham & Orzo

page 130

Spring Pea Soup

page 88

HEARTY SOUPS

Ravioli Chicken Soup

page 125

Confetti
Chicken Soup

page 121

HEARTY SOUPS

Vegetable & Orzo Soup with Pistou

page 161

Smoked Sausage & Lentil Soup

page 93

HEARTY SOUPS

Beef & Cabbage Soup

page 79

**Ham & Bean Soup
with Vegetables**

page 86

HEARTY SOUPS

Pea Soup

page 87

HEARTY SOUPS

**Roasted Tomato
& Vegetable Soup**

page 154

**Chicken Sausage
& Tortellini Soup**

page 136

HEARTY SOUPS

Mexican Corn Soup

page 132

HEARTY SOUPS

Soba Noodles in Broth

page 148

Quick & Easy Italian Meatball Soup

page 71

CHOWDERS & BISQUES

Spicy Tortellini
Chowder

page 209

Curried Sweet
Potato Chowder

page 210

CHOWDERS & BISQUES

Seafood & Corn Chowder

page 201

Salmon Pan Chowder

page 189

Garlic lovers will cheer for this easy soup. The 10 cloves of garlic mellow during cooking, delivering wonderful flavor.

GARLICKY BLACK BEAN & SAUSAGE SOUP

12	ounces bulk mild Italian sausage
1½	cups chopped onions
½	teaspoon fennel seeds, crushed
10	cloves garlic, minced
2	15-ounce cans black beans, rinsed and drained
1	14-ounce can beef broth or 1¾ cups homemade beef broth
2	cups chopped tomatoes
2	tablespoons snipped fresh oregano
	Dash cayenne pepper (optional)
¼	cup dairy sour cream

START TO FINISH:

40 minutes

MAKES:

5 servings

1 In a 4-quart Dutch oven cook sausage, onions, fennel seeds, and garlic over medium heat until sausage is brown; drain off fat. Stir in beans and broth. Bring to boiling; reduce heat. Simmer, covered, for 15 minutes. Stir in tomatoes and oregano; heat through. (If a thinner consistency is desired, add a small amount of water.)

2 If desired, stir cayenne pepper into sour cream. Top each serving with the sour cream mixture.

Nutrition Facts per serving: 429 cal., 20 g total fat (8 g sat. fat), 55 mg chol., 1,453 mg sodium, 42 g carbo., 12 g fiber, 30 g pro.

Kale is a nutritionally supercharged leafy green. Be sure to wash kale well before using—its frilly edges often hide soil.

LAMB & ORZO SOUP WITH KALE

PREP:

15 minutes

COOK:

1 1/2 hours

MAKES:

6 servings

2 1/2   pounds meaty lamb shanks

4   cups water

4   cups chicken or vegetable broth

2   bay leaves

1   tablespoon snipped fresh oregano or 1 teaspoon dried oregano, crushed

1 1/2   teaspoons snipped fresh marjoram or 1/2 teaspoon dried marjoram, crushed

1/4   teaspoon black pepper

2   medium carrots, cut into thin bite-size strips (1 cup)

1   cup sliced celery

3/4   cup dried orzo

3   cups torn fresh kale or spinach

Finely shredded Parmesan cheese (optional)

1 In a large Dutch oven combine lamb shanks, water, broth, bay leaves, dried oregano (if using), dried marjoram (if using), and pepper. Bring to boiling; reduce heat. Simmer, covered, for 1 1/4 to 1 1/2 hours or until meat is tender.

2 Remove lamb shanks from Dutch oven. When cool enough to handle, remove meat from bones. Discard bones. Coarsely chop meat. Strain broth, discarding solids. Skim fat from broth.

3 Return broth to Dutch oven. Stir in chopped meat, carrots, celery, and orzo. Return to boiling; reduce heat. Simmer, covered, about 15 minutes or until vegetables and orzo are tender. Stir in fresh oregano (if using), fresh marjoram (if using), and kale. Cook for 1 to 2 minutes more or just until kale wilts. If desired, sprinkle each serving with Parmesan cheese.

Nutrition Facts per serving: 206 cal., 3 g total fat (1 g sat. fat), 55 mg chol., 764 mg sodium, 23 g carbo., 2 g fiber, 22 g pro.

This old-world recipe proves that going camping doesn't mean your taste buds have to suffer.

CAMPFIRE ITALIAN SOUP

12   ounces very lean ground lamb or beef

⅔   cup chopped fennel

3   14-ounce cans beef broth with onion or 5¼ cups homemade beef broth

1½   teaspoons dried oregano, crushed

¼   teaspoon garlic powder

¼   teaspoon coarsely cracked black pepper

¾   cup uncooked instant white rice

4   cups fresh baby spinach

3   ounces Parmesan cheese, cut into 4 wedges (optional)

PREP:
20 minutes
COOK:
30 minutes
STAND:
5 minutes
MAKES:
4 servings

1 Place a 10-inch cast-iron Dutch oven over medium-high heat on a camp stove, grill rack, or grate over an open fire. Add lamb and fennel. Cook, uncovered, about 12 minutes or until meat is brown and fennel is nearly tender, stirring occasionally.

2 Add broth, oregano, garlic powder, and pepper. Cover and bring to boiling, stirring occasionally. Add uncooked rice. Remove Dutch oven from heat; let stand for 5 minutes. Stir in spinach. If desired, serve with Parmesan cheese wedges.

Nutrition Facts per serving: 273 cal., 12 g total fat (5 g sat. fat), 57 mg chol., 1,184 mg sodium, 20 g carbo., 1 g fiber, 19 g pro.

A tagine (ta-ZHEEN) is a Moroccan stew featuring vegetables, fruits, spices, and meat. In this version, lamb joins ginger, apples, and raisins. Add saffron for extra flavor and a brighter color.

MOROCCAN LAMB TAGINE

START TO FINISH:

35 minutes

MAKES:

4 servings

12   ounces lean ground lamb

1   cup chopped onion

3   cloves garlic, minced

2   cups water

1   14-ounce can chicken broth or 1¾ cups homemade chicken broth

½   cup snipped fresh cilantro

1   tablespoon grated fresh ginger

¼   teaspoon black pepper

¼   teaspoon paprika

⅛   teaspoon thread saffron, crushed, or dash ground saffron (optional)

2   medium apples or pears, cored and thinly sliced

¼   cup raisins or snipped pitted dates

1 In a large saucepan cook lamb, onion, and garlic over medium heat until lamb is brown; drain off fat. Stir in water, broth, cilantro, ginger, pepper, paprika, and, if desired, saffron. Bring to boiling; reduce heat. Simmer, covered, for 10 minutes.

2 Stir in apples and raisins. Return to boiling; reduce heat. Simmer, uncovered, for 1 to 2 minutes more or until apples are just slightly softened.

Nutrition Facts per serving: 260 cal., 12 g total fat (5 g sat. fat), 58 mg chol., 464 mg sodium, 23 g carbo., 3 g fiber, 17 g pro.

Cayenne pepper and green chile peppers add a spicy spark to this creamy soup.

CREAMY CHICKEN & CHILE PEPPER SOUP

8	ounces uncooked ground chicken or turkey
1/4	cup chopped onion
2	cloves garlic, minced
2	cups milk
1	10¾-ounce can condensed cream of chicken soup
1	7-ounce can whole kernel corn with sweet peppers, drained
1/2	cup chopped tomato
1	4-ounce can diced green chile peppers, drained
2	tablespoons snipped fresh cilantro or parsley
1/8	to 1/4 teaspoon cayenne pepper
1	cup shredded Monterey Jack cheese (4 ounces)

START TO FINISH:

25 minutes

MAKES:

4 servings

1 In a large saucepan cook ground chicken, onion, and garlic over medium heat until chicken is no longer pink and onion is tender. Drain off fat, if necessary.

2 Stir in milk, soup, corn, tomato, chile peppers, cilantro, and cayenne pepper. Bring to boiling; reduce heat. Simmer, uncovered, for 5 minutes, stirring occasionally. Add cheese; cook and stir until cheese is melted.

Nutrition Facts per serving: 388 cal., 21 g total fat (9 g sat. fat), 41 mg chol., 1,062 mg sodium, 26 g carbo., 3 g fiber, 24 g pro.

Tortilla soup has grown in popularity over the years. While there are many great versions out there, few are quite as easy as this one!

SPEEDY CHICKEN & SALSA SOUP

PREP:

20 minutes

COOK:

13 minutes

MAKES:

4 servings

1¾ cups water

1 14-ounce can reduced-sodium chicken broth or 1¾ cups homemade chicken broth

8 ounces skinless, boneless chicken breast halves or thighs, cut into bite-size pieces

1 to 2 teaspoons chili powder

1 11-ounce can whole kernel corn with sweet peppers, drained

1 cup bottled chunky salsa

3 cups broken baked tortilla chips

½ cup shredded Monterey Jack cheese with jalapeño peppers (2 ounces)

1 In a large saucepan combine water, broth, chicken, and chili powder. Bring to boiling; reduce heat. Simmer, covered, for 8 minutes. Add corn. Simmer, uncovered, for 5 minutes more. Stir in salsa; heat through. Top each serving with tortilla chips and sprinkle with cheese.

Nutrition Facts per serving: 295 cal., 6 g total fat (3 g sat. fat), 45 mg chol., 1,133 mg sodium, 30 g carbo., 4 g fiber, 22 g pro.

The Italian word minestrone means "big soup," and countless variations of the bean and vegetable soup are prepared in American kitchens. This version introduces chicken breasts and broth for extra flavor.

CHICKEN MINESTRONE

1	tablespoon olive oil
1	cup sliced carrots
$\frac{1}{2}$	cup chopped celery
$\frac{1}{2}$	cup chopped onion
3	14-ounce cans chicken broth or $5\frac{1}{4}$ cups homemade chicken broth
2	19-ounce cans white kidney beans (cannellini), rinsed and drained
8	to 10 ounces skinless, boneless chicken breast halves, cut into bite-size pieces
1	cup fresh green beans cut into $\frac{1}{2}$-inch pieces
$\frac{1}{4}$	teaspoon black pepper
1	cup dried bow ties
1	medium zucchini, quartered lengthwise and cut into $\frac{1}{2}$-inch slices
1	$14\frac{1}{2}$-ounce can diced tomatoes with basil, garlic, and oregano, undrained

START TO FINISH:
45 minutes
MAKES:
8 servings

1 In a 5- to 6-quart Dutch oven heat oil. Add carrots, celery, and onion; cook and stir over medium heat for 5 minutes. Add broth, white kidney beans, chicken, green beans, and pepper. Bring to boiling; add pasta. Reduce heat. Simmer, uncovered, for 5 minutes.

2 Add zucchini. Return to boiling; reduce heat. Simmer, uncovered, for 8 to 10 minutes more or until pasta is tender and green beans are crisp-tender. Stir in undrained tomatoes; heat through.

Nutrition Facts per serving: 183 cal., 4 g total fat (1 g sat. fat), 16 mg chol., 1,115 mg sodium, 27 g carbo., 7 g fiber, 16 g pro.

If you have never tried chipotle (chih-POHT-lay) peppers, this soup provides a great introduction. As well as adding heat, chipotle chile peppers add a pleasant smoky flavor.

CHIPOTLE CHILE PEPPER & CHICKEN SOUP

START TO FINISH:

35 minutes

MAKES:

3 servings

1	tablespoon olive oil or cooking oil
1	cup finely chopped onion
4	cloves garlic, minced
12	ounces skinless, boneless chicken breast halves, cut into bite-size pieces
1	14-ounce can chicken broth or 1¾ cups homemade chicken broth
2	teaspoons chopped canned chipotle peppers in adobo sauce
½	teaspoon sugar
¼	teaspoon salt
2	cups chopped tomatoes or one 14½-ounce can diced tomatoes, undrained
¼	cup snipped fresh cilantro

1 In a large saucepan heat oil. Add onion and garlic; cook and stir over medium-high heat about 4 minutes or until tender. Add chicken; cook and stir for 2 minutes more.

2 Stir in broth, chipotle peppers, sugar, and salt. Bring to boiling; reduce heat. Simmer, uncovered, for 15 minutes. Remove saucepan from heat; stir in tomatoes and cilantro.

Nutrition Facts per serving: 233 cal., 7 g total fat (1 g sat. fat), 67 mg chol., 823 mg sodium, 13 g carbo., 3 g fiber, 29 g pro.

Find coconut milk in most large supermarkets. Don't confuse it, however, with sweetened cream of coconut, which is used to make mixed drinks. (Recipe pictured on page 104.)

CONFETTI CHICKEN SOUP

2	tablespoons cooking oil
1	pound skinless, boneless chicken breast halves, cut into 1-inch pieces
4	teaspoons grated fresh ginger
1	tablespoon red curry paste or ¼ teaspoon cayenne pepper
1	teaspoon ground cumin
8	cloves garlic, minced
4	cups water
1	14-ounce can unsweetened coconut milk
2	cups shredded carrots
2	cups small broccoli florets
1	medium red sweet pepper, cut into bite-size strips
2	3-ounce packages chicken-flavored ramen noodles, coarsely broken
2	cups fresh snow pea pods, tips removed and halved crosswise
2	tablespoons soy sauce
4	teaspoons lime juice
1	cup slivered fresh basil
⅓	cup snipped fresh cilantro

PREP:
30 minutes
COOK:
6 minutes
MAKES:
6 servings

1 In a 4-quart Dutch oven heat 1 tablespoon of the oil. Add chicken; cook and stir over medium-high heat for 3 to 4 minutes or until no longer pink. Remove chicken; set aside.

2 Add remaining oil to Dutch oven. Add ginger, curry paste, cumin, and garlic; cook and stir for 30 seconds. Stir in water, coconut milk, carrots, broccoli, sweet pepper, and noodles (set seasoning packets aside). Bring to boiling; reduce heat. Simmer, covered, for 3 minutes. Stir in cooked chicken, seasoning packets, pea pods, soy sauce, and lime juice; heat through. Stir in basil and cilantro.

Nutrition Facts per serving: 454 cal., 25 g total fat (12 g sat. fat), 44 mg chol., 1,087 mg sodium, 33 g carbo., 4 g fiber, 26 g pro.

Make thin cheese curls using a vegetable peeler on a wedge of hard cheese.

GARDEN CHICKEN SOUP

PREP:

25 minutes

COOK:

11 minutes

MAKES:

4 servings

1	tablespoon cooking oil
12	ounces packaged skinless, boneless chicken breast strips
3	cups reduced-sodium chicken broth
12	fresh packaged peeled baby carrots
2	medium onions, cut into thin wedges
2	cloves garlic, minced
1	large yellow summer squash, halved lengthwise and thinly sliced (about 2 cups)
2	cups shredded Swiss chard
1	tablespoon snipped fresh lemon thyme or thyme
	Asiago or Parmesan cheese curls

1 In a very large skillet heat oil. Add chicken; cook and stir over medium-high heat about 3 minutes or until chicken is no longer pink.

2 Add broth, carrots, onions, and garlic. Bring to boiling; reduce heat. Simmer, covered, for 5 minutes. Add squash and Swiss chard. Return to boiling; reduce heat. Simmer, covered, about 3 minutes more or until vegetables are just tender. Stir in lemon thyme. Top each serving with cheese curls.

Nutrition Facts per serving: 217 cal., 8 g total fat (3 g sat. fat), 57 mg chol., 643 mg sodium, 12 g carbo., 3 g fiber, 26 g pro.

If working with a grill wok, use long-handled tongs or a metal spatula to stir the vegetables as they're grilling.

GRILLED CHICKEN & VEGETABLE SOUP

1	cup sliced carrots
1	large red, green, or yellow sweet pepper, cut into bite-size pieces
1	medium zucchini, cut into bite-size pieces
1/3	cup coarsely chopped onion
2	tablespoons olive oil
1/2	teaspoon black pepper
1/4	teaspoon salt
2	cloves garlic, minced
8	ounces skinless, boneless chicken breast halves and/or thighs
2	14-ounce cans reduced-sodium chicken broth or 3 1/2 cups homemade chicken broth
2	cups water
1	cup dried radiatore, cavatelli, or bow ties
2	tablespoons snipped fresh basil, cilantro, or parsley

PREP:
10 minutes

COOK:
15 minutes

GRILL:
32 minutes

MAKES:
4 servings

1 In a small saucepan cook carrots in a small amount of boiling water for 2 minutes; drain.

2 In a large bowl combine cooked carrots, sweet pepper, zucchini, and onion. Combine olive oil, black pepper, salt, and garlic; drizzle over vegetables, tossing lightly to coat. Spoon vegetable mixture onto a large piece of heavy foil.

3 For a charcoal grill, grill vegetables on the rack of an uncovered grill directly over medium coals about 20 minutes or until lightly charred, stirring often. Remove vegetables from grill; set aside. Add chicken to grill rack. Grill, uncovered, for 12 to 15 minutes or until chicken is no longer pink (170°F for breasts; 180°F for thighs), turning once halfway through grilling. (For a gas grill, preheat grill. Reduce heat to medium. Cover and grill vegetables and chicken as above.) Cool chicken slightly; cut into bite-size pieces.

4 Meanwhile, in a 4-quart Dutch oven bring broth and water to boiling; add pasta. Cook according to package directions. Do not drain. Stir in grilled vegetables, chicken, and basil; heat through.

Nutrition Facts per serving: 268 cal., 10 g total fat (2 g sat. fat), 58 mg chol., 734 mg sodium, 24 g carbo., 3 g fiber, 19 g pro.

Just seven ingredients make up this intriguing, easy-to-prepare soup.

PARMESAN-PESTO CHICKEN SOUP

START TO FINISH:

30 minutes

MAKES:

4 servings

2 14-ounce cans reduced-sodium chicken broth or 3½ cups homemade chicken broth

1 teaspoon dried Italian seasoning, crushed

1 clove garlic, minced

12 ounces skinless, boneless chicken breast halves, cut into bite-size pieces

¾ cup dried small shell macaroni

¾ cup frozen peas

¼ cup thinly sliced green onions

1 recipe Cheesy Toasted Bread

1 In a medium saucepan combine broth, Italian seasoning, and garlic. Bring to boiling. Add chicken and pasta. Return to boiling; reduce heat. Simmer, uncovered, for 8 to 9 minutes or until pasta is tender and chicken is no longer pink, stirring occasionally.

2 Add peas and green onions; cook for 2 minutes more. Top each serving with a slice of Cheesy Toasted Bread.

CHEESY TOASTED BREAD: Cut two ½-inch slices Italian bread in half crosswise. Spread one side of halved bread slices with 2 tablespoons purchased basil pesto; sprinkle with ¼ cup finely shredded Parmesan cheese. Place bread on a baking sheet. Broil 3 to 4 inches from the heat about 2 minutes or until cheese just begins to melt.

Nutrition Facts per serving: 329 cal., 9 g total fat (2 g sat. fat), 57 mg chol., 622 mg sodium, 29 g carbo., 3 g fiber, 30 g pro.

Just a pinch of saffron goes a long way in adding flavor and an intense color to food. The aromatic spice is expensive, however, and can be omitted. This soup is terrific with or without it. (Recipe pictured on page 104.)

RAVIOLI CHICKEN SOUP

Nonstick cooking spray

12 ounces skinless, boneless chicken breast halves, cut into 1/2-inch pieces

6 cups reduced-sodium chicken broth

1/2 cup sliced leek or chopped onion

1 tablespoon finely chopped fresh ginger

1/4 teaspoon thread saffron, slightly crushed (optional)

1 9-ounce package refrigerated vegetable-filled ravioli or herb chicken-filled tortellini

1/2 cup fresh baby spinach or shredded fresh spinach

1 Lightly coat a large saucepan with nonstick cooking spray. Heat saucepan over medium-high heat. Add chicken; cook and stir over medium heat about 3 minutes or until no longer pink.

2 Add broth, leek, ginger, and, if desired, saffron. Bring to boiling. Add ravioli. Return to boiling; reduce heat. Boil gently, uncovered, for 5 to 9 minutes or until ravioli is tender, stirring occasionally. Top each serving with spinach leaves.

Nutrition Facts per serving: 222 cal., 3 g total fat (0 g sat. fat), 59 mg chol., 1,221 mg sodium, 21 g carbo., 3 g fiber, 29 g pro.

START TO FINISH:
25 minutes
MAKES:
4 servings

Straw mushrooms, popular in Asian cooking, are so named because they're grown on straw that's been used in a rice paddy. These mushrooms are dark colored and have a meaty texture.

ASIAN-INSPIRED CHICKEN & SHRIMP SOUP

START TO FINISH:

45 minutes

MAKES:

6 to 8 servings

8 ounces fresh or frozen peeled and deveined small shrimp

12 ounces skinless, boneless chicken breast halves

2 cups water

4 cups chicken broth

8 ounces fresh bean sprouts

1 cup small broccoli florets

½ of a 15-ounce jar whole straw mushrooms or one 8-ounce can sliced mushrooms, drained

½ cup chopped red and/or green sweet pepper

4 green onions, bias-sliced into 1-inch pieces

1 tablespoon soy sauce

Black pepper

1 Thaw shrimp, if frozen; set aside. In a 4-quart Dutch oven combine chicken and water. Bring to boiling; reduce heat. Simmer, covered, for 12 to 14 minutes or until chicken is no longer pink (170°F). Remove chicken from Dutch oven. When cool enough to handle, chop chicken; set aside.

2 Meanwhile, strain cooking liquid and return to Dutch oven. Add broth. Bring to boiling. Add chopped chicken, shrimp, bean sprouts, broccoli, mushrooms, sweet pepper, green onions, and soy sauce. Return to boiling. Cook, uncovered, for 5 minutes. Season to taste with black pepper.

Nutrition Facts per serving: 152 cal., 3 g total fat (1 g sat. fat), 76 mg chol., 849 mg sodium, 7 g carbo., 2 g fiber, 26 g pro.

Stewing chickens are 10 to 18 months old and weigh 3 to 6 pounds.

OLD-FASHIONED CHICKEN NOODLE SOUP

1	4- to 5-pound stewing chicken, cut up
6	cups water
½	cup chopped onion
2	teaspoons salt
¼	teaspoon black pepper
1	bay leaf
1½	cups dried medium noodles
1	cup chopped carrots
1	cup chopped celery
2	tablespoons snipped fresh parsley

PREP:

20 minutes

COOK:

2¼ hours

MAKES:

8 servings

1 In a 6- to 8-quart Dutch oven combine chicken, water, onion, salt, pepper, and bay leaf. Bring to boiling; reduce heat. Simmer, covered, about 2 hours or until chicken is tender.

2 Remove chicken from Dutch oven. When cool enough to handle, remove meat from bones. Discard bones. Cut meat into bite-size pieces; set aside. Remove and discard bay leaf. Skim fat from broth.

3 Bring broth to boiling. Stir in noodles, carrots, and celery. Simmer, covered, about 8 minutes or until noodles are tender but still firm. Stir in chicken and parsley; heat through.

Nutrition Facts per serving: 210 cal., 6 g total fat (2 g sat. fat), 84 mg chol., 665 mg sodium, 10 g carbo., 1 g fiber, 26 g pro.

The roux should be cooked to a coppery color, similar to that of a tarnished penny.
Be patient and keep stirring!

CHICKEN-SAUSAGE GUMBO

PREP:
45 minutes

COOK:
1 hour

MAKES:
10 servings

1	cup all-purpose flour
²⁄₃	cup cooking oil
1	cup sliced celery
1	cup chopped green sweet pepper
½	cup chopped onion
2	cloves garlic, minced
8	ounces cooked smoked turkey sausage, cut into 1-inch pieces
8	ounces andouille sausage, cut into ½-inch pieces
5	cups water
2	pounds meaty chicken pieces (breast halves, thighs, and drumsticks), skinned
1	teaspoon salt
¼	to ½ teaspoon cayenne pepper
¼	teaspoon black pepper
	Hot cooked rice (optional)

1 For roux, in large heavy Dutch oven stir together flour and oil until smooth. Cook over medium-high heat for 5 minutes, stirring constantly. Reduce heat to medium. Cook and stir constantly for 10 to 15 minutes more or until roux is reddish brown in color. Stir in celery, sweet pepper, onion, and garlic; cook for 5 minutes more, stirring occasionally. Add turkey sausage and andouille sausage; cook until lightly browned.

2 Add water, chicken pieces, salt, cayenne pepper, and black pepper. Bring to boiling; reduce heat. Simmer, covered, for 40 to 50 minutes or until chicken is tender and no longer pink (170°F for breasts; 180°F for thighs and drumsticks).

3 Remove chicken from Dutch oven. When cool enough to handle, remove meat from bones. Discard bones. Coarsely chop chicken. Skim off fat. Return chicken to Dutch oven. Cook for 2 to 3 minutes or until chicken is heated through. If desired, serve with rice.

Nutrition Facts per serving: 460 cal., 34 g total fat (9 g sat. fat), 72 mg chol., 961 mg sodium, 12 g carbo., 1 g fiber, 25 g pro.

This traditional Mexican soup is known as caldo Maya, which means "soup of the Maya."
Toppings include avocado, cilantro, green onions, and tortilla strips; serve it with one or all of them.

CHICKEN TORTILLA SOUP

2   to 2½ pounds meaty chicken pieces (breast halves, thighs, and drumsticks), skinned

2   cups coarsely chopped onions

2   cups coarsely chopped celery

2   cups coarsely chopped tomatoes

½   cup snipped fresh cilantro

1   teaspoon ground cumin

¼   to ½ teaspoon cayenne pepper

1½   cups chopped carrots

1   recipe Roasted Poblano Chile Peppers

1   recipe Fried Corn Tortilla Strips (optional)

PREP:
20 minutes
COOK:
1 hour
MAKES:
6 servings

1 In a 4- to 5-quart Dutch oven combine chicken pieces, 6 cups *water*, 1 cup of the onions, 1 cup of the celery, the tomatoes, cilantro, 1½ teaspoons *salt*, cumin, cayenne pepper, and ¼ to ½ teaspoon *black pepper*. Bring to boiling; reduce heat. Simmer, covered, for 40 to 50 minutes or until chicken is tender and no longer pink (170°F for breasts; 180°F for thighs and drumsticks). Remove chicken pieces from Dutch oven. When cool enough to handle, remove meat from bones. Discard bones. Chop chicken; set aside.

2 Meanwhile, strain cooking liquid, reserving liquid and discarding the vegetables. Return cooking liquid to Dutch oven. Add the remaining 1 cup onions, the remaining 1 cup celery, and the carrots. Bring to boiling; reduce heat. Simmer, covered, about 20 minutes or until vegetables are tender.

3 Stir in chopped chicken and Roasted Poblano Chile Peppers; heat through. If desired, garnish each serving with *avocado slices,* additional snipped *fresh cilantro,* sliced *green onions,* and Fried Corn Tortilla Strips.

ROASTED POBLANO CHILE PEPPERS: Cut 1 or 2 fresh poblano chile peppers in half lengthwise; remove stems, membranes, and seeds. Place peppers, cut sides down, on a foil-lined baking sheet. Roast in a 425°F oven for 20 to 25 minutes or until tender. Bring foil up and around pepper halves. Let stand until cool enough to handle. Use a sharp knife to pull the skin off gently and slowly. Discard skin. Chop peppers.

Nutrition Facts per serving: 158 cal., 5 g total fat (1 g sat. fat), 61 mg chol., 638 mg sodium, 7 g carbo., 2 g fiber, 21 g pro.

FRIED CORN TORTILLA STRIPS: Cut six 6-inch corn tortillas into thin strips. In a large skillet heat 3 tablespoons cooking oil. Add about one-third of the tortilla strips; cook and stir over medium heat for 2 to 3 minutes or until crisp. Using a slotted spoon, lift strips from skillet, reserving oil in skillet. Drain strips on paper towels. Repeat with remaining tortilla strips, one-third at a time, adding a little additional oil, if necessary.

Although orzo means "barley" in Italian, it's actually tiny, rice-shape pasta. (Recipe pictured on page 103.)

CHICKEN SOUP WITH HAM & ORZO

START TO FINISH:

35 minutes

MAKES:

6 servings

2   chicken breast halves with skin and bone (about 1 pound)

4   14-ounce cans reduced-sodium chicken broth or 7 cups homemade chicken broth

1   cup dried orzo

12   ounces fresh asparagus spears, bias-sliced into 1½-inch pieces

4   cups lightly packed, thinly sliced Swiss chard

4   tomatoes, seeded and chopped

⅓   cup cubed cooked ham

Coarse salt

Black pepper

Snipped fresh chives

Snipped fresh Italian (flat-leaf) parsley

1 In a 4-quart Dutch oven combine chicken and broth. Bring to boiling; reduce heat. Simmer, covered, about 20 minutes or until chicken is tender and no longer pink (170°F). Remove chicken from Dutch oven. When cool enough to handle, remove meat from bones. Discard skin and bones. Shred chicken; set aside.

2 Return broth to boiling; add orzo. Return to boiling; reduce heat. Cook, uncovered, for 7 minutes. Add asparagus; cook for 3 minutes more.

3 Stir in shredded chicken, Swiss chard, tomatoes, and ham; heat through. Season to taste with salt and pepper. Sprinkle each serving with chives and parsley.

Nutrition Facts per serving: 286 cal., 8 g total fat (2 g sat. fat), 44 mg chol., 1,115 mg sodium, 26 g carbo., 2 g fiber, 25 g pro.

This soup originated in southern India, where, in Victorian times, English visitors enjoyed it and adopted the recipe for cooks at home.

MULLIGATAWNY SOUP

2	tablespoons butter or margarine
2	cups chopped onions
2	cups chopped potatoes
1	cup chopped carrots
2	cloves garlic, minced
3	14-ounce cans chicken broth or 5¼ cups homemade chicken broth
1	15-ounce can garbanzo beans (chickpeas), rinsed and drained
1	cup finely chopped cooked chicken
1	cup unsweetened coconut milk
4	teaspoons curry powder
⅔	cup chopped apple
¼	cup snipped fresh cilantro

1 In a 4-quart Dutch oven melt butter over medium heat. Add onions, potatoes, carrots, and garlic; cook and stir about 10 minutes or until onion is tender. Add broth. Cook, uncovered, over medium-low heat about 20 minutes or until vegetables are tender. Stir in garbanzo beans, chicken, coconut milk, and curry powder; heat through. Top each serving with apple and cilantro.

Nutrition Facts per serving: 267 cal., 14 g total fat (9 g sat. fat), 24 mg chol., 878 mg sodium, 26 g carbo., 6 g fiber, 12 g pro.

PREP:

25 minutes

COOK:

30 minutes

MAKES:

8 servings

Corn shares the spotlight with chicken in this well-seasoned soup. Blending part of the corn with the chicken broth is an easy way to thicken the soup and boost the flavor. (Recipe pictured on page 109.)

MEXICAN CORN SOUP

PREP:

15 minutes

COOK:

10 minutes

MAKES:

6 servings

1   16-ounce package frozen whole kernel corn, thawed

1   cup chicken broth

1   4-ounce can diced green chile peppers

2   tablespoons butter or margarine

1   tablespoon snipped fresh oregano or 1 teaspoon dried oregano, crushed

¼   teaspoon salt

¼   teaspoon black pepper

1   clove garlic, minced

2   cups milk

1   cup chopped cooked chicken

1   cup chopped tomatoes

1   cup shredded Monterey Jack cheese (4 ounces)

Snipped fresh parsley (optional)

Fresh oregano sprigs (optional)

1 In a blender combine half of the corn and the broth. Cover and blend until nearly smooth.

2 In a large saucepan combine corn puree, the remaining corn, chile peppers, butter, dried oregano (if using), salt, pepper, and garlic. Bring to boiling; reduce heat. Simmer, uncovered, for 10 minutes. Stir in fresh oregano (if using), milk, chicken, and tomatoes; heat through.

3 Remove saucepan from heat. Stir in cheese until melted. If desired, sprinkle each serving with parsley and garnish with oregano sprigs.

Nutrition Facts per serving: 279 cal., 14 g total fat (8 g sat. fat), 56 mg chol., 479 mg sodium, 23 g carbo., 0 g fiber, 18 g pro.

The rice thickens the broth as it cooks, giving this soup a just-right consistency.

HEARTY CHICKEN & RICE SOUP

2   14-ounce cans reduced-sodium chicken broth or 3½ cups homemade chicken broth

1   cup water

1   cup chopped fresh mushrooms

½   cup sliced carrot

½   cup chopped celery

¾   cup uncooked long grain rice

1   teaspoon dried basil, crushed (optional)

⅛   to ¼ teaspoon black pepper

2   cups chopped cooked chicken

2   tablespoons snipped fresh parsley

1 In a large saucepan combine broth, water, mushrooms, carrot, and celery. Bring to boiling; reduce heat. Stir in uncooked rice, basil (if desired), and pepper. Simmer, covered, about 15 minutes or until rice is tender. Stir in chicken; heat through. Stir in parsley.

Nutrition Facts per serving: 288 cal., 6 g total fat (2 g sat. fat), 62 mg chol., 558 mg sodium, 31 g carbo., 1 g fiber, 25 g pro.

START TO FINISH:

30 minutes

MAKES:

4 servings

You won't have to call your children twice when you serve this mushroom-, carrot-, and rice-loaded creamy chicken soup for dinner.

CREAMY CHICKEN & RICE SOUP

PREP:

25 minutes

COOK:

30 minutes

MAKES:

6 servings

1	tablespoon butter or margarine
½	cup chopped onion
½	cup sliced celery
½	cup sliced carrot or sliced fresh mushrooms
1	14-ounce can reduced-sodium chicken broth or 1¾ cups homemade chicken broth
1	10¾-ounce can reduced-fat and reduced-sodium condensed cream of chicken soup
1	cup water
1	6¼-ounce package chicken-flavored rice pilaf mix
⅛	teaspoon black pepper
2½	cups milk
2	cups chopped cooked chicken
	Snipped fresh parsley (optional)

1 In a large saucepan melt butter over medium heat. Add onion, celery, and carrot; cook and stir about 5 minutes or until tender.

2 Add broth, soup, and water. Stir in pilaf mix with the seasoning packet and pepper. Bring to boiling; reduce heat. Simmer, covered, about 20 minutes or until rice is tender, stirring occasionally.

3 Stir in milk and chicken; heat through. If desired, sprinkle each serving with parsley.

Nutrition Facts per serving: 303 cal., 9 g total fat (4 g sat. fat), 60 mg chol., 979 mg sodium, 34 g carbo., 1 g fiber, 22 g pro.

If you think dumplings are something only your grandmother had the time and talent to make, think again! These dumplings stir together quickly and puff up magically in this easy soup.

CHICKEN-BROCCOLI SOUP

START TO FINISH:

30 minutes

MAKES:

4 or 5 servings

2	10¾-ounce cans condensed cream of chicken soup
3	cups milk
1½	cups frozen cut broccoli
1	9-ounce package frozen chopped, cooked chicken breast
½	cup coarsely shredded carrot
1	teaspoon Dijon-style mustard
¼	teaspoon dried thyme, crushed
1	recipe Dumplings
½	cup shredded cheddar cheese (2 ounces)

1 In a 4-quart Dutch oven combine soup, milk, broccoli, chicken, carrot, mustard, and thyme. Bring to boiling; reduce heat.

2 Meanwhile, prepare Dumplings. Spoon batter in 4 or 5 mounds onto bubbling soup. Reduce heat. Simmer, covered, for 10 to 12 minutes or until a wooden toothpick inserted into a dumpling comes out clean. Sprinkle dumplings with cheese.

DUMPLINGS: In a small bowl combine ⅔ cup all-purpose flour and 1 teaspoon baking powder. Add ¼ cup milk and 2 tablespoons cooking oil. Stir just until moistened.

Nutrition Facts per serving: 535 cal., 26 g total fat (9 g sat. fat), 75 mg chol., 1,701 mg sodium, 42 g carbo., 3 g fiber, 23 g pro.

Keep soups and stews warm longer by serving them in warmed bowls. Just before ladling, rinse bowls under hot tap water and dry. (Recipe pictured on page 108.)

CHICKEN SAUSAGE & TORTELLINI SOUP

PREP:

15 minutes

COOK:

20 minutes

MAKES:

6 to 8 servings

Nonstick cooking spray

1 pound cooked smoked chicken sausage, halved lengthwise and cut into 1-inch pieces

1 large onion, cut into thin wedges

2 cloves garlic, minced

2 14-ounce cans chicken broth or 3½ cups homemade chicken broth

1 14½-ounce can diced tomatoes with basil, oregano, and garlic, undrained

1 cup water

2 9-ounce packages refrigerated mushroom- or 3-cheese-filled tortellini

1 10-ounce package frozen baby lima beans

¼ cup slivered fresh basil

2 tablespoons shredded Parmesan cheese

1 Lightly coat a 5-quart Dutch oven with nonstick cooking spray. Heat Dutch oven over medium heat. Add sausage, onion, and garlic; cook and stir until sausage is brown and onion is tender. Drain off fat.

2 Add broth, undrained tomatoes, and water. Bring to boiling; reduce heat. Simmer, covered, for 10 minutes. Add tortellini and lima beans. Return to boiling; reduce heat. Simmer, uncovered, for 5 to 6 minutes more or until tortellini and beans are tender. Stir in basil. Sprinkle each serving with Parmesan cheese.

Nutrition Facts per serving: 499 cal., 17 g total fat (8 g sat. fat), 55 mg chol., 1,837 mg sodium, 59 g carbo., 6 g fiber, 28 g pro.

The Chinese and Mediterranean technique of cooking egg drops in soup is featured here. The egg cooks in thin, swirling threads as it is stirred slowly into the hot soup.

EGG DROP & TURKEY SOUP

2   14-ounce cans chicken broth or 3½ cups homemade chicken broth

2   cups sliced fresh mushrooms

3   tablespoons rice vinegar or white vinegar

2   tablespoons soy sauce or reduced-sodium soy sauce

1   teaspoon sugar

1   teaspoon grated fresh ginger

¼   to ½ teaspoon black pepper

1   tablespoon cornstarch

1   tablespoon cold water

2   cups shredded cooked turkey or chicken

2   cups sliced bok choy

1   6-ounce package frozen pea pods

1   beaten egg

3   tablespoons thinly sliced green onions

START TO FINISH:

30 minutes

MAKES:

4 servings

1 In a large saucepan combine broth, mushrooms, vinegar, soy sauce, sugar, ginger, and pepper. Bring to boiling.

2 Stir together cornstarch and cold water; stir into broth mixture. Cook and stir until thickened and bubbly. Cook and stir for 2 minutes more. Stir in turkey, bok choy, and pea pods.

3 Pour the egg into the soup in a steady stream, stirring a few times to create shreds. Remove saucepan from heat. Stir in green onions.

Nutrition Facts per serving: 216 cal., 6 g total fat (2 g sat. fat), 108 mg chol., 1,368 mg sodium, 10 g carbo., 2 g fiber, 28 g pro.

This soup takes advantage of any leftover meat and the bones from a turkey dinner.

TURKEY FRAME SOUP

PREP:

30 minutes

COOK:

1³/₄ hours

MAKES:

6 servings

1	meaty turkey frame
8	cups water
2	large onions, quartered
2	stalks celery, sliced
1	tablespoon instant chicken bouillon granules
3	cloves garlic, minced
	Chopped cooked turkey (if needed)
1	14¹/₂-ounce can diced tomatoes, undrained
1¹/₂	teaspoons dried oregano, basil, marjoram, or thyme, crushed
¹/₄	teaspoon black pepper
3	cups (any combination) sliced celery, carrots, parsnips, or mushrooms; chopped onion or rutabagas; or broccoli or cauliflower florets
1¹/₂	cups dried medium noodles

1 Break turkey frame or cut in half with kitchen shears. Place in an 8- to 10-quart Dutch oven. Add water, onions, celery, bouillon granules, and garlic. Bring to boiling; reduce heat. Simmer, covered, for 1¹/₂ hours.

2 Remove turkey frame. When cool enough to handle, remove meat from bones. Discard bones. Coarsely chop meat. If necessary, add enough turkey to equal 2 cups; set aside.

3 Strain broth, discarding solids. Skim fat from broth. Return broth to Dutch oven. Stir in undrained tomatoes, oregano, and pepper. Stir in vegetables. Return to boiling; reduce heat. Simmer, covered, for 10 minutes. Stir in noodles. Simmer for 8 to 10 minutes more or until noodles are tender but still firm and vegetables are tender. Stir in turkey; heat through.

Nutrition Facts per serving: 182 cal., 4 g total fat (1 g sat. fat), 52 mg chol., 608 mg sodium, 17 g carbo., 2 g fiber, 20 g pro.

Enhance this savory potato soup with a splash of cream for a richer flavor. Bright yellow-green napa cabbage or a little pile of baby spinach leaves are great options for colorful garnish. (Recipe pictured on page 102.)

NEW POTATO SIMMER

1½   pounds tiny new potatoes

1   pound smoked turkey or chicken breast, shredded

2   14-ounce cans reduced-sodium chicken broth or 3½ cups homemade chicken broth

⅓   cup sliced leek (white part only)

⅓   cup whipping cream

3   tablespoons Dijon-style mustard

1   tablespoon snipped fresh lemon thyme

1½   cups shredded napa cabbage

PREP:

15 minutes

COOK:

20 minutes

MAKES:

6 servings

1 Cut any large potatoes in half. In a 4-quart Dutch oven combine potatoes, turkey, broth, and leek. Bring to boiling; reduce heat. Simmer, covered, for 15 minutes.

2 In a small bowl stir together cream and mustard; add to Dutch oven along with lemon thyme. Simmer, uncovered, about 5 minutes more or until potatoes are tender, stirring occasionally. Top each serving with ¼ cup cabbage.

Nutrition Facts per serving: 243 cal., 8 g total fat (4 g sat. fat), 57 mg chol., 1,297 mg sodium, 23 g carbo., 3 g fiber, 19 g pro.

Make this soup extra special with a medley of mushrooms.

TURKEY & MUSHROOM SOUP

START TO FINISH:

35 minutes

MAKES:

4 servings

1	tablespoon butter or margarine
2	cups sliced fresh mushrooms (such as cremini, shiitake, porcini, and/or button)
1/2	cup thinly sliced celery
1/2	cup thinly sliced carrot
1/3	cup chopped onion
4 1/2	cups water
1	tablespoon instant beef bouillon granules
1/8	teaspoon black pepper
1/2	cup dried orzo
1 1/2	cups chopped cooked turkey
2	tablespoons snipped fresh parsley
1	teaspoon snipped fresh thyme

1 In a large saucepan melt butter over medium heat. Add mushrooms, celery, carrot, and onion; cook and stir until crisp-tender. Add water, bouillon granules, and pepper.

2 Bring to boiling; stir in orzo. Return to boiling; reduce heat. Simmer, uncovered, for 5 to 8 minutes or until orzo is tender but still firm. Stir in turkey, parsley, and thyme; heat through.

Nutrition Facts per serving: 227 cal., 7 g total fat (3 g sat. fat), 48 mg chol., 661 mg sodium, 21 g carbo., 2 g fiber, 20 g pro.

Besides the familiar onions, this soup contains three other members of the onion family—leeks, green onions, and shallots.

TURKEY-ONION SOUP

1	tablespoon cooking oil
1½	cups chopped onions
1½	cups sliced carrots
1½	cups sliced celery
1	cup chopped leeks (white parts only)
½	cup sliced green onions
⅓	cup finely chopped shallots
1	2½-pound turkey breast half with bone, skinned
5½	cups water
¼	cup snipped fresh parsley
1½	teaspoons dried oregano, crushed
1½	teaspoons Greek seasoning
1	teaspoon salt
1	teaspoon fennel seeds, crushed
½	teaspoon black pepper
2	bay leaves

PREP:
40 minutes
COOK:
1 hour
MAKES:
6 servings

1 In a 4-quart Dutch oven heat oil. Add onions, carrots, celery, leeks, green onions, and shallots; cook and stir over medium-high heat for 7 to 10 minutes or until tender. Add the turkey breast half, water, parsley, oregano, Greek seasoning, salt, fennel seeds, pepper, and bay leaves. Bring to boiling; reduce heat. Simmer, covered, for 1 to 2 hours or until turkey breast is tender.

2 Remove turkey from Dutch oven. When cool enough to handle, remove meat from bones. Discard bones. Chop turkey. Return turkey to Dutch oven; heat through. Remove and discard bay leaves.

Nutrition Facts per serving: 28 cal., 5 g total fat (1 g sat. fat), 80 mg chol., 516 mg sodium, 13 g carbo., 3 g fiber, 33 g pro.

Cooked, smoked turkey sausage has a long shelf life when kept in the refrigerator. Keep some on hand, along with the other ingredients, and you can stir together this soup in a hurry. Refrigerated bread sticks and apple slices make quick, easy sides.

WHITE BEAN & TURKEY SAUSAGE SOUP

START TO FINISH:

30 minutes

MAKES:

4 servings

2   15-ounce cans Great Northern or white kidney beans (cannellini), rinsed and drained

1   10¾-ounce can condensed cream of celery soup

8   ounces cooked smoked turkey sausage, halved lengthwise and sliced

1½   cups milk

1   teaspoon dried minced onion

½   teaspoon dried thyme, crushed

⅛   to ¼ teaspoon black pepper

2   cloves garlic, minced, or ¼ teaspoon garlic powder

1 In a large saucepan combine beans, soup, and turkey sausage. Stir in milk, onion, thyme, pepper, and garlic. Bring to boiling over medium-high heat, stirring occasionally; reduce heat. Simmer, covered, for 10 minutes, stirring occasionally.

Nutrition Facts per serving: 434 cal., 11 g total fat (3 g sat. fat), 54 mg chol., 1,129 mg sodium, 57 g carbo., 11 g fiber, 29 g pro.

Hot cooked rice makes a tasty accompaniment to this soup.

BLACK BEAN SOUP WITH SAUSAGE

1   cup dry black beans, rinsed

8   cups water

2   cups chicken broth

1   cup chopped onion

1   cup chopped celery

1   teaspoon ground coriander

¼   teaspoon salt

⅛   to ¼ teaspoon cayenne pepper

4   cloves garlic, minced

8   ounces cooked smoked turkey sausage
     or Polish sausage, chopped

     Dairy sour cream or shredded Monterey
     Jack cheese (optional)

     Snipped fresh cilantro (optional)

PREP:
1½ hours
COOK:
1¼ hours
MAKES:
6 servings

❶ In a large saucepan combine beans and 6 cups of the water. Bring to boiling; reduce heat. Simmer for 2 minutes. Remove from heat. Cover and let stand for 1 hour. (Or place beans in water in pan. Cover and let soak in a cool place for 6 to 8 hours or overnight.) Drain and rinse beans.

❷ Return beans to saucepan. Stir in the remaining 2 cups water, broth, onion, celery, coriander, salt, cayenne pepper, and garlic. Bring to boiling; reduce heat. Simmer, covered, for 1 to 1½ hours or until beans are tender.

❸ If desired, mash beans slightly. Stir in sausage; heat through. If desired, top each serving with sour cream and cilantro.

Nutrition Facts per serving: 198 cal., 6 g total fat (2 g sat. fat), 29 mg chol., 682 mg sodium, 24 g carbo., 6 g fiber, 14 g pro.

SHORTCUT BLACK BEAN SOUP WITH SAUSAGE: Prepare as above, except omit dry black beans and the 6 cups soaking water. Decrease chicken broth to 1½ cups. Rinse and drain two 15-ounce cans black beans. In a large saucepan combine beans, broth, 2 cups water, onion, celery, coriander, salt, cayenne pepper, and garlic. Bring to boiling; reduce heat. Simmer, covered, about 15 minutes or until vegetables are tender. Stir in sausage; heat through.

Nutrition Facts per serving: 268 cal., 8 g total fat (2 g sat. fat), 44 mg chol., 1,421 mg sodium, 35 g carbo., 11 g fiber, 25 g pro.

This tongue-tingling soup gets its spirited flavor from Cajun seasoning, a blend of ingredients such as garlic, chile peppers, black pepper, and mustard. The combination of ingredients may vary, depending on the brand of seasoning you buy.

CAJUN FISH SOUP

START TO FINISH:

25 minutes

MAKES:

4 servings

12 ounces fresh or frozen fish fillets or peeled and deveined shrimp

1 14-ounce can vegetable or chicken broth or 1¾ cups homemade vegetable or chicken broth

1 cup sliced fresh mushrooms

1 small yellow summer squash or zucchini, halved lengthwise and sliced

½ cup chopped onion

1 to 1½ teaspoons Cajun seasoning

1 clove garlic, minced

2 14½-ounce cans reduced-sodium stewed tomatoes, undrained

2 tablespoons snipped fresh oregano

½ teaspoon finely shredded lemon peel

1 Thaw fish or shrimp, if frozen. Rinse fish or shrimp. If using fish, cut into 1-inch pieces; set aside.

2 In a large saucepan combine broth, mushrooms, squash, onion, Cajun seasoning, and garlic. Bring to boiling; reduce heat. Simmer, covered, about 5 minutes or until vegetables are tender.

3 Stir in the fish or shrimp and undrained tomatoes. Bring just to boiling; reduce heat. Simmer, covered, for 2 to 3 minutes or until fish flakes easily with a fork or shrimp turn opaque. Remove saucepan from heat. Stir in oregano and lemon peel.

Nutrition Facts per serving: 159 cal., 1 g total fat (0 g sat. fat), 36 mg chol., 568 mg sodium, 21 g carbo., 4 g fiber, 18 g pro.

The sweet essence of fresh fennel blends nicely with fish, tomatoes, garlic, and onion in this classic French soup.

FISH PROVENÇALE

8	ounces fresh or frozen skinless haddock, grouper, or halibut fillets
1	small fennel bulb
3	cups vegetable or chicken broth
1	cup finely chopped onion
1	cup cubed yellow summer squash
1	cup dry white wine
1	teaspoon finely shredded orange peel or lemon peel
3	cloves garlic, minced
2	cups chopped tomatoes or one 14½-ounce can diced tomatoes, undrained
2	tablespoons snipped fresh thyme

START TO FINISH:

30 minutes

MAKES:

4 servings

1 Thaw fish, if frozen. Rinse fish; cut into 1-inch pieces; set aside.

2 Cut off and discard upper stalks of fennel. Remove any wilted outer layers and cut a thin slice from the base. Wash fennel; cut in half lengthwise and thinly slice.

3 In a large saucepan combine fennel, broth, onion, squash, wine, orange peel, and garlic. Bring to boiling; reduce heat. Simmer, covered, for 10 minutes. Stir in fish, tomatoes, and thyme. Cook about 3 minutes more or until fish flakes easily with a fork.

Nutrition Facts per serving: 165 cal., 1 g total fat (0 g sat. fat), 32 mg chol., 798 mg sodium, 17 g carbo., 4 g fiber, 13 g pro.

For a little extra kick, opt for medium salsa instead of mild.

FISH & SALSA SOUP

PREP:

30 minutes

COOK:

25 minutes

MAKES:

4 servings

12	ounces fresh or frozen orange roughy fillets
2	tablespoons olive oil
1	cup chopped, peeled potato
1	cup chopped onion
1	cup chopped carrot
½	cup chopped celery
1	clove garlic, minced
1	14-ounce can chicken or vegetable broth or 1¾ cups homemade chicken or vegetable broth
1¼	cups bottled mild salsa
½	teaspoon lemon-pepper seasoning
2	cups shredded fresh spinach
	Snipped fresh cilantro or parsley

1 Thaw fish, if frozen. Rinse fish; cut into 1-inch pieces; set aside.

2 In a large saucepan heat oil. Add potato, onion, carrot, celery, and garlic; cook and stir over medium heat for 5 minutes. Stir in broth, salsa, and lemon-pepper seasoning. Bring to boiling; reduce heat. Simmer, covered, for 15 minutes. Add fish and spinach. Cook, uncovered, about 5 minutes more or until fish flakes easily with a fork. Sprinkle each serving with cilantro.

Nutrition Facts per serving: 216 cal., 8 g total fat (1 g sat. fat), 18 mg chol., 1,182 mg sodium, 20 g carbo., 3 g fiber, 15 g pro.

*When the weather turns chilly, ladle up steaming bowls of this sassy soup.
If you can't get red snapper or orange roughy, substitute cod or sole.*

RED PEPPER & RED SNAPPER SOUP

1¼ pound fresh or frozen skinless red snapper, orange roughy, or other firm-fleshed fish fillets

2 tablespoons olive oil

2¼ cups coarsely chopped red sweet peppers

1 cup chopped shallots or onion

3 14-ounce cans reduced-sodium chicken broth or 5¼ cups homemade chicken broth

¼ teaspoon salt

¼ teaspoon black pepper

⅛ teaspoon cayenne pepper

½ cup snipped fresh Italian (flat-leaf) parsley

Fresh Italian (flat-leaf) parsley sprigs (optional)

PREP:
25 minutes
COOK:
25 minutes
MAKES:
5 servings

1 Thaw fish, if frozen. Rinse fish; cut into 1-inch pieces; set aside. In a large saucepan heat oil. Add sweet peppers and shallots; cook and stir over medium heat for 5 minutes. Add 1 can of the broth. Bring to boiling; reduce heat. Simmer, covered, about 20 minutes or until sweet peppers are very tender. Remove saucepan from heat; cool slightly.

2 Pour half of the sweet pepper mixture into a blender. Cover and blend until nearly smooth. Pour into a medium bowl. Repeat with remaining sweet pepper mixture.

3 Return all to saucepan. Add the remaining 2 cans of broth, the salt, black pepper, and cayenne pepper. Bring to boiling; reduce heat. Add fish. Simmer, covered, about 5 minutes or until fish flakes easily with a fork, stirring once or twice. Stir in parsley. If desired, garnish each serving with parsley sprigs.

Nutrition Facts per serving: 223 cal., 8 g total fat (1 g sat. fat), 42 mg chol., 859 mg sodium, 10 g carbo., 0 g fiber, 27 g pro.

For this Japanese one-bowl dinner, look for soba noodles, mirin, and dashi in the Asian section of your local supermarket or at an Asian grocery store. (Recipe pictured on page 110.)

SOBA NOODLES IN BROTH

START TO FINISH:

20 minutes

MAKES:

2 servings

8	ounces fresh or frozen shrimp in shells
6	ounces soba (buckwheat noodles) or dried vermicelli
2	cups reduced-sodium chicken broth
1/4	cup mirin (Japanese sweet rice wine)
1/4	cup reduced-sodium soy sauce
2	teaspoons sugar
1/2	teaspoon instant dashi granules (dried tuna-and-seaweed-flavored soup stock)
2	green onions, thinly bias-sliced

1 Thaw shrimp, if frozen. Peel and devein shrimp, leaving tails intact. Rinse and pat dry; set shrimp aside. In a large saucepan cook soba noodles in a large amount of boiling water about 4 minutes or until tender.

2 Meanwhile, in a medium saucepan combine broth, mirin, soy sauce, sugar, and dashi granules. Bring to boiling; reduce heat. Add shrimp; simmer, uncovered, about 2 minutes or until shrimp turn opaque.

3 Drain noodles; divide noodles between 2 soup bowls. Pour the shrimp mixture over the noodles. Sprinkle each serving with green onions.

Nutrition Facts per serving: 515 cal., 2 g total fat (0 g sat. fat), 129 mg chol., 2,698 mg sodium, 93 g carbo., 4 g fiber, 35 g pro.

The lemongrass for this simple soup can be found in Asian specialty markets or larger supermarkets. This lemon-flavored root resembles a fibrous green onion. (Recipe pictured on page 101.)

THAI-STYLE SHRIMP SOUP

12	ounces fresh or frozen peeled and deveined small shrimp
1	14-ounce can chicken broth or 1³⁄₄ cups homemade chicken broth
1	small zucchini, cut into thin bite-size strips (about 1¹⁄₂ cups)
1	green onion, bias-sliced into 1¹⁄₄-inch pieces
2	tablespoons very finely chopped fresh ginger
2	tablespoons very finely chopped fresh lemongrass or 1¹⁄₂ teaspoons finely shredded lemon peel
¹⁄₄	teaspoon crushed red pepper
1	14-ounce can unsweetened coconut milk
2	tablespoons slivered fresh basil
2	tablespoons shaved coconut, toasted

PREP:
20 minutes
COOK:
5 minutes
MAKES:
3 or 4 servings

1 Thaw shrimp, if frozen. Rinse shrimp; pat dry. Set shrimp aside. In a large saucepan bring broth to boiling. Add zucchini, green onion, ginger, lemongrass, and crushed red pepper. Return to boiling; reduce heat. Simmer, uncovered, for 3 minutes, stirring occasionally.

2 Add shrimp. Return to boiling; reduce heat. Simmer, uncovered, for 2 to 3 minutes or until shrimp turn opaque. Add coconut milk; heat through (do not boil). Sprinkle each serving with basil and coconut.

Nutrition Facts per serving: 445 cal., 37 g total fat (31 g sat. fat), 115 mg chol., 708 mg sodium, 12 g carbo., 4 g fiber, 21 g pro.

The savory combination of shrimp, shredded bok choy, and leek is embellished with an accent of lemon pepper.

SHRIMP & GREENS SOUP

START TO FINISH:

20 minutes

MAKES:

4 servings

12 ounces fresh or frozen peeled and deveined shrimp

1 tablespoon olive oil

½ cup thinly sliced leek (white part only)

2 cloves garlic, minced

3 14-ounce cans reduced-sodium chicken or vegetable broth or 5¼ cups homemade chicken or vegetable broth

1 tablespoon snipped fresh parsley

1 teaspoon snipped fresh marjoram or thyme or ¼ teaspoon dried marjoram or thyme, crushed

¼ teaspoon lemon-pepper seasoning

3 cups shredded bok choy or fresh spinach

❶ Thaw shrimp, if frozen. Rinse shrimp; pat dry. Set shrimp aside. In a large saucepan heat oil. Add leek and garlic; cook and stir over medium-high heat about 2 minutes or until leek is tender. Add broth, parsley, marjoram, and lemon-pepper seasoning.

❷ Bring to boiling; add shrimp. Return to boiling; reduce heat. Simmer, uncovered, about 2 minutes or until shrimp turn opaque. Stir in bok choy. Cook about 1 minute more or until bok choy is wilted.

Nutrition Facts per serving: 165 cal., 5 g total fat (1 g sat. fat), 129 mg chol., 1,289 mg sodium, 7 g carbo., 2 g fiber, 22 g pro.

Silken tofu, used in this flavorful soup, has a much finer consistency than other forms of tofu.

EGG DROP SOUP WITH SHRIMP

8	ounces fresh or frozen peeled and deveined shrimp
3½	cups chicken broth
½	of a 15-ounce jar whole straw mushrooms or one 6-ounce jar sliced mushrooms, drained
¼	cup rice vinegar or white vinegar
2	tablespoons soy sauce
1	teaspoon sugar
1	teaspoon grated fresh ginger
½	teaspoon black pepper
4	ounces firm, silken-style tofu (fresh bean curd), drained and cut into bite-size pieces
1	tablespoon cornstarch
1	tablespoon cold water
½	cup frozen peas
½	cup shredded carrot
2	tablespoons thinly sliced green onion
1	beaten egg

START TO FINISH:

35 minutes

MAKES:

4 servings

1 Thaw shrimp, if frozen. Rinse shrimp; pat dry. Set shrimp aside. In a large saucepan combine broth, mushrooms, vinegar, soy sauce, sugar, ginger, and pepper. Bring to boiling; reduce heat. Simmer, covered, for 2 minutes. Stir in shrimp and tofu. Return to boiling; reduce heat. Simmer, covered, for 1 minute more.

2 Stir together cornstarch and cold water; stir into broth mixture. Cook and stir until slightly thickened and bubbly. Cook and stir for 2 minutes more. Stir in peas, carrot, and green onion. Pour the egg into the soup in a steady stream, stirring a few times to create shreds.

Nutrition Facts per serving: 195 cal., 6 g total fat (1 g sat. fat), 139 mg chol., 1,703 mg sodium, 11 g carbo., 3 g fiber, 22 g pro.

Enjoy the flavor of gumbo with much less effort. This soup incorporates familiar gumbo ingredients— rice, tomatoes, sausage, and shrimp—minus the long cooking time.

BAYOU SHRIMP SOUP

START TO FINISH:

35 minutes

MAKES:

4 servings

8   ounces andouille sausage or cooked smoked sausage, thinly sliced

¾   cup chopped green sweet pepper

½   cup chopped onion

1   14-ounce can reduced-sodium chicken broth or 1¾ cups homemade chicken broth

1   tablespoon steak sauce

2   tablespoons snipped fresh thyme or 1½ teaspoons dried thyme, crushed

¼   teaspoon crushed red pepper (optional)

8   ounces frozen peeled, cooked shrimp

2   cups chopped tomatoes

1½   cups cooked rice

1 In a large saucepan cook and stir sausage, sweet pepper, and onion over medium-high heat for 6 to 7 minutes or until vegetables are tender.

2 Add broth, steak sauce, and, if using, dried thyme. (If not using andouille sausage, add the crushed red pepper.) Bring to boiling; reduce heat. Simmer, covered, for 10 minutes.

3 Add shrimp, fresh thyme (if using), tomatoes, and cooked rice; heat through.

Nutrition Facts per serving: 394 cal., 19 g total fat (7 g sat. fat), 149 mg chol., 1,278 mg sodium, 26 g carbo., 2 g fiber, 28 g pro.

Portobello mushrooms lend the heartiness to this flavor-packed soup, while swirls of baby spinach add bright color.

HEARTY VEGETABLE SOUP

2	tablespoons olive oil
⅔	cup sliced leeks (white parts only)
8	ounces fresh portobello mushrooms, stemmed and coarsely chopped
4	14-ounce cans vegetable broth or 7 cups homemade vegetable broth
2½	cups sliced carrots
2	cups chopped, peeled butternut squash
1	medium zucchini, coarsely chopped
1	cup quick-cooking barley
½	teaspoon salt
½	teaspoon dried thyme, crushed
⅛	teaspoon black pepper
1	6-ounce package fresh baby spinach
¼	cup finely shredded Parmesan cheese

PREP:
30 minutes
COOK:
35 minutes
MAKES:
6 servings

1 In a 4- to 5-quart Dutch oven heat oil. Add leeks; cook and stir over medium-low heat about 10 minutes or until softened. Add mushrooms; cook for 5 minutes more. Add broth, carrots, squash, zucchini, barley, salt, thyme, and pepper. Bring to boiling; reduce heat. Simmer, covered, for 8 to 10 minutes or until vegetables and barley are tender.

2 Gradually add spinach, stirring until wilted. Sprinkle each serving with Parmesan cheese.

Nutrition Facts per serving: 302 cal., 12 g total fat (5 g sat. fat), 16 mg chol., 1,705 mg sodium, 35 g carbo., 6 g fiber, 14 g pro.

Look for fire-roasted tomatoes at a health food store if your supermarket doesn't stock them or substitute a can of diced tomatoes. (Recipe pictured on page 108.)

ROASTED TOMATO & VEGETABLE SOUP

PREP:

30 minutes

COOK:

25 minutes

MAKES:

6 servings

2	tablespoons olive oil
1¼	cups chopped onions
1	cup sliced celery
¾	cup chopped carrot
2	cloves garlic, minced
6	cups chicken broth
2	cups chopped, peeled butternut squash
1	14-ounce can fire-roasted diced tomatoes, undrained
1	15-ounce can white kidney beans (cannellini), rinsed and drained
1	medium zucchini, halved lengthwise and sliced
1	cup small broccoli florets
1	cup small cauliflower florets
1½	teaspoons snipped fresh oregano or ½ teaspoon dried oregano, crushed
⅛	teaspoon black pepper
	Freshly grated Parmesan cheese (optional)

1 In a 4-quart Dutch oven heat oil. Add onions, celery, carrot, and garlic; cook and stir over medium heat for 5 minutes. Stir in broth, squash, and undrained tomatoes. Bring to boiling; reduce heat. Simmer, covered, for 20 minutes.

2 Add beans, zucchini, broccoli, cauliflower, oregano, and pepper. Cook for 5 minutes more. If desired, sprinkle each serving with Parmesan cheese.

Nutrition Facts per serving: 161 cal., 5 g total fat (1 g sat. fat), 3 mg chol., 1,279 mg sodium, 25 g carbo., 6 g fiber, 9 g pro.

If you can't find udon noodles—Japanese noodles that are made from either wheat or corn flour—angel hair pasta makes a good substitute, as it cooks in the same amount of time.

TOFU-MUSHROOM NOODLE SOUP

1	16-ounce package extra-firm tofu (fresh bean curd), drained and cut into 1/2-inch pieces
1	tablespoon soy sauce
1	tablespoon toasted sesame oil
1	tablespoon cooking oil
3	cups sliced fresh button mushrooms
1	clove garlic, minced
2	14-ounce cans vegetable broth or 3 1/2 cups homemade vegetable broth
1	10-ounce can condensed vegetarian vegetable soup
1	10-ounce package frozen chopped broccoli
2	ounces udon noodles or dried angel hair pasta, broken
1	to 2 tablespoons snipped fresh cilantro

START TO FINISH:

25 minutes

MAKES:

4 to 6 servings

1 In a bowl gently stir together tofu, soy sauce, and sesame oil; set aside.

2 In a large saucepan heat cooking oil. Add mushrooms and garlic; cook and stir over medium heat for 4 minutes. Add broth, soup, broccoli, and udon noodles. Bring to boiling; reduce heat. Simmer, covered, for 4 to 6 minutes or until vegetables and noodles are tender, stirring occasionally. Gently stir in tofu; heat through. Stir in cilantro.

Nutrition Facts per serving: 295 cal., 15 g total fat (2 g sat. fat), 0 mg chol., 1,545 mg sodium, 29 g carbo., 5 g fiber, 18 g pro.

If you substitute brown or yellow lentils for the red lentils, increase the cooking time in Step 1 to about 30 minutes or until lentils are very tender.

RED LENTIL SOUP

START TO FINISH:

30 minutes

MAKES:

6 to 8 servings

2	tablespoons olive oil
1	cup chopped onion
¼	cup chopped carrot
¼	cup chopped celery
½	teaspoon fennel seeds, crushed
¼	teaspoon ground turmeric
¼	teaspoon ground coriander
⅛	teaspoon black pepper
⅛	teaspoon cayenne pepper
4	cups chicken broth
2½	cups red lentils, rinsed and drained
2¼	cups water
1	7-ounce jar roasted red sweet peppers, drained
⅓	cup plain low-fat yogurt (optional)
2	tablespoons snipped fresh cilantro (optional)
1	recipe Cheese Crisps (optional)

1 In a large saucepan heat 1 tablespoon of the oil. Add onion, carrot, and celery; cook and stir over medium heat about 5 minutes or until onion is tender. Stir in fennel seeds, turmeric, coriander, black pepper, and cayenne pepper. Stir in broth, lentils, and water. Bring to boiling; reduce heat. Simmer, covered, about 5 minutes or until lentils are very tender.

2 Meanwhile, in a blender or food processor combine the roasted sweet peppers and the remaining 1 tablespoon olive oil. Cover and blend or process until nearly smooth. Stir into saucepan; heat through.

3 If desired, top each serving with yogurt, cilantro, and/or Cheese Crisps.

Nutrition Facts per serving: 337 cal., 6 g total fat (1 g sat. fat), 0 mg chol., 551 mg sodium, 50 g carbo., 13 g fiber, 22 g pro.

CHEESE CRISPS: Line a baking sheet with foil; grease foil. Place six to eight 1-tablespoon mounds of finely shredded cheddar cheese on prepared baking sheet. Bake in a 350°F oven for 3 to 4 minutes or until cheese melts. Cool crisps on baking sheet. Carefully peel off foil.

Serve this fiber-rich, meatless soup with a salad of fresh romaine, marinated artichoke hearts, and thinly sliced red onions, tossed with Caesar dressing.

CURRY-GINGER LENTIL SOUP

1	tablespoon olive oil
½	cup chopped onion
1	fresh jalapeño chile pepper, seeded and finely chopped*
1	teaspoon grated fresh ginger
3	cloves garlic, minced
2	14-ounce cans vegetable broth or 3½ cups homemade vegetable broth
2	cups cubed, peeled sweet potatoes
2	cups chopped tomatoes
1	cup water
1	cup brown lentils, rinsed and drained
1	tablespoon curry powder
	Dash salt
	Plain yogurt or dairy sour cream (optional)

PREP:
20 minutes
COOK:
30 minutes
MAKES:
4 to 6 servings

1 In a 4-quart Dutch oven heat oil. Add onion, chile pepper, ginger, and garlic; cook and stir over medium heat about 2 minutes or until tender. Add broth, sweet potatoes, tomatoes, water, lentils, curry powder, and salt. Bring to boiling; reduce heat. Simmer, covered, for 25 to 30 minutes until lentils are tender. If desired, top each serving with yogurt.

*NOTE: When working with chile peppers, wear plastic or rubber gloves. If your bare hands do touch the chile peppers, wash your hands well with soap and water.

Nutrition Facts per serving: 328 cal., 5 g total fat (1 g sat. fat), 0 mg chol., 886 mg sodium, 57 g carbo., 19 g fiber, 18 g pro.

You can keep a batch of this "big soup" in the freezer for up to 3 months.

MINESTRONE

PREP:

45 minutes

COOK:

25 minutes

MAKES:

8 servings

6	cups water
1	28-ounce can tomatoes, cut up and undrained
1	8-ounce can tomato sauce
1	cup chopped onion
1	cup chopped cabbage
½	cup chopped carrot
½	cup chopped celery
1	tablespoon instant beef bouillon granules
1	tablespoon dried Italian seasoning, crushed
1	teaspoon salt
¼	teaspoon black pepper
2	cloves garlic, minced
1	15-ounce can white kidney beans (cannellini) or Great Northern beans, undrained
1	10-ounce package frozen lima beans or one 9-ounce package frozen Italian green beans
1	small zucchini, halved lengthwise and sliced
4	ounces dried linguine or spaghetti, broken
2	to 3 tablespoons purchased basil pesto (optional)
	Grated Parmesan cheese (optional)

1 In a 5- to 6-quart Dutch oven combine water, undrained tomatoes, tomato sauce, onion, cabbage, carrot, celery, bouillon granules, Italian seasoning, salt, pepper, and garlic. Bring to boiling; reduce heat. Simmer, covered, for 10 minutes. Stir in undrained white kidney beans, lima beans, zucchini, and pasta. Return to boiling; reduce heat. Simmer, uncovered, for 15 minutes.

2 If desired, top each serving with pesto and sprinkle with Parmesan cheese.

Nutrition Facts per serving: 176 cal., 1 g total fat (0 g sat. fat), 0 mg chol., 1,011 mg sodium, 37 g carbo., 7 g fiber, 10 g pro.

Tender spinach and sugar snap peas team with cheese tortellini in this lemon-scented soup. Sprinkle each serving with fresh Parmesan cheese for a sharp flavor accent.

ITALIAN-STYLE GREENS & TORTELLINI SOUP

1	tablespoon olive oil
1½	cups finely chopped onions
1	teaspoon dried Italian seasoning, crushed
5	cloves garlic, minced
2	14-ounce cans reduced-sodium chicken broth or 3½ cups homemade chicken broth
1½	cups water
1	9-ounce package refrigerated 3-cheese-filled tortellini
2	cups fresh sugar snap peas, strings and tips removed
2	cups shredded fresh spinach
2	teaspoons lemon juice
2	tablespoons finely shredded Parmesan cheese

START TO FINISH:
35 minutes
MAKES:
4 servings

1 In a 4-quart Dutch oven heat oil. Add onions, Italian seasoning, and garlic; cook and stir over medium heat about 5 minutes or until onion is tender. Add broth and water. Bring to boiling; add tortellini. Return to boiling; reduce heat. Simmer, uncovered, for 4 minutes.

2 Meanwhile, halve sugar snap peas crosswise. Add peas, spinach, and lemon juice to Dutch oven. Return to boiling; reduce heat. Simmer, uncovered, for 2 minutes more. Sprinkle each serving with Parmesan cheese.

Nutrition Facts per serving: 289 cal., 8 g total fat (2 g sat. fat), 20 mg chol., 717 mg sodium, 40 g carbo., 4 g fiber, 14 g pro.

This soup freezes well, so make an extra batch.

BUTTERNUT SQUASH SOUP WITH RAVIOLI

START TO FINISH:

30 minutes

MAKES:

4 servings

2   pounds butternut squash

2   14-ounce cans vegetable broth or 3½ cups homemade vegetable broth

½   cup water

⅛   teaspoon cayenne pepper

1   tablespoon butter or margarine

1   9-ounce package refrigerated 3-cheese-filled ravioli

1   tablespoon mild-flavored molasses (optional)

1 Peel squash; halve lengthwise. Remove seeds and discard. Cut squash into ¾-inch pieces.

2 In a large saucepan combine squash, broth, water, and cayenne pepper. Cook, covered, over medium heat about 20 minutes or until squash is tender.

3 Transfer one-fourth of the squash mixture to a blender or food processor. Cover and blend or process until smooth. Repeat with remaining portions, one at a time, until all of the mixture is blended.

4 Return blended mixture to the saucepan. Bring just to boiling; reduce heat. Simmer, uncovered, for 5 minutes. Add butter; stir just until melted.

5 Meanwhile, cook ravioli according to package directions; drain. Ladle hot soup into bowls. Divide cooked ravioli among bowls. If desired, drizzle each serving with molasses.

Nutrition Facts per serving: 301 cal., 12 g total fat (6 g sat. fat), 64 mg chol., 1,101 mg sodium, 39 g carbo., 2 g fiber, 11 g pro.

Homemade pistou, a basil-based condiment similar to pesto, garnishes this vegetable-filled soup. (Recipe pictured on the cover and on page 105.)

VEGETABLE & ORZO SOUP WITH PISTOU

½	cup dry Great Northern beans
1	tablespoon extra-virgin olive oil
½	cup chopped onion
3	cloves garlic, minced
1	recipe Herb Bag
3	cups chicken broth or homemade chicken broth
8	ounces fresh green beans, halved
1	medium zucchini, chopped
2	cups chopped tomatoes
⅔	cup chopped fennel
2	sprigs fresh thyme
⅓	cup dried orzo
1	recipe Pistou

PREP:
1¼ hours
COOK:
1¼ hours
MAKES:
4 to 5 servings

1 Rinse beans. In a large saucepan combine beans and 2 cups *water*. Bring to boiling; reduce heat. Simmer for 2 minutes. Remove from heat. Cover and let stand 1 hour. (Or place beans in water in saucepan. Cover and let soak in a cool place for 6 to 8 hours or overnight.) Drain and rinse beans; set aside.

2 In a 4-quart Dutch oven heat oil. Add onion and garlic; cook and stir until tender. Add beans and 2 cups fresh *water*. Add Herb Bag. Bring to boiling; reduce heat. Simmer, covered, for 55 minutes. Remove and discard Herb Bag.

3 Add broth, green beans, zucchini, tomatoes, fennel, thyme sprigs, and ½ teaspoon *salt*. Bring to boiling; reduce heat. Simmer, covered, for 20 minutes. Add orzo. Simmer, covered, for 10 minutes more. Remove and discard thyme sprigs.

4 Top each serving with some of the Pistou. If desired, sprinkle each serving with grated *Parmesan cheese*.

HERB BAG: Cut a 10-inch square of 100-percent-cotton cheesecloth. Place 2 bay leaves, ½ teaspoon whole black peppercorns, 3 sprigs fresh thyme, and 3 sprigs fresh parsley on cheesecloth. Bring up corners and tie closed with clean string.

PISTOU: In a food processor or blender combine 2 cups firmly packed basil; 6 cloves garlic, halved; 2 tablespoons grated Parmesan cheese; and 2 tablespoons olive oil. Cover and process or blend until finely chopped. Thin to desired consistency with an additional 1 to 2 tablespoons olive oil.

Nutrition Facts per serving: 340 cal., 16 g total fat (2 g sat. fat), 4 mg chol., 1,096 mg sodium, 41 g carbo., 10 g fiber, 13 g pro.

Cannellini beans (white kidney beans) bring creamy texture and mellow, meaty flavor to an old favorite.

WHITE BEAN & CABBAGE SOUP

PREP:

20 minutes

COOK:

10 minutes

MAKES:

6 servings

1	tablespoon olive oil
3	cups thinly sliced cabbage
1	cup sliced carrots
1	teaspoon dried thyme, crushed
1/4	teaspoon black pepper
6	cloves garlic, minced
2	14-ounce cans chicken broth or 3 1/2 cups homemade chicken broth
1	14 1/2-ounce can tomatoes, cut up and undrained
1	cup water
1/4	cup tomato paste
2	15-ounce cans white kidney beans (cannellini), rinsed and drained

1 In a 4-quart Dutch oven heat oil. Add cabbage, carrots, thyme, pepper, and garlic; cook and stir for 2 to 3 minutes or until cabbage starts to wilt. Stir in broth, undrained tomatoes, water, and tomato paste. Bring to boiling; reduce heat. Simmer, covered, for 7 to 9 minutes or until vegetables are tender, stirring occasionally.

2 Meanwhile, slightly mash half of the drained beans with a potato masher or fork. Add all of the beans to Dutch oven; heat through.

Nutrition Facts per serving: 164 cal., 4 g total fat (1 g sat. fat), 0 mg chol., 1,006 mg sodium, 30 g carbo., 9 g fiber, 11 g pro.

CHOWDERS & BISQUES

3

A treasure of spring—tender, purple-tinged asparagus—is featured in this soup. Sour cream lends a tangy flavor to this creamy delight.

ASPARAGUS & CHEESE POTATO SOUP

START TO FINISH:

35 minutes

MAKES:

4 servings

4	teaspoons cooking oil
1	cup chopped onion
3	tablespoons all-purpose flour
2	cups 1-inch pieces asparagus spears or broccoli florets
1½	cups cubed red potatoes
2	cups milk
1	14-ounce can chicken broth or 1¾ cups homemade chicken broth
¼	teaspoon salt
⅛	teaspoon cayenne pepper
1	cup shredded sharp cheddar cheese (4 ounces)
½	cup chopped, seeded tomato
⅓	cup dairy sour cream

1 In a large saucepan heat oil over medium heat. Add onion; cook and stir until tender. Sprinkle flour over onion; stir to coat.

2 Add asparagus, potatoes, milk, broth, salt, and cayenne pepper. Cook and stir until thickened and bubbly; reduce heat. Simmer, covered, for 10 to 12 minutes or until vegetables are just tender, stirring occasionally. Add cheese, tomato, and sour cream; stir until cheese melts.

Nutrition Facts per serving: 353 cal., 20 g total fat (10 g sat. fat), 48 mg chol., 801 mg sodium, 29 g carbo., 3 g fiber, 16 g pro.

Rye bread is a snappy complement to the rich, nutty, buttery flavor of the Jarlsberg cheese, a Swiss-style cheese.

CHEESY POTATO & CAULIFLOWER CHOWDER

2	tablespoons butter or margarine
1	cup chopped onion
4	cups chicken broth
2	cups diced, peeled Yukon gold or white potatoes
2½	cups cauliflower florets
1	cup half-and-half, light cream, or milk
2	tablespoons all-purpose flour
2½	cups shredded Jarlsberg cheese (10 ounces)
	Salt
	Black pepper
3	slices dark rye or pumpernickel bread, halved crosswise (optional)
½	cup shredded Jarlsberg cheese (2 ounces) (optional)
2	tablespoons snipped fresh Italian (flat-leaf) parsley (optional)

PREP:

20 minutes

BAKE:

8 minutes

COOK:

10 minutes

OVEN:

350°F

MAKES:

6 servings

1 In a large saucepan or Dutch oven melt butter over medium heat. Add onion; cook until tender. Add broth and potatoes. Bring to boiling; reduce heat. Simmer, covered, for 6 minutes. Add cauliflower. Return to boiling; reduce heat. Simmer, covered, for 4 to 6 minutes more or until vegetables are tender.

2 In a bowl combine half-and-half and flour; add to the cauliflower mixture. Cook and stir over medium heat until thickened and bubbly. Reduce heat to low. Stir in the 2½ cups cheese until melted. Do not boil. Season to taste with salt and pepper.

3 Meanwhile, if desired, trim crusts from bread. Place halved bread slices on a baking sheet. Bake in a 350° oven about 3 minutes or until crisp. Turn slices over; sprinkle with the ½ cup cheese and the parsley. Bake for 5 minutes more or until cheese melts. If desired, place one piece of bread on top of each serving.

Nutrition Facts per serving: 267 cal., 17 g total fat (10 g sat. fat), 48 mg chol., 533 mg sodium, 14 g carbo., 2 g fiber, 15 g pro.

You can roast your own peppers, if you like. If you use purchased roasted red peppers, you'll shave significant time off of total preparation.

ROASTED RED PEPPER & JALAPEÑO BISQUE

PREP:

45 minutes

BAKE:

20 minutes

COOK:

15 minutes

OVEN:

425°F

MAKES:

4 servings

2   14-ounce cans chicken broth or 3½ cups homemade chicken broth

2   medium red sweet peppers, roasted, peeled, and chopped,* or one 7-ounce jar roasted red sweet peppers, drained and chopped

1   cup finely chopped sweet onion

½   cup finely chopped celery

2   cloves garlic, minced

4   teaspoons finely chopped seeded fresh jalapeño chile pepper**

⅛   teaspoon seasoned salt

3   tablespoons butter or margarine

3   tablespoons all-purpose flour

1   cup milk

1   cup shredded smoked cheddar or Swiss cheese (6 ounces)

1   cup half-and-half, light cream, or milk

½   cup finely chopped cooked ham

1 In a large saucepan combine broth, roasted sweet peppers, onion, celery, garlic, half of the jalapeño peppers, seasoned salt, and ⅛ teaspoon *black pepper.* Bring to boiling; reduce heat. Simmer, covered, about 7 minutes or until celery is tender. Remove from heat; cool slightly.

2 Place sweet pepper mixture, half at a time, in a blender or food processor. Cover and blend or process until smooth.

3 In the same saucepan melt butter over medium heat. Stir in flour. Add milk and pureed mixture. Cook and stir until bubbly. Add shredded cheese, half-and-half, ham, and remaining jalapeño peppers. Cook and stir until cheese is melted.

***TO ROAST PEPPERS:** Halve peppers lengthwise; remove stems, seeds, and membranes. Place pepper halves, cut sides down, on a foil-lined baking sheet. Bake in a 425° oven for 20 to 25 minutes or until skins are blistered and dark. Bring foil up and around pepper halves to enclose. Let stand about 15 minutes. Use a sharp knife to loosen the edges of the skins from the peppers; slowly pull off the skin. Discard skin. Chop peppers.

****NOTE:** When working with chile peppers, wear plastic or rubber gloves. If your bare hands do touch the chile peppers, wash your hands well with soap and water.

Nutrition Facts per serving: 473 cal., 35 g total fat (21 g sat. fat), 105 mg chol., 1,549 mg sodium, 20 g carbo., 2 g fiber, 21 g pro.

Garnish this cream soup with your favorite baked potato toppers—cheese, green onion, and bacon.

BAKED POTATO SOUP

2	large baking potatoes (about 8 ounces each)
3	tablespoons butter or margarine
6	tablespoons thinly sliced green onions
3	tablespoons all-purpose flour
2	teaspoons snipped fresh dill or chives, or 1/4 teaspoon dried dill
1/4	teaspoon salt
1/4	teaspoon black pepper
4	cups milk
1 1/4	cups shredded American cheese (5 ounces)
4	slices bacon, crisp-cooked, drained, and crumbled

1 Scrub potatoes thoroughly with a vegetable brush; pat dry. Prick potatoes several times with a fork. Bake in a 425° oven for 40 to 60 minutes or until tender. Let cool. Cut potatoes in half lengthwise; gently scoop out pulp, breaking up any large pieces. Discard potato skins.

2 In a large saucepan melt butter over medium heat. Add half of the green onions; cook and stir until tender. Stir in flour, dill, salt, and pepper. Add milk all at once. Cook and stir for 12 to 15 minutes or until thickened and bubbly. Add the potato pulp and 1 cup of the cheese; stir until cheese melts.

3 Top each serving with the remaining cheese, remaining green onions, and bacon.

Nutrition Facts per serving: 377 cal., 23 g total fat (14 g sat. fat), 67 mg chol., 801 mg sodium, 26 g carbo., 1 g fiber, 17 g pro.

PREP:
20 minutes
BAKE:
40 minutes
COOK:
20 minutes
OVEN:
425°F
MAKES:
5 to 6 servings

Add ham and cream-style corn to a package of macaroni and cheese for a speedy dinner sure to satisfy hungry kids.

MACARONI & CHEESE CHOWDER

START TO FINISH:

25 minutes

MAKES:

4 servings

1   14-ounce can reduced-sodium chicken broth or 1¾ cups homemade chicken broth

1   cup water

1   5½-ounce package macaroni and cheese dinner mix

1   14¾-ounce can cream-style corn

1   cup chopped cooked ham

½   cup milk

1 In a large saucepan bring broth and water to boiling. Add macaroni from mix; reduce heat to medium-low. Simmer, covered, for 11 to 14 minutes or until macaroni is tender.

2 Stir in contents of cheese packet from mix, corn, ham, and milk. Cook and stir over medium heat until heated through.

Nutrition Facts per serving: 301 cal., 6 g total fat (2 g sat. fat), 27 mg chol., 1,324 mg sodium, 48 g carbo., 2 g fiber, 16 g pro.

You'll love this old-fashioned cheese soup with lots of ham and vegetables throughout.

CHEESE & HAM CHOWDER

1	cup water
1½	cups chopped, peeled potatoes
½	cup chopped carrot
½	cup chopped celery
¼	cup chopped onion
2	tablespoons butter or margarine
2	tablespoons all-purpose flour
1	cup milk
1	cup diced cooked ham
8	ounces process cheese spread, cubed

1 In a large saucepan bring the water to boiling. Add potatoes, carrot, celery, and onion. Cook, covered, for 12 to 15 minutes or until tender. Do not drain.

2 Meanwhile, in a small saucepan melt butter over medium heat; stir in flour until smooth. Add milk all at once. Cook and stir until mixture is thickened and bubbly. Stir into potato mixture; stir in ham and cheese. Stir until cheese melts and soup is heated through.

Nutrition Facts per serving: 410 cal., 25 g total fat (15 g sat. fat), 88 mg chol., 1,344 mg sodium, 24 g carbo., 2 g fiber, 23 g pro.

START TO FINISH:

30 minutes

MAKES:

4 servings

Brimming with chunks of ham and potato, this hearty soup is an all-time favorite.
Slightly mashing the potatoes thickens the chowder to a pleasing consistency.

CHUNKY POTATO & HAM CHOWDER

PREP:

20 minutes

COOK:

20 minutes

MAKES:

4 servings

1	cup chicken broth
3	medium potatoes, peeled and finely chopped
1/3	cup sliced leek (white part only) or chopped onion
2	cups milk
1	tablespoon butter or margarine
1/2	teaspoon snipped fresh thyme or 1/8 teaspoon dried thyme, crushed
1/4	teaspoon black pepper
1 1/2	cups finely chopped cooked ham or smoked turkey
1	tablespoon snipped fresh basil (optional)
	Cracked black pepper

1 In a large saucepan combine broth, potatoes, and leeks. Bring to boiling; reduce heat. Simmer, covered, about 15 minutes or until potatoes are tender. Mash potato mixture slightly.

2 Add milk, butter, thyme, black pepper, ham, and, if desired, basil. Cook and stir until heated through. Sprinkle each serving with cracked pepper.

Nutrition Facts per serving: 262 cal., 11 g total fat (5 g sat. fat), 47 mg chol., 959 mg sodium, 24 g carbo., 1 g fiber, 16 g pro.

The earthy flavor and chewy texture of wild rice make this soup an outstanding choice for the first course of a special meal.

WILD RICE CHOWDER

1	tablespoon butter or margarine
½	cup chopped onion
½	cup finely chopped celery
½	cup finely chopped carrot
⅔	cup uncooked wild rice, rinsed and drained
4	cups mushroom broth or chicken broth
1	tablespoon snipped fresh rosemary or 1 teaspoon dried rosemary, crushed
4	teaspoons snipped fresh thyme or ¾ teaspoon dried thyme, crushed
2	cups half-and-half or light cream
3	to 4 strips bacon, crisp-cooked, drained, and crumbled
	Dash black pepper

PREP:
25 minutes
COOK:
45 minutes
MAKES:
6 servings

1 In a medium saucepan melt butter over medium heat. Add onion, celery, and carrot; cook and stir for 3 to 4 minutes or until tender. Stir in uncooked wild rice; cook and stir for 1 minute more.

2 Add broth, dried rosemary (if using), and dried thyme (if using). Bring to boiling; reduce heat. Simmer, covered, about 45 minutes or until rice is tender.

3 Stir in half-and-half. Cook until heated through. Stir in bacon, fresh rosemary (if using), fresh thyme (if using), and pepper.

Nutrition Facts per serving: 235 cal., 14 g total fat (8 g sat. fat), 38 mg chol., 520 mg sodium, 23 g carbo., 2 g fiber, 8 g pro.

If you love the flavor of Reuben sandwiches, you'll enjoy this chowder. Be sure to use process Swiss cheese—it melts more smoothly than natural Swiss.

REUBEN CHOWDER

PREP:
15 minutes
BAKE:
15 minutes
OVEN:
325°F
MAKES:
4 servings

1 tablespoon butter or margarine, softened

4 slices rye bread

½ teaspoon caraway seeds

3 cups milk

1 10¾-ounce can condensed cream of celery soup

2 ounces process Swiss cheese slices, torn into pieces

1 14- or 16-ounce can sauerkraut, rinsed, drained, and snipped

2 5-ounce packages sliced corned beef, chopped

1 Butter both sides of each slice of the bread; sprinkle with caraway seeds. Cut bread into triangles; place on a baking sheet. Bake in a 325° oven about 15 minutes or until toasted, turning once halfway through baking time.

2 Meanwhile, in a large saucepan combine milk, soup, and cheese. Cook and stir just until boiling. Stir in sauerkraut and corned beef; heat through. Serve soup with toasted bread.

Nutrition Facts per serving: 456 cal., 23 g total fat (11 g sat. fat), 77 mg chol., 2,696 mg sodium, 35 g carbo., 5 g fiber, 27 g pro.

This hearty soup is brimming with corn and chunks of pork sausage. Slices of garlic toast make perfect partners.

CORN-SAUSAGE CHOWDER

1	pound bulk pork sausage
1	cup coarsely chopped onion
3	cups ½-inch pieces red potatoes
2	cups water
1	teaspoon salt
½	teaspoon dried marjoram, crushed
⅛	teaspoon black pepper
1	15¼-ounce can whole kernel corn, drained
1	14¾-ounce can cream-style corn, undrained
1	12-ounce can evaporated milk (1½ cups)

START TO FINISH:
30 minutes
MAKES:
6 servings

1 In a Dutch oven cook pork sausage and onion over medium heat until sausage is brown and onion is tender. Drain well.

2 Return sausage mixture to Dutch oven. Stir in potatoes, water, salt, marjoram, and pepper. Bring to boiling; reduce heat. Simmer, covered, about 10 minutes or until potatoes are tender.

3 Stir in the drained whole kernel corn, undrained cream-style corn, and evaporated milk. Cook and stir until heated through.

Nutrition Facts per serving: 491 cal., 27 g total fat (12 g sat. fat), 60 mg chol., 1,135 mg sodium, 43 g carbo., 4 g fiber, 17 g pro.

To speed up the final soup-making process, bake the butternut squash ahead of time. Store, covered, in the refrigerator.

CURRIED BUTTERNUT CHICKEN BISQUE

PREP:
40 minutes

BAKE:
50 minutes

OVEN:
350°F

MAKES:
5 or 6 servings

2	pounds butternut squash
1	tablespoon olive oil
½	cup chopped onion
2	cloves garlic, minced
2	tablespoons grated fresh ginger
2	cups cubed cooked chicken
1	14-ounce can chicken broth or 1¾ cups homemade chicken broth
1	13½-ounce can unsweetened coconut milk
¼	cup water
2	to 3 teaspoons curry powder
½	teaspoon salt
⅛	teaspoon black pepper
2	cups hot cooked brown rice
¼	cup snipped fresh cilantro
¼	cup chopped cashews

1 Cut squash in half lengthwise; remove and discard seeds. Arrange squash halves, cut sides down, in a 3-quart rectangular baking dish. Bake in a 350° oven for 30 minutes. Turn squash halves cut sides up. Bake, covered, for 20 to 25 minutes more or until squash is tender. Cool slightly. Carefully scoop the pulp from squash halves. Place pulp in a medium bowl; discard shells. Mash squash slightly with a potato masher; set aside.

2 In a large saucepan heat oil. Add onion; cook and stir over medium heat for 3 to 4 minutes or until tender. Add garlic and ginger; cook and stir for 1 minute more. Stir in squash, chicken, broth, coconut milk, water, curry powder, salt, and pepper. Cook over medium heat until heated through, stirring occasionally.

3 Serve bisque over hot rice; sprinkle each serving with cilantro and cashews.

Nutrition Facts per serving: 465 cal., 26 g total fat (15 g sat. fat), 50 mg chol., 684 mg sodium, 37 g carbo., 4 g fiber, 24 g pro.

Team this creamy, stick-to-the-ribs soup with a garden-fresh salad and crisp breadsticks for a satisfying meal.

CORN-CHICKEN CHOWDER

6	ears fresh sweet corn or 3 cups frozen whole kernel corn
1	tablespoon cooking oil
³⁄₄	cup chopped onion
³⁄₄	cup chopped green and/or red sweet pepper
1	14-ounce can chicken broth or 1³⁄₄ cups homemade chicken broth
1	cup cubed, peeled potato
1	cup half-and-half, light cream, or milk
2	tablespoons all-purpose flour
2	teaspoons snipped fresh thyme or ¹⁄₂ teaspoon dried thyme, crushed
¹⁄₄	teaspoon salt
¹⁄₄	teaspoon black pepper
1¹⁄₄	cups chopped cooked chicken
2	slices bacon, crisp-cooked, drained, and crumbled
	Fresh thyme sprigs (optional)

START TO FINISH:

40 minutes

MAKES:

4 servings

1 Cut kernels from ears of corn; scrape cobs to remove milky portion. Set aside.

2 In a large saucepan heat oil. Add onion and sweet pepper; cook and stir until onion is tender. Stir in corn, broth, and potato. Bring to boiling; reduce heat. Simmer, covered, about 20 minutes or until potato is tender, stirring occasionally.

3 In a small bowl combine half-and-half, flour, snipped or dried thyme, salt, and black pepper; stir into corn mixture. Cook and stir until thickened and bubbly; cook and stir for 1 minute more. Add chicken and bacon; cook and stir until heated through. If desired, garnish with thyme.

Nutrition Facts per serving: 410 cal., 18 g total fat (7 g sat. fat), 65 mg chol., 612 mg sodium, 43 g carbo., 6 g fiber, 24 g pro.

Chopped red sweet pepper and green spinach give this creamy chicken chowder its festive name.

CONFETTI CHICKEN CHOWDER

START TO FINISH:

25 minutes

MAKES:

6 servings

¼ cup butter or margarine

½ cup chopped red sweet pepper

½ cup all-purpose flour

6 cups chicken broth

2 cups chopped, cooked chicken

1 10-ounce package frozen chopped spinach, thawed and drained

¼ teaspoon ground nutmeg

1 cup half-and-half or light cream

Croutons (optional)

1 In a large saucepan melt butter over medium heat. Add sweet pepper; cook and stir for 2 to 3 minutes or until tender. Stir in flour; cook and stir for 1 minute. Stir in broth; cook and stir until thickened and bubbly.

2 Add chicken, spinach, and nutmeg. Stir in half-and-half; heat through. If desired, top each serving with croutons.

Nutrition Facts per serving: 292 cal., 18 g total fat (9 g sat. fat), 78 mg chol., 1,205 mg sodium, 12 g carbo., 2 g fiber, 19 g pro.

Flecks of jalapeño pepper in the cheese spread add just a hint of heat to this thick and chunky chowder.

CREAMY CHICKEN CHOWDER

1	tablespoon cooking oil
1	pound skinless, boneless chicken breasts, cut into ½-inch pieces
1	11-ounce can whole kernel corn with sweet peppers, drained
1	4-ounce can diced green chile peppers, undrained
2	tablespoons snipped fresh cilantro
2	teaspoons chili powder
½	teaspoon ground cumin
¼	teaspoon garlic powder
1	14-ounce can reduced-sodium chicken broth or 1¾ cups homemade chicken broth
1	10¾-ounce can condensed cream of potato soup
1	8-ounce carton dairy sour cream
½	of an 8-ounce package process cheese spread with jalapeño peppers, cubed

PREP:
20 minutes
COOK:
15 minutes
MAKES:
6 servings

1 In a large saucepan heat oil over medium-high heat. Add chicken and cook until browned on all sides. Add corn, undrained chile peppers, cilantro, chili powder, cumin, and garlic powder. Stir in broth. Heat to boiling; reduce heat. Simmer, covered, about 15 minutes or until chicken is tender and no longer pink.

2 In a medium bowl combine potato soup and sour cream. Stir in about 1 cup of the hot soup; return mixture to saucepan. Stir in cheese. Heat through, stirring to melt cheese.

Nutrition Facts per serving: 325 cal., 18 g total fat (8 g sat. fat), 74 mg chol., 1,054 mg sodium, 20 g carbo., 2 g fiber, 24 g pro.

This hearty chowder lives up to its name: It only takes about 30 minutes to make and it's very cheesy!

EASY CHEESY VEGETABLE-CHICKEN CHOWDER

START TO FINISH:

30 minutes

MAKES:

4 servings

1	cup small broccoli florets
1	cup frozen whole kernel corn
$\frac{1}{2}$	cup water
$\frac{1}{4}$	cup chopped onion
$\frac{1}{2}$	teaspoon dried thyme, crushed
2	cups milk
$1\frac{1}{2}$	cups chopped cooked chicken
1	$10\frac{3}{4}$-ounce can condensed cream of potato soup
1	cup shredded cheddar cheese (4 ounces)
	Black pepper

1 In a large saucepan combine broccoli, corn, water, onion, and thyme. Bring to boiling; reduce heat. Simmer, covered, for 8 to 10 minutes or until vegetables are tender. Do not drain.

2 Stir in milk, chicken, soup, and cheese; cook and stir over medium heat until cheese melts and mixture is heated through. Sprinkle each serving with pepper.

Nutrition Facts per serving: 374 cal., 18 g total fat (9 g sat. fat), 92 mg chol., 858 mg sodium, 24 g carbo., 2 g fiber, 29 g pro.

Chipotles (dried smoked jalapeño chile peppers) add heat and a distinctive smoky sweetness to this chowder. You'll find canned chipotle peppers in adobo sauce in supermarkets or at a Mexican market.

CHIPOTLE-CHICKEN CHOWDER

1	tablespoon olive oil
1½	cups chopped red and/or green sweet pepper
¾	cup chopped onion
¼	teaspoon ground cumin
1	14-ounce can reduced-sodium chicken broth or 1¾ cups homemade chicken broth
2	cups cubed, peeled potatoes
½	cup water
1	to 2 teaspoons chopped canned chipotle chile peppers in adobo sauce
1½	cups chopped cooked chicken
1	12-ounce can evaporated milk (1½ cups)
3	tablespoons cornstarch
	Sliced green onion (optional)

PREP:
10 minutes
COOK:
20 minutes
MAKES:
4 servings

1 In a large saucepan heat oil. Add sweet pepper, onion, and cumin; cook for 3 minutes, stirring occasionally.

2 Add broth, potatoes, water, and chipotle peppers. Bring to boiling; reduce heat. Simmer, covered, about 8 minutes or until potatoes are tender. Stir in chicken.

3 In a small bowl gradually stir about ⅓ cup of the milk into the cornstarch. Stir milk mixture into the chicken mixture. Add remaining milk. Cook and stir over medium heat until thickened and bubbly. Cook and stir for 2 minutes more. If desired, garnish with green onion.

Nutrition Facts per serving: 360 cal., 14 g total fat (5 g sat. fat), 71 mg chol., 385 mg sodium, 34 g carbo., 3 g fiber, 24 g pro.

Green chile peppers, cilantro, and taco seasoning mix add a south-of-the-border flavor to chicken chowder.

MEXICAN-STYLE CHICKEN CHOWDER

START TO FINISH:

30 minutes

MAKES:

4 servings

2½ cups chopped cooked chicken

1 14-ounce can reduced-sodium chicken broth or 1¾ cups homemade chicken broth

1 11-ounce can whole kernel corn with sweet peppers, drained

1 10¾-ounce can condensed cream of potato soup or cream of chicken soup

1 cup water

1 4-ounce can diced green chile peppers, undrained

½ of a 1¼-ounce package taco seasoning mix (about 2 tablespoons)

1 cup dairy sour cream

½ cup shredded cheddar cheese (2 ounces)

2 tablespoons snipped fresh cilantro

Tortilla chips (optional)

1 In a large saucepan combine chicken, broth, corn, soup, water, chile peppers, and taco seasoning mix. Bring to boiling; reduce heat. Simmer, covered, for 15 minutes.

2 In a small bowl combine 1 cup of the hot chicken mixture and the sour cream; stir into soup. Heat through (do not boil).

3 Sprinkle cheddar cheese and cilantro over each serving. If desired, serve with tortilla chips.

Nutrition Facts per serving: 465 cal., 25 g total fat (12 g sat. fat), 120 mg chol., 1,763 mg sodium, 28 g carbo., 3 g fiber, 36 g pro.

A Minnesota staple—nutty and chewy wild rice—stars in this creamy soup. Wild rice isn't truly rice at all. It is a long-grain marsh grass native to the northern Great Lakes area.

CHICKEN & WILD RICE SOUP

1	tablespoon butter or margarine
1/3	cup finely chopped carrot
1/3	cup finely chopped onion
1/3	cup finely chopped celery
4	cups chicken broth
1/2	cup uncooked wild rice, rinsed and drained
12	ounces skinless, boneless chicken breast halves, cut into 3/4-inch pieces
1/4	cup all-purpose flour
1/4	cup butter or margarine, softened
4	cups whipping cream, half-in-half, or light cream
	Salt
	Black pepper

PREP:
30 minutes
COOK:
40 minutes
MAKES:
8 servings

1 In a Dutch oven melt the tablespoon butter over medium heat. Add carrot, onion, and celery; cook and stir about 5 minutes or until tender. Add broth and wild rice. Bring to boiling; reduce heat. Simmer, covered, for 20 minutes. Add chicken pieces. Simmer, covered, for 20 to 25 minutes more or until wild rice is tender.

2 In a small bowl combine flour and the 1/4 cup softened butter to make a smooth paste. Stir the flour mixture into the rice mixture. Cook and stir until thickened and bubbly. Cook and stir for 1 minute more. Add whipping cream. Cook and stir over medium heat until heated through. Season to taste with salt and pepper.

Nutrition Facts per serving: 341 cal., 23 g total fat (14 g sat. fat), 89 mg chol., 728 mg sodium, 17 g carbo., 1 g fiber, 16 g pro.

The cornstarch-thickened broth is ultrasmooth, giving the soup its name.

VELVET CHICKEN SOUP

PREP:

20 minutes

COOK:

45 minutes

MAKES:

4 servings

1   pound meaty chicken pieces (breast halves, thighs, and drumsticks), skinned

2   cups water

1   cup chopped carrots

1   cup chopped celery

1   cup chopped onion

2   teaspoons instant chicken bouillon granules

2   tablespoons snipped fresh parsley or 2 teaspoons dried parsley flakes

2   cloves garlic, minced

$\frac{1}{2}$ teaspoon salt

$\frac{1}{4}$ teaspoon black pepper

2   cups milk

1   cup half-and-half or light cream

3   tablespoons cornstarch

1 In a large saucepan combine chicken and water. Bring to boiling; reduce heat. Simmer, covered, about 20 minutes or until chicken is tender and no longer pink. Remove chicken from cooking liquid.

2 Meanwhile, skim fat from cooking liquid; set aside. Add carrots, celery, onion, bouillon granules, dried parsley (if using), garlic, salt, and pepper. Bring to boiling; reduce heat. Simmer, covered, about 20 minutes or until vegetables are tender.

3 When cool enough to handle, remove chicken meat from bones. Discard bones. Coarsely chop meat; return to cooking liquid. Stir in milk and $\frac{1}{2}$ cup of the half-and-half. In a small bowl combine the remaining $\frac{1}{2}$ cup half-and-half and the cornstarch; stir into chicken mixture. Cook and stir over medium heat until thickened and bubbly; cook and stir for 2 minutes more. Stir in fresh parsley, if using.

Nutrition Facts per serving: 297 cal., 13 g total fat (7 g sat. fat), 78 mg chol., 901 mg sodium, 23 g carbo., 2 g fiber, 22 g pro.

A sprinkling of cheese perfectly complements this soup's fresh ingredients. The flavor is complex; the soup is not.

BROCCOLI-CHICKEN CHOWDER

6	cups broccoli florets
2	14-ounce cans chicken broth or 3½ cups homemade chicken broth
¼	cup all-purpose flour
2	cups half-and-half or light cream
2	cups chopped cooked chicken
1	tablespoon snipped fresh basil or 1 teaspoon dried basil, crushed
¼	teaspoon black pepper
	Salt (optional)
½	cup shredded Swiss or American cheese (2 ounces)

START TO FINISH:

30 minutes

MAKES:

5 or 6 servings

1 In a large saucepan combine broccoli and 1 can of the broth. Bring to boiling; reduce heat. Simmer, covered, for 3 minutes.

2 Meanwhile, in a covered jar combine remaining broth and the flour. Cover and shake well; stir into soup. Stir in half-and-half. Cook and stir over medium-high heat until thickened and bubbly. Cook and stir for 1 minute more.

3 Stir in chicken, basil, and pepper; heat through. If desired, season to taste with salt. Sprinkle each serving with cheese.

Nutrition Facts per serving: 347 cal., 20 g total fat (10 g sat. fat), 96 mg chol., 845 mg sodium, 16 g carbo., 3 g fiber, 27 g pro.

Because they hold their shape well, Golden Delicious, Granny Smith, Rome, Jonathan, or Newtown Pippin are good apple options for this soup.

CHICKEN & APPLE CURRY CHOWDER

START TO FINISH:

45 minutes

MAKES:

4 servings

2	tablespoons olive oil
2	cups chopped celery
1	cup chopped carrots
½	cup chopped onion
2	14-ounce cans chicken broth or 3½ cups homemade chicken broth
1	cup chopped apple
¼	cup uncooked long grain rice
2	teaspoons curry powder
⅛	teaspoon dried thyme, crushed
½	cup half-and-half or light cream
2	tablespoons all-purpose flour
1	cup chopped cooked chicken
	Thinly sliced apple (optional)
	Fresh thyme sprigs (optional)

1 In a large saucepan heat oil. Add celery, carrots, and onion; cook and stir over medium heat about 5 minutes or until tender. Add broth, chopped apple, rice, curry powder, and thyme. Bring to boiling; reduce heat. Simmer, covered, for 15 to 20 minutes or until rice is tender.

2 In a small bowl combine half-and-half and flour. Stir into rice mixture. Cook and stir until thickened and bubbly. Stir in chicken; heat through. If desired, garnish each serving with sliced apple and thyme sprigs.

Nutrition Facts per serving: 281 cal., 14 g total fat (4 g sat. fat), 44 mg chol., 924 mg sodium, 25 g carbo., 3 g fiber, 15 g pro.

Chances are, you have most of the ingredients for this chowder in your kitchen. Add turkey sausage links to your list of on-hand items, and you can make this one-dish warmer at a few minutes' notice.

TURKEY & WILD RICE CHOWDER

6	ounces cooked smoked turkey sausage, halved lengthwise and cut into $\frac{1}{2}$-inch slices
2	cups milk
1$\frac{1}{2}$	cups water
$\frac{1}{2}$	cup chopped onion
$\frac{1}{2}$	cup chopped red or green sweet pepper
$\frac{1}{2}$	cup frozen whole kernel corn
2	teaspoons instant chicken bouillon granules
2	teaspoons snipped fresh marjoram or $\frac{1}{2}$ teaspoon dried marjoram, crushed
$\frac{1}{4}$	teaspoon black pepper
2	tablespoons all-purpose flour
1$\frac{1}{2}$	cups cooked wild or brown rice

START TO FINISH:

25 minutes

MAKES:

4 servings

1 In a large saucepan combine sausage, 1$\frac{3}{4}$ cups of the milk, the water, onion, sweet pepper, corn, bouillon granules, dried marjoram (if using), and black pepper. Bring to boiling.

2 Meanwhile, in a covered jar combine flour and remaining $\frac{1}{4}$ cup milk. Cover and shake well. Stir into soup. Cook and stir until thickened and bubbly. Cook and stir for 1 minute more. Stir in cooked rice and fresh marjoram (if using); heat through.

Nutrition Facts per serving: 244 cal., 6 g total fat (2 g sat. fat), 38 mg chol., 876 mg sodium, 32 g carbo., 3 g fiber, 15 g pro.

For a quick and easy meal, prep the ingredients ahead of time. Peel and chop the potatoes, turkey, and parsley. Refrigerate the potatoes, covered, in water. Refrigerate the turkey and parsley separately in airtight containers.

TURKEY & SWEET POTATO CHOWDER

START TO FINISH:

35 minutes

MAKES:

4 servings

1½ cups chopped, peeled potatoes

1 14-ounce can chicken broth or 1¾ cups homemade chicken broth

2 small ears frozen corn on the cob, thawed

12 ounces cooked turkey breast, cut into ½-inch cubes (2¼ cups)

1½ cups milk

1½ cups ¾-inch cubed, peeled sweet potato

¼ teaspoon black pepper

¼ cup coarsely snipped fresh Italian (flat-leaf) parsley

1 In a medium saucepan combine potatoes and broth. Bring to boiling; reduce heat. Simmer, uncovered, about 12 minutes or until potato is tender, stirring occasionally. Remove from heat. Using potato masher, mash mixture until thickened and smooth.

2 Cut the kernels from one of the ears of corn. Carefully cut the second ear of corn crosswise into ½-inch circles.

3 Stir corn, turkey, milk, sweet potato, and pepper into potato mixture. Bring to boiling; reduce heat. Simmer, uncovered, for 12 to 15 minutes or until the sweet potato is tender. Sprinkle each serving with parsley.

Nutrition Facts per serving: 309 cal., 5 g total fat (2 g sat. fat), 66 mg chol., 381 mg sodium, 32 g carbo., 4 g fiber, 33 g pro.

This colorful chowder gets an extra dose of freshness from some snipped fresh basil. In a pinch, dried basil will do, but use only a teaspoon and add it in the first step when you're boiling the vegetables.

TURKEY-VEGETABLE CHOWDER

1 cup small broccoli florets

½ cup coarsely shredded carrot

½ cup diced peeled potato or ½ cup loose-pack frozen diced hash brown potatoes

½ cup water

¼ cup chopped onion

2 cups milk

1½ cups chopped cooked turkey or chicken

1 10½-ounce can condensed cream of chicken or cream of mushroom soup

1 tablespoon snipped fresh basil

¼ teaspoon salt

¼ teaspoon black pepper

Fresh basil leaves, slivered (optional)

START TO FINISH:
30 minutes
MAKES:
4 servings

1 In a medium saucepan combine broccoli, carrot, potato, water, and onion. Bring to boiling; reduce heat. Simmer, covered, about 6 minutes or until vegetables are tender. Do not drain.

2 Stir in milk, turkey, soup, snipped basil, salt, and pepper. Cook and stir over medium heat until heated through. If desired, top each serving with slivered basil.

Nutrition Facts per serving: 272 cal., 10 g total fat (4 g sat. fat), 59 mg chol., 825 mg sodium, 20 g carbo., 2 g fiber, 24 g pro.

Frozen stir-fry vegetables, refrigerated packaged potatoes, and canned salmon guarantee off-the-shelf convenience.

SALMON CONFETTI CHOWDER

PREP:

15 minutes

COOK:

10 minutes

MAKES:

4 servings

1   tablespoon butter or margarine

2   cups frozen stir-fry vegetables (yellow, green, and red sweet peppers and onion)

2   tablespoons finely chopped seeded fresh jalapeño chile pepper*

2   tablespoons all-purpose flour

2   cups milk

1   cup half-and-half or light cream

2   cups refrigerated diced potatoes with onions

1   15-ounce can salmon, drained and flaked

¼   cup snipped watercress leaves

2   tablespoons lemon juice

½   teaspoon salt

½   teaspoon black pepper

1 In a large saucepan melt butter over medium heat. Add stir-fry vegetables and jalapeño pepper; cook and stir for 3 to 5 minutes or until tender. Stir in flour. Stir in milk and half-and-half. Cook and stir until slightly thickened and bubbly. Cook and stir for 2 minutes more.

2 Stir in potatoes, salmon, watercress, lemon juice, salt, and pepper. Cook and stir until heated through.

***NOTE:** When working with chile peppers, wear plastic or rubber gloves. If your bare hands do touch the chile peppers, wash your hands well with soap and water.*

Nutrition Facts per serving: 411 cal., 19 g total fat (9 g sat. fat), 98 mg chol., 1,128 mg sodium, 29 g carbo., 3 g fiber, 30 g pro.

For a spicier soup, substitute a dark green poblano pepper and a fresh red jalapeño chile pepper for the green and red sweet peppers. (Recipe pictured on page 112.)

SALMON PAN CHOWDER

4	2-ounce fresh or frozen skinless salmon fillets
	Nonstick cooking spray
1¼	cups white and/or purple pearl onions, peeled
1	medium red sweet pepper, cut into ½-inch strips
1	medium yellow sweet pepper, cut into ½-inch strips
1	medium green sweet pepper, cut into ½-inch strips
1	large fresh banana pepper, cut into ¼-inch rings
1	14-ounce can vegetable broth or chicken broth, or 1¾ cup homemade vegetable or chicken broth
1	cup whipping cream
½	teaspoon caraway seeds, lightly crushed
¼	teaspoon salt
	Fresh dill sprigs (optional)

PREP:
25 minutes
COOK:
28 minutes
MAKES:
4 servings

1 Thaw fish, if frozen. Rinse fish and pat dry with paper towels; set fish aside.

2 Coat a 4- to 6-quart Dutch oven with cooking spray; heat pan. Add onions; cook and stir, uncovered, over medium-high heat about 7 minutes or until tender. Add sweet peppers and banana pepper; cook and stir for 1 minute. Add broth. Bring just to boiling; reduce heat. Simmer, uncovered, for 10 minutes. Stir in whipping cream. Return to boiling; reduce heat. Simmer, uncovered, for 10 minutes.

3 Meanwhile, rub caraway seeds and salt on both sides of fish. Coat a medium skillet with nonstick cooking spray; heat skillet. Cook fillets, uncovered, over medium-high heat for 3 to 4 minutes per side or until fish flakes easily when tested with a fork.

4 Place a salmon fillet in each of four shallow soup bowls; ladle soup mixture over salmon fillets. If desired, garnish with dill sprigs.

Nutrition Facts per serving: 332 cal., 25 g total fat (14 g sat. fat), 112 mg chol., 613 mg sodium, 15 g carbo., 3 g fiber, 14 g pro.

This broth-based chowder sings with fresh flavors—corn, potatoes, spinach, and thyme.

SPRING SALMON CHOWDER

PREP:

15 minutes

COOK:

12 minutes

MAKES:

6 servings

12 ounces fresh or frozen skinless salmon

1 ear fresh sweet corn or $1/2$ cup frozen whole kernel corn, thawed

2 14-ounce cans vegetable broth or $3^1/2$ cups homemade vegetable broth

6 tiny new potatoes, quartered

6 2-inch fresh thyme sprigs or $1/2$ teaspoon dried thyme, crushed

1 cup packed baby spinach leaves

$1/4$ cup sliced green onions

Salt

Black pepper

1 Thaw fish, if frozen. Rinse fish and pat dry with paper towels. Cut salmon into 1-inch pieces; set aside.

2 Cut kernels from ear of corn; scrape cob to remove milky portion. Set aside.

3 In a large saucepan heat broth to boiling. Add potatoes. Cook, covered, about 5 minutes or until tender but not cooked through. Add corn and thyme. Return to boiling; reduce heat. Simmer, covered, about 4 minutes or until vegetables are tender. Reduce heat.

4 Add salmon to saucepan. Simmer, uncovered, for 3 to 5 minutes or until salmon flakes easily when tested with a fork. If desired, remove thyme sprigs. Stir in spinach and green onions; cook about 1 minute or until spinach begins to wilt. Season to taste with salt and pepper.

Nutrition Facts per serving: 169 cal., 7 g total fat (1 g sat. fat), 37 mg chol., 639 mg sodium, 14 g carbo., 2 g fiber, 14 g pro.

Evaporated milk gives this salmon bisque a creamy richness. Mustard lends an interesting flavor note.

DILLY DIJON SALMON BISQUE

8	ounces fresh or frozen skinless salmon fillet
1	tablespoon olive oil
½	cup chopped onion
1¼	cups water
½	cup uncooked long grain white rice
1	14-ounce can chicken broth or 1¾ cups homemade chicken broth
2	cups fresh or frozen whole kernel corn
1	12-ounce can evaporated milk (1½ cups)
1	tablespoon Dijon-style mustard
1	teaspoon snipped fresh dill or ½ teaspoon dried dill
½	teaspoon salt
½	teaspoon black pepper
	Fresh dill sprigs (optional)

PREP:
10 minutes
COOK:
25 minutes
MAKES:
4 servings

1 Thaw fish, if frozen. Rinse fish and pat dry with paper towels. Cut salmon into 1-inch pieces; set aside.

2 In a large saucepan heat oil. Add onion; cook and stir over medium heat until tender. Add water and bring to boiling. Stir in rice. Reduce heat. Simmer, covered, for 15 minutes.

3 Add broth; return to boiling. Add salmon and corn. Simmer, covered, for 5 minutes or until rice is tender and salmon flakes easily when tested with a fork. Stir in evaporated milk, mustard, dill, salt, and pepper; heat through. If desired, garnish with fresh dill sprigs.

Nutrition Facts per serving: 390 cal., 13 g total fat (5 g sat. fat), 55 mg chol., 927 mg sodium, 47 g carbo., 3 g fiber, 23 g pro.

This chowder takes 20 minutes from start to finish, making it perfect busy-night fare. Keep the staples on hand, then stop off for the fish on your way home from work.

SEA BASS CHOWDER

START TO FINISH:

20 minutes

MAKES:

4 to 6 servings

1   pound fresh or frozen skinless sea bass, red snapper, and/or catfish fillets

1   tablespoon butter or olive oil

½   cup chopped onion

2   cloves garlic, minced

4   cups water

2   fish bouillon cubes

1   tablespoon lemon juice

½   teaspoon instant chicken bouillon granules

½   teaspoon dried thyme, crushed

¼   teaspoon fennel seeds, slightly crushed

Dash powdered saffron (optional)

1   bay leaf

4   Roma tomatoes, halved lengthwise and thinly sliced

Fresh thyme sprigs (optional)

1 Thaw fish, if frozen. Rinse fish; pat dry with paper towels. Cut fish into ¾-inch cubes; set aside.

2 In a large saucepan melt butter over medium heat. Add onion and garlic; cook and stir until tender. Stir in water, fish bouillon cubes, lemon juice, chicken bouillon granules, thyme, fennel seeds, saffron (if using), and bay leaf. Cook and stir until boiling.

3 Add fish and tomatoes. Return to boiling; reduce heat. Simmer, covered, for 10 minutes. Remove and discard bay leaf. If desired, garnish each serving with fresh thyme sprigs.

Nutrition Facts per serving: 160 cal., 5 g total fat (2 g sat. fat), 55 mg chol., 683 mg sodium, 6 g carbo., 1 g fiber, 22 g pro.

Choose a mild, firm-textured whitefish for this chowder, then prepare to be complimented for a delicious meal.

FISH & CLAM CHOWDER

1	pound fresh or frozen skinless whitefish fillets
1	10-ounce can whole baby clams, rinsed and drained
3	cups chopped, peeled potatoes
1½	cups chopped carrots
1½	cups chopped celery stalks with leaves
1	cup chopped onion
1	clove garlic, minced
½	teaspoon salt
½	teaspoon lemon-pepper seasoning
2	cups water
1	cup half-and-half or light cream
1	cup milk
	Butter (optional)
	Black pepper (optional)

PREP:
25 minutes
COOK:
20 minutes
MAKES:
6 servings

1 Thaw fish, if frozen. Rinse fish and pat dry with paper towels. If necessary, cut fish into large pieces to fit into a 4- to 6-quart Dutch oven.

2 In Dutch oven combine fish, clams, potatoes, carrots, celery, onion, garlic, salt, and lemon-pepper seasoning. Add water. Bring to boiling; reduce heat. Simmer, covered, for 20 to 25 minutes or until potatoes are tender, stirring occasionally. Stir in half-and-half and milk. Cook and stir until heated through. If desired, top each serving with a piece of butter and some black pepper.

Nutrition Facts per serving: 285 cal., 7 g total fat (4 g sat. fat), 76 mg chol., 455 mg sodium, 29 g carbo., 3 g fiber, 26 g pro.

You can walk away from this chowder for about an hour while it bakes in the oven.

BAKED FISH CHOWDER

PREP:

20 minutes

BAKE:

1 hour

OVEN:

350°F

MAKES:

4 servings

1	pound fresh or frozen fish fillets (such as cod, haddock, or orange roughy)
1¼	cups chopped, peeled potatoes
1	cup chopped onion
¼	cup chopped celery
2	tablespoons butter or margarine, cut up
1	bay leaf
1	teaspoon salt
¼	teaspoon black pepper
¼	teaspoon dried dill
4	whole cloves (optional)*
1	cup water
¼	cup dry vermouth, dry white wine, or water
1	cup whipping cream or evaporated milk

1 Thaw fish, if frozen. Rinse fish and pat dry with paper towels. Cut fish into 2-inch pieces; set aside.

2 In a 2-quart casserole combine fish, potatoes, onion, celery, butter, bay leaf, salt, pepper, and dill. If using, add bag of cloves to fish mixture.

3 Combine the water and vermouth. Pour over fish mixture.

4 Bake, covered, in a 350° oven about 1 hour or until potatoes are tender, stirring halfway through cooking time. Remove and discard bay leaf and spice bag, if using. Stir in cream.

*NOTE: If using whole cloves, place cloves on a double-thick 3-inch square of 100-percent-cotton cheesecloth. Bring corners together; tie with a clean kitchen string.

Nutrition Facts per serving: 424 cal., 29 g total fat (16 g sat. fat), 147 mg chol., 721 mg sodium, 15 g carbo., 1 g fiber, 23 g pro.

New England-style chowders like this one have a creamy base; Manhattan-style chowder contain tomatoes.

NEW ENGLAND CLAM CHOWDER

2	slices bacon, chopped
1	cup chopped onion
1	cup chopped celery
½	cup chopped carrot
2	cups chopped, peeled (if desired) potatoes
1	8-ounce bottle clam juice or 1 cup chicken broth
1	cup water
2	teaspoons snipped fresh thyme or ½ teaspoon dried thyme, crushed
¼	teaspoon black pepper
1	bay leaf
2	10-ounce cans whole baby clams, drained*
1½	cups whipping cream, half-and-half, or light cream
½	cup frozen whole kernel corn

PREP:

20 minutes

COOK:

20 minutes

MAKES:

5 servings

1 In a large saucepan cook bacon over medium heat until crisp. Add onion, celery, and carrot; reduce heat to medium-low. Cook, uncovered, for 10 minutes, stirring frequently.

2 Add potatoes, clam juice, water, dried thyme (if using), pepper, and bay leaf. Bring to boiling; reduce heat. Simmer, covered, about 10 minutes or until potatoes are tender. Remove and discard bay leaf.

3 Stir in fresh thyme (if using), clams, cream, and corn; heat through.

*NOTE: If you prefer to use fresh clams, substitute 48 littleneck clams for the canned clams. Scrub live clams under cold running water. In an 8-quart Dutch oven combine 4 quarts (16 cups) cold water and ¹⁄₃ cup salt. Add clams; soak for 1 hour. Drain and rinse. Discard water. Steam clams, half at a time, over boiling water, covered, for 5 to 7 minutes or until clams open and are thoroughly cooked. Discard any clams that do not open. Cool for 15 minutes. Remove from shells; coarsely chop.

Nutrition Facts per serving: 551 cal., 33 g total fat (19 g sat. fat), 181 mg chol., 330 mg sodium, 26 g carbo., 3 g fiber, 34 g pro.

If you prefer to use purchased bacon pieces instead of regular bacon, use 2 tablespoons olive oil to cook the celery, carrot, and onion.

MANHATTAN CLAM CHOWDER

START TO FINISH:

40 minutes

MAKES:

4 servings

1	pint shucked clams or two 6½-ounce cans minced clams
2	slices bacon
1	cup chopped celery
¼	cup chopped carrot
⅓	cup chopped onion
1	8-ounce bottle clam juice or 1 cup chicken broth
2	cups cubed red potatoes
1	teaspoon dried thyme, crushed
⅛	teaspoon cayenne pepper
⅛	teaspoon black pepper
1	14½-ounce can diced tomatoes, undrained

1 Chop fresh clams, if using, reserving juice; set clams aside. Strain clam juice to remove bits of shell. (Or drain canned clams, reserving juice.) If necessary, add enough water to reserved clam juice to equal 1½ cups. Set juice aside.

2 In a large saucepan cook bacon over medium heat until crisp. Remove bacon and drain on paper towels; crumble. Reserve 2 tablespoons drippings in pan.

3 Heat bacon drippings over medium heat. Add celery, carrot, and onion; cook and stir until tender. Stir in the reserved 1½ cups clam juice and the 8 ounces clam juice. Stir in potatoes, thyme, cayenne pepper, and black pepper. Bring to boiling; reduce heat. Simmer, covered, for 10 minutes. Stir in clams, bacon, and undrained tomatoes. Return to boiling; reduce heat. Cook for 1 to 2 minutes more or until heated through.

Nutrition Facts per serving: 254 cal., 9 g total fat (1 g sat. fat), 41 mg chol., 507 mg sodium, 24 g carbo., 3 g fiber, 19 g pro.

With clams, onion, celery, tomatoes, and thyme, this version of clam chowder has its roots in the time-honored Eastern seaboard tradition. Sweet potatoes, chile peppers, and lime juice give this chowder a new twist.

CARIBBEAN CLAM CHOWDER

1	6½-ounce can minced clams
2	cups cubed, peeled sweet potatoes
½	cup chopped onion
½	cup chopped celery
¼	cup chopped red sweet pepper
2	cloves garlic, minced
1½	teaspoons snipped fresh thyme or ½ teaspoon dried thyme, crushed
1	10-ounce can chopped tomatoes and green chile peppers, undrained
1	tablespoon lime juice
1	tablespoon dark rum (optional)

START TO FINISH:

35 minutes

MAKES:

4 servings

1 Drain clams, reserving juice. Add enough water to clam juice to make 2½ cups liquid.

2 In a large saucepan bring the clam liquid to boiling. Stir in sweet potatoes, onion, celery, sweet pepper, garlic, and dried thyme, if using. Return to boiling; reduce heat. Simmer, covered, about 10 minutes or until sweet potatoes are tender.

3 Mash sweet potato mixture slightly with a potato masher. Stir in clams, undrained tomatoes, lime juice, and fresh thyme, if using. If desired, stir in rum. Return to boiling; reduce heat. Cook for 1 to 2 minutes more or until heated through.

Nutrition Facts per serving: 128 cal., 1 g total fat (0 g sat. fat), 19 mg chol., 337 mg sodium, 22 g carbo., 3 g fiber, 9 g pro.

Remember this flavor-packed soup the next time you need to fix a meal in a hurry.

BROCCOLI-CLAM CHOWDER

START TO FINISH:

20 minutes

MAKES:

4 servings

⅓	cup water
1	10-ounce package frozen chopped broccoli or spinach
⅓	cup chopped onion
½	teaspoon dried thyme, crushed
1½	cups milk
1	10¾-ounce can condensed cream of shrimp soup
1	6½-ounce can minced clams, drained
1	teaspoon Worcestershire sauce

1 In a medium saucepan bring the water to boiling; add frozen broccoli, onion, and thyme. Return to boiling; reduce heat. Simmer, covered, about 8 minutes or until broccoli is tender. Do not drain.

2 Stir in milk, soup, clams, and Worcestershire sauce. Cook until heated through, stirring occasionally.

Nutrition Facts per serving: 181 cal., 7 g total fat (2 g sat. fat), 41 mg chol., 676 mg sodium, 16 g carbo., 3 g fiber, 15 g pro.

If you think fresh oyster chowder takes a long time to make, you're in for a surprise. When you buy shucked oysters from the seafood section of the supermarket, cook them in 5 minutes. This creamy jalapeño-spiced meal-in-a-bowl takes 40 minutes more to prepare.

OYSTER & CORN CHOWDER

2	teaspoons olive oil
1	cup chopped onion
½	cup chopped red sweet pepper
1	clove garlic, minced
1	14-ounce can reduced-sodium chicken broth or 1¾ cups homemade chicken broth
1½	cups coarsely chopped, peeled potato
1	fresh jalapeño chile pepper, seeded and finely chopped*
¼	teaspoon salt
	Dash black pepper
8	ounces shucked oysters, undrained
1	cup fresh or frozen whole kernel corn
1	tablespoon snipped fresh oregano
½	cup half-and-half or light cream
	Fresh oregano sprigs (optional)

START TO FINISH:

45 minutes

MAKES:

3 servings

1 In a medium saucepan heat oil. Add onion, sweet pepper, and garlic; cook and stir over medium heat until vegetables are tender.

2 Stir in broth, potato, jalapeño pepper, salt, and black pepper. Bring to boiling; reduce heat. Simmer, covered, about 10 minutes or until potato is nearly tender.

3 Stir in undrained oysters, corn, and oregano. Return to boiling; reduce heat. Simmer, covered, about 5 minutes or until oysters curl around the edges. Stir in half-and-half. Cook until heat through, stirring occasionally. If desired, garnish with oregano sprigs.

***NOTE:** When working with chile peppers, wear plastic or rubber gloves. If your bare hands do touch the chile peppers, wash your hands well with soap and water.*

Nutrition Facts per serving: 276 cal., 10 g total fat (4 g sat. fat), 55 mg chol., 728 mg sodium, 36 g carbo., 4 g fiber, 13 g pro.

Shrimp and bay scallops pair up for this elegant and flavorful chowder.

MUSHROOM, LEEK & SEAFOOD CHOWDER

PREP:

20 minutes

COOK:

20 minutes

MAKES:

8 servings

8   ounces fresh or frozen peeled and deveined shrimp

8   ounces fresh or frozen bay scallops

2   ounces thinly sliced pancetta or bacon (2 slices), chopped

3   cups sliced fresh shiitake or other mushrooms

3   leeks, thinly sliced (white parts only)

2   cloves garlic, minced

3   cups chopped potatoes

2   14$\frac{1}{2}$-ounce cans chicken broth or 3$\frac{1}{2}$ cups homemade chicken broth

$\frac{1}{4}$ teaspoon black pepper

$\frac{1}{2}$ cup shredded carrot

3   tablespoons butter or margarine, melted

3   tablespoons all-purpose flour

2   cups half-and-half or light cream

Lemon slices (optional)

Fresh thyme (optional)

1 Thaw shrimp and scallops, if frozen. Rinse seafood and pat dry with paper towels. Cover and chill.

2 In a 4- to 6-quart Dutch oven cook pancetta over medium heat until brown. Remove with a slotted spoon, reserving drippings in pan. Drain pancetta on paper towels; set aside.

3 Add mushrooms, leeks, and garlic to Dutch oven; cook and stir about 3 minutes or until tender. Add potatoes, broth, and pepper. Bring to boiling; reduce heat. Simmer, covered, about 15 minutes or until potatoes are tender. Add carrot to potato mixture; bring to boiling.

4 Combine melted butter and flour. Add flour mixture and half-and-half to potato mixture. Cook and stir over medium heat until thickened and bubbly. Add shrimp, scallops, and pancetta. Cook and stir for 2 to 3 minutes or until shrimp and scallops turn opaque. If desired, garnish each serving with lemon slices and thyme.

Nutrition Facts per serving: 278 cal., 14 g total fat (6 g sat. fat), 76 mg chol., 543 mg sodium, 24 g carbo., 3 g fiber, 16 g pro.

For a striking garnish, float one shrimp with tail intact on each serving. (Recipe pictured on page 112.)

SEAFOOD & CORN CHOWDER

1	14-ounce can chicken broth or 1¾ cups homemade chicken broth
1	cup sliced celery
1	cup chopped onion
½	cup sliced carrot
1	14¾-ounce can cream-style corn
1	cup whipping cream
½	teaspoon snipped fresh thyme or ¼ teaspoon dried thyme, crushed
⅛	teaspoon black pepper
	Few dashes bottled hot pepper sauce
10	to 12 ounces cooked or canned lump crabmeat and/or peeled, deveined, and cooked shrimp
	Croutons (optional)
	Fresh thyme sprigs (optional)

PREP:
15 minutes
COOK:
20 minutes
MAKES:
4 or 5 servings

1 In a medium saucepan combine broth, celery, onion, and carrot. Bring to boiling; reduce heat. Simmer, covered, about 20 minutes or until vegetables are very tender. Cool slightly.

2 Transfer half of the broth mixture to a blender or food processor. Cover and blend or process until smooth. Repeat with remaining broth mixture. Return mixture to saucepan. Stir in corn, whipping cream, thyme, black pepper, and hot pepper sauce. Bring to boiling; reduce heat. Stir in crabmeat and/or shrimp; heat through. If desired, garnish each serving with croutons and fresh thyme.

Nutrition Facts per serving: 394 cal., 25 g total fat (14 g sat. fat), 153 mg chol., 965 mg sodium, 27 g carbo., 3 g fiber, 19 g pro.

You can also serve this flavorful soup as an appetizer for 12 servings.

ROASTED CORN & CRAB SOUP

PREP:

30 minutes

ROAST:

20 minutes

COOK:

20 minutes

OVEN:

450°F

MAKES:

6 servings

1	16-ounce package frozen whole kernel corn
1	tablespoon cooking oil
2	cups chopped onions
1½	cups coarsely chopped red sweet peppers
4	14-ounce cans chicken broth or 7 cups homemade chicken broth
½	teaspoon dried thyme, crushed
⅛	to ¼ teaspoon cayenne pepper
⅓	cup all-purpose flour
½	cup half-and-half or light cream
⅔	cup chopped cooked crabmeat

1 Thaw frozen corn; pat dry with paper towels. Line a 15×10×1-inch baking pan with foil; lightly grease the foil.

2 Spread corn in a single layer in prepared pan. Roast in a 450° oven for 10 minutes; stir. Roast about 10 minutes more until golden brown, stirring once or twice. Remove from oven; set aside.

3 In a 4- to 6-quart Dutch oven heat oil. Add onions and sweet peppers; cook and stir over medium heat for 3 to 4 minutes or until almost tender. Add roasted corn, 3 cans of the broth, the thyme, and cayenne pepper. Bring to boiling; reduce heat. Simmer, uncovered, for 15 minutes.

4 Meanwhile, in a large screw-top jar combine remaining 1 can broth and the flour. Cover and shake well; stir into soup. Cook and stir until slightly thickened and bubbly. Cook and stir for 1 minute more. Stir in half-and-half; heat through.

5 To serve, ladle soup into bowls. Divide crabmeat among each serving.

Nutrition Facts per serving: 229 cal., 7 g total fat (2 g sat. fat), 26 mg chol., 907 mg sodium, 30 g carbo., 4 g fiber, 14 g pro.

This winning chowder features the prize of all seafood—crabmeat. It's even more enticing with bouquet garni seasoning—a mixture of several herbs—and a small amount of cream cheese.

CRAB CHOWDER

1   6-ounce package frozen crabmeat or one 6½-ounce can crabmeat, drained, flaked, and cartilage removed

2   tablespoons butter or margarine

1   medium zucchini, cut into 2-inch strips

1   cup chopped red or green sweet pepper

2   tablespoons all-purpose flour

4   cups milk

2   tablespoons sliced green onion

½   teaspoon bouquet garni seasoning

¼   teaspoon salt

⅛   teaspoon black pepper

1   3-ounce package cream cheese, cut up

1   teaspoon snipped fresh thyme

   Fresh thyme sprigs (optional)

START TO FINISH:

25 minutes

MAKES:

4 servings

1 Thaw crabmeat, if frozen. Rinse and pat dry with paper towels. Set crabmeat aside.

2 In a medium saucepan melt butter over medium heat. Add zucchini and sweet pepper; cook and stir 3 to 4 minutes or until crisp-tender. Stir in flour. Add milk, green onion, bouquet garni seasoning, salt, and black pepper. Cook and stir over medium-high heat until thickened and bubbly. Add cream cheese; cook and stir until cream cheese melts. Stir in crabmeat and snipped thyme; heat through. If desired, garnish each serving with additional fresh thyme.

Nutrition Facts per serving: 314 cal., 19 g total fat (9 g sat. fat), 64 mg chol., 844 mg sodium, 18 g carbo., 1 g fiber, 19 g pro.

Two flavors of canned soup—asparagus and mushroom—come together to create an elegant soup that takes only 20 minutes to make.

EASY CRAB BISQUE

START TO FINISH:

20 minutes

MAKES:

6 servings

1   10³⁄₄-ounce can condensed cream of asparagus soup

1   10³⁄₄-ounce can condensed cream of mushroom soup

2³⁄₄ cups milk

1   cup half-and-half or light cream

1   6¹⁄₂-ounce can crabmeat, drained, flaked, and cartilage removed, or one 6-ounce package frozen crabmeat, thawed

3   tablespoons dry sherry or milk

1 In a large saucepan combine soups, milk, and half-and-half. Cook over medium heat until boiling, stirring frequently.

2 Stir in crabmeat and dry sherry; heat through.

Nutrition Facts per serving: 227 cal., 12 g total fat (6 g sat. fat), 63 mg chol., 921 mg sodium, 16 g carbo., 1 g fiber, 12 g pro.

This elegant, easy bisque is perfect for an intimate dinner. Don't tell anyone that it starts with two cans of soup.

CRAB-TOMATO BISQUE

1   19-ounce can ready-to-eat tomato basil soup

1   $10^3/_4$-ounce can condensed cream of shrimp soup

1   cup vegetable broth

1   cup half-and-half, light cream, or milk

1   tablespoon dried minced onion

1   teaspoon dried parsley flakes or 1 tablespoon snipped fresh parsley

1   $6^1/_2$-ounce can crabmeat, drained, flaked, and cartilage removed

1 In a large saucepan combine soups, vegetable broth, half-and-half, onion, and dried parsley, if using. Cook over medium heat until bubbly, stirring occasionally.

2 Stir in crabmeat and fresh parsley, if using; heat through.

Nutrition Facts per serving: 242 cal., 12 g total fat (6 g sat. fat), 73 mg chol., 1,447 mg sodium, 20 g carbo., 1 g fiber, 15 g pro.

START TO FINISH:

15 minutes

MAKES:

4 servings

Crab, creamy Brie cheese, and earthy mushrooms combine for a soup you won't soon forget.
Serve it in a bowl for a satisfying main dish or in a small cup for a first-course appetizer.

BRIE, CRAB & MUSHROOM SOUP

START TO FINISH:

35 minutes

MAKES:

4 servings

3	tablespoons butter or margarine
3	cups thinly sliced fresh mushrooms
½	cup finely chopped onion
¼	cup all-purpose flour
¼	teaspoon ground white pepper
⅛	teaspoon salt
1	14-ounce can vegetable broth
2	cups milk
1	4½-ounce round Brie cheese, rind removed and cut into 1-inch pieces
1½	cups chopped Roma tomatoes
2	6½-ounce cans crabmeat, drained, flaked, and cartilage removed
2	tablespoons snipped fresh parsley
4	teaspoons finely shredded Romano cheese

1 In a large saucepan melt butter over medium heat. Add mushrooms and onion; cook and stir about 5 minutes or until vegetables are tender. Stir in flour, white pepper, and salt. Add broth all at once. Cook and stir until thickened and bubbly.

2 Stir in milk, Brie, and tomatoes. Cook and stir about 7 minutes more or until Brie is melted. Stir in crabmeat; heat through. Top each serving with parsley and Romano cheese.

Nutrition Facts per serving: 418 cal., 23 g total fat (12 g sat. fat), 149 mg chol., 1,137 mg sodium, 19 g carbo., 2 g fiber, 34 g pro.

If thawing puff pastry toppers isn't in your schedule, use croutons or crackers instead of the pastry.

RED SEAFOOD CHOWDER

PREP:
15 minutes
COOK:
20 minutes
BAKE:
10 minutes
OVEN:
400°F
MAKES:
4 servings

1	tablespoon olive oil or cooking oil
½	cup chopped onion
½	cup chopped fennel (half of a medium fennel bulb) (if desired, reserve leafy tops for garnish)
4	medium tomatoes, peeled, seeded, and chopped
2	14-ounce cans reduced-sodium chicken broth or 3½ cups homemade chicken broth
¼	teaspoon curry powder
¼	teaspoon black pepper
12	ounces seafood and/or fish (fresh bay scallops; peeled and deveined medium shrimp; and/or skinless red snapper or halibut fillets)
½	of a 17.3-ounce package frozen puff pastry (1 sheet), thawed

1 In a large saucepan heat oil. Add onion and fennel; cook and stir over medium heat until tender but not brown. Stir in tomatoes, broth, curry powder, and pepper. Bring to boiling; reduce heat. Simmer, covered, for 15 minutes.

2 Rinse seafood and/or fish; pat dry with paper towels. Cut fillets into bite-size pieces. Stir in desired seafood and/or fish. Return to boiling; reduce heat. Simmer, uncovered, for 2 to 3 minutes more or until scallops and/or shrimp are opaque and fish flakes easily when tested with a fork.

3 Meanwhile, unfold pastry onto a floured surface. Cut into 8 squares, triangles, rounds, and/or other shapes with a sharp knife or cookie cutter. Place pastry pieces on an ungreased baking sheet. Bake in a 400° oven about 10 minutes or until golden brown and puffed.

4 Top each serving with 2 pieces baked puff pastry. If desired, garnish with reserved fennel tops.

Nutrition Facts per serving: 419 cal., 23 g total fat (1 g sat. fat), 28 mg chol., 850 mg sodium, 32 g carbo., 2 g fiber, 20 g pro.

Most of the ingredients for this chowder can be kept on hand for a need-quick meal. The Gouda cheese adds a pleasantly smoky flavor and aroma.

TORTELLINI-VEGETABLE CHOWDER

START TO FINISH:

30 minutes

MAKES:

6 servings

2 14-ounce cans reduced-sodium chicken broth or 3½ cups homemade chicken broth

1 16-ounce package frozen broccoli, cauliflower, and carrots

1 9-ounce package refrigerated cheese- or meat-filled tortellini

2 cups milk

¼ cup all-purpose flour

1 cup shredded process smoked Gouda cheese (4 ounces)

1 tablespoon shredded fresh basil

Black pepper (optional)

1 In large saucepan combine broth and frozen vegetables. Bring to boiling; add tortellini. Return to boiling; reduce heat. Simmer, uncovered, about 4 minutes or just until vegetables are tender.

2 Meanwhile, in a covered jar combine about half of the milk and the flour. Cover and shake well. Stir into soup.

3 Add remaining milk. Cook and stir until thickened and bubbly. Cook and stir for 1 minute more. Stir in cheese until melted. Stir in basil. If desired, season to taste with pepper.

Nutrition Facts per serving: 302 cal., 10 g total fat (5 g sat. fat), 41 mg chol., 878 mg sodium, 39 g carbo., 3 g fiber, 17 g pro.

The tortellini is Italian and the seasonings are Mexican. The combination may not be authentic, but it is delicious. (Recipe pictured on page 111.)

SPICY TORTELLINI CHOWDER

1	tablespoon butter or margarine
2/3	cup chopped onion
1/2	cup chopped red sweet pepper
1/3	cup chopped fresh green chile peppers (such as Anaheim or poblano)*
2	tablespoons minced garlic
1	fresh jalapeño chile pepper, seeded and chopped*
3	cups chicken broth
2	cups cubed, peeled potatoes
1	teaspoon ground cumin
1/4	teaspoon salt
1/4	teaspoon black pepper
1/8	teaspoon cayenne pepper
2	tablespoons all-purpose flour
2	tablespoons butter or margarine, melted
1	15¼-ounce can whole kernel corn, drained
2	cups half-and-half or light cream
2	cups refrigerated or frozen cheese-filled tortellini, cooked according to package directions and drained
	Corn tortillas, cut into strips and crisp-fried, or tortilla chips, broken

PREP:
35 minutes
COOK:
30 minutes
MAKES:
6 to 8 servings

1 In a 4- to 6-quart Dutch oven melt the 1 tablespoon butter over medium heat. Add onion, sweet pepper, chile peppers, garlic, and jalapeño pepper; cook and stir about 5 minutes or until vegetables are tender.

2 Stir in broth, potatoes, cumin, salt, black pepper, and cayenne pepper. Bring to boiling; reduce heat. Simmer, covered, for 25 to 30 minutes or until potatoes are tender.

3 In a small bowl combine flour and the 2 tablespoons melted butter; add to soup mixture. Cook and stir over medium heat until thickened and bubbly. Cook and stir for 1 minute more; reduce heat. Add corn, half-and-half, and cooked tortellini. Heat through. Top each serving with fried tortilla strips.

*NOTE: When working with chile peppers, wear plastic or rubber gloves. If your bare hands do touch the peppers, wash your hands well with soap and warm water.

Nutrition Facts per serving: 394 cal., 20 g total fat (11 g sat. fat), 66 mg chol., 730 mg sodium, 45 g carbo., 3 g fiber, 13 g pro.

This creamy soup's rich combination of flavors will dazzle you. (Recipe pictured on page 111.)

CURRIED SWEET POTATO CHOWDER

START TO FINISH:

30 minutes

MAKES:

3 servings

2   teaspoons butter or margarine

1⅓ cups ½-inch cubes sweet potatoes

⅓   cup minced shallot

½   teaspoon curry powder

1   tablespoon all-purpose flour

1½ cups milk

½   cup half-and-half

¼   teaspoon salt

¼   teaspoon black pepper

1   cup frozen baby peas

4   teaspoons curried pumpkin seeds or pumpkin seeds

Crackers (optional)

1 In a medium saucepan melt butter over medium heat. Add sweet potatoes and shallot; cook and stir for 2 minutes. Add curry powder; cook and stir for 30 seconds. Stir in flour. Gradually stir in milk until smooth. Add half-and-half, salt, and pepper. Bring to boiling; reduce heat. Simmer, covered, for 10 minutes, stirring occasionally.

2 Add peas. Simmer, covered, about 5 minutes more or until potatoes and peas are tender, stirring occasionally.

3 Sprinkle each serving with 1 teaspoon curried pumpkin seeds. If desired, serve with crackers.

Nutrition Facts per serving: 254 cal., 11 g total fat (5 g sat. fat), 32 mg chol., 359 mg sodium, 29 g carbo., 4 g fiber, 11 g pro.

CHILIES

4

Two cans of soup give you a head start on this incredibly beefy, flavorful chili. Serve with sliced apple wedges, chunks of cheddar cheese, and crackers.

BEER CHILI

PREP:

25 minutes

COOK:

30 minutes

MAKES:

4 or 5 servings

1	pound ground beef
½	cup chopped onion
1	15½-ounce can red kidney beans, undrained
1	12-ounce can beer or nonalcoholic beer
1	11¼-ounce can condensed chili beef soup
1	10¾-ounce can condensed tomato soup
½	cup water
½	cup chopped green sweet pepper
2	teaspoons chili powder
1	teaspoon Worcestershire sauce
½	teaspoon garlic powder
	Shredded cheddar cheese (optional)
	Dairy sour cream (optional)

1 In a 4-quart Dutch oven cook ground beef and onion over medium-high heat until beef is brown and onion is tender. Drain off fat.

2 Stir in undrained kidney beans, beer, chili beef soup, tomato soup, water, sweet pepper, chili powder, Worcestershire sauce, and garlic powder. Bring to boiling; reduce heat. Simmer, covered, for 30 minutes. If desired, sprinkle each serving with cheddar cheese and top with sour cream.

Nutrition Facts per serving: 472 cal., 15 g total fat (6 g sat. fat), 79 mg chol., 1,341 mg sodium, 49 g carbo., 14 g fiber, 34 g pro.

If you can't find flavored biscuit mix, any biscuit mix will do, or flavor your own.
Stir ¼ cup finely shredded cheddar cheese and ¼ teaspoon garlic powder into plain biscuit mix.

EASY CHILI & DUMPLINGS

1	pound ground beef
1	15-ounce can red kidney beans, rinsed and drained
1	14½-ounce can diced tomatoes, undrained
1	11½-ounce can tomato juice
½	cup water
4	teaspoons chili powder
½	teaspoon salt
1	7¾-ounce package cheese-garlic complete biscuit mix
	Snipped fresh cilantro or parsley (optional)

In a large saucepan cook ground beef over medium-high heat until brown. Drain off fat.

Stir in beans, undrained tomatoes, tomato juice, water, chili powder, and salt. Bring to boiling; reduce heat. Simmer, uncovered, for 5 minutes.

Meanwhile, prepare biscuit mix according to package directions. Spoon biscuit dough in mounds onto the simmering chili mixture. Simmer, covered, for 12 to 15 minutes or until a wooden toothpick inserted into dumplings comes out clean. If desired, garnish with cilantro.

Nutrition Facts per serving: 482 cal., 28 g total fat (10 g sat. fat), 64 mg chol., 1,155 mg sodium, 38 g carbo., 6 g fiber, 19 g pro.

PREP:
25 minutes
COOK:
12 minutes
MAKES:
6 servings

An unusual mix of apples, cocoa, curry, cinnamon, and almonds, lends a tantalizing Asian essence to chili.

CURRIED FRUIT-&-NUT CHILI

PREP:

45 minutes

COOK:

1 hour

MAKES:

8 servings

1½	pounds ground beef
2	cups chopped onions
3	cloves garlic, minced
2	14½-ounce cans diced tomatoes, undrained
1	15-ounce can tomato sauce
1	15-ounce can red kidney beans, rinsed and drained
1	14-ounce can chicken broth or 1¾ cups homemade chicken broth
2¼	cups chopped green, red, and/or yellow sweet peppers
1⅓	cups chopped cooking apples, such as Granny Smith or Jonathan (2 medium)
2	4-ounce cans diced green chile peppers, drained
3	tablespoons chili powder
2	tablespoons unsweetened cocoa powder
1	tablespoon curry powder
1	teaspoon ground cinnamon
⅔	cup slivered almonds
	Cheddar cheese, plain yogurt, and/or raisins (optional)

1 In a 6-quart Dutch oven cook ground beef, onions, and garlic over medium-high heat until beef is brown and onion is tender. Drain off fat.

2 Stir in undrained tomatoes, tomato sauce, beans, and broth. Add sweet peppers, apples, chile peppers, chili powder, cocoa powder, curry powder, and cinnamon. Bring to boiling; reduce heat. Simmer, covered, for 1 hour. Stir in almonds. If desired, serve with cheddar cheese, yogurt, and/or raisins.

Nutrition Facts per serving: 357 cal., 16 g total fat (4 g sat. fat), 54 mg chol., 782 mg sodium, 34 g carbo., 10 g fiber, 26 g pro.

This crowd-pleaser is great for potlucks and tailgating. Reduce the black pepper and chili powder to turn down the spiciness.

CHILI FOR A CROWD

1⅓	cups dry pinto beans, rinsed
4	cups water
3	14½-ounce cans diced tomatoes, undrained
3	cups chopped green sweet peppers
2	cups chopped onions
2	cloves garlic, minced
2½	pounds coarsely ground beef*
1	pound lean ground pork
⅓	cup chili powder
2	teaspoons salt
2	teaspoons black pepper
2	teaspoons cumin seeds
½	cup snipped fresh parsley

PREP:
25 minutes
STAND:
1 hour
COOK:
2½ hours
MAKES:
16 servings

1 In a 5- to 6-quart Dutch oven combine beans and enough water to cover them. Bring to boiling; reduce heat. Simmer, uncovered, for 2 minutes. Remove from heat. Cover and let stand for 1 hour. (Or place beans in water in Dutch oven. Cover and let soak in a cool place for 6 to 8 hours or overnight.) Drain and rinse beans.

2 In the same Dutch oven combine beans and the 4 cups water. Bring to boiling; reduce heat. Simmer, covered, for 1 to 1½ hours or until beans are tender. Drain, reserving ¾ cup liquid. Return beans and the reserved liquid to Dutch oven. Add undrained tomatoes, sweet peppers, onions, and garlic.

3 Meanwhile, in a large skillet cook and stir ground beef and ground pork, one-third at a time, over medium heat until brown. Drain off fat.

4 Add cooked beef and pork to the bean mixture. Stir in chili powder, salt, black pepper, and cumin seeds. Bring to boiling; reduce heat. Simmer, covered, for 1 hour. Uncover and simmer about 30 minutes more or until desired consistency, stirring occasionally. Stir in parsley.

*NOTE: For coarsely ground beef, ask your butcher to coarsely grind beef chuck roast or coarsely chop beef chuck roast in a food processor.

Nutrition Facts per serving: 235 cal., 10 g total fat (4 g sat. fat), 58 mg chol., 458 mg sodium, 17 g carbo., 5 g fiber, 21 g pro.

Fire up your crowd with a batch of chili that combines flavors from two different cuisines. Fiery Madras curry powder, coconut milk, and naan, an Indian flatbread, are available at shops that carry Indian food.

INDO-TEXAN CURRY CHILI

PREP:

20 minutes

COOK:

1¹/₂ hours

MAKES:

6 servings

2 pounds coarsely ground beef*

4 cloves garlic, minced

1 tablespoon hot Madras curry powder, salt-free curry seasoning blend, or curry powder

2 teaspoons ground coriander

1 teaspoon ground cumin

1 teaspoon finely shredded lemon peel

2 cups chopped red sweet peppers

1 15-ounce can tomato puree

2 10-ounce cans chopped tomatoes and green chile peppers, undrained

1 10¹/₂-ounce can condensed beef broth

1 cup canned unsweetened coconut milk

¹/₄ cup ketchup

Indian flatbread (naan) or flour tortillas (optional)

Snipped fresh basil (optional)

Chopped peanuts, raisins, and/or chutney (optional)

1 In a 4-quart Dutch oven cook ground beef and garlic over medium-high heat until beef is brown. Drain off fat.

2 Stir in curry powder, coriander, cumin, and lemon peel. Stir in sweet peppers, tomato puree, undrained tomatoes, broth, coconut milk, and ketchup. Bring to boiling; reduce heat. Simmer, uncovered, for 1¹/₂ hours or until desired consistency. If desired, serve with flatbread and top with basil and peanuts, raisins, and/or chutney.

*NOTE: For coarsely ground beef, ask your butcher to coarsely grind beef chuck roast or coarsely chop beef chuck roast in a food processor.

Nutrition Facts per serving: 511 cal., 23 g total fat (12 g sat. fat), 95 mg chol., 923 mg sodium, 42 g carbo., 3 g fiber, 34 g pro.

If you like your chili seriously hot, this recipe is for you. For an even bigger kick, use the whole teaspoon of cayenne pepper. (Recipe pictured on page 273.)

KICKIN' HOT CHILI

2	pounds ground beef
2	cups chopped onions
½	cup chopped green or red sweet pepper
6	cloves garlic, minced
3½	cups water
1	15-ounce can dark red kidney beans, rinsed and drained
1	15-ounce can Great Northern beans, rinsed and drained
1	10-ounce can diced tomatoes and green chile peppers, undrained
1	12-ounce can tomato paste
1	tablespoon yellow mustard
1	teaspoon salt
1	teaspoon chili powder
1	teaspoon black pepper
½	to 1 teaspoon cayenne pepper
½	teaspoon ground cumin
	Green sweet pepper strips (optional)

PREP:
20 minutes
COOK:
30 minutes
MAKES:
8 servings

1 In a 5- to 6-quart Dutch oven cook ground beef, onions, the ½ cup sweet pepper, and the garlic over medium-high heat until beef is brown and onion is tender. Drain off fat.

2 Stir in the water, beans, undrained tomatoes, tomato paste, mustard, salt, chili powder, black pepper, cayenne pepper, and cumin. Bring to boiling; reduce heat. Simmer, covered, for 30 minutes, stirring occasionally. If desired, garnish each serving with sweet pepper strips.

Nutrition Facts per serving: 373 cal., 15 g total fat (6 g sat. fat), 71 mg chol., 802 mg sodium, 31 g carbo., 8 g fiber, 31 g pro.

Liven up your chili routine with this out-of-the-ordinary version! Hominy and pinto beans add pleasant surprises, while nacho cheese soup makes it irresistibly cheesy.

MEXICAN BEEF CHILI

PREP:

20 minutes

COOK:

20 minutes

MAKES:

6 servings

1   pound ground beef

1   15-ounce can pinto beans, rinsed and drained

1   15-ounce can golden hominy, rinsed and drained

1   14½-ounce can diced tomatoes and green chile peppers, undrained

1   11-ounce can condensed nacho cheese soup

1   cup water

1   1¼-ounce envelope taco seasoning mix

Corn chips (optional)

Dairy sour cream (optional)

Sliced pitted ripe olives (optional)

1 In a large saucepan cook ground beef over medium-high heat until brown. Drain off fat.

2 Stir in beans, hominy, undrained tomatoes, nacho cheese soup, water, and taco seasoning mix. Bring to boiling, stirring often; reduce heat. Simmer, covered, for 20 minutes, stirring occasionally. If desired, serve with corn chips, sour cream, and olives.

Nutrition Facts per serving: 331 cal., 15 g total fat (6 g sat. fat), 54 mg chol., 1,581 mg sodium, 27 g carbo., 6 g fiber, 23 g pro.

This chili is extra thick and spicy. For a milder chili, substitute two 14-ounce cans diced tomatoes for the cans of chopped tomatoes and green chile peppers.

SPICY CHILI

1	pound ground beef
1	cup chopped onion
½	cup chopped green sweet pepper
2	cloves garlic, minced
2	10-ounce cans chopped tomatoes and green chile peppers, undrained
1	15-ounce can dark red kidney beans, rinsed and drained
1	8-ounce can tomato sauce
½	cup water
1	teaspoon chili powder
½	teaspoon ground cumin
¼	teaspoon salt
¼	teaspoon black pepper
1	recipe Cheesy Cornmeal Dumplings
	Dairy sour cream (optional)

PREP:
25 minutes
COOK:
20 minutes
MAKES:
4 servings

1 In a large saucepan or Dutch oven cook ground beef, onion, sweet pepper, and garlic over medium heat until beef is brown and onion is tender. Drain off fat.

2 Stir in undrained tomatoes, beans, tomato sauce, water, chili powder, cumin, salt, and black pepper. Bring to boiling; reduce heat. Simmer, uncovered, for 5 minutes.

3 Spoon Cheesy Cornmeal Dumplings by tablespoonfuls in mounds onto bubbling chili. Simmer, covered, for 15 to 20 minutes or until a wooden toothpick inserted into dumplings comes out clean. If desired, top each serving with sour cream.

CHEESY CORNMEAL DUMPLINGS: In a medium bowl combine ½ cup all-purpose flour, ½ cup shredded cheddar cheese (2 ounces), ½ cup yellow cornmeal, 1 teaspoon baking powder, and dash black pepper. In a small bowl combine 1 beaten egg, 2 tablespoons milk, and 2 tablespoons cooking oil; add to flour mixture. Stir with a fork just until moistened.

Nutrition Facts per serving: 646 cal., 31 g total fat (12 g sat. fat), 145 mg chol., 1,515 mg sodium, 58 g carbo., 10 g fiber, 40 g pro.

This family-pleasing chili is part of what Cincinnati natives call a "five-way," a plate of spaghetti topped with beans, chili, onions, and grated cheese. (Recipe pictured on page 276.)

CINCINNATI CHILI

PREP:
25 minutes

COOK:
45 minutes

MAKES:
8 servings

5   bay leaves
1   teaspoon whole allspice
2   pounds ground beef
2   cups chopped onions
1   clove garlic, minced
2   tablespoons chili powder
1   teaspoon ground cinnamon
½   teaspoon cayenne pepper
4   cups water
1   15-ounce can red kidney beans, rinsed and drained
1   8-ounce can tomato sauce
1   tablespoon vinegar
1   teaspoon Worcestershire sauce
½   teaspoon salt
¼   teaspoon black pepper
    Hot cooked spaghetti (optional)
    Grated cheddar cheese (optional)

1 Wrap bay leaves and allspice in a double thickness of 100-percent-cotton cheesecloth. Tie closed with clean kitchen string; set aside.

2 In a 4-quart Dutch oven cook ground beef, onions, and garlic over medium-high heat until the beef is brown and onions are tender. Drain off fat. Stir in chili powder, cinnamon, and cayenne pepper. Cook and stir for 1 minute.

3 Stir in water, beans, tomato sauce, vinegar, Worcestershire sauce, salt, and pepper. Add spice bag. Bring to boiling; reduce heat. Simmer, covered, for 30 minutes. Uncover; simmer for 15 to 20 minutes more or until desired consistency. Remove and discard spice bag. If desired, serve over spaghetti and sprinkle with cheese.

Nutrition Facts per serving: 256 cal., 11 g total fat (4 g sat. fat), 71 mg chol., 435 mg sodium, 15 g carbo., 5 g fiber, 25 g pro.

Mole (MOH-lay) is a rich, dark sauce of chile peppers, bitter chocolate, ground seeds, and spices that is served with meat and poultry in Mexican cuisine. In this beefy chili, coffee helps intensify the deep color and pungent flavor of purchased mole sauce.

CHILI WITH COFFEE & MOLE

2	tablespoons cooking oil
2½	pounds beef round steak, cut into ½-inch cubes
½	cup chopped onion
4	cloves garlic, minced
2	teaspoons ground cumin
¼	to ½ teaspoon crushed red pepper
3	cups peeled, seeded, and coarsely chopped tomatoes (6 medium)
2	cups strong brewed coffee
1	16-ounce can red kidney beans, rinsed and drained
¼	cup purchased mole sauce
1	teaspoon salt
½	teaspoon dried oregano, crushed
½	cup dairy sour cream

PREP:
30 minutes
COOK:
1¼ hours
MAKES:
6 servings

1 In a 4-quart Dutch oven heat oil. Add half of the beef; cook over medium heat until brown. Using a slotted spoon remove beef; set aside. Add remaining beef, onion, garlic, cumin, and crushed red pepper; cook until beef is brown.

2 Return all of the beef to the Dutch oven. Stir in tomatoes, coffee, beans, mole sauce, salt, and oregano. Bring to boiling; reduce heat. Simmer, covered, for 1¼ to 1½ hours or until beef is tender, stirring occasionally. Top each serving with sour cream.

Nutrition Facts per serving: 432 cal., 18 g total fat (5 g sat. fat), 116 mg chol., 659 mg sodium, 20 g carbo., 6 g fiber, 49 g pro.

Red alert! In addition to simple heat, this chili also offers well-blended taste. Ancho chile peppers are dried poblano peppers and are the sweetest of all dried chile pepper varieties.

TEXAS CHILI

PREP:
35 minutes

COOK:
1¼ hours

MAKES:
8 servings

2	tablespoons cooking oil
2½	pounds beef round steak, cut into ½-inch cubes
1	cup chopped onion
4	cloves garlic, minced
3	dried ancho or Anaheim chile peppers, seeded and crumbled
2	teaspoons ground cumin
1	to 1½ teaspoons crushed red pepper
2	15-ounce cans pinto beans or red kidney beans, rinsed and drained
2	14½-ounce cans diced tomatoes, undrained
1	14-ounce can beef broth or 1¾ cups homemade beef broth
½	cup water
½	teaspoon dried oregano, crushed
	Pickled chile peppers (optional)

1 In a 4-quart Dutch oven heat oil. Add one-third of the beef; cook over medium heat until brown. Using a slotted spoon, remove beef, reserving drippings in pan. Set aside. Repeat with another one-third of the beef. Add remaining beef, the onion, garlic, ancho peppers, cumin, and crushed red pepper. Cook until beef is brown.

2 Return all of the beef to the Dutch oven. Stir in beans, undrained tomatoes, broth, water, and oregano. Bring to boiling; reduce heat. Simmer, uncovered, for 1¼ to 1½ hours or until beef is tender, stirring occasionally. If desired, top each serving with pickled peppers.

Nutrition Facts per serving: 424 cal., 16 g total fat (5 g sat. fat), 81 mg chol., 706 mg sodium, 29 g carbo., 8 g fiber, 40 g pro.

Texans have strong opinions about their chili. The meat must be cubed, never ground. Beans and canned tomatoes may be served alongside but are never stirred into the mixture. (Recipe pictured on page 275.)

TEXAS BOWLS O' RED CHILI

3	pounds boneless beef chuck roast, cut into ½-inch cubes
1	teaspoon salt
½	teaspoon freshly ground black pepper
1	tablespoon cooking oil
4	cups chopped onions
3	tablespoons chili powder
3	tablespoons yellow cornmeal
6	cloves garlic, minced
1	tablespoon ground cumin
2	teaspoons dried oregano, crushed
¼	teaspoon cayenne pepper
1	14-ounce can beef broth or 1¾ cups homemade beef broth
1¼	cups water
1	tablespoon packed brown sugar
	Chopped onion (optional)

PREP:
30 minutes
COOK:
1½ hours
MAKES:
6 servings

1 Sprinkle beef with ½ teaspoon of the salt and ¼ teaspoon of the black pepper. In a 4-quart Dutch oven heat oil. Add one-third of the beef; cook over medium heat until brown. Using a slotted spoon, remove beef, reserving drippings in pan. Repeat with remaining beef, cooking one-third at a time and adding more oil, if necessary.

2 Add the 4 cups chopped onions to drippings; cook over medium-high heat about 5 minutes or until tender. Stir in chili powder, cornmeal, garlic, cumin, oregano, and cayenne pepper; cook and stir for 30 seconds. Stir in the beef, remaining ½ teaspoon salt, remaining ¼ teaspoon pepper, broth, water, and brown sugar. Bring to boiling; reduce heat. Simmer, covered, for 1½ to 2 hours or until beef is tender. If desired, top each serving with additional chopped onion.

Nutrition Facts per serving: 448 cal., 17 g total fat (5 g sat. fat), 107 mg chol., 812 mg sodium, 19 g carbo., 4 g fiber, 53 g pro.

Pull out this chili when the gang assembles for an afternoon of football—either in the backyard or on TV. Italian sausage and beef cubes provide heartiness. Bacon adds an interesting flavor note.

BEST-EVER CHILI WITH BEANS

PREP:

45 minutes

COOK:

1¹⁄₄ hours

MAKES:

6 servings

¹⁄₂	pound uncooked Italian sausage links (casings removed, if present)
1¹⁄₂	pounds boneless beef chuck roast, cut into ¹⁄₂-inch cubes
³⁄₄	cup chopped green sweet pepper
2¹⁄₂	cups water
1	15-ounce can pinto or kidney beans, rinsed and drained
1	14¹⁄₂-ounce can diced tomatoes with onion and garlic, undrained
1	6-ounce can tomato paste or Italian-style tomato paste
1	to 2 fresh jalapeño chile peppers, seeded and finely chopped*
1	tablespoon chili powder
¹⁄₄	teaspoon salt
6	slices bacon, crisp-cooked, drained, and crumbled

1 In a 4-quart Dutch oven cook sausage over medium-high heat until brown. Using a slotted spoon, remove sausage, reserving drippings in Dutch oven. Cook half of the beef in the hot drippings until beef is brown; remove beef from pan. Add remaining beef and sweet pepper. Cook until beef is brown; drain off fat. Return all the beef and the sausage to Dutch oven.

2 Stir in the water, beans, undrained tomatoes, tomato paste, jalapeño chile peppers, chili powder, and salt. Bring to boiling; reduce heat. Simmer, covered, about 1¹⁄₄ hours or until beef is tender. Stir in bacon; heat through.

*NOTE: When working with chile peppers, wear plastic or rubber gloves. If your bare hands do touch the chile peppers, wash your hands well with soap and water.

Nutrition Facts per serving: 510 cal., 30 g total fat (11 g sat. fat), 104 mg chol., 1,064 mg sodium, 24 g carbo., 6 g fiber, 36 g pro.

Chipotle peppers in adobo sauce are doubly delicious. The smoky jalapeño is a direct hit of heat, while the adobo sauce is a slow burn. Together they flavor this chili with a deep richness that only slow simmering can produce.

BEEF & RED BEAN CHILI

1   cup dry red beans or dry kidney beans, rinsed

1   tablespoon olive oil

2   pounds boneless beef chuck roast, cut into 1-inch cubes

1   cup coarsely chopped onion

1   15-ounce can tomato sauce

1   14½-ounce can diced tomatoes and green chile peppers, undrained

1   14-ounce can beef broth or 1¾ cups homemade beef broth

1   or 2 chipotle chile peppers in adobo sauce, finely chopped, plus 2 teaspoons adobo sauce

2   teaspoons dried oregano, crushed

1   teaspoon ground cumin

½   teaspoon salt

¾   cup chopped red sweet pepper

¼   cup snipped fresh cilantro

PREP:

1¼ hours

COOK:

1½ hours

MAKES:

6 servings

1 In a 4- to 5-quart Dutch oven combine beans and enough water to cover them. Bring to boiling; reduce heat. Simmer, uncovered, for 2 minutes. Remove from heat. Cover and let stand for 1 hour. (Or place beans in water in Dutch oven. Cover and let soak in a cool place for 6 to 8 hours or overnight.) Drain and rinse beans; set side.

2 In the same Dutch oven heat the oil. Add half of the beef and the onion; cook over medium-high heat until mixture is light brown. Using a slotted spoon, remove beef and onion; set aside. Repeat with remaining beef. Return beef and onion to the Dutch oven. Add the beans, tomato sauce, undrained tomatoes, broth, chipotle peppers and adobo sauce, oregano, cumin, and salt.

3 Bring to boiling; reduce heat. Simmer, covered, for 1½ to 2 hours or until beef and beans are tender. Top each serving with sweet pepper and cilantro.

Nutrition Facts per serving: 516 cal., 26 g total fat (9 g sat. fat), 98 mg chol., 1,162 mg sodium, 32 g carbo., 8 g fiber, 38 g pro.

The three sources of heat—pickled jalapeños, chili powder, and crushed red pepper—provide flavor beyond the burn.

RED-HOT CHILI

PREP:

20 minutes

COOK:

2 hours

MAKES:

5 servings

2	tablespoons cooking oil
2	pounds boneless beef chuck roast, cut into ³/₄-inch cubes
1	cup chopped onion
³/₄	cup chopped green sweet pepper
1	clove garlic, minced
2¹/₂	cups water
2	6-ounce cans tomato paste
2	pickled jalapeño chile peppers, rinsed, seeded, and chopped
4	teaspoons chili powder
³/₄	teaspoon salt
¹/₂	teaspoon crushed red pepper
¹/₂	teaspoon dried oregano, crushed
¹/₂	teaspoon ground cumin
1	15- to 16-ounce can pinto beans, rinsed and drained

1 In a large heavy saucepan or Dutch oven heat oil. Add half of the beef; cook in hot oil over medium heat until beef is brown. Using a slotted spoon, remove beef, reserving drippings in pan. Set aside. Repeat with remaining beef.

2 Add onion, sweet pepper, and garlic to drippings; cook and stir for 5 minutes. Return all the beef to the pan.

3 Stir in water, tomato paste, pickled jalapeño peppers, chili powder, salt, crushed red pepper, oregano, and cumin. Bring to boiling; reduce heat. Simmer, covered, about 1¹/₂ hours, stirring occasionally.

4 Stir in beans; simmer, covered, about 30 minutes more or until beef is tender.

Nutrition Facts per serving: 465 cal., 16 g total fat (5 g sat. fat), 132 mg chol., 761 mg sodium, 30 g carbo., 9 g fiber, 50 g pro.

This chili is a terrific way to use lean, flavorful bison or venison. Both of these meats match well with the strong flavors of garlic, cumin, and oregano, but if you don't have access to them, substitute ground beef.

FREE-RANGE GAME CHILI

PREP:

20 minutes

COOK:

50 minutes

MAKES:

6 servings

Nonstick cooking spray

1 pound ground bison (buffalo) or venison

1 cup chopped onion

3 cloves garlic, minced

4½ teaspoons chili powder

2 teaspoons dried oregano, crushed

1 teaspoon ground cumin

2 14½-ounce cans diced tomatoes, undrained

1 14-ounce can beef broth or 1¾ cups homemade beef broth

1 cup water

1 15-ounce can red kidney beans or black beans, rinsed and drained

4 ounces soft goat cheese (chèvre), crumbled (optional)

½ cup chopped green onions (optional)

1 Coat a 4-quart saucepan or Dutch oven with cooking spray; heat over medium heat. Add ground meat, onion, and garlic; cook about 15 minutes or until meat is brown, stirring occasionally. Drain off fat, if necessary.

2 Stir in chili powder, oregano, and cumin; cook for 5 minutes more. Add undrained tomatoes, broth, and water. Bring to boiling; reduce heat. Simmer, uncovered, for 30 minutes, stirring occasionally. Add beans; heat through. If desired, sprinkle each serving with goat cheese and green onions.

Nutrition Facts per serving: 187 cal., 2 g total fat (1 g sat. fat), 48 mg chol., 600 mg sodium, 22 g carbo., 7 g fiber, 24 g pro.

If you like meat cubes in your chili but are short on time, try this fast-to-fix offering. Pork tenderloin cooks in just 5 minutes, yet the smoky chipotle chile peppers give a simmered-all-day flavor. (Recipe pictured on page 276.)

CHUNKY CHIPOTLE PORK CHILI

START TO FINISH:

35 minutes

MAKES:

4 servings

1	tablespoon cooking oil
1/3	cup chopped onion
4	cloves garlic, minced
12	ounces pork tenderloin, cut into 3/4-inch cubes
2	teaspoons chili powder
2	teaspoons ground cumin
1	yellow or red sweet pepper, cut into 1/2-inch pieces
1	cup beer or beef broth
1/2	cup bottled picante sauce or salsa
1	to 2 tablespoons finely chopped canned chipotle chile pepper in adobo sauce
1	15- to 16-ounce can small red beans or pinto beans, rinsed and drained
1/2	cup dairy sour cream
	Fresh cilantro or Italian (flat-leaf) parsley sprigs (optional)

1 In a large saucepan heat oil. Add onion and garlic; cook over medium heat about 4 minutes or until onion is tender.

2 In a medium bowl toss pork with chili powder and cumin. Add to onion mixture; cook and stir until pork is brown. Add sweet pepper, beer, picante sauce, and chipotle pepper. Bring to boiling; reduce heat. Simmer, covered, about 5 minutes or until pork is tender. Stir in beans; heat through. Top each serving with sour cream. If desired, garnish with cilantro sprigs.

Nutrition Facts per serving: 328 cal., 11 g total fat (4 g sat. fat), 65 mg chol., 625 mg sodium, 29 g carbo., 7 g fiber, 26 g pro.

This traditional Mexican chili features pork, hominy, and tomatillos instead of the more common mixture of beef, beans, and tomatoes.

CHILI VERDE

2	tablespoons cooking oil
2	pounds lean boneless pork, cut into ³⁄₄-inch cubes
¹⁄₂	cup chopped onion
¹⁄₂	cup chopped green sweet pepper
¹⁄₄	cup chopped celery
2	tablespoons chopped green onion
1	clove garlic, minced
2	tablespoons all-purpose flour
2¹⁄₄	cups water
1	15-ounce can golden hominy, rinsed and drained
1	11- to 13-ounce can tomatillos, drained and cut up
2	4-ounce cans diced green chile peppers, drained
	Flour tortillas (optional)
	Dairy sour cream (optional)
	Chopped tomatoes (optional)
	Snipped fresh cilantro (optional)

PREP:

55 minutes

COOK:

30 minutes

MAKES:

6 to 8 servings

1 In a 4-quart Dutch oven heat 1 tablespoon of the oil. Add half of the pork; cook over medium heat until brown. Using a slotted spoon, remove pork; set aside. Repeat with remaining pork, reserving drippings in pan. Add onion, sweet pepper, celery, green onion, and garlic to drippings; cook and stir about 5 minutes or until vegetables are tender. Stir in the remaining 1 tablespoon oil and flour; cook and stir for 5 minutes more.

2 Stir pork and the water into vegetable mixture. Bring to boiling. Stir in hominy, tomatillos, and green chile peppers. Return to boiling; reduce heat. Simmer, uncovered, about 30 minutes or until pork is tender, stirring occasionally. If desired, serve with tortillas, sour cream, tomatoes, and cilantro.

Nutrition Facts per serving: 327 cal., 13 g total fat (3 g sat. fat), 95 mg chol., 701 mg sodium, 16 g carbo., 3 g fiber, 35 g pro.

Honor the stars in your home with this spicy chili garnished with tortilla stars. To make the stars, cut flour tortillas with a 2-inch star-shaped cutter. Fry in a little oil until light brown, drain on paper towels, and sprinkle with chili powder.

ALL-STAR WHITE CHILI

START TO FINISH:

35 minutes

MAKES:

6 to 8 servings

1½   pounds bulk pork sausage

1   cup chopped onion

4   cloves garlic, minced

2   19-ounce cans white kidney (cannellini) beans, rinsed and drained

2   14-ounce cans reduced-sodium chicken broth or 3½ cups homemade chicken broth

1   14½-ounce can white or yellow whole kernel corn, drained

1   fresh poblano chile pepper, seeded and finely chopped* (¾ cup)

⅓   cup lime juice

¼   teaspoon ground white pepper

  Crushed white corn tortilla chips or tortilla stars

1 In a 4-quart Dutch oven cook sausage, onion, and garlic over medium heat until meat is brown and onion is tender. Drain off fat.

2 Stir in beans, broth, corn, chile pepper, lime juice, and white pepper. Bring to boiling; reduce heat. Simmer, covered, for 20 minutes. Top each serving with crushed chips or tortilla stars.

*NOTE: When working with chile peppers, wear plastic or rubber gloves. If your bare hands do touch the chile peppers, wash your hands well with soap and water.

Nutrition Facts per serving: 660 cal., 37 g total fat (14 g sat. fat), 65 mg chol., 1,464 mg sodium, 54 g carbo., 10 g fiber, 28 g pro.

Without the red beans and tomatoes, this bowl may not look like your usual chili, but it sure tastes like it. It's seasoned with Southwest-style chile peppers, garlic, and cumin.

CHILI BLANCO

1	pound uncooked ground chicken or ground turkey
1	pound lean ground pork
1½	cups chopped onions
6	cloves garlic, minced
3	14-ounce cans chicken broth or 5¼ cups homemade chicken broth
2	15-ounce cans Great Northern beans, rinsed and drained
1	15-ounce can golden hominy, rinsed and drained
2	4-ounce cans diced green chile peppers, undrained
1	medium fresh poblano chile pepper, seeded and chopped* (¾ cup)
1	large fresh jalapeño chile pepper, seeded and chopped*
3	tablespoons lime juice
2	tablespoons ground cumin
½	teaspoon ground white pepper
½	cup snipped fresh cilantro

PREP:
30 minutes
COOK:
40 minutes
MAKES:
10 servings

1 In a 4-quart Dutch oven cook chicken, pork, onions, and garlic over medium heat until pork is brown and onion is tender. Drain off fat.

2 Stir in broth, beans, hominy, green chile peppers, poblano pepper, jalapeño pepper, lime juice, cumin, and white pepper. Bring to boiling; reduce heat. Simmer, covered, for 40 minutes, stirring occasionally. Stir in cilantro.

*NOTE: When working with chile peppers, wear plastic or rubber gloves. If your bare hands do touch the chile peppers, wash your hands well with soap and water.

Nutrition Facts per serving: 318 cal., 15 g total fat (4 g sat. fat), 32 mg chol., 875 mg sodium, 22 g carbo., 6 g fiber, 23 g pro.

This hearty meal-in-a-pot adds chicken, rather than beef, to chili fixings. For a soup buffet, prepare the chili ahead, chill, and reheat it while guests gather.

SPICY CHICKEN CHILI

PREP:

1¹⁄₂ hours

COOK:

2 hours

MAKES:

12 servings

1	pound dry Great Northern beans, rinsed
1	tablespoon cooking oil
2	cups chopped onions
2	4-ounce cans diced green chile peppers, undrained
4	cloves garlic, minced
2	teaspoons ground cumin
1¹⁄₂	teaspoons dried oregano, crushed
¹⁄₄	teaspoon ground cloves
¹⁄₄	teaspoon cayenne pepper
4	14-ounce cans chicken broth or 7 cups homemade chicken broth
4	cups coarsely chopped cooked chicken*
1	12-ounce can beer or nonalcoholic beer
1	cup shredded Monterey Jack cheese or Monterey Jack cheese with jalapeño peppers (4 ounces)
	Dairy sour cream (optional)
	Bottled salsa (optional)
	Snipped fresh cilantro (optional)
	Shredded Monterey Jack cheese (optional)

1 In a 4- to 5-quart Dutch oven combine beans and enough water to cover them. Bring to boiling; reduce heat. Simmer, uncovered, for 2 minutes. Remove from heat. Cover and let stand for 1 hour. (Or place beans in water in Dutch oven. Cover and let soak in a cool place for 6 to 8 hours or overnight.) Drain and rinse beans; set aside.

2 In the same Dutch oven heat oil. Add onions; cook over medium heat for 5 to 8 minutes or until tender. Stir in chile peppers, garlic, cumin, oregano, cloves, and cayenne pepper. Cook and stir for 2 minutes more. Stir in beans and broth. Bring to boiling; reduce heat. Simmer, covered, about 2 hours or until beans are very tender. Stir in chicken, beer, and the 1 cup cheese; cook and stir until cheese is melted. If desired, serve with sour cream, salsa, cilantro, and additional cheese.

*NOTE: For cooked chicken, place 2 pounds boneless, skinless chicken breast halves in a large skillet or saucepan; add enough water to cover. Bring to boiling; reduce heat. Simmer, covered, for 15 to 20 minutes or until chicken is tender and no longer pink. Drain; cool slightly. Coarsely chop chicken.

Nutrition Facts per serving: 306 cal., 7 g total fat (3 g sat. fat), 52 mg chol., 834 mg sodium, 29 g carbo., 9 g fiber, 30 g pro.

Tomatillos are sometimes called Mexican green tomatoes because they resemble small green tomatoes and are frequently used in Mexican cooking. Their flavor hints of lemon and apple, adding a unique taste to salads, salsas, and this chunky soup.

CHICKEN CHILI WITH RICE

1	tablespoon cooking oil
3	cloves garlic, minced
1	fresh jalapeño chile pepper, seeded and finely chopped*
2	cups frozen small whole onions
1	cup reduced-sodium chicken broth or homemade chicken broth
2	teaspoons chili powder
1	teaspoon ground cumin
1	teaspoon dried oregano, crushed
¼	teaspoon salt
⅛	teaspoon ground white pepper
⅛	teaspoon cayenne pepper
1	19-ounce can white kidney (cannellini) beans, rinsed and drained
1	cup chopped cooked chicken
1	cup chopped tomatillos
2	cups hot cooked rice or couscous

START TO FINISH:
35 minutes
MAKES:
4 servings

1 In a large saucepan heat oil. Add garlic and jalapeño pepper; cook over medium heat for 30 seconds. Carefully stir in onions, broth, chili powder, cumin, oregano, salt, white pepper, and cayenne pepper. Bring to boiling; reduce heat. Simmer, covered, for 20 minutes.

2 Stir in beans, chicken, and tomatillos; cook and stir until heated through. Serve over rice.

*NOTE: When working with chile peppers, wear plastic or rubber gloves. If your bare hands do touch the chile peppers, wash your hands well with soap and water.

Nutrition Facts per serving: 312 cal., 7 g total fat (1 g sat. fat), 31 mg chol., 514 mg sodium, 48 g carbo., 8 g fiber, 20 g pro.

Black beans, preferred in cuisines of the Caribbean, also make a fine chili.

TURKEY & BLACK BEAN CHILI

PREP:

20 minutes

COOK:

40 minutes

MAKES:

4 servings

1	tablespoon cooking oil
½	cup chopped onion
4	teaspoons chili powder
2	teaspoons ground cumin
2	cloves garlic, minced
1	teaspoon anise seeds, crushed
1	bay leaf
½	teaspoon ground coriander
8	ounces uncooked ground turkey
1	15-ounce can black beans, rinsed and drained
1	14½-ounce can diced tomatoes, undrained
1	14-ounce can chicken broth or 1¾ cups homemade chicken broth
¾	cup chopped red sweet pepper
1	to 2 fresh jalapeño chile peppers, seeded and finely chopped*
¼	teaspoon salt
¼	teaspoon cayenne pepper
2	tablespoons snipped fresh cilantro
	Shredded Monterey Jack or cheddar cheese (optional)
	Thinly sliced green onions (optional)

1 In a 4-quart Dutch oven heat oil. Add onion; cook over medium heat about 4 minutes or until tender. Stir in chili powder, cumin, garlic, anise seeds, bay leaf, and coriander. Cook and stir for 1 minute.

2 Stir in ground turkey; cook for 5 to 7 minutes or until turkey is no longer pink, stirring to break up turkey.

3 Add beans, undrained tomatoes, broth, sweet pepper, jalapeño pepper, salt, and cayenne pepper. Bring to boiling; reduce heat. Simmer, covered, for 30 minutes, stirring occasionally. Remove and discard bay leaf. Stir in snipped cilantro. If desired, serve with cheese and green onions.

*NOTE: When working with chile peppers, wear plastic or rubber gloves. If your bare hands do touch the chile peppers, wash your hands well with soap and water.

Nutrition Facts per serving: 252 cal., 10 g total fat (2 g sat. fat), 35 mg chol., 1,085 mg sodium, 26 g carbo., 8 g fiber, 21 g pro.

Adding raisins, olives, and almonds makes this chili similar to picadillo, a popular dish in many Spanish-speaking countries.

PICADILLO CHILI

1	pound uncooked ground turkey
1	cup chopped onion
2	cloves garlic, minced
1½	teaspoons chili powder
½	teaspoon ground cumin
¼	teaspoon ground cinnamon
⅛	teaspoon cayenne pepper
1	28-ounce can diced tomatoes, undrained
1	15-ounce can tomato sauce
1	15-ounce can black beans, rinsed and drained
1	4-ounce can diced green chile peppers, undrained
½	cup golden raisins
½	cup sliced pimiento-stuffed green olives
½	cup slivered almonds, toasted
⅓	cup sliced green onions

PREP:

20 minutes

COOK:

45 minutes

MAKES:

6 servings

1 In a 4-quart Dutch oven cook turkey and onion over medium heat until turkey is no longer pink and onion is tender, stirring to break up ground turkey. Drain off fat.

2 Add garlic, chili powder, cumin, cinnamon, and cayenne pepper; cook and stir for 2 minutes more. Stir in undrained tomatoes, tomato sauce, beans, chile peppers, and raisins. Bring to boiling; reduce heat. Simmer, covered, for 45 minutes. Stir in olives, almonds, and green onions.

Nutrition Facts per serving: 349 cal., 14 g total fat (2 g sat. fat), 60 mg chol., 1,086 mg sodium, 37 g carbo., 8 g fiber, 23 g pro.

With just five ingredients and 20 minutes, you can have this flavorful chili for dinner any day of the week. Be sure to keep the fixings on hand.

TURKEY CHILI WITH HOMINY

START TO FINISH:

20 minutes

MAKES:

4 or 5 servings

12	ounces bulk turkey Italian sausage or uncooked ground turkey
2	15-ounce cans chili beans with chili gravy
1	15-ounce can golden hominy, rinsed and drained
1	cup bottled salsa with lime
$^2/_3$	cup water
$^1/_3$	cup sliced green onions

1 In a large saucepan cook the turkey sausage over medium-high heat until brown. Stir in the undrained chili beans, hominy, salsa, and water. Heat through. Sprinkle each serving with sliced green onion.

Nutrition Facts per serving: 470 cal., 11 g total fat (3 g sat. fat), 45 mg chol., 1,897 mg sodium, 64 g carbo., 16 g fiber, 28 g pro.

Turkey kielbasa packs a heap of flavor into this easy chili while keeping the fat content low.

ZESTY BLACK BEAN CHILI

1	16-ounce jar thick and chunky salsa
1	15-ounce can black beans, rinsed and drained
1½	cups vegetable juice or hot-style vegetable juice
8	ounces fully cooked turkey kielbasa (Polish sausage), halved lengthwise and sliced (1¾ cups)
¼	cup water
2	teaspoons chili powder
2	cloves garlic, minced, or ¼ teaspoon garlic powder
	Dairy sour cream or plain low-fat yogurt (optional)
	Sliced green onion and/or chopped red onion (optional)
	Chopped avocado (optional)
	Corn bread (optional)

START TO FINISH:

30 minutes

MAKES:

4 servings

1 In a large saucepan combine salsa, beans, vegetable juice, turkey kielbasa, water, chili powder, and garlic. Bring to boiling; reduce heat. Simmer, covered, for 20 minutes, stirring occasionally. If desired, top each serving with sour cream, onion, and avocado and serve with corn bread.

Nutrition Facts per serving: 219 cal., 4 g total fat (1 g sat. fat), 35 mg chol., 1,891 mg sodium, 28 g carbo., 6 g fiber, 17 g pro.

Three beans are better than one. Each type has a distinctive flavor and texture, making every spoonful of this chili an adventure. (Recipe pictured on page 274.)

BEAN MEDLEY CHILI

PREP:

30 minutes

COOK:

40 minutes

MAKES:

8 servings

1	tablespoon cooking oil
2	cups chopped onions
12	cloves garlic, minced
1	canned chipotle chile pepper in adobo sauce, finely chopped
3	tablespoons chili powder
1	teaspoon ground cumin
1	teaspoon salt
1	28-ounce can diced tomatoes, undrained
1	14-ounce can vegetable broth or chicken broth or $1\frac{3}{4}$ cups homemade vegetable broth or chicken broth
1	15-ounce can black beans, rinsed and drained
1	15-ounce can red kidney beans, rinsed and drained
1	cup chopped red sweet pepper
1	cup chopped green sweet pepper
1	15-ounce can garbanzo beans (chickpeas), rinsed and drained
$\frac{1}{4}$	cup snipped fresh cilantro
4	cups hot cooked rice
	Fresh cilantro sprigs (optional)

1 In a 4-quart Dutch oven heat oil. Add onions and garlic; cook and stir over medium heat for 4 to 5 minutes or until onion is tender. Stir in chipotle pepper, chili powder, cumin, and salt; cook and stir for 1 minute. Add undrained tomatoes and broth. Bring to boiling; reduce heat. Simmer, covered, for 15 minutes.

2 Stir in black beans, kidney beans, and sweet peppers. Return to boiling; reduce heat. Simmer, covered, about 20 minutes more or until sweet peppers are tender.

3 Add garbanzo beans and snipped cilantro; heat through. Serve with rice. If desired, garnish with cilantro sprigs.

Nutrition Facts per serving: 314 cal., 4 g total fat (0 g sat. fat), 0 mg chol., 1,082 mg sodium, 61 g carbo., 11 g fiber, 14 g pro.

Toasting cumin seeds brings out a deep, nutty flavor. You'll know the cumin seeds are ready when your kitchen fills with a fragrant aroma. Avoid overcooking, which makes cumin bitter.

WHITE BEAN CHILI WITH TOASTED CUMIN

3	tablespoons cooking oil
2	cups chopped onions
6	cloves garlic, minced
4	14½-ounce cans diced tomatoes, undrained
2	12-ounce cans beer or nonalcoholic beer
2	chipotle chile peppers in adobo sauce, chopped
2	tablespoons cumin seeds, toasted*
2	teaspoons sugar
1	teaspoon salt
4	19-ounce cans baby or regular white kidney (cannellini) or white navy beans, rinsed and drained
3	cups coarsely chopped, seeded, and peeled golden nugget, butternut, and/or acorn squash (about 12 ounces)
1	8-ounce carton dairy sour cream
¼	cup lime juice
2	tablespoons snipped fresh chives

PREP:
30 minutes
COOK:
1 hour
MAKES:
8 servings

1 In a 6- to 8-quart Dutch oven heat oil. Add onions and garlic; cook and stir over medium heat about 4 minutes or until onions are tender. Stir in the undrained tomatoes, beer, chipotle peppers, cumin, sugar, and salt. Stir in beans. Bring to boiling; reduce heat. Stir in squash. Simmer, covered, for 1 hour.

2 Meanwhile, in a small bowl combine sour cream, lime juice, and chives. Top each serving with sour cream mixture.

*NOTE: **To toast cumin seeds, place the seeds in a dry skillet over low heat. Cook about 8 minutes, stirring often.**

Nutrition Facts per serving: 365 cal., 15 g total fat (5 g sat. fat), 13 mg chol., 995 mg sodium, 52 g carbo., 13 g fiber, 17 g pro.

If you think all-vegetable chilies tend to be bland, try this one and think again.
Tomatoes with green chile peppers give it a powerful taste.

TOUCHDOWN VEGGIE CHILI

START TO FINISH:

35 minutes

MAKES:

8 servings

2　15-ounce cans garbanzo beans (chickpeas), rinsed and drained

2　15-ounce cans red kidney beans, rinsed and drained

2　14-ounce cans beef broth or 3½ cups homemade beef broth

2　11-ounce cans whole kernel corn with sweet peppers, drained

1　10-ounce can chopped tomatoes and green chile peppers, undrained

1　cup chopped onion

4　teaspoons chili powder

2　cloves garlic, minced, or ¼ teaspoon garlic powder

¼　teaspoon crushed red pepper

¼　teaspoon black pepper

½　cup dairy sour cream

　　Corn chips (optional)

1 In a 4-quart Dutch oven combine beans, broth, corn, undrained tomatoes, onion, chili powder, garlic, crushed red pepper, and black pepper. Bring to boiling; reduce heat. Simmer, covered, for 20 minutes.

2 Top each serving with sour cream and, if desired, corn chips.

Nutrition Facts per serving: 301 cal., 5 g total fat (2 g sat. fat), 5 mg chol., 1,395 mg sodium, 53 g carbo., 14 g fiber, 14 g pro.

Bottled hot pepper sauce provides the kick in this chili. If you prefer, leave it out of the recipe and pass the bottle of hot pepper sauce so guests can adjust the heat as they please.

EASY VEGETARIAN CHILI

2	tablespoons olive oil
1½	cups sliced celery
1½	cups chopped green sweet peppers
4	14½-ounce cans diced tomatoes with onion and garlic, undrained
3	15-ounce cans red kidney beans, rinsed and drained
1	15-ounce can Great Northern beans or navy beans, rinsed and drained
1	12-ounce can beer or 1½ cups water
1	tablespoon chili powder
1	bay leaf
1½	teaspoons dried basil, crushed
1½	teaspoons dried oregano, crushed
½	teaspoon salt
½	teaspoon black pepper
¼	teaspoon bottled hot pepper sauce
	Shredded cheddar cheese (optional)

PREP:
20 minutes
COOK:
1 hour
MAKES:
8 to 10 servings

1 In a 4-quart Dutch oven heat oil. Add celery and sweet peppers; cook over medium heat about 5 minutes or until tender, stirring occasionally. Stir in undrained tomatoes, beans, beer, chili powder, bay leaf, basil, oregano, salt, black pepper, and hot pepper sauce. Bring to boiling; reduce heat. Simmer, uncovered, for 1 hour, stirring occasionally.

2 Remove and discard bay leaf. If desired, sprinkle each serving with shredded cheese.

Nutrition Facts per serving: 338 cal., 8 g total fat (2 g sat. fat), 7 mg chol., 1,869 mg sodium, 51 g carbo., 15 g fiber, 17 g pro.

Frozen hash brown potatoes and zucchini are the surprise ingredients in this meatless chili. Polenta makes a pleasant alternative to traditional corn bread.

SPICY VEGETARIAN CHILI & POLENTA

START TO FINISH:

30 minutes

MAKES:

4 servings

1	tablespoon olive oil
½	cup chopped onion
1	cup frozen loose-pack hash brown potatoes
1	cup chopped zucchini
1	10-ounce can diced tomatoes and green chiles, undrained
1	8-ounce can tomato sauce
2	teaspoons chili powder
2	cloves garlic, minced
1	15-ounce can kidney beans, rinsed and drained
1	16-ounce package refrigerated cooked polenta, cut into 8 slices
½	cup shredded Monterey Jack cheese (2 ounces)
	Dairy sour cream (optional)

1 In a large skillet heat oil. Add onion; cook and stir over medium heat about 4 minutes or until tender. Stir in potatoes, zucchini, undrained tomatoes, tomato sauce, chili powder, and garlic. Bring to boiling; reduce heat. Simmer, covered, for 15 minutes. Stir in beans. Simmer, uncovered, for 5 minutes more or until desired consistency.

2 Meanwhile, heat polenta according to package directions; serve with chili. Sprinkle each serving with cheese and, if desired, top with sour cream.

Nutrition Facts per serving: 350 cal., 9 g total fat (3 g sat. fat), 15 mg chol., 1,251 mg sodium, 58 g carbo., 12 g fiber, 17 g pro.

Ripe avocado and snipped fresh cilantro provide a refreshing flavor counterpoint to this easy chili.

TWO-BEAN CHILI WITH AVOCADO

2   teaspoons canola or olive oil

1   cup chopped onion

2   teaspoons dried oregano, crushed

2   14½-ounce cans diced tomatoes, undrained

1   15-ounce can black or kidney beans, rinsed and drained

1   15-ounce can pinto beans, rinsed and drained

½   cup salsa (preferably guajillo chile salsa)

1   medium ripe avocado, peeled, seeded, and diced

¼   cup snipped fresh cilantro

PREP:
15 minutes
COOK:
30 minutes
MAKES:
4 or 5 servings

1 In a large saucepan heat oil. Add onion and oregano; cook and stir over medium-high heat about 4 minutes or until onion is tender.

2 Stir in undrained tomatoes, beans, and salsa. Bring to boiling; reduce heat. Simmer, uncovered, for 25 minutes. Top each serving with avocado and cilantro.

Nutrition Facts per serving: 326 cal., 9 g total fat (1 g sat. fat), 0 mg chol., 1,017 mg sodium, 51 g carbo., 15 g fiber, 16 g pro.

Balsamic vinegar, olives, and a topping of mozzarella cheese lend an Italian flair to this meatless chili. (Recipe pictured on page 274.)

ITALIAN THREE-BEAN CHILI

PREP:

20 minutes

COOK:

30 minutes

MAKES:

6 servings

2 tablespoons olive oil

½ cup chopped red onion

1 clove garlic, minced

1 15-ounce can tomato sauce

1 15-ounce can black beans, rinsed and drained

1 15- to 16-ounce can Great Northern beans, rinsed and drained

1 14½-ounce can diced tomatoes, undrained

1 cup frozen green soybeans (edamame)

1 4-ounce can diced green chile peppers, undrained

½ cup water

1 tablespoon balsamic vinegar

⅓ cup sliced pitted ripe olives

2 tablespoons snipped fresh cilantro

3 cups hot cooked rice, pasta, or couscous

Shredded mozzarella cheese (optional)

1 In a large saucepan heat oil. Add onion and garlic; cook and stir over medium heat about 4 minutes or until onion is tender. Add tomato sauce, beans, undrained tomatoes, soybeans, chile peppers, water, and vinegar. Bring to boiling; reduce heat. Simmer, covered, for 20 minutes, stirring occasionally.

2 Stir in olives and cilantro. Simmer, covered, for 5 minutes. Serve over rice and, if desired, top with mozzarella cheese.

Nutrition Facts per serving: 436 cal., 12 g total fat (3 g sat. fat), 11 mg chol., 828 mg sodium, 62 g carbo., 10 g fiber, 23 g pro.

Apples and apricots offer a hint of sweetness to this spicy bean chili. For a totally vegetarian chili, use vegetable broth in place of the chicken broth.

FRUIT & NUT CHILI

	Nonstick cooking spray
½	cup chopped onion
1	clove garlic, minced
1	14½-ounce can diced tomatoes, undrained
1	14-ounce can chicken broth or 1¾ cups homemade chicken broth
1	8-ounce can tomato sauce
¾	cup chopped green sweet pepper
⅔	cup chopped, peeled tart apple
1	4-ounce can diced green chile peppers, drained
1	tablespoon chili powder
1½	teaspoons unsweetened cocoa powder
½	teaspoon ground cinnamon
1	15-ounce can red kidney beans, rinsed and drained
¼	cup slivered almonds
¼	cup snipped dried apricots
	Shredded cheddar cheese (optional)

PREP:
30 minutes
COOK:
40 minutes
MAKES:
4 servings

1 Coat a 4-quart Dutch oven with cooking spray; heat over medium heat. Add onion and garlic; cook and stir about 4 minutes or until onion is tender.

2 Stir in undrained tomatoes, broth, tomato sauce, sweet pepper, apple, chile peppers, chili powder, cocoa powder, and cinnamon. Bring to boiling; reduce heat. Simmer, covered, for 30 minutes, stirring occasionally. Stir in beans, almonds, and apricots. Return to boiling; reduce heat. Simmer, uncovered, for 10 minutes more. If desired, sprinkle each serving with cheese.

Nutrition Facts per serving: 258 cal., 6 g total fat (1 g sat. fat), 0 mg chol., 1,018 mg sodium, 44 g carbo., 11 g fiber, 14 g pro.

You would swear there is meat in this hearty chili, but you would be mistaken—it's chock-full of mushrooms. As brown mushrooms mature into portobellos, they gain a meaty texture. (Recipe pictured on page 275.)

CHILI CON PORTOBELLO

PREP:

30 minutes

COOK:

1 hour

MAKES:

4 servings

2 tablespoons olive oil

1 cup chopped onion

2 cloves garlic, minced

8 ounces portobello mushroom caps, coarsely chopped (about 4 cups)

1 28-ounce can diced tomatoes, undrained

1 15-ounce can red kidney beans, rinsed and drained

1 tablespoon ground cumin

1 tablespoon medium or hot chili powder

Dairy sour cream (optional)

1 In a large saucepan heat oil. Add onion and garlic; cook and stir over medium-high heat about 4 minutes or until onion is tender. Stir in mushrooms. Cook and stir for 3 minutes more.

2 Stir in undrained tomatoes, beans, cumin, and chili powder. Bring to boiling; reduce heat. Simmer, covered, for 1 hour. If desired, top each serving with sour cream.

Nutrition Facts per serving: 157 cal., 5 g total fat (1 g sat. fat), 0 mg chol., 377 mg sodium, 23 g carbo., 8 g fiber, 6 g pro.

The smoky flavor in this vegetable-laden chili comes from toasted spices and the chipotle chile pepper, which is a smoked jalapeño. (Recipe pictured on the cover.)

CHAMPION CHILI WITH THE WORKS

2	teaspoons chili powder
1	teaspoon ground cumin
½	teaspoon salt
¼	teaspoon dried oregano, crushed
2	tablespoons olive oil
½	cup chopped onion
6	cloves garlic, minced
1	pound butternut squash, peeled, seeded, and cut into ¾-inch chunks
1½	cups sliced carrots
¾	cup chopped green sweet pepper
1	cup frozen whole kernel corn
2	15-ounce cans black beans, red kidney beans, and/or pinto beans, rinsed and drained
1	28-ounce can diced tomatoes, undrained
1	12-ounce can beer or nonalcoholic beer
1	canned chipotle chile pepper in adobo sauce, finely chopped
¼	teaspoon black pepper
1	cup chopped zucchini

PREP:
45 minutes
COOK:
35 minutes
MAKES:
6 to 8 servings

1 In a small nonstick skillet toast chili powder, cumin, salt, and oregano over medium heat about 2 minutes or until spices are fragrant, shaking skillet occasionally. Set aside.

2 In a 4-quart Dutch oven heat oil. Add onion and garlic; cook and stir over medium-high heat about 4 minutes or until onion is tender. Stir in squash, carrots, sweet pepper, and corn. Stir in the toasted spice mixture, beans, undrained tomatoes, beer, chipotle pepper, and black pepper. Bring to boiling; reduce heat. Simmer, covered, for 30 minutes.

3 Stir in zucchini; simmer, covered, about 5 minutes more or until vegetables are tender.

Nutrition Facts per serving: 268 cal., 6 g total fat (1 g sat. fat), 0 mg chol., 788 mg sodium, 46 g carbo., 11 g fiber, 13 g pro.

Calling all hearty appetites! This satisfying blend of black beans, white kidney beans, jicama, and chile peppers boasts a pronounced south-of-the-border flavor.

BLACK & WHITE BEAN CHILI

START TO FINISH:

35 minutes

MAKES:

4 servings

1   tablespoon cooking oil

½   cup chopped onion

1   clove garlic, minced

1   15-ounce can white kidney (cannellini) beans, rinsed and drained

1   15-ounce can black beans, rinsed and drained

1   14-ounce can chicken broth or 1¾ cups homemade chicken broth

1   cup chopped, peeled jicama or potato

1   4-ounce can diced green chile peppers, undrained

1   teaspoon ground cumin

2   tablespoons snipped fresh cilantro

1   tablespoon lime juice

¼   cup crumbled queso fresco or feta cheese (1 ounce)

1 In a large saucepan heat oil. Add onion and garlic; cook and stir over medium-high heat about 4 minutes or until onion is tender. Stir in beans, broth, jicama, chile peppers, and cumin. Bring to boiling; reduce heat. Simmer, covered, about 10 minutes or until jicama is crisp-tender or potato is tender.

2 Stir in snipped cilantro and lime juice; heat through. Top each serving with cheese.

Nutrition Facts per serving: 254 cal., 9 g total fat (3 g sat. fat), 15 mg chol., 1,012 mg sodium, 37 g carbo., 10 g fiber, 19 g pro.

STEWS & RAGOÛTS

5

Pork stew meat and boneless lamb are equally good in this colorful stew. If you use pork, simmer it only about 30 minutes in Step 1.

OLD-FASHIONED BEEF STEW

PREP:

20 minutes

COOK:

1¹/₂ hours

MAKES:

5 servings

2	tablespoons all-purpose flour
12	ounces beef stew meat, cut into ³/₄-inch cubes
2	tablespoons cooking oil
3	cups vegetable juice
1	cup water
1	medium onion, cut into thin wedges
1	tablespoon Worcestershire sauce
1¹/₂	teaspoons instant beef bouillon granules
1	teaspoon dried oregano, crushed
¹/₂	teaspoon dried marjoram, crushed
¹/₄	teaspoon black pepper
1	bay leaf
3	cups cubed potatoes
1¹/₂	cups frozen cut green beans
1	cup frozen whole kernel corn
1	cup sliced carrots

1 Place flour in a self-sealing plastic bag. Add beef cubes, a few at a time, shaking to coat. In a large saucepan heat oil. Add beef cubes; cook and stir over medium heat until beef is brown. Drain off fat. Stir in vegetable juice, water, onion, Worcestershire sauce, bouillon granules, oregano, marjoram, pepper, and bay leaf. Bring to boiling; reduce heat. Simmer, covered, for 1 to 1¹/₄ hours or until beef is nearly tender.

2 Stir in potatoes, green beans, corn, and carrots. Return to boiling; reduce heat. Simmer, covered, about 30 minutes more or until beef and vegetables are tender. Remove and discard bay leaf.

Nutrition Facts per serving: 331 cal., 13 g total fat (4 g sat. fat), 43 mg chol., 744 mg sodium, 36 g carbo., 6 g fiber, 18 g pro.

Before serving, cut up any large vegetable chunks.

EASY OVEN STEW

1	pound beef stew meat, cut into 1-inch cubes
¼	teaspoon salt
¼	teaspoon black pepper
1	16-ounce package frozen stew vegetables
1	4½-ounce jar whole mushrooms, drained
1	10¾-ounce can condensed cream of celery soup
1	10¾-ounce can condensed beefy mushroom or cream of mushroom soup
1¼	cups water
¼	cup dry sherry (optional)

1 Place beef in a 4-quart Dutch oven. Sprinkle with salt and pepper. Stir in stew vegetables and mushrooms. In a medium bowl combine cream of celery soup, beefy mushroom soup, water, and, if desired, sherry. Stir into Dutch oven.

2 Bake, covered, in a 350° oven for 2 to 2½ hours or until beef and vegetables are tender.

Nutrition Facts per serving: 199 cal., 6 g total fat (2 g sat. fat), 53 mg chol., 1,053 mg sodium, 15 g carbo., 2 g fiber, 20 g pro.

PREP:
15 minutes
BAKE:
2 hours
OVEN:
350°F
MAKES:
6 servings

Green salsa, hominy, green chile peppers, and cilantro lend a south-of-the-border accent to this beef stew. For an extra kick, use medium-hot green salsa instead of mild.

GREEN CHILE STEW

PREP:

15 minutes

COOK:

1³/₄ hours

MAKES:

8 servings

¼ cup all-purpose flour

2 pounds beef stew meat

¼ cup butter or margarine

6 cloves garlic, minced

3 cups beef broth

1 12-ounce bottle dark beer or ale

1 cup bottled mild or medium-hot green salsa

2 tablespoons snipped fresh oregano or 2 teaspoons dried oregano, crushed

1 teaspoon ground cumin

2 cups cubed potatoes

1 14½-ounce can hominy, drained

2 4-ounce cans diced green chile peppers

12 green onions, bias-sliced into 1-inch pieces

½ cup snipped fresh cilantro

1 Place flour in a self-sealing plastic bag. Add beef cubes, a few at a time, shaking to coat. In a 4½-quart Dutch oven melt butter over medium heat. Add beef cubes, half at a time, to hot butter; cook and stir until brown. Remove beef, reserving drippings in Dutch oven. Add garlic; cook and stir in reserved drippings for 1 minute.

2 Return beef to Dutch oven along with broth, beer, salsa, oregano, and cumin. Bring to boiling; reduce heat. Simmer, covered, about 1¼ hours or until beef is nearly tender. Add potatoes. Simmer, covered, about 30 minutes more or until beef and potatoes are tender. Stir in hominy, chile peppers, green onions, and cilantro; heat through.

Nutrition Facts per serving: 392 cal., 16 g total fat (4 g sat. fat), 82 mg chol., 720 mg sodium, 28 g carbo., 1 g fiber, 32 g pro.

A carbonnade is a thick Belgian stew made with beef, beer, onions, and brown sugar. It's known for its rich, meaty flavor. Carrots and parsnips provide extra sweetness and a bit of color.

CARBONNADE OF BEEF & VEGETABLES

4	slices bacon
2	pounds boneless beef top round steak, cut into 1-inch cubes
3	large leeks or medium onions, sliced
2	12-ounce bottles dark beer or ale
1/4	cup red wine vinegar
3	tablespoons brown sugar
2	tablespoons instant beef bouillon granules
2	teaspoons dried thyme, crushed
1/2	teaspoon black pepper
4	cloves garlic, minced
1 1/2	pounds carrots and/or parsnips, bias-sliced into 1/2-inch pieces
1/4	cup water
1/4	cup all-purpose flour
	Hot cooked wide noodles (optional)
	Fresh thyme sprigs (optional)

PREP:
15 minutes
COOK:
1 1/4 hours
MAKES:
8 servings

1 In a 4-quart Dutch oven cook bacon over medium heat until crisp. Remove bacon, reserving drippings in Dutch oven. Drain bacon on paper towels. Crumble bacon; set aside.

2 Brown beef cubes, half at a time, in reserved bacon drippings. Drain off fat. Return all beef to Dutch oven. Add leeks, beer, vinegar, brown sugar, bouillon granules, thyme, pepper, and garlic. Bring to boiling; reduce heat. Simmer, covered, for 45 minutes, stirring occasionally. Add carrots. Return to boiling; reduce heat. Simmer, covered, for 30 to 35 minutes more or until beef and vegetables are tender.

3 In a screw-top jar combine water and flour. Cover and shake until smooth. Add flour mixture to Dutch oven. Cook and stir over medium heat until thickened and bubbly. Cook and stir for 1 minute more. Stir in bacon. If desired, serve over noodles and garnish each serving with thyme.

Nutrition Facts per serving: 390 cal., 6 g total fat (2 g sat. fat), 94 mg chol., 813 mg sodium, 42 g carbo., 4 g fiber, 33 g pro.

This robust beef-and-vegetable stew is seasoned with herbs, olives, and capers and served with tender green beans. (Recipe pictured on page 282.)

FRENCH-STYLE BEEF STEW

PREP:

35 minutes

COOK:

1³/₄ hours

MAKES:

4 servings

1	tablespoon olive oil
1	pound boneless beef top round steak, cut into 1-inch cubes
¹/₂	cup chopped onion
1	cup dry white wine
2	cups water
1	teaspoon dried herbes de Provence, crushed
¹/₄	teaspoon salt
¹/₄	teaspoon black pepper
16	fresh packaged peeled baby carrots
8	tiny new potatoes, halved or quartered
8	pearl onions, peeled
1	large tomato, peeled, seeded, and chopped
¹/₄	cup pitted niçoise or kalamata olives
2	tablespoons capers, drained
8	ounces steamed haricots verts or small green beans
1	tablespoon snipped fresh Italian (flat-leaf) parsley

1 In a 4-quart Dutch oven heat oil. Add beef cubes and onion, half at a time, to hot oil; cook and stir over medium heat until beef is brown. Drain off fat. Return all beef mixture to Dutch oven.

2 Add wine to Dutch oven. Cook and stir to loosen any browned bits in bottom of Dutch oven. Add water, herbes de Provence, salt, and pepper. Bring to boiling; reduce heat. Simmer, covered, about 1¹/₄ hours or until beef is nearly tender. Add carrots, potatoes, and pearl onions. Return to boiling; reduce heat. Simmer, covered, about 30 minutes more or until meat and vegetables are tender. Stir in tomato, olives, and capers; heat through.

3 Place haricots verts in shallow soup bowls; top with stew. Sprinkle each serving with parsley.

Nutrition Facts per serving: 377 cal., 10 g total fat (2 g sat. fat), 72 mg chol., 399 mg sodium, 31 g carbo., 5 g fiber, 31 g pro.

This slow-cooking, thick and chunky stew fills the bowl with rib-sticking goodness.

BAKED BEEF-VEGETABLE STEW

2	pounds boneless beef chuck roast, cut into 1-inch cubes
4	medium potatoes, cut into 1-inch pieces
3	medium onions, cut into wedges
3	medium carrots, bias-sliced into ½-inch pieces
8	fresh mushrooms, halved
1	16-ounce package frozen whole kernel corn
1	bay leaf
1	10¾-ounce can condensed tomato soup
1	cup water or dry red wine
¼	cup all-purpose flour
2	teaspoons instant beef bouillon granules
2	teaspoons dried Italian seasoning, crushed
1	teaspoon freshly ground black pepper

PREP:

25 minutes

BAKE:

3 hours

OVEN:

300°F

MAKES:

8 servings

1 In a 6-quart Dutch oven combine beef, potatoes, onions, carrots, mushrooms, corn, and bay leaf. In a medium bowl whisk together soup, water, flour, bouillon granules, Italian seasoning, and pepper; stir into Dutch oven.

2 Bake, covered, in a 300° oven about 3 hours until meat and vegetables are tender. Remove and discard bay leaf.

Nutrition Facts per serving: 318 cal., 6 g total fat (2 g sat. fat), 68 mg chol., 541 mg sodium, 38 g carbo., 4 g fiber, 30 g pro.

Long served at political rallies in the South, burgoo is a dish for which no two recipes seem to be alike. Country cooks use whatever meat, poultry, and vegetables they have on hand in this spicy stew.

KENTUCKY BURGOO

PREP:

40 minutes

COOK:

1 hour 35 minutes

MAKES:

6 to 8 servings

4 cups water

1 14½-ounce can diced tomatoes, undrained

12 ounces boneless beef chuck roast, cut into ¾-inch cubes

2 teaspoons instant chicken bouillon granules

1 pound meaty chicken pieces (breast halves, thighs, and/or drumsticks), skinned

1 10-ounce package frozen succotash

1 10-ounce package frozen cut okra

1 cup cubed, peeled potatoes

1 cup sliced carrots

½ cup chopped onion

2 teaspoons curry powder

1 teaspoon sugar

Salt

Black pepper

1 In a 5- to 6-quart Dutch oven combine water, undrained tomatoes, beef, and bouillon granules. Bring to boiling; reduce heat. Simmer, covered, for 30 minutes. Add chicken pieces. Return to boiling; reduce heat. Simmer, covered, about 45 minutes more or until beef is tender and chicken is no longer pink (170°F for breast halves; 180°F for thighs and drumsticks). Remove chicken pieces from Dutch oven.

2 Stir in succotash, okra, potatoes, carrots, onion, curry powder, and sugar. Return to boiling; reduce heat. Simmer, covered, about 20 minutes or until vegetables are tender.

3 Meanwhile, when chicken is cool enough to handle, remove meat from bones. Discard bones. Cut chicken into bite-size pieces. Return chicken to Dutch oven; heat through. Season to taste with salt and black pepper.

Nutrition Facts per serving: 273 cal., 5 g total fat (1 g sat. fat), 64 mg chol., 585 mg sodium, 30 g carbo., 5 g fiber, 26 g pro.

To peel pearl onions, place them in boiling water for 30 seconds; drain and rinse with cold water. Cut off the root end and squeeze from the other end.

BEEF BOURGUIGNON

1	tablespoon cooking oil
1	pound boneless beef chuck roast, cut into ¾-inch cubes
1½	cups chopped onions
2	cloves garlic, minced
1½	cups Pinot Noir or Burgundy wine
¾	cup beef broth
1	teaspoon dried thyme, crushed
¾	teaspoon dried marjoram, crushed
½	teaspoon salt
¼	teaspoon black pepper
2	bay leaves
3	cups whole fresh mushrooms
4	medium carrots, cut into ¾-inch pieces
1	cup pearl onions, peeled, or frozen small whole onions
2	tablespoons all-purpose flour
2	tablespoons butter or margarine, softened
2	slices bacon, crisp-cooked, drained, and crumbled
3	cups hot cooked noodles

PREP:

30 minutes

COOK:

1¼ hours

MAKES:

6 servings

1 In a 4-quart Dutch oven heat oil. Add beef cubes, chopped onion, and garlic, half at a time, to hot oil; cook and stir over medium heat until beef is brown. Return all beef mixture to Dutch oven.

2 Stir in wine, broth, thyme, marjoram, salt, pepper, and bay leaves. Bring to boiling; reduce heat. Simmer, covered, for 45 minutes. Add mushrooms, carrots, and pearl onions. Return to boiling; reduce heat. Cook, covered, for 25 to 30 minutes more or until beef and vegetables are tender. Discard bay leaves.

3 In a small bowl combine flour and butter; stir until smooth. Stir into Dutch oven. Cook and stir until thickened and bubbly. Cook and stir 1 minute more. Stir in bacon. Serve with noodles.

Nutrition Facts per serving: 395 cal., 14 g total fat (5 g sat. fat), 87 mg chol., 436 mg sodium, 35 g carbo., 4 g fiber, 23 g pro.

*Dried tomatoes and molasses add depth and richness to the flavor of this meat dish.
Baking uncovered for the last hour thickens the sauce to a perfect consistency.*

OVEN-BAKED BEEF RAGÙ

PREP:

30 minutes

BAKE:

2 1/2 hours

OVEN:

350°F

MAKES:

6 servings

2   pounds boneless beef chuck roast, cut into 1-inch cubes

2   medium red onions, cut into thin wedges

4   carrots, cut into 1/2-inch slices

3   cloves garlic, minced

1/4   cup butter or margarine

1/3   cup all-purpose flour

1   14-ounce can beef broth or 1 3/4 cups homemade beef broth

1   cup water

1/2   cup dry red wine

1 1/4   cups dried porcini and/or shiitake mushrooms (1 ounce)

1/2   cup snipped dried tomatoes (not oil-packed)

1/2   cup snipped fresh parsley

1   tablespoon mild-flavored molasses

3/4   teaspoon dried thyme, crushed

1/2   teaspoon caraway seeds, crushed

1/4   teaspoon salt

1/4   teaspoon black pepper

1   bay leaf

1 In a 2 1/2- to 3-quart casserole combine beef cubes, onions, carrots, and garlic; set aside.

2 In a medium saucepan melt butter over medium-low heat. Stir in the flour. Cook and stir for 1 minute. Add broth, water, and wine all at once. Cook and stir until thickened and bubbly. Stir in mushrooms, tomatoes, parsley, molasses, thyme, caraway seeds, salt, pepper, and bay leaf. Pour over beef-vegetable mixture in casserole.

3 Bake, covered, in a 350° oven for 1 1/2 hours. Stir stew. Bake, uncovered, about 1 hour more or until beef and vegetables are tender, stirring occasionally. Remove and discard bay leaf.

Nutrition Facts per serving: 395 cal., 18 g total fat (8 g sat. fat), 118 mg chol., 593 mg sodium, 22 g carbo., 3 g fiber, 34 g pro.

Nothing warms the soul on a snowy winter day like a steaming bowl of this all-time favorite.

WINTER BEEF RAGOÛT

2	tablespoons cooking oil
1	pound boneless beef chuck roast, cut into ¾-inch cubes
2	14-ounce cans beef broth or 3½ cups homemade beef broth
2	teaspoons snipped fresh oregano or ¾ teaspoon dried oregano, crushed
2	teaspoons snipped fresh basil or ¾ teaspoon dried basil, crushed
2	teaspoons Worcestershire sauce
½	teaspoon black pepper
2	cups cubed Yukon gold potatoes or other potatoes
1	cup frozen cut green beans
1	cup sliced carrots
1	cup sliced celery
1	15-ounce can Great Northern beans, rinsed and drained
1	14½-ounce can diced tomatoes, undrained
1	small yellow summer squash or zucchini, sliced
	Fresh dill (optional)

PREP:
30 minutes
COOK:
1½ hours
MAKES:
6 servings

1 In a 4-quart Dutch oven heat oil. Add beef cubes, half at a time, to hot oil; cook and stir over medium heat until brown. Drain off fat. Return all beef to Dutch oven. Add broth, dried oregano and basil (if using), Worcestershire sauce, and pepper. Bring to boiling; reduce heat. Simmer, covered, for 1 hour.

2 Add potatoes, green beans, carrots, and celery. Return to boiling; reduce heat. Simmer, covered, for 20 minutes. Stir in beans, undrained tomatoes, squash, and fresh oregano and basil, if using. Return to boiling; reduce heat. Simmer, covered, about 5 minutes more or just until squash is tender. If desired, garnish each serving with dill.

Nutrition Facts per serving: 307 cal., 7 g total fat (2 g sat. fat), 36 mg chol., 552 mg sodium, 33 g carbo., 6 g fiber, 27 g pro.

Accompany this stick-to-your-ribs meat stew with a loaf of rustic bread and a crisp salad of mixed greens, grapes, and toasted walnuts. (Recipe pictured on page 279.)

BEEF RAGÙ WITH GRAVY

(Recipe pictured on page 279.)

PREP:
45 minutes

COOK:
1 hour 50 minutes

MAKES:
6 to 8 servings

¼ cup all-purpose flour

2 pounds boneless beef chuck roast, cut into 1-inch cubes

3 tablespoons cooking oil

½ cup chopped onion

1 clove garlic, minced

2 bay leaves

2 teaspoons Worcestershire sauce

1 teaspoon sugar

1 teaspoon lemon juice

½ teaspoon paprika

Dash ground allspice

6 tiny new potatoes, halved

6 medium carrots, quartered

1 pound boiling onions, peeled

2 tablespoons cold water

1 tablespoon all-purpose flour

¼ cup dry sherry (optional)

Snipped fresh parsley (optional)

1 Place the ¼ cup flour in a self-sealing plastic bag. Add beef cubes, a few at a time, shaking to coat. In a 4-quart Dutch oven heat oil. Add beef cubes, one-third at a time, to hot oil; cook and stir over medium heat until beef is brown. Drain off fat. Return all beef to Dutch oven. Add chopped onion, garlic, bay leaves, and 4 cups *water*. Stir in Worcestershire sauce, sugar, lemon juice, paprika, allspice, ½ teaspoon *salt*, and ½ teaspoon *black pepper*. Bring to boiling; reduce heat. Simmer, covered, for 1½ to 2 hours or until beef is nearly tender.

2 Add potatoes, carrots, and boiling onions. Return to boiling; reduce heat. Simmer, covered, for 20 to 30 minutes more or until vegetables are tender. Remove and discard bay leaves. Transfer beef and vegetables to a serving dish. Cover and keep warm.

3 For gravy, in a small bowl combine the 2 tablespoons cold water and the 1 tablespoon flour; stir into Dutch oven. Cook and stir until thickened and bubbly. Cook and stir for 1 minute more. If desired, stir in sherry. Pour gravy over beef and vegetables. If desired, sprinkle with parsley.

Nutrition Facts per serving: 320 cal., 8 g total fat (2 g sat. fat), 89 mg chol., 348 mg sodium, 26 g carbo., 4 g fiber, 35 g pro.

You can make the stew ahead of time and reheat it. Be sure to stir frequently while reheating so the cornmeal does not settle.

RED CHILI STEW

PREP:

35 minutes

COOK:

1 hour 40 minutes

MAKES:

6 servings

2	tablespoons cooking oil
2½	pounds boneless beef chuck roast, cut into ¾-inch cubes
½	cup chopped onion
4	cloves garlic, minced
2	15- to 16-ounce cans pinto and/or red kidney beans, rinsed and drained
2	14½-ounce cans diced tomatoes, undrained
1	10½-ounce can condensed beef broth
1	10-ounce can enchilada sauce
½	cup cold water
¼	cup cornmeal or tortilla flour
¼	cup snipped fresh cilantro
1	recipe Fry Bread or flour tortillas (optional)
2	ounces queso blanco or Monterey Jack cheese, shredded

1 In a 5- to 6-quart Dutch oven heat oil. Add beef cubes, onion, and garlic, half at a time, to hot oil; cook and stir over medium heat until brown. Drain off fat. Return all beef mixture to Dutch oven.

2 Stir in beans, undrained tomatoes, broth, and enchilada sauce. Bring to boiling; reduce heat. Simmer, covered, for 1 hour, stirring occasionally. Simmer, uncovered, about 30 minutes more or until beef is tender, stirring occasionally. Stir together cold water and cornmeal; stir into Dutch oven. Cook and stir about 10 minutes more or until thickened. Stir in cilantro.

3 If desired, place Fry Bread in shallow soup bowls; top with stew. Sprinkle each serving with cheese.

Nutrition Facts per serving: 764 cal., 27 g total fat (7 g sat. fat), 123 mg chol., 1,728 mg sodium, 71 g carbo., 9 g fiber, 56 g pro.

FRY BREAD: In a large bowl stir together 1½ cups all-purpose flour, ½ cup cornmeal, 1 teaspoon salt, and ¼ teaspoon baking powder. Use a pastry blender to cut in ¼ cup shortening until mixture is the consistency of small peas. Add ¾ cup water and ⅓ cup snipped fresh cilantro; stir just until dough forms a ball (dough will be slightly sticky). Divide dough into 6 portions. On a floured surface, roll each portion of dough into a 7-inch circle. In a heavy 10-inch skillet heat 1 tablespoon shortening over medium heat. Fry one dough circle at a time for 2 to 3 minutes on each side or until golden brown, turning once. (Add additional shortening as needed.) If fry bread begins to brown too quickly, reduce heat to medium-low.

This inviting stew comes from a region of Switzerland near the border of Italy. Swiss cooking is among the heartiest in Europe—and the use of polenta is traditional.

POLENTA BEEF STEW

PREP:
25 minutes

COOK:
2 hours

MAKES:
8 servings

¼ cup all-purpose flour

1 teaspoon garlic powder

1 teaspoon dried thyme, crushed

1 teaspoon dried basil, crushed

2 pounds boneless beef chuck steak, cut into 1-inch cubes

2 tablespoons olive oil

½ cup chopped onion

1 teaspoon snipped fresh rosemary or ¼ teaspoon dried rosemary, crushed

6 cloves garlic, minced

1 14-ounce can beef broth or 1¾ cups homemade beef broth

1½ cups dry red wine

8 ounces boiling onions, peeled

5 medium carrots, cut into 1-inch pieces

½ cup snipped fresh Italian (flat-leaf) parsley

¼ cup tomato paste

1 recipe Polenta

1 Combine flour, garlic powder, thyme, basil, ½ teaspoon *salt*, and ½ teaspoon *black pepper* in a self-sealing plastic bag. Add beef cubes, a few at a time, shaking to coat. In a 4- to 5-quart Dutch oven heat oil. Add beef cubes, half at a time, to hot oil; cook and stir over medium heat until beef is brown. Drain off fat. Return all beef to Dutch oven. Add onion, dried rosemary (if using), and garlic; cook and stir for 3 to 4 minutes. Stir in broth and wine. Bring to boiling; reduce heat. Simmer, covered, for 1½ hours.

2 Stir in boiling onions and carrots. Bring to boiling; reduce heat. Simmer, covered, about 30 minutes more or until beef and vegetables are tender.

3 Stir in parsley, tomato paste, and the fresh rosemary, if using. Serve with Polenta.

POLENTA: In a large saucepan bring 3 cups milk just to a simmer over medium heat. In a medium bowl combine 1 cup cornmeal, 1 cup water, and 1 teaspoon salt. Stir cornmeal mixture slowly into hot milk. Cook and stir until mixture comes to a boil; reduce heat to low. Cook for 10 to 15 minutes or until mixture is very thick, stirring occasionally. (If mixture is too thick, stir in additional milk.) Stir in 2 tablespoons butter or margarine until melted.

Nutrition Facts per serving: 508 cal., 26 g total fat (10 g sat. fat), 88 mg chol., 736 mg sodium, 32 g carbo., 4 g fiber, 29 g pro.

Fast, delicious, and sure to please, this stew has everything your family wants for a weeknight dinner.

MEATBALL STEW

2 14-ounce cans reduced-sodium beef broth or 3½ cups homemade beef broth

1 14½-ounce can diced tomatoes, undrained

1 cup finely chopped carrots

1 cup sliced celery

1 cup chopped onion

½ cup water

⅓ cup quick-cooking barley

1 teaspoon dried basil, crushed

1 bay leaf

1 16-ounce package frozen cooked meatballs (about 32)

1 In a large saucepan or Dutch oven combine broth, undrained tomatoes, carrots, celery, onion, water, barley, basil, and bay leaf. Bring to boiling, stirring occasionally; reduce heat. Simmer, covered, for 5 minutes.

2 Add frozen meatballs. Return to boiling; reduce heat. Simmer, covered, about 5 minutes more or until meatballs are heated through and barley is tender, stirring once or twice. Remove and discard bay leaf.

Nutrition Facts per serving: 330 cal., 22 g total fat (9 g sat. fat), 30 mg chol., 1,518 mg sodium, 21 g carbo., 5 g fiber, 13 g pro.

START TO FINISH:
30 minutes
MAKES:
6 servings

With a mere five ingredients, you can have an easy, family-pleasing weeknight meal on the table in under 30 minutes.

SPEEDY BEEF STEW

START TO FINISH:

25 minutes

MAKES:

4 servings

1   17-ounce package refrigerated cooked beef pot roast with juices

2   10¾-ounce cans condensed beefy mushroom soup

1   16-ounce package frozen mixed vegetables

4   teaspoons snipped fresh basil or 1½ teaspoons dried basil, crushed

1½   cups milk

① Cut beef into bite-size pieces, if necessary. In a 4-quart Dutch oven combine beef and juices, soup, frozen vegetables, and dried basil, if using. Bring to boiling; reduce heat. Simmer, covered, for 10 minutes. Stir in milk and fresh basil, if using; heat through.

Nutrition Facts per serving: 386 cal., 15 g total fat (7 g sat. fat), 80 mg chol., 1,688 mg sodium, 33 g carbo., 5 g fiber, 33 g pro.

Step aside, sandwiches—here's a tastier way to use leftover roast beef.

HURRY-UP BEEF-VEGETABLE STEW

2   cups water

1   10¾-ounce can condensed golden mushroom soup

1   10¾-ounce can condensed tomato soup

½   cup dry red wine or beef broth

2   cups chopped cooked beef

1   16-ounce package frozen sugar snap stir-fry vegetables
or one 16-ounce package frozen cut broccoli

½   teaspoon dried thyme, crushed

START TO FINISH:

20 minutes

MAKES:

5 servings

1 In a 4-quart Dutch oven combine water, mushroom soup, tomato soup, and wine. Stir in beef, frozen vegetables, and thyme. Cook over medium heat until bubbly, stirring frequently. Continue cooking, uncovered, for 4 to 5 minutes more or until vegetables are crisp-tender, stirring occasionally.

Nutrition Facts per serving: 231 cal., 4 g total fat (1 g sat. fat), 42 mg chol., 906 mg sodium, 21 g carbo., 4 g fiber, 20 g pro.

Browning the lamb adds flavor, seals in juices, and helps develop a rich color.

LAMB & VEGETABLE STEW

PREP:
30 minutes

COOK:
50 minutes

MAKES:
4 or 5 servings

1 tablespoon cooking oil

1 pound lean boneless lamb, cut into ¾-inch cubes

1 14-ounce can beef broth or 1¾ cups homemade beef broth

1 cup dry red wine or beef broth

1 tablespoon snipped fresh thyme or 1 teaspoon dried thyme, crushed

2 cloves garlic, minced

1 bay leaf

2 cups cubed, peeled butternut squash

1 cup parsnips cut into ½-inch slices

1 cup chopped, peeled sweet potatoes

1 cup sliced celery

1 medium onion, cut into thin wedges

½ cup plain low-fat yogurt or dairy sour cream

3 tablespoons all-purpose flour

Salt

Black pepper

1 In a large saucepan heat oil. Add lamb cubes, half at a time, to hot oil; cook and stir over medium heat until lamb is brown. Drain off fat. Return all lamb to saucepan. Stir in broth, wine, dried thyme (if using), garlic, and bay leaf. Bring to boiling; reduce heat. Simmer, covered, for 20 minutes.

2 Stir in squash, parsnips, sweet potatoes, celery, and onion. Return to boiling; reduce heat. Simmer, covered, about 30 minutes more or until lamb and vegetables are tender. Remove and discard bay leaf.

3 In a small bowl combine fresh thyme (if using), yogurt, and flour. Stir ½ cup of the hot liquid into the yogurt mixture. Add yogurt mixture to saucepan. Cook and stir until thickened and bubbly. Cook and stir for 1 minute more. Season to taste with salt and pepper.

Nutrition Facts per serving: 365 cal., 9 g total fat (2 g sat. fat), 75 mg chol., 397 mg sodium, 32 g carbo., 4 g fiber, 30 g pro.

Classic French cassoulet is a garlic-flavored bean stew that features various meats, depending on the version.

LAMB CASSOULET

2	cups dry navy beans
12	cups water
1	tablespoon cooking oil
1	pound lean boneless lamb, cut into 1-inch cubes
1	cup chopped carrots
½	cup chopped green sweet pepper
½	cup chopped onion
1	tablespoon instant beef bouillon granules
1	tablespoon Worcestershire sauce
2	teaspoons snipped fresh thyme or 1 teaspoon dried thyme, crushed
3	cloves garlic, minced
2	bay leaves
8	ounces skinless, boneless chicken thighs, cut into 1-inch pieces
1	14½-ounce can diced tomatoes, undrained
½	teaspoon salt

PREP:
1½ hours
COOK:
1½ hours
MAKES:
8 servings

1 Rinse beans. In a 4-quart Dutch oven combine beans and 8 cups of the water. Bring to boiling; reduce heat. Simmer for 2 minutes. Remove from heat. Cover and let stand for 1 hour. (Or place beans in water in Dutch oven. Cover and let stand in a cool place for 6 to 8 hours or overnight.) Drain and rinse beans. Return beans to Dutch oven.

2 Meanwhile, in a large skillet heat oil. Add lamb cubes, half at a time, to hot oil; cook and stir over medium heat until lamb is brown. Drain off fat. Add lamb, carrots, sweet pepper, onion, bouillon granules, Worcestershire sauce, dried thyme (if using), garlic, and bay leaves to Dutch oven. Add the remaining 4 cups water. Bring to boiling; reduce heat. Simmer, covered, for 1 to 1½ hours or until beans are tender.

3 Stir in chicken, undrained tomatoes, salt, and fresh thyme, if using. Return to boiling; reduce heat. Simmer, covered, for 30 minutes more. Remove and discard bay leaves. Skim off fat.

Nutrition Facts per serving: 313 cal., 6 g total fat (1 g sat. fat), 60 mg chol., 693 mg sodium, 37 g carbo., 14 g fiber, 29 g pro.

This full-flavored stew, based on the classic French dish, is perfect for casual entertaining. Its slow simmering allows the cook plenty of time to relax and converse with guests.

CASSOULET-STYLE STEW

PREP:

2 hours

COOK:

1³/₄ hours

MAKES:

6 servings

8	ounces dry navy beans
1	tablespoon olive oil or cooking oil
1	to 1¹/₂ pounds meaty lamb shanks
1	cup chopped celery
1	cup coarsely chopped, peeled potato
¹/₂	cup coarsely chopped carrot
¹/₂	cup coarsely chopped, peeled parsnip
2	cloves garlic, minced
1¹/₂	cups sliced fresh mushrooms
²/₃	cup dry black-eyed peas, rinsed and drained
¹/₄	cup dry red wine or beef broth
1¹/₄	teaspoons salt
1	tablespoon snipped fresh thyme or 1 teaspoon dried thyme, crushed
2	teaspoons snipped fresh rosemary or ¹/₂ teaspoon dried rosemary, crushed
¹/₄	teaspoon black pepper
1	14¹/₂-ounce can diced tomatoes, undrained
	Fresh rosemary or thyme sprigs (optional)

1 Rinse beans. In a large Dutch oven combine beans and 3 cups *water*. Bring to boiling; reduce heat. Simmer, uncovered, for 2 minutes. Remove from heat. Cover and let stand for 1 hour. (Or place beans in water in a Dutch oven. Cover and let stand in a cool place for 6 to 8 hours or overnight.) Drain and rinse beans.

2 In a 4- to 5-quart Dutch oven heat oil. Add lamb shanks; cook over medium-high heat until brown. Add celery, potato, carrot, parsnip, and garlic; cook and stir for 5 minutes. Return beans to Dutch oven along with mushrooms, black-eyed peas, wine, salt, dried thyme and dried rosemary (if using), pepper, and 3¹/₂ cups *water*. Bring to boiling; reduce heat. Simmer, covered, about 1¹/₂ hours or until the beans and peas are tender.

3 Remove lamb shanks from Dutch oven. When cool enough to handle, remove meat from bones. Discard bones. Chop meat. Return meat to Dutch oven along with undrained tomatoes and fresh thyme and fresh rosemary (if using). Return to boiling; reduce heat. Simmer, covered, for 15 minutes more. If desired, garnish each serving with rosemary.

Nutrition Facts per serving: 310 cal., 8 g total fat (2 g sat. fat), 35 mg chol., 654 mg sodium, 39 g carbo., 12 g fiber, 20 g pro.

Lamb lovers will savor every bite of this flavorful, chunky stew. (Recipe pictured on page 281.)

LUCK O' THE IRISH STEW

1	pound lean boneless lamb, cut into ¾-inch cubes
4	cups beef broth
2	medium onions, cut into wedges
¼	teaspoon black pepper
1	bay leaf
4	medium potatoes, peeled and quartered
6	medium carrots, cut into ½-inch slices
½	teaspoon dried thyme, crushed
¼	teaspoon dried basil, crushed
½	cup cold water
¼	cup all-purpose flour
	Salt
	Black pepper
	Fresh thyme sprigs (optional)

PREP:
30 minutes
COOK:
1¼ hours
MAKES:
6 servings

1 In a large saucepan combine lamb, broth, onions, the ¼ teaspoon pepper, and bay leaf. Bring to boiling; reduce heat. Simmer, covered, for 45 minutes. Skim off fat.

2 Add potatoes, carrots, thyme, and basil. Bring to boiling; reduce heat. Simmer, covered, for 30 to 35 minutes more or until vegetables are tender. Remove and discard bay leaf.

3 In a small bowl combine cold water and flour; stir into saucepan. Cook and stir until thickened and bubbly. Cook and stir for 1 minute more. Season to taste with salt and additional pepper. If desired, garnish each serving with thyme.

Nutrition Facts per serving: 230 cal., 3 g total fat (1 g sat. fat), 48 mg chol., 649 mg sodium, 30 g carbo., 4 g fiber, 20 g pro.

Gremolata, a combination of parsley, lemon peel, and garlic, is not just another pretty garnish. It adds a fresh, bright accent to meat dishes that otherwise might seem dull.

VEAL STEW WITH GREMOLATA

PREP:

30 minutes

COOK:

1 hour

MAKES:

4 servings

3   tablespoons all-purpose flour

1   pound boneless veal or pork sirloin, cut into 1-inch cubes

2   tablespoons olive oil

½   cup dry white wine

1   large onion, cut into wedges

2   cloves garlic, minced

1   14½-ounce can diced tomatoes, undrained

1   14-ounce can beef broth or 1¾ cups homemade beef broth

1   cup sliced carrots

1   cup chopped celery

¼   teaspoon dried thyme, crushed

1   bay leaf

1   strip (4×1-inch) lemon peel*

1   recipe Gremolata

1   cup dried orzo, cooked and drained

Lemon peel strips (optional)

1 Combine flour, ½ teaspoon *black pepper*, and ¼ teaspoon *salt* in a self-sealing plastic bag. Add veal cubes, a few at a time, shaking to coat. In a large saucepan or Dutch oven heat 1 tablespoon of the oil. Add veal cubes; cook and stir until brown. Drain off fat. Transfer veal from saucepan to a medium bowl. Add wine to saucepan. Cook and stir to loosen any browned bits in bottom of saucepan. Add wine mixture to veal in bowl.

2 Add the remaining 1 tablespoon oil to saucepan. Add onion; cook and stir over medium heat for 4 minutes. Add garlic; cook and stir for 1 minute more. Return veal mixture to saucepan along with undrained tomatoes, broth, carrots, celery, thyme, bay leaf, and lemon peel. Bring to boiling; reduce heat. Simmer, covered, about 1 hour or until veal is tender.

3 If desired, cook, uncovered, for 5 to 10 minutes more or until stew thickens slightly. Remove and discard bay leaf and lemon peel. Serve stew with Gremolata and orzo. If desired, garnish each serving with additional lemon peel.

GREMOLATA: In a small bowl stir together ¼ cup snipped fresh Italian (flat-leaf) parsley, 2 teaspoons finely shredded lemon peel and 4 cloves garlic, minced.

*NOTE: Use a vegetable peeler to peel the strip of lemon peel. A peeler will give you a good-size piece of peel, but leave the bitter white pith behind.

Nutrition Facts per serving: 491 cal., 14 g total fat (3 g sat. fat), 71 mg chol., 748 mg sodium, 51 g carbo., 4 g fiber, 33 g pro.

Until recently, yucca (cassava) and plantains were found only in Hispanic produce markets and American border towns. With the exploding interest in foods of Central and South America, however, these wonderful starches are in practically every well-stocked supermarket.

JAMAICAN PORK STEW

1	small yucca (about 12 ounces), peeled
2	tablespoons olive oil
1½	pounds boneless pork sirloin, cut into 1-inch cubes
1	plantain, peeled and cut into ¾-inch slices
1	large onion, sliced
1	to 1½ teaspoons Jamaican jerk seasoning
½	teaspoon salt
3	cloves garlic, minced
1	cup chicken broth
2	large sweet potatoes, peeled and cut into ½- to 1-inch cubes
½	cup dried apricots, halved
	Salt
	Black pepper

PREP:

40 minutes

COOK:

50 minutes

MAKES:

6 servings

1 Halve yucca lengthwise; discard fibrous center. Cut yucca into 1-inch pieces; set aside.

2 In a 4-quart Dutch oven heat oil. Add pork cubes, plantain, and onion, half at a time, to hot oil; cook and stir over medium heat until brown. Return all pork mixture to Dutch oven. Add jerk seasoning, the ½ teaspoon salt, and garlic; cook and stir for 30 seconds. Add broth. Bring to boiling; reduce heat. Simmer, covered, for 30 minutes.

3 Add yucca, sweet potatoes, and apricots. Return to boiling; reduce heat. Simmer, covered, for 20 to 30 minutes more or until pork and vegetables are tender. Season to taste with additional salt and pepper.

Nutrition Facts per serving: 480 cal., 11 g total fat (3 g sat. fat), 62 mg chol., 566 mg sodium, 65 g carbo., 6 g fiber, 31 g pro.

The flavor of a plantain will depend on the ripeness. A ripe, black-skinned plantain tastes like a banana. An almost-ripe, yellow plantain tastes similar to sweet potatoes. Unripe, green plantains taste starchy but lose the starchy flavor upon cooking.

CARIBBEAN-STYLE PORK STEW

START TO FINISH:

30 minutes

MAKES:

6 servings

1   15-ounce can black beans, rinsed and drained

1   14-ounce can beef broth or 1¾ cups homemade beef broth

1¾   cups water

12   ounces cooked lean boneless pork, cut into thin bite-size strips

3   plantains, peeled and cubed

1   cup chopped tomatoes

½   of a 16-ounce package (2 cups) frozen pepper stir-fry vegetables

1   tablespoon grated fresh ginger

1   teaspoon ground cumin

¼   teaspoon crushed red pepper

¼   teaspoon salt

3   cups hot cooked rice

     Crushed red pepper (optional)

     Fresh pineapple slices (optional)

1 In a 4-quart Dutch oven combine beans, broth, and water; bring to boiling. Add pork, plantains, and tomatoes. Stir in frozen vegetables, ginger, cumin, the ¼ teaspoon crushed red pepper, and salt. Return to boiling; reduce heat. Simmer, covered, about 10 minutes or until plantains are tender.

2 Serve with rice. If desired, sprinkle each serving with additional crushed red pepper and garnish with pineapple.

Nutrition Facts per serving: 367 cal., 5 g total fat (1 g sat. fat), 32 mg chol., 555 mg sodium, 64 g carbo., 7 g fiber, 22 g pro.

CHILIES

Kickin' Hot Chili

page 217

CHILIES

Bean Medley Chili

page 238

**Italian
Three-Bean Chili**

page 244

CHILIES

**Texas Bowls
O' Red Chili**

page 223

**Chili con
Portobello**

pages 246

CHILIES

Cincinnati Chili

page 220

Chunky Chipotle
Pork Chili

page 228

STEWS & RAGOÛTS

**Harvest
Vegetable Stew**

page 317

STEWS & RAGOÛTS

Caribbean Chicken
Stew

page 298

Moroccan Stew

page 290

STEWS & RAGOÛTS

**Beef Ragù
with Gravy**

page 260

STEWS & RAGOÛTS

Cioppino with
Chile Peppers

page 310

Spanish
Chicken Stew

Page 299

STEWS & RAGOÛTS

Luck O' the Irish
Stew

Page 269

STEWS & RAGOÛTS

Three-Bean Ragoût

page 304

French-Style
Beef Stew

page 254

STEWS & RAGOÛTS

Pork & Ale Ragoût

page 289

Savory Baked Vegetable Stew

page 320

SLOW COOKER FAVORITES

Lamb & Lentil Soup

page 341

**Sausage &
Tortellini Soup**

page 360

SLOW COOKER FAVORITES

Confetti White Chili

page 366

**New Mexico
Beef Stew**

page 332

SLOW COOKER FAVORITES

Fireside Beef Stew

page 334

Split Pea & Smoked Turkey Soup

page 361

SALADS & BREADS

Fruit Cups with Strawberry Dressing

page 385

SALADS & BREADS

Cornmeal Skillet Rolls

page 398

Tomato-Cheese Breadsticks

page 392

This robust pork stew takes on an autumn orange from the russet-colored sweet potatoes. It celebrates the season with assorted root vegetables, tomatoes, and apples simmered with melt-in-your-mouth pork sirloin. (Recipe pictured on page 283.)

PORK & ALE RAGOÛT

2	tablespoons all-purpose flour
½	teaspoon crushed red pepper
1	pound boneless pork sirloin, cut into ¾-inch cubes
1	tablespoon cooking oil
2	cloves garlic, minced
3	cups vegetable broth
1	12-ounce can beer or 1½ cups vegetable broth
3	medium parsnips, peeled and cut into ¾-inch slices
2	large sweet potatoes, peeled and cut into 1-inch cubes
1	medium onion, cut into thin wedges
2	tablespoons snipped fresh thyme or 1½ teaspoons dried thyme, crushed
1	tablespoon brown sugar
1	tablespoon Dijon-style mustard
4	large tomatoes, coarsely chopped
2	small green apples, cored and cut into wedges

PREP:
25 minutes
COOK:
35 minutes
MAKES:
6 servings

1 Combine flour and crushed red pepper in a self-sealing plastic bag. Add pork cubes, a few at a time, shaking to coat.

2 In a 4-quart Dutch oven heat oil. Add pork cubes and garlic, half at a time, to hot oil; cook and stir over medium heat until pork is brown. Add broth, beer, parsnips, sweet potatoes, onion, thyme, brown sugar, and Dijon-style mustard. Bring to boiling; reduce heat. Simmer, covered, for 30 minutes.

3 Stir in tomatoes and apples. Return to boiling; reduce heat. Simmer, covered, about 5 minutes more or until pork, vegetables, and apples are tender.

Nutrition Facts per serving: 288 cal., 7 g total fat (2 g sat. fat), 48 mg chol., 571 mg sodium, 36 g carbo., 6 g fiber, 20 g pro.

As this stew bakes, the exotic aromas of a North African spice market will fill your kitchen. (Recipe pictured on page 278.)

MOROCCAN STEW

PREP:

40 minutes

BAKE:

1 hour 20 minutes

OVEN:

325°F

MAKES:

6 servings

3	tablespoons all-purpose flour
1	teaspoon ground cumin
2	pounds boneless pork shoulder roast, cut into ¾-inch cubes
2	tablespoons cooking oil
½	cup chopped onion
2	14½-ounce cans diced tomatoes, undrained
2	cups chopped red potatoes
2	cups frozen cut green beans
1½	cups frozen baby lima beans
1	cup sliced carrots
¾	cup chopped, peeled sweet potato
⅓	cup water
1	teaspoon salt
1	teaspoon ground ginger
1	teaspoon ground cinnamon
½	teaspoon sugar
½	teaspoon black pepper
2	tablespoons snipped fresh cilantro or parsley
½	cup plain yogurt
	Pita bread (optional)

1 Combine flour and cumin in a self-sealing plastic bag. Add pork cubes, a few at a time, shaking to coat. In a 4- to 5-quart Dutch oven heat oil. Add pork cubes and onion, half at a time, to hot oil; cook and stir over medium heat until pork is brown. Drain off fat. Return all pork mixture to Dutch oven.

2 Stir in undrained tomatoes, red potatoes, green beans, lima beans, carrots, sweet potato, water, salt, ginger, cinnamon, sugar, and pepper. Bring just to boiling. Remove from heat.

3 Bake, covered, in a 325° oven about 1 hour and 20 minutes or until meat and vegetables are tender. Sprinkle each serving with cilantro and top with yogurt. If desired, serve with pita bread.

Nutrition Facts per serving: 445 cal., 14 g total fat (4 g sat. fat), 99 mg chol., 792 mg sodium, 40 g carbo., 7 g fiber, 38 g pro.

This version of the classic Cajun stew contains shrimp, andouille sausage, and ham.

JAMBALAYA

1	pound fresh or frozen peeled and deveined shrimp
2	tablespoons cooking oil
1/2	cup chopped onion
1/3	cup chopped celery
1/4	cup chopped green sweet pepper
2	cloves garlic, minced
2	cups chicken broth
1	14 1/2-ounce can diced tomatoes, undrained
8	ounces andouille or kielbasa sausage, halved lengthwise and cut into 1/2-inch slices
3/4	cup uncooked long grain rice
1	teaspoon dried thyme, crushed
1/2	teaspoon dried basil, crushed
1/4	teaspoon black pepper
1/4	teaspoon cayenne pepper
1	bay leaf
1	cup cubed cooked ham

PREP:
25 minutes
COOK:
20 minutes
MAKES:
6 servings

1 Thaw shrimp, if frozen. Rinse shrimp; set aside.

2 In a 12-inch skillet heat oil. Add onion, celery, sweet pepper, and garlic; cook and stir over medium heat for 5 minutes. Stir in broth, undrained tomatoes, sausage, rice, thyme, basil, black pepper, cayenne pepper, and bay leaf. Bring to boiling; reduce heat. Simmer, covered, for 15 minutes.

3 Stir in shrimp. Return to boiling. Simmer, covered, about 5 minutes more or until shrimp turn opaque and rice is tender. Stir in ham; heat through. Remove and discard bay leaf.

Nutrition Facts per serving: 416 cal., 20 g total fat (6 g sat. fat), 154 mg chol., 1,199 mg sodium, 27 g carbo., 1 g fiber, 30 g pro.

This thick stew is a simplified version of the traditional Brazilian dish feijoada (fay-ZHWAH-duh). The flavor is as rich as its color.

BRAZILIAN PORK & BLACK BEAN STEW

PREP:

1²/₃ hours

COOK:

2 hours 40 minutes

MAKES:

10 servings

1	pound dry black beans
12	cups water
3	tablespoons cooking oil
2	pounds boneless pork shoulder roast, cut into 1½-inch cubes
1½	pounds meaty smoked pork hocks
2	cups chopped onions
6	cloves garlic, minced
1	teaspoon cayenne pepper
1	14½-ounce can diced tomatoes, undrained
8	ounces cooked garlic sausage or kielbasa, cut into ½-inch slices
½	cup snipped fresh parsley
½	teaspoon salt
5	cups hot cooked rice
	Hot cooked collard greens
2	oranges, cut into wedges

1 Rinse beans. In a 4-quart Dutch oven combine beans and 8 cups of the water. Bring to boiling; reduce heat. Simmer for 2 minutes. Remove from heat. Cover and let stand for 1 hour. (Or place beans in water in Dutch oven. Cover and let stand in a cool place for 6 to 8 hours or overnight.) Drain and rinse beans.

2 In the same Dutch oven heat 2 tablespoons of the oil. Add pork cubes, half at a time, to hot oil; cook and stir over medium heat until brown. Drain off fat. Return all pork cubes to Dutch oven. Add beans, pork hocks, and the remaining 4 cups water. Bring to boiling; reduce heat. Simmer, covered, for 2 hours. Remove pork hocks from Dutch oven. When cool enough to handle, remove meat from bones. Discard bones. Shred meat. Return meat to Dutch oven.

3 Meanwhile, in a large skillet heat the remaining 1 tablespoon oil. Add onions; cook and stir over medium-high heat for 5 minutes. Add garlic and cayenne pepper; cook and stir for 30 seconds. Add undrained tomatoes. Cook for 10 minutes more, stirring occasionally. Add tomato mixture, sausage, parsley, and salt to Dutch oven. Simmer, uncovered, for 30 minutes. Serve with rice and greens. Pass orange wedges to squeeze over stew.

Nutrition Facts per serving: 726 cal., 33 g total fat (11 g sat. fat), 110 mg chol., 1,017 mg sodium, 64 g carbo., 10 g fiber, 43 g pro.

This savory combination could be described as a posole (poh-SOH-leh)—a thick, hearty Mexican soup traditionally served as a main course at Christmas. Sprinkle shredded radishes on top for a festive presentation.

PORK & HOMINY STEW

12	ounces lean boneless pork
1	tablespoon cooking oil
1	cup chopped onion
2	cloves garlic, minced
4	cups chicken broth
1	cup thinly sliced carrots
¼	teaspoon ground cumin
¼	teaspoon crushed red pepper
1	14½-ounce can hominy, drained
3	tablespoons snipped fresh cilantro
¼	cup shredded radishes

START TO FINISH:

30 minutes

MAKES:

4 servings

1 If desired, partially freeze pork for easier slicing. Thinly slice pork across the grain into bite-size strips.

2 In a large saucepan heat oil. Add pork strips, onion, and garlic; cook and stir over medium heat until brown. Remove pork mixture from saucepan; set aside.

3 Add broth, carrots, cumin, and crushed red pepper to saucepan. Bring to boiling; reduce heat. Simmer, covered, about 8 minutes or until carrots are just tender. Return pork mixture to saucepan along with hominy and cilantro; heat through. Top each serving with radishes.

Nutrition Facts per serving: 281 cal., 10 g total fat (2 g sat. fat), 49 mg chol., 1,262 mg sodium, 24 g carbo., 4 g fiber, 23 g pro.

This fiery stew contains two different fresh chile peppers—mild poblanos and hot jalapeños. If the heat is too much, remove the seeds from the jalapeños.

PORK & CHILE PEPPER STEW

PREP:

35 minutes

BAKE:

1¹/₂ hours

OVEN:

425°F/325°F

MAKES:

8 servings

4	fresh poblano chile peppers* or 2 green sweet peppers
1¹/₂	pounds boneless pork shoulder roast, cut into bite-size pieces
3	cups chopped onions
¹/₄	cup finely chopped fresh jalapeño chile peppers*
1	teaspoon salt
¹/₂	teaspoon dried oregano, crushed
6	cloves garlic, minced
1¹/₂	pounds red potatoes, cut into 1-inch pieces
3	medium zucchini, halved lengthwise and cut into ¹/₂-inch slices
1	10-ounce package frozen whole kernel corn, thawed
¹/₂	cup snipped fresh cilantro
	Lime wedges (optional)

1 To roast poblano peppers, halve peppers lengthwise; remove stems, membranes, and seeds. Place peppers, cut sides down, on a foil-lined baking sheet. Bake in a 425° oven for 20 to 25 minutes or until tender. Bring foil up and around pepper halves. Let stand until cool enough to handle. Use a sharp knife to pull the skin off gently and slowly. Discard skin. Coarsely chop peppers.

2 In a 5- to 6-quart Dutch oven combine roasted poblano peppers, pork, onions, jalapeño peppers, salt, oregano, and garlic. Bake, covered, in a 325° oven for 45 minutes.

3 Stir in potatoes. Bake, covered, for 30 minutes more. Stir in zucchini and corn. Bake, covered, about 15 minutes more or until pork and vegetables are tender. Stir in cilantro. If desired, serve with lime wedges.

*NOTE: When working with chile peppers, wear plastic or rubber gloves. If your bare hands do touch the chile peppers, wash your hands well with soap and water.

Nutrition Facts per serving: 269 cal., 6 g total fat (2 g sat. fat), 55 mg chol., 377 mg sodium, 34 g carbo., 5 g fiber, 22 g pro.

Cabbage, tomatoes, onion, and sausage turn this bean soup into a hearty, home-style stew.

ITALIAN SAUSAGE-NAVY BEAN STEW

2⅓	cups dry navy beans
6¾	cups water
1	pound uncooked Italian sausage links, cut into ½-inch slices
1	cup chopped onion
1	clove garlic, minced
2	14-ounce cans beef broth or 3½ cups homemade beef broth
1	teaspoon dried oregano, crushed
2	bay leaves
3	cups chopped cabbage
1	14½-ounce can diced tomatoes, undrained
	Salt
	Black pepper

PREP:
1½ hours
COOK:
1¼ hours
MAKES:
8 servings

1 Rinse beans. In a 4-quart Dutch oven combine beans and 6 cups of the water. Bring to boiling; reduce heat. Simmer for 2 minutes. Remove from heat. Cover and let stand for 1 hour. (Or place beans in water in Dutch oven. Cover and let soak in a cool place for 6 to 8 hours or overnight.) Drain and rinse beans; set aside.

2 In same Dutch oven cook sausage, onion, and garlic over medium-high heat until meat is brown and onion is tender. Drain off fat. Stir in the remaining ¾ cup water, beans, broth, oregano, and bay leaves. Bring to boiling; reduce heat. Simmer, covered, for 1 to 1½ hours or until beans are tender, stirring occasionally. Stir in cabbage and undrained tomatoes. Return to boiling; reduce heat. Simmer, covered, about 15 minutes more or until cabbage is tender. Remove and discard bay leaves. Skim off fat. Season to taste with salt and pepper.

Nutrition Facts per serving: 391 cal., 14 g total fat (6 g sat. fat), 38 mg chol., 840 mg sodium, 41 g carbo., 15 g fiber, 22 g pro.

Rye bread makes a snappy accompaniment to this kid-pleasing stew.

CREAMY HAM & VEGETABLE STEW

START TO FINISH:

35 minutes

MAKES:

4 servings

1½	cups water
2	carrots, cut into 1-inch pieces
1	cup very finely chopped, peeled potato
1	medium onion, cut into chunks
1	cup frozen peas
1	cup cubed cooked ham
1	10¾-ounce can reduced-sodium condensed cream of celery soup
½	of an 8-ounce jar (½ cup) process cheese sauce

1 In a large saucepan combine water, carrots, potato, and onion. Bring to boiling; reduce heat. Simmer, covered, for 10 minutes. Add peas and ham. Return to boiling; reduce heat. Cook, covered, for 5 minutes more. Stir in soup and cheese sauce; heat through.

Nutrition Facts per serving: 260 cal., 11 g total fat (6 g sat. fat), 40 mg chol., 1,269 mg sodium, 27 g carbo., 4 g fiber, 14 g pro.

Originally a concoction of squirrel meat and onions, this stew originated in Brunswick County, Virginia. Through the years, the ingredients have changed, with the squirrel meat often being left out along the way. This more recent version, incorporating chicken, makes a great family meal.

BRUNSWICK STEW

2	pounds meaty chicken pieces (breast halves, thighs, and/or drumsticks), skinned
1½	to 2 pounds meaty smoked pork hocks
3	medium onions, cut into thin wedges
1	14½-ounce can diced tomatoes, undrained
½	cup chicken broth
1	tablespoon Worcestershire sauce
1	teaspoon dry mustard
1	teaspoon dried thyme, crushed
¼	teaspoon black pepper
¼	teaspoon bottled hot pepper sauce
4	cloves garlic, minced
2	cups frozen cut okra
1	cup frozen baby lima beans
1	cup frozen whole kernel corn
¼	cup cold water
2	tablespoons all-purpose flour

PREP:
30 minutes
COOK:
50 minutes
MAKES:
4 or 5 servings

1 In a 4-quart Dutch oven combine chicken pieces, pork hocks, onions, undrained tomatoes, broth, Worcestershire sauce, mustard, thyme, pepper, hot pepper sauce, and garlic. Bring to boiling; reduce heat. Simmer, covered, for 35 to 45 minutes or until chicken is tender and no longer pink (170°F for breast halves; 180°F for thighs and drumsticks). Remove chicken and pork hocks from Dutch oven.

2 Add okra, lima beans, and corn. Return to boiling; reduce heat. Simmer, covered, for 10 to 15 minutes more or just until vegetables are tender.

3 Meanwhile, when cool enough to handle, remove meat from pork hocks. Discard bones. Chop meat. Remove chicken from bones. Discard bones. Cut chicken into bite-size pieces.

4 Combine cold water and flour; stir into Dutch oven. Cook and stir until thickened and bubbly. Cook and stir 1 minute more. Stir in pork and chicken; heat through. If desired, season to taste with *salt* and additional *black pepper.*

Nutrition Facts per serving: 454 cal., 10 g total fat (3 g sat. fat), 109 mg chol., 794 mg sodium, 44 g carbo., 5 g fiber, 48 g pro.

Coconut milk, a staple in Caribbean kitchens, gives this stew a rich, thick body.
(Recipe pictured on page 278.)

CARIBBEAN CHICKEN STEW

PREP:

50 minutes

COOK:

40 minutes

MAKES:

8 servings

1	tablespoon cooking oil
2	medium onions, cut into 1-inch pieces
1	3- to 3½-pound whole broiler-fryer chicken, cut into 8 pieces (wing tips removed)
2	14-ounce cans chicken broth
2½	pounds sweet potatoes, peeled and cut into 1-inch pieces
1	14½-ounce can diced tomatoes, undrained
1	10-ounce package frozen whole kernel corn
½	to 1 teaspoon crushed red pepper
½	teaspoon salt
1	cup purchased unsweetened coconut milk
2	tablespoons grated fresh ginger or 1 teaspoon ground ginger
4	cups hot cooked rice

1 In a 4- to 5-quart Dutch oven heat oil. Add onions; cook and stir over medium heat about 5 minutes or until tender. Add chicken pieces and broth. Bring to boiling; reduce heat. Simmer, covered, for 30 minutes. Remove chicken from Dutch oven.

2 Add sweet potatoes, undrained tomatoes, corn, crushed red pepper, and salt to Dutch oven. Return to boiling; reduce heat. Simmer, covered, for 10 to 15 minutes or until vegetables are tender.

3 Meanwhile, when cool enough to handle, remove chicken from bones. Discard skin and bones. Chop chicken. Skim fat from broth.

4 Using a slotted spoon, remove 1½ cups of the vegetables from the Dutch oven. Remove 1 cup of the broth from Dutch oven. Cool slightly. Transfer vegetables and broth to a blender or food processor. Cover and blend or process until smooth. Return all to Dutch oven. Add chicken, coconut milk, and ginger; heat through. Serve over cooked rice.

Nutrition Facts per serving: 587 cal., 26 g total fat (10 g sat. fat), 86 mg chol., 731 mg sodium, 60 g carbo., 5 g fiber, 28 g pro.

Though olives may not be the first condiment most cooks would think of to season a stew, they give grand flavor to this Spanish-inspired chicken dish. (Recipe pictured on page 280.)

SPANISH CHICKEN STEW

1¼	pounds skinless, boneless chicken thighs, cut into 1½-inch pieces
¼	teaspoon salt
¼	teaspoon black pepper
1	tablespoon olive oil
1	medium onion, thinly sliced
1	red sweet pepper, cut into thin bite-size strips
2	cloves garlic, minced
12	ounces red potatoes, cut into ½-inch wedges
1	cup chicken broth
½	teaspoon dried savory, crushed
¼	teaspoon dried thyme, crushed
1	14½-ounce can diced tomatoes, undrained
⅓	cup small pimiento-stuffed olives, cut up

PREP:
15 minutes
COOK:
20 minutes
MAKES:
4 servings

1 Sprinkle chicken with salt and pepper. In a 4-quart Dutch oven heat oil. Add chicken; cook and stir over medium-high heat until no longer pink.

2 Add onion and sweet pepper; cook and stir about 3 minutes or until crisp-tender. Add garlic; cook and stir for 30 seconds more. Add potatoes, broth, savory, and thyme. Bring to boiling; reduce heat. Simmer, covered, about 15 minutes or until chicken and potatoes are tender. Add undrained tomatoes. Return to boiling; reduce heat. Simmer, covered, for 5 minutes. Stir in olives.

Nutrition Facts per serving: 334 cal., 11 g total fat (2 g sat. fat), 113 mg chol., 918 mg sodium, 24 g carbo., 3 g fiber, 32 g pro.

Serrano chile peppers give this stew a real Southwestern kick. Serranos are classified as very hot, but cool sour cream helps mellow the heat.

TEX-MEX CHICKEN STEW

PREP:

25 minutes

COOK:

20 minutes

MAKES:

4 to 6 servings

2 tablespoons butter or margarine

1 pound skinless, boneless chicken breast halves, cut into bite-size pieces

1 large sweet potato, peeled and sliced

½ cup chopped onion

1 to 2 fresh serrano chile peppers, halved and seeded*

½ teaspoon ground coriander

¼ teaspoon ground cumin

3 cups chicken broth

1 14½-ounce can hominy, drained, or 1 cup frozen whole kernel corn, thawed

Dairy sour cream (optional)

1 In a large saucepan or Dutch oven melt butter. Add chicken, half at a time, to hot butter; cook and stir over medium heat until no longer pink. Remove chicken, reserving drippings in saucepan.

2 Add sweet potato, onion, chile pepper halves, coriander, and cumin to saucepan. Add 1½ cups of the broth. Bring to boiling; reduce heat. Simmer, covered, about 20 minutes or until vegetables are very tender. Cool slightly.

3 Transfer sweet potato mixture to a blender. Cover and blend until smooth. Return to saucepan. Stir in chicken, the remaining 1½ cups broth, and hominy; heat through. If desired, top each serving with sour cream.

*NOTE: When working with chile peppers, wear plastic or rubber gloves. If your bare hands do touch the chile peppers, wash your hands well with soap and water.

Nutrition Facts per serving: 330 cal., 9 g total fat (4 g sat. fat), 84 mg chol., 1,080 mg sodium, 29 g carbo., 5 g fiber, 31 g pro.

Dress up leftover chicken by stirring it into this easy-to-prepare stew. Chunks of yellow squash and sweet pepper accompany plump tortellini and spinach.

CHICKEN STEW WITH TORTELLINI

2	14-ounce cans reduced-sodium chicken broth or 3½ cups homemade chicken broth
1½	cups water
1	medium yellow summer squash, halved lengthwise and cut into ½-inch slices
1	cup sliced carrots
1	cup dried 3-cheese-filled tortellini
¾	cup chopped green sweet pepper
1	medium onion, cut into thin wedges
½	teaspoon salt
¼	teaspoon garlic-pepper seasoning
2½	cups chopped cooked chicken
2	cups torn fresh spinach
2	tablespoons snipped fresh basil
	Fresh Italian (flat-leaf) parsley (optional)

START TO FINISH:
35 minutes

MAKES:
6 servings

1 In a 4-quart Dutch oven bring broth and water to boiling. Add squash, carrots, tortellini, sweet pepper, onion, salt, and garlic-pepper seasoning. Return to boiling; reduce heat. Simmer, covered, about 15 minutes or until tortellini and vegetables are nearly tender.

2 Stir in chicken and spinach. Cook, covered, about 5 minutes more or until tortellini and vegetables are tender. Stir in basil. If desired, garnish each serving with parsley.

Nutrition Facts per serving: 219 cal., 6 g total fat (1 g sat. fat), 52 mg chol., 761 mg sodium, 17 g carbo., 2 g fiber, 23 g pro.

This stew version of shepherd's pie gets a colorful and tasty twist with mashed sweet potatoes instead of regular mashed potatoes and poultry instead of meat.

SWEET POTATO-TOPPED CHICKEN STEW

START TO FINISH:

35 minutes

MAKES:

4 servings

1	17-ounce can sweet potatoes, drained
1	tablespoon butter or margarine, melted
2	tablespoons butter or margarine
$\frac{1}{2}$	cup chopped onion
2	cups chopped cooked chicken
1	$10\frac{3}{4}$-ounce can condensed cream of mushroom soup
1	10-ounce package frozen peas and carrots
$\frac{1}{2}$	teaspoon dried sage, crushed

1 In a medium bowl mash sweet potatoes with an electric mixer on low to medium speed; beat in the 1 tablespoon melted butter. Set aside.

2 In a large skillet melt the 2 tablespoons butter. Add onion; cook and stir over medium heat for 4 minutes. Stir in chicken, soup, peas and carrots, and sage. Cook and stir until bubbly.

3 Drop mashed sweet potatoes into 4 mounds on top of chicken mixture. Simmer, covered, about 10 minutes more or until heated through.

Nutrition Facts per serving: 436 cal., 19 g total fat (9 g sat. fat), 88 mg chol., 815 mg sodium, 41 g carbo., 6 g fiber, 25 g pro.

If broccoli rabe is not available, substitute a small head of escarole, a mildly bitter green. Coarsely chop and add to stew during the last 2 minutes of cooking. Or substitute regular broccoli, cooking it the same amount of time as the broccoli rabe.

TUSCAN RAVIOLI STEW

1	tablespoon olive oil
⅓	cup sliced leek (white part only)
3	cloves garlic, minced
1	14-ounce can beef broth or 1¾ cups homemade beef broth
¾	cup water
¼	teaspoon crushed red pepper (optional)
5	cups coarsely chopped broccoli rabe
1	14½-ounce can no-salt-added stewed tomatoes, undrained
1	9-ounce package refrigerated chicken- or 3-cheese-filled ravioli
1	tablespoon snipped fresh rosemary or 1 teaspoon dried rosemary, crushed
¼	cup grated Asiago cheese

START TO FINISH:

20 minutes

MAKES:

4 servings

1 In a large saucepan heat oil. Add leek and garlic; cook and stir over medium heat for 5 minutes. Add broth, water, and, if desired, crushed red pepper. Bring to boiling.

2 Add broccoli rabe, undrained tomatoes, ravioli, and rosemary. Return to boiling; reduce heat. Simmer, covered, for 7 to 8 minutes or until broccoli rabe and ravioli are tender. Sprinkle each serving with cheese.

Nutrition Facts per serving: 320 cal., 13 g total fat (2 g sat. fat), 65 mg chol., 704 mg sodium, 38 g carbo., 5 g fiber, 15 g pro.

Pale, delicate flageolet beans originated in France. New Mexico red appaloosa beans have large white splotches, resembling the markings of Appaloosa horses. Scarlet runner beans have distinctive red streaks. Look for all three varieties at a health food store. (Recipe pictured on page 282.)

THREE-BEAN RAGOÛT

PREP:

1 1/2 hours

COOK:

1 1/4 hours

MAKES:

4 to 6 servings

1/2 cup dry flageolet beans

1/2 cup dry New Mexico red appaloosa beans

1/2 cup dry scarlet runner beans

9 cups water

2 bay leaves

1 tablespoon butter or margarine

12 ounces fresh chanterelle or shiitake mushrooms, coarsely chopped

1 cup chopped celery

1 cup chopped carrots

1/3 cup chopped onion

2 cups chicken broth

1 cup shredded smoked chicken or turkey

1 tablespoon snipped fresh sage

Salt

Black pepper

Fresh sage sprigs (optional)

1 Rinse beans. In a large saucepan combine beans and 5 cups of the water. Bring to boiling; reduce heat. Simmer for 2 minutes. Remove from heat. Cover and let stand for 1 hour. (Or place beans in water in a large saucepan. Cover and let soak in a cool place for 6 to 8 hours or overnight.) Drain and rinse beans.

2 Return beans to saucepan. Stir in bay leaves and the remaining 4 cups water. Bring to boiling; reduce heat. Simmer, covered, about 1 hour or until beans are tender. Drain beans. Remove and discard bay leaves.

3 Meanwhile, in another large saucepan melt butter over medium heat. Add mushrooms, celery, carrots, and onion; cook and stir for 5 to 7 minutes over until vegetables are tender. Stir in cooked beans, broth, chicken, and snipped sage. Bring to boiling; reduce heat. Simmer, uncovered, for 10 minutes. Season to taste with salt and pepper. If desired, garnish each serving with sage sprigs.

Nutrition Facts per serving: 400 cal., 10 g total fat (3 g sat. fat), 34 mg chol., 735 mg sodium, 55 g carbo., 10 g fiber, 26 g pro.

Most of this country's peanut crop goes into peanut butter and snacks. In Africa, however, peanuts often are stirred into chicken and pork dishes. Here they're a perfect partner for smoked turkey.

PEANUT STEW

1⅔   cups unsalted dry-roasted peanuts

1½   to 2 cups water

8   ounces fresh mushrooms, coarsely chopped

3   green or red sweet peppers, finely chopped

2   medium tomatoes, coarsely chopped

2   medium onions, finely chopped

½   to 1 teaspoon crushed red pepper

1   teaspoon salt

1   teaspoon grated fresh ginger

¾   teaspoon ground turmeric

½   teaspoon black pepper

2   cloves garlic, minced

3½   cups chopped smoked turkey

¼   cup thinly sliced green onions

Hot cooked couscous (optional)

PREP:
40 minutes
COOK:
40 minutes
MAKES:
8 servings

1 Place peanuts, half at a time, in a food processor or blender. Cover and process or blend until coarsely ground.

2 In a 4½-quart Dutch oven combine peanuts and 1½ cups of the water. Add mushrooms, sweet peppers, tomatoes, onions, crushed red pepper, salt, ginger, turmeric, black pepper, and garlic. Bring to boiling; reduce heat. Simmer, covered, for 30 minutes. If necessary, as stew thickens, gradually stir in the remaining ½ cup water. If oil from the peanuts surfaces, skim off with a spoon. (Mixture should be like a medium-thick gravy.)

3 Add turkey. Return to simmering. Cook, covered, for 10 minutes more. Sprinkle each serving with green onions. If desired, serve with couscous.

Nutrition Facts per serving: 286 cal., 18 g total fat (3 g sat. fat), 37 mg chol., 1,016 mg sodium, 13 g carbo., 2 g fiber, 23 g pro.

Two 5-ounce cans of chunk-style chicken make an easy substitution for the chopped cooked turkey.

TURKEY STEW WITH CORNMEAL DUMPLINGS

START TO FINISH:

40 minutes

MAKES:

4 servings

1   14-ounce can chicken broth or $1\frac{3}{4}$ cups homemade chicken broth

1   10-ounce package frozen mixed vegetables

1   cup frozen small whole onions

$\frac{1}{2}$ cup water

2   teaspoons snipped fresh basil or oregano or $\frac{1}{2}$ teaspoon dried basil or oregano, crushed

$\frac{1}{2}$ teaspoon salt

$\frac{1}{8}$ teaspoon garlic powder

$\frac{1}{8}$ teaspoon black pepper

1   cup milk

$\frac{1}{3}$ cup all-purpose flour

2   cups cubed cooked turkey or chicken

1   recipe Cornmeal Dumplings

1 In a large saucepan combine broth, frozen vegetables, onions, water, dried basil (if using), salt, garlic powder, and pepper. Bring to boiling. Meanwhile, combine milk and flour; stir into saucepan. Stir in turkey. Cook and stir until thickened and bubbly. Stir in fresh basil, if using.

2 Drop Cornmeal Dumplings mixture from a tablespoon into 4 to 8 mounds on top of the bubbling stew. Simmer, covered (do not lift cover), over low heat for 10 to 12 minutes or until a wooden toothpick inserted in a dumpling comes out clean.

CORNMEAL DUMPLINGS: In a medium bowl stir together $\frac{1}{2}$ cup all-purpose flour, $\frac{1}{2}$ cup shredded cheddar cheese, $\frac{1}{3}$ cup yellow cornmeal, 1 teaspoon baking powder, and dash black pepper. In a small bowl combine 1 slightly beaten egg, 2 tablespoons milk, and 2 tablespoons cooking oil; add to flour mixture, stirring with a fork just until combined.

Nutrition Facts per serving: 510 cal., 21 g total fat (7 g sat. fat), 135 mg chol., 1,045 mg sodium, 46 g carbo., 5 g fiber, 35 g pro.

Turn a can of tomato soup into a full meal with some hearty stir-ins, including that ever-favorite comfort food smoked sausage.

TURKEY SAUSAGE & SWEET PEPPER STEW

1 pound cooked smoked turkey sausage or cooked turkey kielbasa, halved lengthwise and cut into $\frac{1}{2}$-inch pieces

4 medium red, yellow, and/or green sweet peppers, cut into 1-inch pieces

2 stalks celery, cut into $\frac{1}{2}$-inch pieces

1 cup chopped onion

1 15-ounce can Great Northern or navy beans, rinsed and drained

1 14$\frac{1}{2}$-ounce can diced tomatoes, undrained

1 10$\frac{3}{4}$-ounce can condensed tomato soup

1 cup water

START TO FINISH:
40 minutes

MAKES:
6 servings

1 In a 4-quart Dutch oven combine sausage, sweet peppers, celery, and onion. Add beans, undrained tomatoes, tomato soup, and water. Bring to boiling; reduce heat. Simmer, covered, for 15 to 20 minutes or until vegetables are tender.

Nutrition Facts per serving: 258 cal., 7 g total fat (2 g sat. fat), 51 mg chol., 1,275 mg sodium, 31 g carbo., 7 g fiber, 18 g pro.

Smoked turkey sausage stars in this hearty Cajun-style stew.

HEARTY SAUSAGE GUMBO

PREP:

20 minutes

COOK:

25 minutes

MAKES:

8 servings

1	tablespoon olive oil
1	cup chopped onion
½	cup chopped red sweet pepper
½	cup chopped green sweet pepper
½	cup chopped celery
1	clove garlic, minced
5½	cups water
1	pound cooked smoked turkey sausage, quartered lengthwise and sliced
1	16-ounce package frozen cut okra
1	14½-ounce can diced tomatoes, undrained
1	7-ounce package gumbo mix with rice
1	teaspoon snipped fresh rosemary
½	teaspoon snipped fresh thyme
⅛	teaspoon cayenne pepper (optional)

1 In a 4-quart Dutch oven heat oil. Add onion, red sweet pepper, green sweet pepper, celery, and garlic; cook and stir over medium heat for 4 minutes. Add water, sausage, okra, undrained tomatoes, gumbo mix, rosemary, thyme, and, if desired, cayenne pepper. Bring to boiling; reduce heat. Simmer, covered, about 20 minutes or until rice is tender.

Nutrition Facts per serving: 224 cal., 7 g total fat (1 g sat. fat), 38 mg chol., 1,329 mg sodium, 29 g carbo., 3 g fiber, 13 g pro.

Rabbit is available, fresh or frozen, in most supermarkets. This tender, mild-flavored meat needs less cooking time than many other meats.

RABBIT STEW WITH FENNEL

PREP:

20 minutes

COOK:

1 hour

MAKES:

4 servings

1	2½-pound domestic rabbit, cut up, or 2½ pounds meaty chicken pieces (breast halves, thighs, and drumsticks), skinned
1	tablespoon olive oil
2	large fennel bulbs (1 pound each)
1	cup chopped onion
1	cup chopped carrots
⅓	cup sliced shallots
4	cloves garlic, minced
1	14-ounce can chicken broth or 1¾ cups homemade chicken broth
1	cup dry white wine
½	teaspoon dried thyme, crushed, or 1 teaspoon snipped fresh thyme
¼	teaspoon dried rosemary, crushed, or ½ teaspoon snipped fresh rosemary
¼	teaspoon fennel seeds, crushed
1	bay leaf
1	teaspoon finely shredded lemon peel

1 Sprinkle rabbit with ¼ teaspoon *salt* and ¼ teaspoon *black pepper*. In a 4-quart Dutch oven heat oil. Add rabbit; cook over medium-high heat about 8 minutes or until well browned, turning occasionally to brown evenly. Remove rabbit from Dutch oven; set aside.

2 Meanwhile, cut off and discard upper stalks of fennel bulbs. Snip enough of the feathery tops to make 2 tablespoons; set aside for garnish. Remove any wilted outer layers and cut a thin slice from bulb base. Wash and chop fennel.

3 Add fennel, onion, carrots, and shallots to Dutch oven. Cook and stir over medium heat about 6 minutes or just until tender. Add garlic; cook and stir for 30 seconds more. Return rabbit to Dutch oven along with broth, wine, dried thyme and dried rosemary (if using), fennel seeds, bay leaf, ¼ teaspoon *salt*, and ¼ teaspoon *black pepper*. Bring to boiling; reduce heat. Simmer, covered, for 45 to 55 minutes for rabbit (35 to 40 minutes for chicken) or until meat is tender. Remove and discard bay leaf. Stir in fresh thyme and fresh rosemary, if using.

4 In a small bowl combine reserved fennel tops and lemon peel; sprinkle over each serving.

Nutrition Facts per serving: 570 cal., 19 g total fat (5 g sat. fat), 162 mg chol., 957 mg sodium, 28 g carbo., 9 g fiber, 62 g pro.

This interesting version of San Francisco's fish stew gets a kick from dried pasilla chile peppers and some chili powder too. (Recipe pictured on page 280.)

CIOPPINO WITH CHILE PEPPERS

PREP:

55 minutes

COOK:

25 minutes

MAKES:

6 servings

1 pound fresh or frozen whitefish fillets

1 pound fresh or frozen monkfish

8 ounces fresh or frozen peeled and deveined medium shrimp

2 dried pasilla chile peppers*

¾ teaspoon chili powder

4 teaspoons olive oil

1 cup chopped onion

1 cup frozen whole kernel corn

6 cloves garlic, minced

1 15-ounce can white kidney beans (cannellini), rinsed and drained

1 14½-ounce can diced tomatoes, undrained

1 8-ounce bottle clam juice

1 cup dry white wine

2 tablespoons canned diced green chile peppers

1 Thaw fish and shrimp, if frozen. Rinse fish; cut into 1-inch pieces.

2 Place dried peppers in a small bowl. Add enough boiling *water* to cover. Let stand 20 minutes. Remove peppers with a slotted spoon, reserving ¼ cup soaking liquid. Remove seeds and stems; discard. In blender combine peppers and reserved liquid. Cover; blend until smooth. Set aside.

3 Meanwhile, place fish and shrimp in a large shallow bowl. Combine chili powder and ½ teaspoon *salt*; sprinkle over fish and shrimp.

4 In a 4-quart nonstick Dutch oven heat 2 teaspoons of the oil. Add half of the fish and half of the shrimp to hot oil; cook about 4 minutes or just until done, gently turning occasionally. Transfer fish and shrimp to another bowl. Repeat with remaining fish and shrimp (add additional oil, if necessary). Chill.

5 In same Dutch oven heat remaining 2 teaspoons oil. Add onion, corn, and garlic; cook and stir over medium heat 3 minutes. Stir in pureed chile pepper mixture, beans, undrained tomatoes, clam juice, wine, green chile peppers, 1 cup *water*, and ½ teaspoon *salt*. Bring to boiling; reduce heat. Simmer, covered, 20 minutes. Add fish and shrimp. Simmer, uncovered, for 5 minutes more. If desired, serve with *chopped avocado* and *snipped fresh cilantro*.

*NOTE: When working with chile peppers, wear plastic or rubber gloves. If your bare hands do touch the chile peppers, wash your hands well with soap and water.

Nutrition Facts per serving: 285 cal., 6 g total fat (1 g sat. fat), 74 mg chol., 774 mg sodium, 23 g carbo., 5 g fiber, 32 g pro.

This speedy version of the classic Italian fish stew is very easy to make.

QUICK CIOPPINO

6   ounces fresh or frozen cod fillets

6   ounces fresh or frozen peeled and deveined shrimp

1   tablespoon olive oil or cooking oil

1   medium green sweet pepper, cut into thin bite-size strips

1   cup chopped onion

2   cloves garlic, minced

2   14½-ounce cans Italian-style stewed tomatoes, undrained

½   cup water

3   tablespoons snipped fresh basil

Thaw fish and shrimp, if frozen. Rinse fish and shrimp. Cut fish into 1-inch pieces; set aside.

In a large saucepan heat oil. Add sweet pepper, onion, and garlic; cook and stir for 4 to 5 minutes. Stir in undrained tomatoes and water. Bring to boiling. Stir in cod and shrimp. Return to boiling; reduce heat. Simmer, covered, for 2 to 3 minutes or until cod flakes easily when tested with a fork and shrimp turn opaque. Stir in basil.

Nutrition Facts per serving: 222 cal., 6 g total fat (1 g sat. fat), 85 mg chol., 538 mg sodium, 19 g carbo., 3 g fiber, 19 g pro.

START TO FINISH:
20 minutes
MAKES:
4 servings

STEWS & RAGOÛTS   311

Expect this new, easy version of fish chowder to become an old favorite in no time.

FISH STEW WITH ASPARAGUS

START TO FINISH:

20 minutes

MAKES:

4 servings

12 ounces fresh or frozen cod or other whitefish fillets

1 14-ounce can chicken broth or 1¾ cups homemade chicken broth

1 10¾-ounce can condensed cream of onion soup

1 10-ounce package frozen cut asparagus

1 cup water

½ teaspoon dried thyme, crushed

¼ cup grated Parmesan cheese (1 ounce)

1 Thaw fish, if frozen. Rinse fish; cut into ½-inch pieces; set aside.

2 In a large saucepan combine broth, soup, frozen asparagus, water, and thyme. Heat until bubbly, stirring occasionally. Stir in fish. Simmer, covered, for 5 to 7 minutes or until fish flakes easily when tested with a fork. Sprinkle each serving with Parmesan cheese.

Nutrition Facts per serving: 194 cal., 7 g total fat (2 g sat. fat), 53 mg chol., 1,129 mg sodium, 12 g carbo., 2 g fiber, 22 g pro.

This full-bodied stew owes its spiciness to crushed red pepper and a can of Mexican-style stewed tomatoes. A mixture of parsley and lemon peel makes a colorful and flavorful topper.

SPICY MEXICAN-STYLE FISH STEW

1	pound fresh or frozen whitefish fillets (such as cod or haddock)
2	cups chicken or vegetable broth
1	cup sliced fresh mushrooms
1	cup sliced zucchini or yellow summer squash
1/2	cup chopped onion
1/8	teaspoon salt
1/8	teaspoon crushed red pepper
1	clove garlic, minced
1	bay leaf
2	14 1/2-ounce cans Mexican-style stewed tomatoes, undrained
2	tablespoons snipped fresh parsley
1/2	teaspoon finely shredded lemon peel

START TO FINISH:

25 minutes

MAKES:

4 servings

1 Thaw fish, if frozen. Rinse fish; cut into 1-inch pieces. Set aside.

2 In a large saucepan or Dutch oven combine broth, mushrooms, zucchini, onion, salt, crushed red pepper, garlic, and bay leaf. Bring to boiling; reduce heat. Simmer, covered, for 5 minutes.

3 Stir in fish and undrained tomatoes. Bring to boiling; reduce heat. Simmer, covered, about 5 minutes more or just until fish flakes easily when tested with a fork. Remove and discard bay leaf.

4 Combine parsley and lemon peel; sprinkle over each serving.

Nutrition Facts per serving: 194 cal., 2 g total fat (0 g sat. fat), 49 mg chol., 1,216 mg sodium, 18 g carbo., 1 g fiber, 26 g pro.

This version of bouillabaise features the shrimp, scallops, and mussels of the famous French seafood stew, but Moroccan spices—cumin, cinnamon, and cayenne pepper—replace the classic herbs.

MOROCCAN BOUILLABAISSE

PREP:

1 hour

COOK:

11 minutes

MAKES:

4 servings

8	ounces fresh or frozen peeled and deveined shrimp
8	ounces fresh or frozen scallops
8	ounces fresh mussels in shells (about 12)
4	cups water
3	tablespoons salt
1	tablespoon olive oil
1	cup finely chopped onion
4	cloves garlic, minced
1	teaspoon ground cumin
$\frac{1}{2}$	teaspoon ground cinnamon
$\frac{1}{4}$	teaspoon cayenne pepper
1	cup fish or vegetable broth
1	cup finely chopped tomatoes
$\frac{1}{4}$	teaspoon salt
$\frac{1}{8}$	teaspoon ground saffron
	Hot cooked couscous
	Fresh parsley sprigs (optional)

1 Thaw shrimp and scallops, if frozen. Rinse shrimp and scallops. Halve any large scallops. Scrub mussels with a stiff brush under cold running water. Using your fingers, pull out the beards that are visible between the shells. In a large Dutch oven combine water and the 3 tablespoons salt. Add mussels and soak for 15 minutes. Drain and rinse. Repeat soaking mussels twice.

2 In a large saucepan heat oil. Add onion and garlic; cook and stir over medium heat for 4 to 5 minutes. Add cumin, cinnamon, and cayenne pepper; cook and stir for 1 minute.

3 Add broth, tomatoes, the $\frac{1}{4}$ teaspoon salt, and saffron. Bring to boiling; add scallops and mussels. Return to boiling; reduce heat. Simmer, covered, about 5 minutes or until mussel shells open. Add shrimp; cook, covered, 1 to 2 minutes more or until shrimp turn opaque. Discard any unopened mussel shells. Serve with couscous. If desired, garnish each serving with parsley.

Nutrition Facts per serving: 273 cal., 6 g total fat (1 g sat. fat), 90 mg chol., 460 mg sodium, 28 g carbo., 3 g fiber, 26 g pro.

Gumbo—in 25 minutes? Yes! Purchased cooked bacon pieces, canned shrimp, canned soup, and quick-cooking rice make it happen.

EASY SEAFOOD GUMBO

8	ounces fresh or frozen whitefish fillets (such as orange roughy or cod)
1	14½-ounce can stewed tomatoes, undrained
1	10¾-ounce can condensed chicken gumbo soup
1	10-ounce package frozen cut okra
1	cup water
1	teaspoon dried thyme, crushed
¼	teaspoon bottled hot pepper sauce
1	6½-ounce can shrimp, undrained
¼	cup cooked bacon pieces
1	teaspoon filé powder (optional)
	Hot cooked rice

START TO FINISH:
25 minutes
MAKES:
5 servings

1 Thaw fish, if frozen. Rinse fish; cut into 1-inch pieces. Set aside.

2 In a large saucepan combine undrained tomatoes, soup, okra, water, thyme, and hot pepper sauce. Bring to boiling; reduce heat. Simmer, covered, for 10 minutes. Add fish. Simmer, covered, about 5 minutes more or until fish flakes easily when tested with a fork.

3 Stir in undrained shrimp, bacon pieces, and, if desired, filé powder; heat through. Serve over rice.

Nutrition Facts per serving: 283 cal., 4 g total fat (1 g sat. fat), 82 mg chol., 943 mg sodium, 37 g carbo., 4 g fiber, 22 g pro.

No need to wait for cool weather to serve this colorful stew. It is a satisfying meal any time of the year. The feta cheese—an optional addition—lends a tangy, fresh flavor.

GARBANZO BEAN STEW

START TO FINISH:

20 minutes

MAKES:

4 servings

1	tablespoon cooking oil
1	cup chopped onion
¾	cup chopped green sweet pepper
3	cloves garlic, minced
1½	teaspoons ground cumin
½	teaspoon paprika
⅛	to ¼ teaspoon cayenne pepper
2	14-ounce cans vegetable broth or 3½ cups homemade vegetable broth
1	10-ounce package frozen whole kernel corn
1	15-ounce can garbanzo beans (chickpeas), rinsed and drained
½	cup chopped tomato
2	tablespoons snipped fresh oregano
2	tablespoons lemon juice
2	tablespoons thinly sliced green onions
¼	cup crumbled feta cheese (optional)

1 In a large saucepan heat oil. Add onion, sweet pepper, and garlic; cook and stir over medium heat for 4 to 5 minutes. Stir in cumin, paprika, and cayenne pepper; cook and stir for 1 minute.

2 Add broth and corn. Bring to boiling; reduce heat. Simmer, covered, for 5 to 10 minutes or until corn is tender. Stir in beans, tomato, oregano, and lemon juice; heat through. Sprinkle each serving with green onions. If desired, top each serving with feta cheese.

Nutrition Facts per serving: 246 cal., 7 g total fat (1 g sat. fat), 0 mg chol., 1,169 mg sodium, 42 g carbo., 8 g fiber, 10 g pro.

Try a spiced ketchup in this recipe for an extra kick. (Recipe pictured on page 277.)

HARVEST VEGETABLE STEW

3	teaspoons instant beef bouillon granules
5	cups water
1½	cups chopped tomatoes or one 14½-ounce can diced tomatoes, undrained
2	medium Yukon gold potatoes, peeled and cut into 1-inch pieces
1	cup chopped celery
½	cup chopped green sweet pepper
⅓	cup chopped onion
2	cups shredded cabbage
1	15-ounce can red kidney beans, rinsed and drained
1	cup halved green beans
1	cup chopped zucchini
8	to 10 fresh oregano sprigs, tied in a bunch with kitchen string
¼	cup ketchup
¼	teaspoon black pepper
	Dash bottled hot pepper sauce
	Salt
	Black pepper

PREP:
25 minutes
COOK:
30 minutes
MAKES:
6 servings

1 In a 4-quart Dutch oven combine bouillon granules and water. Bring to boiling. Add tomatoes, potatoes, celery, sweet pepper, and onion. Bring to boiling; reduce heat. Simmer, uncovered, for 15 minutes. Add cabbage, kidney beans, green beans, zucchini, oregano, ketchup, the ¼ teaspoon pepper, and hot pepper sauce. Simmer about 15 minutes more or until vegetables are tender. Remove and discard oregano. Season to taste with salt and additional pepper.

Nutrition Facts per serving: 136 cal., 1 g total fat (0 g sat. fat), 0 mg chol., 730 mg sodium, 30 g carbo., 7 g fiber, 8 g pro.

Cumin and curry add depth and heat to this vegetable stew. Ladle the spicy mixture over hot cooked rice in a shallow bowl.

SPICY VEGETABLE STEW

START TO FINISH:

40 minutes

MAKES:

6 servings

5½	cups coarsely chopped, peeled eggplant
3¾	cups coarsely chopped zucchini
1	14½-ounce can diced tomatoes, undrained
1	large red sweet pepper, coarsely chopped
8	ounces fresh mushrooms, quartered
⅓	cup chopped onion
1	teaspoon ground cumin
1	teaspoon curry powder
¼	to ½ teaspoon cayenne pepper
¼	teaspoon salt
	Salt
	Black pepper
4½	cups hot cooked rice

1 In a 4-quart Dutch oven combine eggplant, zucchini, undrained tomatoes, sweet pepper, mushrooms, onion, cumin, curry powder, cayenne pepper, and the ¼ teaspoon salt. Bring to boiling, stirring occasionally; reduce heat. Simmer, covered, for 10 minutes. Simmer, uncovered, for 10 to 15 minutes more or until vegetables are tender. Season to taste with additional salt and black pepper. Serve with rice.

Nutrition Facts per serving: 221 cal., 1 g total fat (0 g sat. fat), 0 mg chol., 265 mg sodium, 47 g carbo., 5 g fiber, 7 g pro.

Pressing the eggplant is an important step because it removes the excess liquid that would otherwise dilute the flavor of the stew.

OVEN-BAKED VEGETABLE & BEAN RAGOÛT

1	small eggplant, cubed (about 12 ounces)
1	tablespoon salt
3	tablespoons olive oil
2	cloves garlic, minced
2	cups cubed potatoes
4	ounces fresh mushrooms, quartered
1	medium onion, cut into 1-inch pieces
1	small zucchini, halved lengthwise and thickly sliced
1	small red sweet pepper, cut into 1-inch pieces
1	small yellow sweet pepper, cut into 1-inch pieces
1	14½-ounce can whole Italian-style tomatoes, cut up and undrained
1	cup cooked dry white beans
½	cup chicken or vegetable broth
⅓	cup tomato paste
¼	teaspoon salt
⅛	teaspoon black pepper
⅛	teaspoon crushed red pepper

PREP:
1½ hours
BAKE:
1 hour
OVEN:
350°F
MAKES:
4 servings

1 Place cubed eggplant in a colander; sprinkle with the 1 tablespoon salt. Place a bowl filled with water on top of eggplant (as a weight), pressing eggplant down. Let stand for 1 hour. Rinse and drain eggplant well. Pat dry with paper towels.

2 In a large nonstick skillet heat 2 tablespoons of the oil. Add eggplant and garlic; cook and stir over medium-high heat for 2 minutes. Transfer to a 2-quart casserole.

3 Add the remaining 1 tablespoon oil, potatoes, mushrooms, onion, zucchini, red sweet pepper, and yellow sweet pepper to skillet; cook and stir over medium heat for 5 minutes. Transfer to the casserole.

4 In a large bowl combine undrained tomatoes, cooked beans, broth, tomato paste, the ¼ teaspoon salt, black pepper, and crushed red pepper. Stir into casserole. Bake, covered, in a 350° oven for 1 hour.

Nutrition Facts per serving: 317 cal., 11 g total fat (2 g sat. fat), 1 mg chol., 1,114 mg sodium, 48 g carbo., 8 g fiber, 10 g pro.

Fresh, frozen, and canned veggies are packed into this robust meatless stew. (Recipe pictured on page 283.)

SAVORY BAKED VEGETABLE STEW

PREP:

30 minutes

BAKE:

1¼ hours

OVEN:

350°F

MAKES:

6 servings

1	tablespoon olive oil
1	large potato, peeled and cut into 1-inch cubes
1	medium sweet potato, peeled and cut into 1-inch cubes
1	large carrot, peeled and sliced
1	cup cubed, peeled rutabaga
5	boiling onions, peeled
1	stalk celery, coarsely chopped
1	teaspoon Cajun seasoning
1	14½-ounce can Mexican-style stewed tomatoes, cut up and undrained
2¼	cups vegetable broth
1	15-ounce can garbanzo beans (chickpeas), rinsed and drained
½	cup coarsely chopped red sweet pepper
½	cup small button mushrooms, halved
½	cup frozen peas
½	cup frozen cut green beans
¼	cup coarsely chopped green sweet pepper
	Salt
	Black pepper
2	tablespoons cornstarch

1 In a 4-quart Dutch oven heat oil. Add potato, sweet potato, carrot, rutabaga, boiling onions, and celery; cook and stir over medium heat for 5 minutes. Stir in Cajun seasoning.

2 Add undrained tomatoes and 2 cups of the broth (broth should cover vegetables). Bake, covered, in a 350° oven about 1 hour or until vegetables are crisp-tender, stirring once or twice.

3 Add garbanzo beans, red sweet pepper, mushrooms, peas, green beans, and green sweet pepper. Return to oven. Bake, uncovered, about 10 minutes more or until heated through. Season to taste with salt and black pepper.

4 Combine cornstarch and the remaining ¼ cup broth. Place Dutch oven on range top; stir in cornstarch mixture. Cook and stir until thickened and bubbly. Cook and stir for 2 minutes more.

Nutrition Facts per serving: 239 cal., 4 g total fat (0 g sat. fat), 0 mg chol., 933 mg sodium, 46 g carbo., 8 g fiber, 7 g pro.

SLOW COOKER FAVORITES

6

Italian sausage brings a touch of the Mediterranean to chili-style soup. Ladled over hot cooked rice, it's a robust meal-in-a-bowl. (Recipe pictured on page 285.)

ITALIAN BEAN SOUP

PREP:

20 minutes

COOK:

6 to 8 hours (low) or 3 to 4 hours (high)

MAKES:

6 to 8 servings

1	pound ground beef
8	ounces bulk Italian sausage
1	cup chopped onion
1	cup chopped green sweet pepper
3	cloves garlic, minced
1	28-ounce can Italian-style tomatoes, cut up and undrained
1	15-ounce can garbanzo beans (chickpeas), rinsed and drained
1	15-ounce can light red kidney beans, rinsed and drained
1	cup water
3	tablespoons Worcestershire sauce
2	to 3 tablespoons chili powder
2	teaspoons dried basil, crushed
2	teaspoons dried oregano, crushed
$\frac{1}{2}$	teaspoon bottled hot pepper sauce (optional)
$\frac{1}{4}$	teaspoon salt
	Hot cooked rice
	Shredded cheddar cheese

1 In a large skillet cook ground beef, sausage, onion, sweet pepper, and garlic over medium heat until meat is brown. Drain off fat.

2 Transfer beef mixture to a 3½- or 4-quart slow cooker. Stir in undrained tomatoes, beans, water, Worcestershire sauce, chili powder, basil, oregano, hot pepper sauce (if desired), and salt.

3 Cover and cook on low-heat setting for 6 to 8 hours or on high-heat setting for 3 to 4 hours. Serve over hot cooked rice and top with cheese.

Nutrition Facts per serving: 436 cal., 20 g total fat (7 g sat. fat), 72 mg chol., 992 mg sodium, 36 g carbo., 10 g fiber, 29 g pro.

Ever notice how nacho cheese dips always disappear quickly at parties?
This similarly flavored soup will have much the same effect at your dinner table.

NACHO CHEESE SOUP

1   pound lean ground pork or ground beef

2   11-ounce cans whole kernel corn with sweet peppers, drained

2   11-ounce cans condensed nacho cheese soup

2   cups water

1   16-ounce jar salsa

2   4-ounce cans diced green chile peppers, undrained

1   cup crushed tortilla chips

$1/2$ cup dairy sour cream

1 In a large skillet cook ground meat over medium heat until brown. Drain off fat.

2 Transfer meat to a $3^{1}/_{2}$- or 4-quart slow cooker. Stir in corn, soup, water, salsa, and green chile peppers.

3 Cover and cook on low-heat setting for 4 to 6 hours or on high-heat setting for 2 to 3 hours. Top each serving with tortilla chips and sour cream.

Nutrition Facts per serving: 396 cal., 23 g total fat (9 g sat. fat), 55 mg chol., 1,252 mg sodium, 33 g carbo., 5 g fiber, 17 g pro.

PREP:

25 minutes

COOK:

4 to 6 hours (low) or
2 to 3 hours (high)

MAKES:

8 servings

The robust Italian flavors of this soup call for wedges of focaccia or thick slices of buttery garlic bread. Brown the meat, if you want a rich brown color, or skip the step to save time.

BEEF & TORTELLINI SOUP

PREP:

20 minutes

COOK:

*7 to 8 hours (low) or
3¹/₂ to 4 hours (high),
plus 30 minutes (high)*

MAKES:

4 servings

8	ounces boneless beef round steak, cut 1 inch thick
1	tablespoon all-purpose flour
¹/₂	teaspoon salt
¹/₂	teaspoon black pepper
1	tablespoon butter or margarine
¹/₂	cup chopped onion
1	14-ounce can beef broth or 1³/₄ cups homemade beef broth
1	14-ounce jar roasted garlic pasta sauce
1	cup sliced carrots
¹/₂	cup water
¹/₂	teaspoon dried Italian seasoning, crushed
1	medium zucchini, cut into thin bite-size strips (1¹/₄ cups)
1	9-ounce package refrigerated cheese-filled tortellini

1 Trim fat from beef. Cut beef into 1-inch pieces. In a self-sealing plastic bag combine flour, salt, and pepper. Add beef pieces, a few at a time, shaking to coat. In a large skillet melt butter over medium heat. Add beef and onion; cook and stir until beef is brown and onion is tender. Drain off fat.

2 Transfer beef mixture to a 3¹/₂- or 4-quart slow cooker. Stir in broth, pasta sauce, carrots, water, and Italian seasoning.

3 Cover and cook on low-heat setting for 7 to 8 hours or on high-heat setting for 3¹/₂ to 4 hours.

4 If using low-heat setting, turn cooker to high-heat setting. Stir in zucchini and tortellini. Cover and cook for 30 minutes more.

Nutrition Facts per serving: 383 cal., 11 g total fat (4 g sat. fat), 71 mg chol., 1,252 mg sodium, 45 g carbo., 3 g fiber, 26 g pro.

Purchased salsa is the shortcut ticket to the bold flavors in this soup. Simply choose your favorite brand for your own "house specialty" version.

SOUTHWEST STEAK & POTATO SOUP

1½ pounds boneless beef sirloin steak, cut 1 inch thick

2 medium potatoes, cut into 1-inch pieces

2 cups frozen cut green beans

1 small onion, sliced and separated into rings

1 16-ounce jar thick and chunky salsa

1 14-ounce can beef broth or 1¾ cups homemade beef broth

1 teaspoon dried basil, crushed

2 cloves garlic, minced

Shredded Monterey Jack or Mexican blend cheese (optional)

PREP:

25 minutes

COOK:

8 to 10 hours (low) or 4 to 5 hours (high)

MAKES:

6 servings

1 Trim fat from beef. Cut beef into 1-inch pieces. Set aside.

2 In a 3½- or 4-quart slow cooker layer potatoes, green beans, and onion. Add beef. In a medium bowl stir together salsa, broth, basil, and garlic. Pour over beef and vegetables in cooker.

3 Cover and cook on low-heat setting for 8 to 10 hours or on high-heat setting for 4 to 5 hours. If desired, sprinkle each serving with cheese.

Nutrition Facts per serving: 206 cal., 4 g total fat (1 g sat. fat), 68 mg chol., 624 mg sodium, 16 g carbo., 3 g fiber, 27 g pro.

One pound of beef stew meat easily makes six servings of hearty soup when you add substantial ingredients like wild rice and rutabaga.

WILD RICE & VEGETABLE BEEF SOUP

PREP:

20 minutes

COOK:

*8 to 10 hours (low) or
4 to 5 hours (high)*

MAKES:

6 servings

1	tablespoon olive oil (optional)
1	pound lean beef stew meat, cut into 1-inch pieces
3	14-ounce cans beef broth or 5¼ cups homemade beef broth
2	cups rutabaga cut into ½-inch pieces
1	cup sliced carrots
1	cup frozen whole kernel corn
½	cup chopped onion
⅓	cup uncooked wild rice, rinsed
1½	teaspoons dried thyme, crushed
¼	teaspoon black pepper
4	cloves garlic, minced

1 If desired, in a large skillet heat oil. Add beef, half at a time; cook and stir over medium heat until brown. Drain off fat.

2 Place beef in a 3½- or 4-quart slow cooker. Stir in broth, rutabaga, carrots, corn, onion, wild rice, thyme, pepper, and garlic.

3 Cover and cook on low-heat setting for 8 to 10 hours or on high-heat setting for 4 to 5 hours.

Nutrition Facts per serving: 203 cal., 4 g total fat (1 g sat. fat), 45 mg chol., 747 mg sodium, 21 g carbo., 3 g fiber, 21 g pro.

Thick with chunks of tender meat, vegetables, and noodles, this soup makes a perfect cold-weather supper for hardworking, hard-playing families.

BEEF & NOODLE SOUP

1	pound beef stew meat, cut into $^1/_2$-inch pieces
1	16-ounce package frozen mixed vegetables
5	cups water
1	14$^1/_2$-ounce can diced tomatoes, undrained
1	8-ounce can tomato sauce
2	bay leaves
2	tablespoons instant beef bouillon granules
1$^1/_2$	teaspoons dried basil, crushed
$^1/_2$	teaspoon dried marjoram, crushed
$^1/_4$	teaspoon black pepper
2	cups uncooked medium noodles

PREP:

15 minutes

COOK:

9 to 11 hours (low) or 4$^1/_2$ to 5$^1/_2$ hours (high), plus 30 minutes (high)

MAKES:

8 servings

1 In a 4$^1/_2$- to 6-quart slow cooker combine beef, frozen vegetables, water, undrained tomatoes, tomato sauce, bay leaves, bouillon granules, basil, marjoram, and pepper.

2 Cover and cook on low-heat setting for 9 to 11 hours or on high-heat setting for 4$^1/_2$ to 5$^1/_2$ hours.

3 If using low-heat setting, turn cooker to high-heat setting. Stir in noodles. Cover and cook for 30 minutes more. Remove and discard bay leaves.

Nutrition Facts per serving: 179 cal., 4 g total fat (1 g sat. fat), 36 mg chol., 1,106 mg sodium, 19 g carbo., 4 g fiber, 17 g pro.

Use curly dried Chinese egg noodles, rather than rice sticks or rice noodles, for this recipe.

TERIYAKI BEEF-NOODLE SOUP

PREP:

20 minutes

COOK:

*6 to 8 hours (low) or
3 to 4 hours (high)*

STAND:

5 minutes

MAKES:

6 servings

1   pound beef stir-fry strips

2   14-ounce cans beef broth or 3½ cups homemade beef broth

2   cups water

2   medium red or green sweet peppers, cut into ½-inch pieces

1   8-ounce can sliced water chestnuts, drained and chopped

6   green onions, cut into 1-inch pieces

3   tablespoons soy sauce

1   teaspoon ground ginger

¼   teaspoon black pepper

5   to 6 ounces dried Chinese noodles

1 In a 3½- or 4-quart slow cooker combine beef, broth, water, sweet peppers, water chestnuts, green onions, soy sauce, ginger, and black pepper.

2 Cover and cook on low-heat setting for 6 to 8 hours or on high-heat setting for 3 to 4 hours. Turn off cooker. Stir in noodles. Cover and let stand for 5 minutes.

Nutrition Facts per serving: 232 cal., 4 g total fat (1 g sat. fat), 46 mg chol., 1,588 mg sodium, 27 g carbo., 3 g fiber, 22 g pro.

Purchase ready-cut stew meat from the butcher, or buy a beef chuck or shoulder roast and cut it into 1- to 1 1/2-inch pieces.

SLOW-COOKER BEEF STEW

1	tablespoon cooking oil
2	pounds beef stew meat, trimmed and cut into bite-size pieces
1½	pounds small red potatoes, quartered
8	medium carrots, cut into ½-inch pieces
2	small red onions, cut into wedges
3	tablespoons quick-cooking tapioca
2	10¾-ounce cans condensed cream of mushroom soup or condensed cream of celery soup
1	14-ounce can beef broth or 1¾ cups homemade beef broth
1½	teaspoons dried thyme, crushed
½	teaspoon salt
½	teaspoon black pepper
1	16-ounce package frozen cut green beans, thawed

1 In a large skillet heat oil. Add beef, half at a time; cook and stir over medium heat until brown. Drain off fat. Set aside.

2 In a 5½- or 6-quart slow cooker place potatoes, carrots, onions, and tapioca. Toss to mix. Add beef. In a medium bowl stir together soup, broth, thyme, salt, and pepper. Pour over beef and vegetables in cooker. Stir to combine.

3 Cover and cook on low-heat setting for 9 to 10 hours or on high-heat setting for 4½ to 5 hours.

4 If using low-heat setting, turn cooker to high-heat setting. Stir in thawed green beans. Cover and cook for 10 to 15 minutes more or until tender.

Nutrition Facts per serving: 316 cal., 11 g total fat (3 g sat. fat), 38 mg chol., 766 mg sodium, 31 g carbo., 6 g fiber, 24 g pro.

PREP:

30 minutes

COOK:

9 to 10 hours (low) or 4½ to 5 hours (high), plus 10 minutes (high)

MAKES:

10 servings

Cumin, cayenne, cinnamon, and dried fruits give this stew its North African character. The serve-along? Couscous, of course—the quintessential Moroccan staple.

NORTH AFRICAN BEEF STEW

PREP:

20 minutes

COOK:

7¹/₂ to 8¹/₂ hours (low) or 3¹/₂ to 4 hours (high), plus 30 minutes

MAKES:

6 servings

1¹/₂	pounds beef stew meat, cut into 1-inch pieces
2	medium sweet potatoes, peeled, halved lengthwise, and cut into ¹/₂-inch slices
1	medium onion, cut into wedges
1	cup water
1	teaspoon instant beef bouillon granules
³/₄	teaspoon ground cumin
¹/₄	teaspoon cayenne pepper
¹/₈	teaspoon ground cinnamon
4	cloves garlic, minced
1	14¹/₂-ounce can diced tomatoes, undrained
¹/₂	cup dried apricots or pitted dried plums (prunes), quartered Hot cooked couscous (optional)
¹/₄	cup chopped peanuts

1 In a 3¹/₂- or 4-quart slow cooker combine beef, sweet potatoes, and onion. Stir in water, bouillon granules, cumin, cayenne pepper, cinnamon, and garlic.

2 Cover and cook on low-heat setting for 7¹/₂ to 8¹/₂ hours or on high-heat setting for 3¹/₂ to 4 hours.

3 Stir in undrained tomatoes and apricots. Cover and cook for 30 minutes more. If desired, serve stew over hot cooked couscous. Sprinkle each serving with peanuts.

Nutrition Facts per serving: 274 cal., 7 g total fat (2 g sat. fat), 67 mg chol., 373 mg sodium, 24 g carbo., 4 g fiber, 27 g pro.

For a perfect cozy dinner with friends, serve this stew with crusty bread, olives, and a hearty red wine.

PROVENÇAL BEEF STEW

8	small tiny new potatoes
1	pound small carrots with tops, peeled and trimmed, or one 16-ounce package peeled baby carrots
1	cup coarsely chopped shallots or onion
½	cup pitted green or ripe olives
1½	pounds lean boneless beef chuck roast, cut into 2-inch pieces
1	cup beef broth
4	to 6 cloves garlic, minced
1	tablespoon quick-cooking tapioca
1	teaspoon dried herbes de Provence, crushed
¼	teaspoon salt
¼	teaspoon cracked black pepper
¼	cup dry red wine or beef broth
	Snipped fresh parsley (optional)
	Capers, drained (optional)

PREP:

20 minutes

COOK:

*10 to 12 hours (low) or
4 to 5 hours (high)*

MAKES:

6 servings

1 Peel a strip from center of each potato. In a 4-quart slow cooker combine potatoes, carrots, shallots, and olives. Top with beef. In a small bowl combine broth, garlic, tapioca, herbes de Provence, salt, and cracked pepper. Pour over beef.

2 Cover and cook on low-heat setting for 10 to 12 hours or on high-heat setting for 4 to 5 hours. Stir in wine during last 30 minutes of cooking. If desired, sprinkle each serving with parsley and capers.

Nutrition Facts per serving: 198 cal., 5 g total fat (2 g sat. fat), 54 mg chol., 308 mg sodium, 16 g carbo., 3 g fiber, 20 g pro.

Chipotle chile peppers are dried, smoked jalapeño peppers, so they pack considerable heat. Canned in piquant adobo sauce, they're convenient for seasoning stews. You'll find them in the ethnic foods aisle of supermarkets or in Hispanic food markets. (Recipe pictured on page 285.)

NEW MEXICO BEEF STEW

PREP:

30 minutes

COOK:

12 to 14 hours (low) or 6 to 7 hours (high)

MAKES:

6 servings

2 cups fresh corn kernels or one 10-ounce package frozen whole kernel corn, thawed

1 15-ounce can garbanzo beans (chickpeas), rinsed and drained

2 cups chopped, peeled celery root or 1 cup sliced celery

1 cup chopped onion

3 cloves garlic, minced

2 to 3 canned chipotle peppers in adobo sauce, chopped

1½ pounds boneless beef chuck roast, cut into ¾-inch pieces

1 teaspoon salt

½ teaspoon black pepper

1 teaspoon dried thyme, crushed

1 28-ounce can diced tomatoes, undrained

Lime slices (optional)

Fresh cilantro (optional)

1 In a 4- to 5½-quart slow cooker layer corn, beans, celery root, onion, garlic, and chipotle peppers. Add beef. Sprinkle with salt, black pepper, and thyme. Pour undrained tomatoes over beef.

2 Cover and cook on low-heat setting for 12 to 14 hours or on high-heat setting for 6 to 7 hours. Stir before serving. Season to taste with additional salt and black pepper. If desired, garnish each serving with a lime slice and fresh cilantro.

Nutrition Facts per serving: 367 cal., 8 g total fat (2 g sat. fat), 54 mg chol., 1,078 mg sodium, 42 g carbo., 7 g fiber, 33 g pro.

Burgundy wines are made from Pinot Noir grapes, so if you don't want to splurge for a real Burgundy wine from France, simply choose a good Pinot Noir from California.

BURGUNDY BEEF STEW

2 pounds boneless beef chuck roast, trimmed and cut into 1-inch cubes

1 teaspoon salt

¼ teaspoon black pepper

2 tablespoons cooking oil (optional)

2 tablespoons quick-cooking tapioca

6 large carrots, cut into 1-inch pieces

1 9-ounce package frozen cut green beans

½ of a 16-ounce package frozen small whole onions (2 cups)

1 14-ounce can beef broth or 1¾ cups homemade beef broth

1 cup Burgundy or other dry red wine

2 cloves garlic, minced

5 slices bacon, crisp-cooked, drained, and crumbled

1 Sprinkle beef with salt and pepper. If desired, in a large skillet heat oil. Add beef, half at a time; cook and stir over medium heat until brown. Drain off fat.

2 Transfer beef to a 3½- or 4-quart slow cooker. Sprinkle with tapioca. Stir in carrots, green beans, onions, broth, wine, and garlic.

3 Cover and cook on low-heat setting for 10 to 12 hours or on high-heat setting for 5 to 6 hours. Sprinkle each serving with crumbled bacon.

Nutrition Facts per serving: 339 cal., 9 g total fat (3 g sat. fat), 95 mg chol., 862 mg sodium, 19 g carbo., 5 g fiber, 37 g pro.

PREP:

20 minutes

COOK:

10 to 12 hours (low) or 5 to 6 hours (high)

MAKES:

6 servings

Chunks of butternut squash impart just a hint of sweetness to this home-style stew. (Recipe pictured on the cover and on page 286.)

FIRESIDE BEEF STEW

PREP:

25 minutes

COOK:

10 to 12 hours (low) or 5 to 6 hours (high), plus 15 minutes (high)

MAKES:

6 servings

2 tablespoons all-purpose flour

1 pound boneless beef chuck roast, cut into 1-inch pieces

2 tablespoons cooking oil

1 pound tiny new potatoes, quartered

1 pound butternut squash, peeled, seeded, and cut into 1-inch pieces (about 2½ cups)

2 small onions, cut into wedges

2 cloves garlic, minced

1 14-ounce can beef broth or 1¾ cups homemade beef broth

1 cup vegetable juice

2 tablespoons Worcestershire sauce

1 tablespoon lemon juice

½ teaspoon sugar

½ teaspoon paprika

¼ teaspoon black pepper

⅛ teaspoon ground allspice

1 9-ounce package frozen Italian-style green beans or 2 cups frozen peas

1 Place flour in a self-sealing plastic bag. Add beef pieces, a few at time, shaking to coat. In a large skillet heat oil. Add beef; cook and stir over medium heat until brown. Drain off fat.

2 In a 3½- to 4½-quart slow cooker combine beef, potatoes, squash, onions, and garlic. In a large bowl combine broth, vegetable juice, Worcestershire sauce, lemon juice, sugar, paprika, pepper, and allspice. Pour over beef and vegetables in cooker.

3 Cover and cook on low-heat setting for 10 to 12 hours or on high-heat setting for 5 to 6 hours.

4 If using low-heat setting, turn cooker to high-heat setting. Stir in green beans. Cover and cook for 15 minutes more.

Nutrition Facts per serving: 304 cal., 13 g total fat (4 g sat. fat), 48 mg chol., 456 mg sodium, 30 g carbo., 4 g fiber, 19 g pro.

The sweet-tart combination of molasses and vinegar brings out the flavor of the beef in this saucy stew.

BEEF & MUSHROOM STEW

2	pounds boneless beef chuck steak, trimmed and cut into 1-inch cubes
3	tablespoons all-purpose flour
2	tablespoons cooking oil
4	medium carrots, cut into ½-inch slices
1	cup chopped onion
1	14½-ounce can diced tomatoes, undrained
¼	cup cider vinegar
¼	cup mild-flavored molasses
½	teaspoon salt
½	teaspoon celery salt
¼	teaspoon black pepper
¼	teaspoon ground ginger
12	ounces assorted fresh mushrooms, halved
¼	cup raisins
3	cups hot cooked noodles, rice, or mashed potatoes

PREP:
30 minutes
COOK:
*8 hours (low) or
4 hours (high),
plus 1 hour (high)*
MAKES:
6 servings

1 In a self-sealing plastic bag toss beef cubes with flour. In a large skillet heat oil. Add beef, half at a time; cook and stir over medium heat until brown. Drain off fat.

2 In a 3½- or 4-quart slow cooker place carrots and onion. Add beef. In a medium bowl combine undrained tomatoes, vinegar, molasses, salt, celery salt, pepper, and ginger; pour over beef in cooker.

3 Cover and cook on low-heat setting for 8 hours or on high-heat setting for 4 hours.

4 If using low-heat setting, turn cooker to high-heat setting. Stir in mushrooms and raisins. Cover and cook for 1 hour more. Serve over hot cooked noodles.

Nutrition Facts per serving: 483 cal., 16 g total fat (5 g sat. fat), 79 mg chol., 584 mg sodium, 50 g carbo., 3 g fiber, 34 g pro.

Heavenly news! The flavors of Steak Diane, a classic French dish, translate perfectly in this hearty slow-cooker stew.

MUSHROOM STEAK DIANE STEW

PREP:

20 minutes

COOK:

*8 to 10 hours (low) or
4 to 5 hours (high)*

MAKES:

6 servings

1½   pounds boneless beef round steak, cut 1 inch thick

2   medium onions, cut into thin wedges

3   cups sliced fresh button mushrooms (8 ounces)

1   10¾-ounce can condensed golden mushroom soup

¼   cup tomato paste

2   teaspoons Worcestershire sauce

1   teaspoon dry mustard

½   teaspoon cracked black pepper

3   cups hot cooked noodles

1 Trim fat from beef. Cut beef into 1-inch pieces. Set aside.

2 In a 3½- or 4-quart slow cooker place onions; top with mushrooms. Add beef. In a medium bowl combine mushroom soup, tomato paste, Worcestershire sauce, dry mustard, and pepper. Pour over beef mixture in cooker.

3 Cover and cook on low-heat setting for 8 to 10 hours or on high-heat setting for 4 to 5 hours. Serve over hot cooked noodles.

Nutrition Facts per serving: 314 cal., 7 g total fat (2 g sat. fat), 92 mg chol., 569 mg sodium, 30 g carbo., 3 g fiber, 33 g pro.

You'll need a large slow cooker for this thick, meaty chili. Leftovers? Enjoy a second round of chili spooned over baked potatoes or make chili dogs with your favorite franks.

SOUTHWEST CHILI

2	pounds ground beef
2	cups chopped onions
1/2	cup chopped green or red sweet pepper
6	cloves garlic, minced
3 1/2	cups water
1	12-ounce can tomato paste
1	15-ounce can dark red kidney beans, rinsed and drained
1	15-ounce can Great Northern beans, rinsed and drained
1	14 1/2-ounce can diced tomatoes, undrained
1	tablespoon yellow mustard
1	teaspoon chili powder
1	teaspoon black pepper
1/2	teaspoon salt
1/2	to 1 teaspoon cayenne pepper
1/2	teaspoon ground cumin

PREP:

20 minutes

COOK:

8 to 10 hours (low) or 4 to 5 hours (high)

MAKES:

8 servings

1 In a very large skillet cook ground beef, onions, sweet pepper, and garlic over medium-high heat until beef is brown. Drain off fat.

2 Transfer beef mixture to a 4 1/2- to 6-quart slow cooker. Stir together the water and tomato paste; add to beef mixture. Stir in the beans, undrained tomatoes, mustard, chili powder, black pepper, salt, cayenne pepper, and cumin.

3 Cover and cook on low-heat setting for 8 to 10 hours or on high heat setting for 4 to 5 hours.

Nutrition Facts per serving: 414 cal., 18 g total fat (7 g sat. fat), 75 mg chol., 772 mg sodium, 36 g carbo., 9 g fiber, 32 g pro.

Mix up a fresh fruit salad for a serve-along that will contrast pleasingly with this boldly flavored chili.

SOUTHWEST TWO-MEAT & BEER CHILI

PREP:

20 minutes

COOK:

*8 to 10 hours (low) or
4 to 5 hours (high)*

MAKES:

6 servings

12   ounces boneless beef sirloin steak, cut 1 inch thick

12   ounces lean pork stew meat

¼   cup all-purpose flour

1   tablespoon cooking oil

2   14½-ounce cans diced tomatoes with basil, oregano, and garlic, undrained

1   15-ounce can red kidney beans, rinsed and drained

1   12-ounce can beer or nonalcoholic beer

1   8-ounce can tomato sauce

½   cup chopped onion

2   tablespoons chili powder

1   teaspoon ground cumin

¼   teaspoon ground cinnamon

1 Trim fat from beef. Cut beef and pork into 1-inch pieces. In a self-sealing plastic bag place flour. Add meat pieces, a few at a time, shaking to coat. In a large skillet heat oil. Add meat, half at a time; cook and stir over medium heat until brown. Drain off fat.

2 Transfer meat to a 4- to 5-quart slow cooker. Stir in undrained tomatoes, beans, beer, tomato sauce, onion, chili powder, cumin, and cinnamon.

3 Cover and cook on low-heat setting for 8 to 10 hours or on high-heat setting for 4 to 5 hours.

Nutrition Facts per serving: 339 cal., 8 g total fat (2 g sat. fat), 71 mg chol., 1,105 mg sodium, 34 g carbo., 6 g fiber, 32 g pro.

This hearty chili could have been called everything-but-the-kitchen-sink chili, as it boasts three different meats and a variety of chili seasonings.

MEAT LOVERS' CHILI

PREP:

30 minutes

COOK:

8 to 10 hours (low) or 4 to 5 hours (high)

MAKES:

6 servings

8   ounces bulk Italian sausage

1½   pounds boneless beef chuck roast, trimmed and cut into ½-inch pieces

1   cup chopped onion

¾   cup chopped green sweet pepper

1   clove garlic, minced

2   cups water

1   14½-ounce can diced tomatoes, undrained

1   6-ounce can tomato paste

6   slices bacon, crisp-cooked, drained, and crumbled

1   to 2 fresh jalapeño chile peppers, seeded and finely chopped*

1   small dried red chile pepper, seeded and crumbled

1   tablespoon chili powder

¼   teaspoon salt

¼   teaspoon dried oregano, crushed

1   15-ounce can pinto or red kidney beans, rinsed and drained

1 In a 4-quart Dutch oven cook sausage over medium-high heat until brown. Using a slotted spoon, transfer sausage to a 3½- or 4-quart slow cooker, reserving drippings. Cook half of the beef in hot drippings until brown; transfer beef to cooker. Add remaining beef, the onion, sweet pepper, and garlic to drippings in Dutch oven. Cook until beef is brown and onion is tender. Drain off fat. Transfer beef mixture to cooker.

2 Stir in water, undrained tomatoes, tomato paste, bacon, jalapeño peppers, dried chile pepper, chili powder, salt, and oregano.

3 Cover and cook on low-heat setting for 8 to 10 hours or on high-heat setting for 4 to 5 hours. Stir in beans; heat through.

*NOTE: When working with chile peppers, wear plastic or rubber gloves. If your bare hands do touch the chile peppers, wash your hands well with soap and water.

Nutrition Facts per serving: 430 cal., 19 g total fat (4 g sat. fat), 78 mg chol., 658 mg sodium, 25 g carbo., 6 g fiber, 37 g pro.

Texans enjoy their chili with beans on the side, but if you'd rather, stir the Double-Bean Toss into the chili just before serving.

CHILI WITH DOUBLE-BEAN TOSS

PREP:

25 minutes

COOK:

10 to 12 hours (low) or 5 to 6 hours (high)

MAKES:

6 servings

1   tablespoon cooking oil

1   pound boneless beef top round steak, trimmed and cut into ¾-inch pieces

2   14½-ounce cans diced tomatoes, undrained

1   14-ounce can beef broth or 1¾ cups homemade beef broth

1   cup chopped onion

1   or 2 fresh jalapeño or serrano chile peppers, seeded and finely chopped*

2   cloves garlic, minced

4   teaspoons chili powder

1   tablespoon packed brown sugar

1½   teaspoons dried oregano, crushed

½   teaspoon ground cumin

¼   teaspoon black pepper

1   recipe Double-Bean Toss

   Dairy sour cream (optional)

   Fresh cilantro or parsley sprigs (optional)

   Tortilla chips (optional)

1 In a large skillet heat oil. Add beef, half at a time; cook and stir over medium heat until brown. Drain off fat.

2 In a 3½- or 4-quart slow cooker combine undrained tomatoes, broth, onion, chile pepper, garlic, chili powder, brown sugar, oregano, cumin, and black pepper. Stir in beef.

3 Cover and cook on low-heat setting for 10 to 12 hours or on high-heat setting for 5 to 6 hours.

4 Serve the chili with Double-Bean Toss. If desired, top each serving with sour cream and garnish with cilantro and tortilla chips.

DOUBLE-BEAN TOSS: In a medium bowl combine one 15-ounce can pinto beans, rinsed and drained; one 15-ounce can black beans, rinsed and drained; ½ teaspoon finely shredded lime peel; 1 tablespoon lime juice; 1 tablespoon cooking oil; and 1 clove garlic, minced. Toss to mix.

*NOTE: When working with chile peppers, wear plastic or rubber gloves. If your bare hands do touch the chile peppers, wash your hands well with soap and water.

Nutrition Facts per serving: 332 cal., 11 g total fat (3 g sat. fat), 45 mg chol., 924 mg sodium, 35 g carbo., 9 g fiber, 27 g pro.

Lentils make this dish extra easy—they don't require presoaking or precooking; just rinse and add them to the slow cooker with the rest of the ingredients. (Recipe pictured on page 284.)

LAMB & LENTIL SOUP

1	tablespoon cooking oil
12	ounces lean boneless lamb or beef, cut into $\frac{1}{2}$-inch cubes
1	cup thinly sliced celery
1	cup coarsely chopped carrots
1	cup dry lentils, rinsed
1	$10\frac{1}{2}$-ounce can condensed French onion soup
$1\frac{1}{2}$	teaspoons dried thyme, crushed
$\frac{1}{2}$	teaspoon black pepper
$\frac{1}{2}$	teaspoon salt
$3\frac{1}{4}$	cups water

PREP:

20 minutes

COOK:

7 to 8 hours (low) or $3\frac{1}{2}$ to 4 hours (high)

MAKES:

4 or 5 servings

1 In a large skillet heat oil. Add meat; cook and stir over medium heat until brown. Drain off fat.

2 In a $3\frac{1}{2}$- or 4-quart slow cooker place celery, carrots, and lentils. Top with meat. Stir in soup, thyme, pepper, and salt. Gradually stir in water.

3 Cover and cook on low-heat setting for 7 to 8 hours or on high-heat setting for $3\frac{1}{2}$ to 4 hours.

Nutrition Facts per serving: 379 cal., 10 g total fat (2 g sat. fat), 57 mg chol., 989 mg sodium, 38 g carbo., 17 g fiber, 33 g pro.

A longtime food editor in the Better Homes and Gardens family of publications says that she's made this recipe so many times, she doesn't have to measure the ingredients anymore. That's high praise from someone who has seen a lot of recipes over the years!

COUNTRY BEAN STEW

PREP:

1 1/2 hours

COOK:

8 to 10 hours (low) or 4 to 5 hours (high), plus 15 minutes (high)

MAKES:

6 servings

2	cups dry Great Northern beans
1 1/2	cups coarsely chopped carrots
12	ounces lean boneless lamb, trimmed and cut into 3/4-inch pieces
8	ounces bulk Italian sausage
1 1/2	cups coarsely chopped onion
3	cloves garlic, minced
1	teaspoon instant beef bouillon granules
1/2	teaspoon dried thyme, crushed
1/2	teaspoon dried oregano, crushed
3	cups water
1/4	cup dry red wine
1/2	of a 6-ounce can (1/3 cup) tomato paste
1/2	cup cubed cooked ham
1/4	cup snipped fresh parsley

1 Rinse beans. In a large saucepan combine beans and enough water to cover them by 2 inches. Bring to boiling; reduce heat. Simmer, uncovered, for 10 minutes. Remove from heat. Cover and let stand for 1 hour. Drain and rinse beans.

2 In a 3 1/2- to 5-quart slow cooker combine beans and carrots. In a large skillet cook lamb, Italian sausage, onion, and garlic over medium heat until meat is brown and onions are tender. Drain off fat.

3 Transfer meat mixture to cooker. Stir in bouillon granules, thyme, and oregano. Pour water over all.

4 Cover and cook on low-heat setting for 8 to 10 hours or on high-heat setting for 4 to 5 hours.

5 If using low-heat setting, turn cooker to high-heat setting. In a small bowl stir wine into tomato paste; add to stew. Stir in ham and parsley. Cover and cook for 15 minutes more.

Nutrition Facts per serving: 475 cal., 13 g total fat (5 g sat. fat), 72 mg chol., 769 mg sodium, 50 g carbo., 15 g fiber, 37 g pro.

Barley is a good choice for a slow-cooker stew because it retains its shape and chewy texture during the long cooking. Buy regular rather than quick-cooking barley for this dish.

LAMB & BARLEY STEW WITH MINT

1½   pounds lamb stew meat, trimmed and cut into 1-inch cubes

2½   cups reduced-sodium chicken broth or
         homemade chicken broth

1   14½-ounce can diced tomatoes, undrained

½   cup chopped onion

½   cup pearl barley

¼   cup dry white wine (optional)

4   cloves garlic, minced

2   tablespoons snipped fresh dillweed or 1½ teaspoons dried
         dillweed

½   teaspoon salt

¼   teaspoon black pepper

1   7-ounce jar roasted red sweet peppers,
         drained and thinly sliced

¼   cup snipped fresh mint

PREP:

20 minutes

COOK:

*8 to 10 hours (low) or
4 to 5 hours (high)*

MAKES:

4 to 6 servings

1 In a 3½- or 4-quart slow cooker combine lamb, broth, undrained tomatoes, onion, barley, wine (if desired), garlic, dried dill (if using), salt, and black pepper.

2 Cover and cook on low-heat setting for 8 to 10 hours or on high-heat setting for 4 to 5 hours. To serve, stir in the fresh dill (if using), roasted sweet peppers, and fresh mint.

Nutrition Facts per serving: 346 cal., 7 g total fat (2 g sat. fat), 107 mg chol., 1,193 mg sodium, 28 g carbo., 6 g fiber, 40 g pro.

This sweet and savory stew also works well when made with beef. Serve it with a romaine lettuce salad and hot corn bread.

VENISON & CIDER STEW

PREP:

35 minutes

COOK:

*10 to 12 hours (low) or
5 to 6 hours (high),
plus 30 minutes (high)*

MAKES:

6 servings

2	tablespoons cooking oil
1¼	pounds venison stew meat, cut into 1-inch pieces
2	medium red-skinned potatoes, cut up
4	medium carrots and/or parsnips, cut up
2	medium onions, quartered
½	cup sliced celery
1	cup apple cider
1	cup beef broth
2	tablespoons quick-cooking tapioca
¼	teaspoon salt
¼	teaspoon dried marjoram, crushed
¼	teaspoon crushed red pepper (optional)
2	medium apples, cored and cut into wedges

1 In a large skillet heat oil. Add venison, half at a time; cook and stir over medium heat until brown. Drain off fat.

2 In a 3½- to 5-quart slow cooker combine the venison, potatoes, carrots, onions, celery, cider, broth, tapioca, salt, marjoram, and, if desired, crushed red pepper. Stir gently to combine.

3 Cover and cook on low-heat setting for 10 to 12 hours or on high-heat setting for 5 to 6 hours.

4 If using low heat setting, turn cooker to high-heat setting. Stir in the apple wedges. Cover and cook for 30 minutes more.

Nutrition Facts per serving: 286 cal., 7 g total fat (2 g sat. fat), 80 mg chol., 306 mg sodium, 32 g carbo., 4 g fiber, 24 g pro.

If bison or beef stew meat is unavailable, use a 1 1/2-pound bison (buffalo) or beef chuck pot roast. Trim fat from meat and cut the meat into 1-inch cubes.

BUFFALO STEW

4	medium red-skinned potatoes, chopped
4	medium carrots, cut into 1-inch pieces, or 2 cups tiny whole carrots
1	cup coarsely chopped onion
½	cup sliced celery
2	tablespoons quick-cooking tapioca
1	pound bison (buffalo) or beef stew meat, cut into 1-inch cubes
2	14½-ounce cans stewed tomatoes, cut up and undrained
1	tablespoon sugar
1	tablespoon dried Italian seasoning, crushed (optional)
1	teaspoon salt
½	teaspoon black pepper

1 In a 4- to 5-quart slow cooker place potatoes, carrots, onion, and celery. Sprinkle tapioca over vegetables. Add meat. In a medium bowl combine undrained tomatoes, sugar, Italian seasoning (if desired), salt, and pepper; pour over meat.

2 Cover and cook on low-heat setting for 10 to 12 hours or on high-heat setting for 5 to 6 hours.

Nutrition Facts per serving: 263 cal., 3 g total fat (1 g sat. fat), 47 mg chol., 702 mg sodium, 39 g carbo., 5 g fiber, 21 g pro.

PREP:
25 minutes

COOK:
10 to 12 hours (low) or 5 to 6 hours (high)

MAKES:
6 servings

Tuscans love white beans, and you will, too, once you enjoy them in this colorful soup.

TUSCAN HAM & BEAN SOUP

PREP:

25 minutes

COOK:

*6 to 8 hours (low) or
3 to 4 hours (high)*

MAKES:

8 servings

3	15-ounce cans small white beans, rinsed and drained
2½	cups cubed cooked ham
1½	cups chopped carrots
1	cup thinly sliced celery
1	cup chopped onion
¼	teaspoon black pepper
2	14½-ounce cans diced tomatoes with garlic and herbs, undrained
2	14-ounce cans reduced-sodium chicken broth or 3½ cups homemade chicken broth
8	cups torn fresh kale or spinach leaves
	Freshly shredded Parmesan cheese (optional)

1 In a 5- to 6-quart slow cooker combine beans, ham, carrots, celery, onion, and pepper. Stir in undrained tomatoes and broth.

2 Cover and cook on low-heat setting for 6 to 8 hours or on high-heat setting for 3 to 4 hours. Just before serving, stir in kale. If desired, sprinkle each serving with Parmesan cheese.

Nutrition Facts per serving: 323 cal., 3 g total fat (1 g sat. fat), 21 mg chol., 2,099 mg sodium, 53 g carbo., 12 g fiber, 25 g pro.

When you don't have time to shred a head of cabbage, use packaged coleslaw mix instead. The carrot in the mix will add bright spots of color to the soup.

HAM & VEGETABLE SOUP

3   cups cubed cooked ham or 1 pound cooked, smoked kielbasa (Polska kielbasa), halved lengthwise and cut into $\frac{1}{2}$-inch slices

3   cups shredded cabbage

2   14$\frac{1}{2}$-ounce cans stewed tomatoes, undrained

1   15-ounce can Great Northern beans, undrained

1   14$\frac{1}{2}$-ounce can cut green beans, undrained

$\frac{1}{2}$ cup chopped onion

$\frac{1}{4}$ cup ketchup

2   tablespoons packed brown sugar (optional)

1   tablespoon Worcestershire sauce

4   cloves garlic, minced

$\frac{1}{2}$ teaspoon black pepper

$\frac{1}{2}$ teaspoon bottled hot pepper sauce

1 In a 4- to 6-quart slow cooker combine all ingredients.

2 Cover and cook on low-heat setting for 8 to 10 hours or on high-heat setting for 4 to 5 hours.

Nutrition Facts per serving: 421 cal., 23 g total fat (8 g sat. fat), 51 mg chol., 1,348 mg sodium, 37 g carbo., 7 g fiber, 19 g pro.

PREP:
20 minutes

COOK:
8 to 10 hours (low) or 4 to 5 hours (high)

MAKES:
6 servings

Dried cranberries provide just the right amount of tang to complement the smoky flavor of the ham and pungency of the curry powder.

CURRIED SPLIT PEA SOUP

PREP:

10 minutes

COOK:

10 to 12 hours (low) or 5 to 6 hours (high)

MAKES:

6 servings

1	pound dry green split peas, rinsed
1	pound ham hocks
1½	cups cubed cooked ham
1½	cups chopped celery
1	cup chopped onion
1	cup chopped carrots
⅓	cup dried cranberries
4	teaspoons curry powder
1	tablespoon dried marjoram, crushed
2	bay leaves
¼	teaspoon black pepper
6	cups water

1 In a 3½- or 4-quart slow cooker combine split peas, ham hocks, ham, celery, onion, carrots, cranberries, curry powder, marjoram, bay leaves, and pepper. Stir in the water.

2 Cover and cook on low-heat setting for 10 to 12 hours or on high-heat setting for 5 to 6 hours. Remove and discard bay leaves. Remove ham hocks. When ham hocks are cool enough to handle, remove meat from bones; discard bones. Coarsely chop meat. Return ham to soup.

Nutrition Facts per serving: 376 cal., 4 g total fat (1 g sat. fat), 25 mg chol., 626 mg sodium, 58 g carbo., 6 g fiber, 29 g pro.

Tortilla chips make a fun accompaniment to this south-of-the-border spiced stew.

TACO PORK STEW

1	tablespoon cooking oil
1½	pounds lean pork stew meat, cut into 1-inch pieces
1	15-ounce can red kidney beans, rinsed and drained
1½	cups frozen whole kernel corn
1	cup frozen small whole onions
1	14½-ounce can diced tomatoes, undrained
1	8-ounce can tomato sauce
1	cup water
1	1¼-ounce envelope taco seasoning mix
½	teaspoon ground cumin
⅓	cup shredded cheddar cheese
⅓	cup dairy sour cream

PREP:

15 minutes

COOK:

*8 to 10 hours (low) or
4 to 5 hours (high)*

MAKES:

6 servings

1 In a large skillet heat oil. Add pork, half at a time; cook and stir over medium heat until brown. Drain off fat.

2 Transfer pork to a 3½- or 4-quart slow cooker. Stir in beans, corn, and onions. In a medium bowl combine undrained tomatoes, tomato sauce, water, taco seasoning mix, and cumin. Stir into pork mixture in cooker.

3 Cover and cook on low-heat setting for 8 to 10 hours or on high-heat setting for 4 to 5 hours. Top each serving with cheddar cheese and sour cream.

Nutrition Facts per serving: 360 cal., 15 g total fat (5 g sat. fat), 85 mg chol., 1,171 mg sodium, 30 g carbo., 7 g fiber, 33 g pro.

Boneless pork shoulder—a down-home cut of meat—gets a bistro-style update with fresh fennel, roasted sweet peppers, and an herb-cream base.

RED PEPPER, PORK, & FENNEL STEW

PREP:

20 minutes

COOK:

*8 to 10 hours (low) or
4 to 5 hours (high)*

MAKES:

6 servings

1	tablespoon olive or cooking oil
1½	pounds boneless pork shoulder, trimmed and cut into 1-inch pieces
3	medium onions, cut into thin wedges
2	small fennel bulbs, trimmed and cut into ½-inch wedges
1	14-ounce can beef broth or 1¾ cups homemade beef broth
4	teaspoons quick-cooking tapioca
½	teaspoon dried marjoram or savory, crushed
¼	teaspoon salt
¼	teaspoon cracked black pepper
1	12-ounce jar roasted red sweet peppers, drained and cut into thin strips
⅓	cup whipping cream
3	cups hot cooked rice

1 In a large skillet heat oil. Add pork, half at a time; cook and stir over medium heat until brown. Drain off fat. Set aside.

2 In a 3½- or 4-quart slow cooker combine onions and fennel. Stir in broth, tapioca, marjoram, salt, and black pepper. Top with pork.

3 Cover and cook on low-heat setting for 8 to 10 hours or on high-heat setting for 4 to 5 hours. Stir in roasted sweet peppers and cream. Serve over hot cooked rice.

Nutrition Facts per serving: 387 cal., 16 g total fat (7 g sat. fat), 95 mg chol., 425 mg sodium, 32 g carbo., 9 g fiber, 26 g pro.

Satay is an Indonesian specialty of spicy marinated meat broiled or grilled on skewers. Bring its lively flavors home with this easy, full-flavored stew.

PORK SATAY STEW

1½   pounds boneless pork shoulder, trimmed and
     cut into 1-inch pieces

2   medium red and/or green sweet peppers,
     cut into 1-inch pieces

1   large red onion, cut into wedges

1   cup bottled thick and chunky salsa

½   cup creamy peanut butter

1   tablespoon reduced-sodium soy sauce

1   tablespoon lime juice

1½   teaspoons grated fresh ginger

½   teaspoon ground coriander

¾   cup half-and-half or light cream

3   cups hot cooked rice

⅓   cup chopped dry roasted peanuts

¼   cup sliced green onions

PREP:

15 minutes

COOK:

*7 to 8 hours (low) or
3½ to 4 hours (high)*

MAKES:

6 servings

1 In a 3½-quart slow cooker combine pork, sweet peppers, onion, salsa, peanut butter, soy sauce, lime juice, ginger, and coriander.

2 Cover and cook on low-heat setting for 7 to 8 hours or on high-heat setting for 3½ to 4 hours. Stir in half-and-half. Serve over hot cooked rice. Sprinkle each serving with peanuts and green onions.

Nutrition Facts per serving: 502 cal., 25 g total fat (7 g sat. fat), 84 mg chol., 462 mg sodium, 36 g carbo., 3 g fiber, 34 g pro.

Pumpkin pie spice and a hint of sweetness from dried apricots and raisins complement the pork and winter squash. Any type of winter squash will do, although butternut is easiest to peel.

PORK & SQUASH STEW

PREP:

20 minutes

COOK:

7 to 8 hours (low) or 3½ to 4 hours (high)

MAKES:

4 servings

2	tablespoons cooking oil
1½	pounds boneless pork shoulder roast, trimmed and cut into 1-inch pieces
1½	pounds winter squash (such as butternut, Hubbard, or acorn), peeled and cut into 1-inch pieces
½	cup sliced onion
½	cup dried apricots
2	tablespoons raisins
3	tablespoons instant flour or ¼ cup packaged instant mashed potato flakes
1	tablespoon packed brown sugar
¾	teaspoon pumpkin pie spice
¼	teaspoon salt
1	14-ounce can chicken broth or 1¾ cups homemade chicken broth
1	tablespoon bottled steak sauce

1 In a large skillet heat oil. Add pork, half at a time; cook and stir over medium heat until brown. Drain off fat.

2 In a 3½- or 4-quart slow cooker place squash, onion, apricots, and raisins. Add pork. Sprinkle with instant flour, brown sugar, pumpkin pie spice, and salt. Combine broth and steak sauce; pour over pork.

3 Cover and cook on low-heat setting for 7 to 8 hours or on high-heat setting for 3½ to 4 hours. Stir gently before serving.

Nutrition Facts per serving: 469 cal., 21 g total fat (6 g sat. fat), 115 mg chol., 771 mg sodium, 33 g carbo., 2 g fiber, 38 g pro.

Prepare this Asian-influenced soup with good taste—and good nutrition—in mind. Green soybeans (edamame) are good sources of soy, which is associated with a reduced risk of some types of cancer and the maintenance or improvement of bone health.

PORK & EDAMAME SOUP

1	tablespoon cooking oil
2	pounds boneless pork shoulder, trimmed and cut into 1-inch pieces
2	14-ounce cans chicken broth or 3½ cups homemade chicken broth
1	12-ounce package frozen green soybeans (edamame)
1	8-ounce can sliced water chestnuts, drained
1	cup chopped red sweet pepper
2	tablespoons reduced-sodium soy sauce
1	tablespoon bottled hoisin sauce
2	teaspoons grated fresh ginger
¼	to ½ teaspoon crushed red pepper
6	cloves garlic, minced
1	3-ounce package ramen noodles, broken

1 In a large skillet heat oil. Add pork, half at a time; cook and stir over medium heat until brown. Drain off fat.

2 Transfer pork to a 3½- to 4½-quart slow cooker. Stir in broth, soybeans, water chestnuts, sweet pepper, soy sauce, hoisin sauce, ginger, crushed red pepper, and garlic.

3 Cover and cook on low-heat setting for 7 to 8 hours or on high-heat setting for 3½ to 4 hours. Skim off fat. Stir in ramen noodles (discard seasoning packet or reserve for another use). Cover and cook for 5 minutes more.

Nutrition Facts per serving: 400 cal., 15 g total fat (4 g sat. fat), 111 mg chol., 906 mg sodium, 22 g carbo., 7 g fiber, 41 g pro.

PREP:

25 minutes

COOK:

7 to 8 hours (low) or 3½ to 4 hours (high), plus 5 minutes

MAKES:

6 servings

Chicken thighs are the preferred cut for slow-cooker soups because they don't fall apart or become stringy during the long cooking.

GINGER-CHICKEN NOODLE SOUP

PREP:

20 minutes

COOK:

2 to 3 hours (high)
plus 5 minutes (high)

MAKES:

6 servings

1   pound skinless, boneless chicken thighs, cut into 1-inch pieces

1   cup coarsely shredded carrots

2   tablespoons dry sherry (optional)

1   tablespoon soy sauce

1   tablespoon rice vinegar

1   teaspoon grated fresh ginger or $\frac{1}{2}$ teaspoon ground ginger

$\frac{1}{4}$ teaspoon black pepper

3   14-ounce cans chicken broth or $5\frac{1}{4}$ cups homemade chicken broth

1   cup water

2   ounces dried rice vermicelli noodles or medium noodles

1   6-ounce package frozen pea pods, thawed and halved diagonally

    Soy sauce (optional)

1 In a $3\frac{1}{2}$- to 6-quart slow cooker combine chicken, carrots, sherry (if desired), the 1 tablespoon soy sauce, the vinegar, ginger, and pepper. Stir in broth and water.

2 Cover and cook on high-heat setting for 2 to 3 hours.

3 Stir in noodles and pea pods. Cover and cook for 5 to 10 minutes more or until noodles are tender. If desired, serve with additional soy sauce.

Nutrition Facts per serving: 174 cal., 3 g total fat (1 g sat. fat), 44 mg chol., 1,050 mg sodium, 13 g carbo., 1 g fiber, 21 g pro.

This streamlined soup version of the classic French specialty is delicious served with crusty bread.

EASY CASSOULET SOUP

2   medium carrots, cut into $\frac{1}{2}$-inch pieces

1   medium red or green sweet pepper, cut into $\frac{1}{2}$-inch pieces

1   cup chopped onion

3   cloves garlic, minced

2   15-ounce cans white kidney (cannellini) beans or Great Northern beans, rinsed and drained

1   $14\frac{1}{2}$-ounce can Italian-style stewed tomatoes, undrained

8   ounces skinless, boneless chicken thighs, cut into 1-inch pieces

8   ounces cooked smoked turkey sausage, halved lengthwise and cut into $\frac{1}{2}$-inch slices

$1\frac{1}{2}$ cups chicken broth

$\frac{1}{2}$ cup dry white wine or chicken broth

1   tablespoon snipped fresh parsley

1   teaspoon dried thyme, crushed

$\frac{1}{8}$ to $\frac{1}{4}$ teaspoon cayenne pepper

1   bay leaf

PREP:

20 minutes

COOK:

7 to 8 hours (low) or $3\frac{1}{2}$ to 4 hours (high)

MAKES:

6 to 8 servings

1 In a $3\frac{1}{2}$- to 5-quart slow cooker layer carrots, sweet pepper, onion, garlic, beans, undrained tomatoes, chicken, and sausage. Add broth, wine, parsley, thyme, cayenne pepper, and bay leaf.

2 Cover and cook on low-heat setting for 7 to 8 hours or on high-heat setting for $3\frac{1}{2}$ to 4 hours. Remove and discard bay leaf.

Nutrition Facts per serving: 248 cal., 6 g total fat (2 g sat. fat), 55 mg chol., 969 mg sodium, 31 g carbo., 9 g fiber, 23 g pro.

Round out this meal with hot-from-the oven biscuits and a crisp green salad topped with citrus slices and your favorite vinaigrette would round out this meal nicely.

SPINACH, CHICKEN, & WILD RICE SOUP

PREP:

15 minutes

COOK:

7 to 8 hours (low) or 3½ to 4 hours (high)

MAKES:

6 servings

3 cups water

1 14-ounce can chicken broth or 1¾ cups homemade chicken broth

1 10¾-ounce can condensed cream of chicken soup

⅔ cup uncooked wild rice, rinsed

½ teaspoon dried thyme, crushed

¼ teaspoon black pepper

3 cups chopped cooked chicken or turkey

2 cups shredded fresh spinach

1 In a 3½- or 4-quart slow cooker combine water, broth, soup, wild rice, thyme, and pepper.

2 Cover and cook on low-heat setting for 7 to 8 hours or on high-heat setting for 3½ to 4 hours. Stir in chicken and spinach.

Nutrition Facts per serving: 263 cal., 9 g total fat (3 g sat. fat), 66 mg chol., 741 mg sodium, 19 g carbo., 2 g fiber, 25 g pro.

Cream of chicken soup gives you a head start, and the bacon, added as a final touch, brings a crunchy contrast to the creaminess.

CREAMED CHICKEN & CORN SOUP

12	ounces skinless, boneless chicken thighs
1	26-ounce can condensed cream of chicken soup
1	14¾-ounce can cream-style corn
1	14-ounce can reduced-sodium chicken broth or 1¾ cups homemade chicken broth
1	cup chopped carrots
1	cup finely chopped onion
1	cup frozen whole kernel corn
½	cup chopped celery
½	cup water
2	slices bacon, crisp-cooked, drained, and crumbled

PREP:

20 minutes

COOK:

*5 to 6 hours (low) or
2½ to 3 hours (high)*

MAKES:

4 to 6 servings

1 In a 3½- or 4-quart slow cooker combine chicken, soup, cream-style corn, broth, carrots, onion, frozen corn, celery, and water.

2 Cover and cook on low-heat setting for 5 to 6 hours or on high-heat setting for 2½ to 3 hours. Remove chicken from cooker; cool slightly. Chop chicken; stir into soup. Sprinkle each serving with bacon.

Nutrition Facts per serving: 469 cal., 19 g total fat (6 g sat. fat), 87 mg chol., 2,063 mg sodium, 50 g carbo., 5 g fiber, 28 g pro.

This hearty recipe can easily be made into a tasty meatless version by omitting the chicken.

BEAN SOUP WITH CHICKEN & VEGETABLES

PREP:

1¹/₂ hours

COOK:

*8 to 10 hours (low) or
4 to 5 hours (high),
plus 30 minutes (high)*

MAKES:

6 servings

1 cup dry Great Northern beans

1 cup chopped onion

1 medium fennel bulb, trimmed and cut into ¹/₂-inch pieces

1 cup chopped carrots

2 cloves garlic, minced

1 teaspoon dried thyme, crushed

1 teaspoon dried marjoram, crushed

¹/₄ teaspoon black pepper

3 14-ounce cans chicken broth or 5¹/₄ cups homemade chicken broth

2¹/₂ cups chopped cooked chicken

1 14¹/₂-ounce can diced tomatoes, undrained

2 tablespoons snipped fresh parsley

1 Rinse beans. In a large saucepan combine beans and enough water to cover them by 2 inches. Bring to boiling; reduce heat. Simmer, uncovered, for 10 minutes. Remove saucepan from heat. Cover; let stand for 1 hour. Drain and rinse beans; set aside.

2 In a 4- to 5-quart slow cooker combine onion, fennel, carrots, garlic, thyme, marjoram, and pepper. Place beans over vegetables. Pour broth over all.

3 Cover and cook on low-heat setting for 8 to 10 hours or on high-heat setting for 4 to 5 hours.

4 If using low-heat setting, turn cooker to high-heat setting. Stir in chicken and tomatoes. Cover and cook for 30 minutes more. Stir in parsley before serving.

Nutrition Facts per serving: 299 cal., 6 g total fat (2 g sat. fat), 52 mg chol., 834 mg sodium, 31 g carbo., 9 g fiber, 29 g pro.

Dried herbs and herb blends are preferred for slow cooking because they release their flavor gradually. Dried Italian seasoning is a fragrant blend of basil, oregano, rosemary, fennel seeds, and sometimes garlic powder and cayenne pepper.

HEARTY TURKEY SOUP

1	pound uncooked ground raw turkey or chicken
1	cup chopped celery
½	cup thinly sliced carrot
½	cup chopped onion
3	cups tomato juice
2	cups frozen French-cut green beans
1	cup sliced fresh mushrooms
½	cup chopped tomato
2	teaspoons dried Italian seasoning, crushed
1½	teaspoons Worcestershire sauce
¾	teaspoon garlic salt
½	teaspoon sugar
¼	teaspoon black pepper
1	bay leaf

PREP:

30 minutes

COOK:

5 to 6 hours (low) or 2½ to 3 hours (high)

MAKES:

4 or 5 servings

1 In a large skillet cook turkey, celery, carrot, and onion over medium heat until turkey is no longer pink. Drain off liquid.

2 Transfer turkey mixture to a 3½- or 4-quart slow cooker. Stir in tomato juice, frozen green beans, mushrooms, tomato, Italian seasoning, Worcestershire sauce, garlic salt, sugar, pepper, and bay leaf.

3 Cover and cook on low-heat setting for 5 to 6 hours or on high-heat setting for 2½ to 3 hours. Remove and discard bay leaf.

Nutrition Facts per serving: 256 cal., 10 g total fat (3 g sat. fat), 90 mg chol., 970 mg sodium, 20 g carbo., 4 g fiber, 24 g pro.

*For a traditional Italian trattoria presentation, purchase a wedge of Parmesan cheese
and use a vegetable peeler to cut wide shavings of cheese to garnish the soup.*
(Recipe pictured on page 284.)

SAUSAGE & TORTELLINI SOUP

PREP:

10 minutes

COOK:

*8 to 10 hours (low) or
4 to 5 hours (high),
plus 15 minutes (high)*

MAKES:

10 to 12 servings

2   14½-ounce cans Italian-style stewed tomatoes, undrained

3   cups water

2   cups frozen cut green beans or Italian-style green beans

1   10½-ounce can condensed French onion soup

8   ounces cooked smoked turkey sausage, halved
    lengthwise and cut into ½-inch slices

2   cups packaged shredded cabbage with carrot (coleslaw mix)

1   9-ounce package refrigerated cheese-filled tortellini
    Shaved or shredded Parmesan cheese (optional)

1 In a 4- to 5-quart slow cooker combine undrained tomatoes, water,
frozen green beans, soup, and turkey sausage.

2 Cover and cook on low-heat setting for 8 to 10 hours or on high-heat
setting for 4 to 5 hours.

3 If using low-heat setting, turn cooker to high-heat setting. Stir in
cabbage and tortellini; cover and cook for 15 minutes more. If desired,
garnish each serving with Parmesan cheese.

Nutrition Facts per serving: 176 cal., 5 g total fat (1 g sat. fat), 28 mg chol., 717 mg sodium,
23 g carbo., 2 g fiber, 9 g pro.

You can choose from numerous varieties of cooked smoked turkey at your supermarket deli. Also check out the selection of turkey sausage at the meat counter. (Recipe pictured on page 286.)

SPLIT PEA & SMOKED TURKEY SOUP

1	pound dry green split peas, rinsed
2	cups chopped cooked smoked turkey or sliced cooked turkey sausage (8 to 10 ounces)
1½	cups coarsely chopped carrots
1	cup coarsely chopped yellow or green sweet pepper
½	cup chopped onion
2	cloves garlic, minced
1	teaspoon dried basil, crushed
1	teaspoon dried oregano, crushed
3	14-ounce cans chicken broth or 5¼ cups homemade chicken broth

PREP:

25 minutes

COOK:

10 to 12 hours (low) or 5 to 6 hours (high)

MAKES:

4 servings

1 In a 3½- or 4-quart slow cooker combine the split peas, turkey, carrots, sweet pepper, onion, garlic, basil, and oregano. Pour broth over all.

2 Cover and cook on low-heat setting for 10 to 12 hours or on high-heat setting for 5 to 6 hours. Stir before serving.

Nutrition Facts per serving: 551 cal., 5 g total fat (1 g sat. fat), 22 mg chol., 2,258 mg sodium, 86 g carbo., 33 g fiber, 45 g pro.

If you don't have saffron, one of the world's most expensive spices, substitute turmeric, an economical and delicious alternative.

CHICKEN & SAUSAGE PAELLA

PREP:

30 minutes

COOK:

7 to 8 hours (low) or 3½ to 4 hours (high)

STAND:

5 minutes

MAKES:

6 servings

1	tablespoon cooking oil
2½	to 3 pounds meaty chicken pieces (breasts, thighs, and drumsticks), skinned
8	ounces cooked smoked turkey sausage, halved lengthwise and sliced
1	large onion, sliced
3	cloves garlic, minced
2	tablespoons snipped fresh thyme or 2 teaspoons dried thyme, crushed
¼	teaspoon black pepper
⅛	teaspoon thread saffron or ¼ teaspoon ground turmeric
1	14-ounce can reduced-sodium chicken broth or 1¾ cups homemade chicken broth
½	cup water
2	cups chopped tomatoes
2	medium yellow or green sweet peppers, cut into thin bite-size strips (1½ cups)
1	cup frozen peas
3	cups hot cooked rice or one 5-ounce package saffron-flavored yellow rice mix, cooked according to package directions

1 In a large skillet heat oil. Add chicken pieces, half at a time. Cook over medium heat until brown on all sides. Drain off fat.

2 In a 3½- or 4-quart slow cooker layer chicken pieces, turkey sausage, and onion. Sprinkle with garlic, dried thyme (if using), black pepper, and saffron. Pour broth and water over all.

3 Cover and cook on low-heat setting for 7 to 8 hours or on high-heat setting for 3½ to 4 hours. Add the tomatoes, sweet peppers, peas, and fresh thyme (if using). Cover and let stand for 5 minutes. Serve over hot cooked rice.

Nutrition Facts per serving: 394 cal., 12 g total fat (3 g sat. fat), 99 mg chol., 609 mg sodium, 36 g carbo., 3 g fiber, 36 g pro.

Gravy mix adds down-home flavor to this soup, while sour cream brings irresistible creaminess and a mild tang.

CREAMY CHICKEN & VEGETABLE STEW

1	tablespoon cooking oil
1½	pounds boneless, skinless chicken thighs, cut into 1-inch pieces
1	pound potatoes, peeled and cut into 1-inch pieces
2	cups baby carrots, trimmed
2	cups frozen cut green beans
½	cup chopped onion
1	teaspoon dried thyme, crushed
½	teaspoon salt
½	teaspoon poultry seasoning
2	cups water
2	0.87-ounce envelopes chicken gravy mix
1	8-ounce carton dairy sour cream

PREP:

30 minutes

COOK:

8 to 9 hours (low) or 4 to 4½ hours (high)

MAKES:

6 servings

1 In a large skillet heat oil. Add chicken, half at a time; cook and stir over medium heat until brown. Drain off fat.

2 Transfer chicken to a 3½- or 4-quart slow cooker. Stir in potatoes, carrots, green beans, onion, thyme, salt, and poultry seasoning. In a small bowl stir together water and gravy mix; stir into mixture in cooker.

3 Cover and cook on low-heat setting for 8 to 9 hours or on high-heat setting for 4 to 4½ hours.

4 In a medium bowl gradually stir about 1 cup of the hot stew into sour cream. Add sour cream mixture to cooker, stirring gently until combined.

Nutrition Facts per serving: 344 cal., 14 g total fat (6 g sat. fat), 107 mg chol., 769 mg sodium, 26 g carbo., 4 g fiber, 26 g pro.

Diced hash brown potatoes bring rib-sticking goodness to this filling stew; sausage contributes a smoky flavor.

EASY SAUSAGE & CHICKEN STEW

PREP:

10 minutes

COOK:

8 to 10 hours (low) or 4 to 5 hours (high), plus 30 minutes (high)

MAKES:

6 to 8 servings

1   pound cooked smoked turkey sausage, halved lengthwise and sliced

2   cups packaged peeled baby carrots

1   14-ounce can reduced-sodium chicken broth or 1¾ cups homemade chicken broth

1½ cups loose-pack frozen diced hash brown potatoes

1   10¾-ounce can condensed cream of chicken soup

1   teaspoon dried oregano, crushed

2   cups chopped cooked chicken or turkey

1   9-ounce package frozen cut green beans, thawed

1 In a 3½- or 4-quart slow cooker combine turkey sausage, carrots, broth, hash brown potatoes, soup, and oregano.

2 Cover and cook on low-heat setting for 8 to 10 hours or on high-heat setting for 4 to 5 hours.

3 If using low-heat setting, turn cooker to high-heat setting. Stir in chicken and green beans. Cover and cook for 30 minutes more.

Nutrition Facts per serving: 477 cal., 30 g total fat (13 g sat. fat), 79 mg chol., 1,238 mg sodium, 25 g carbo., 4 g fiber, 27 g pro.

A big bowl of this colorful stew is the ideal warm-up after an afternoon of working or playing outdoors.

TURKEY SAUSAGE & SWEET POTATO STEW

1½ pounds cooked smoked turkey sausage, halved lengthwise and cut into 1-inch slices

4 medium sweet potatoes, peeled and cut into ½-inch pieces (about 4 cups)

2 medium green sweet peppers, cut into 1-inch pieces

2 stalks celery, cut into ½-inch pieces

1 cup chopped onion

¼ cup quick-cooking tapioca

2 14½-ounce cans diced tomatoes with roasted garlic, undrained

2 15-ounce cans garbanzo beans (chickpeas), rinsed and drained

2 cups reduced-sodium beef broth or homemade beef broth

PREP:
25 minutes

COOK:
8 to 10 hours (low) or 4 to 5 hours (high)

MAKES:
10 servings

1 In a 3½- to 6-quart slow cooker combine turkey sausage, sweet potatoes, sweet peppers, celery, onion, and tapioca. Add undrained tomatoes, beans, and broth.

2 Cover and cook on low-heat setting for 8 to 10 hours or on high-heat setting for 4 to 5 hours.

Nutrition Facts per serving: 351 cal., 9 g total fat (2 g sat. fat), 61 mg chol., 1,577 mg sodium, 45 g carbo., 7 g fiber, 21 g pro.

Serve this thick chicken chili in bread bowls. To make the bread bowls, slice off the tops and hollow out the centers of 4-inch-diameter sourdough rolls. Ladle the chili into the bread bowls and serve the roll tops alongside. (Recipe pictured on page 285.)

CONFETTI WHITE CHILI

PREP:

25 minutes

COOK:

*6 to 8 hours (low) or
3 to 4 hours (high),
plus 15 minutes (high)*

MAKES:

6 to 8 servings

3	15-ounce cans Great Northern, pinto, or white kidney (cannellini) beans
1½	cups chopped red, green, and/or yellow sweet peppers
1	cup coarsely shredded carrots
½	cup sliced green onions
2	cloves garlic, minced
2	teaspoons dried oregano, crushed
1	teaspoon ground cumin
½	teaspoon salt
2	14-ounce cans chicken broth or 3½ cups homemade chicken broth
2½	cups chopped cooked chicken or turkey*
	Shredded Monterey Jack cheese (optional)

1 Rinse and drain 2 cans of the beans and place in a 3½- or 4-quart slow cooker. Use a potato masher or fork to mash beans. Rinse and drain the remaining 1 can of beans (do not mash). Stir beans, sweet peppers, carrots, green onions, garlic, oregano, cumin, and salt into mashed beans in cooker. Add broth. Stir until well combined.

2 Cover and cook on low-heat setting for 6 to 8 hours or high-heat setting for 3 to 4 hours.

3 If using low-heat setting, turn cooker to high-heat setting. Stir in chicken. Cover and cook for 15 minutes more or until chicken is heated through. If desired, sprinkle each serving with cheese.

*NOTE: For the cooked chicken, poach 3 or 4 skinless, boneless chicken breast halves in boiling water or chicken broth, covered, about 12 minutes or until no pink remains. Drain, cool slightly, and chop.

Nutrition Facts per serving: 707 cal., 10 g total fat (2 g sat. fat), 52 mg chol., 1,536 mg sodium, 110 g carbo., 16 g fiber, 44 g pro.

Thick and chunky, this chowder measures up. Halibut and haddock would be fine substitutes for the cod.

HEARTY FISH CHOWDER

2   cups finely chopped potatoes (2 medium)

1   cup chopped onion

2   cloves garlic, minced

1   10³/₄-ounce can condensed cream of celery soup

1   10-ounce package frozen whole kernel corn

1   10-ounce package frozen baby lima beans or 2 cups
     frozen baby lima beans

1½   cups chicken broth

¹/₃   cup dry white wine or chicken broth

1   teaspoon lemon-pepper seasoning

1   pound cod fillets

1   14½-ounce can stewed tomatoes, undrained

¹/₃   cup nonfat dry milk powder

1 In a 3½- or 4-quart slow cooker combine potatoes, onion, garlic, soup, corn, lima beans, broth, wine, and lemon-pepper seasoning.

2 Cover and cook on low-heat setting for 6 to 7 hours or on high-heat setting for 3 to 3½ hours.

3 Rinse fish; pat dry with paper towels. Place fish on the mixture in the cooker. If using low-heat setting, turn cooker to high-heat setting. Cover and cook for 1 hour more. Add undrained tomatoes and dry milk powder to cooker; stir gently to break up the fish.

Nutrition Facts per serving: 295 cal., 4 g total fat (1 g sat. fat), 39 mg chol., 955 mg sodium, 40 g carbo., 6 g fiber, 23 g pro.

PREP:

25 minutes

COOK:

*6 to 7 hours (low) or
3 to 3¹/₂ hours (high),
plus 1 hour (high)*

MAKES:

6 servings

Easy is right! The dry scalloped potato mix makes this wonderful dill-infused salmon chowder as simple as can be.

EASY POTATO & SALMON CHOWDER

PREP:

15 minutes

COOK:

*6 to 8 hours (low) or
3 to 4 hours (high),
plus 20 minutes (high)*

MAKES:

8 servings

2   14-ounce cans reduced-sodium chicken broth or 3½ cups homemade chicken broth

1½ cups frozen whole kernel corn

1½ cups thinly sliced carrots

1½ cups water

½   cup chopped onion

1   4.9-ounce package dry scalloped potato mix

2   teaspoons dried dillweed

2   cups half-and-half or light cream

½   cup all-purpose flour

2   6-ounce cans skinless, boneless salmon, drained

1 In a 3½- or 4-quart slow cooker combine broth, corn, carrots, water, onion, potato mix (including seasoning packet), and dillweed.

2 Cover and cook on low-heat setting for 6 to 8 hours or on high-heat setting for 3 to 4 hours.

3 If using low-heat setting, turn cooker to high-heat setting. In a medium bowl whisk together cream and flour. Gradually stir cream mixture into mixture in cooker. Gently stir in salmon. Cover and cook for 20 to 30 minutes more or until thickened.

Nutrition Facts per serving: 269 cal., 10 g total fat (5 g sat. fat), 45 mg chol., 827 mg sodium, 32 g carbo., 2 g fiber, 14 g pro.

This slow cooker version of the classic New Orleans dish boasts all the traditional spicy-hot seasonings.

SHRIMP CREOLE

1	14½-ounce can diced tomatoes, undrained
1	14-ounce can chicken broth or 1¾ cups homemade chicken broth
1½	cups chopped onions
1	cup chopped green sweet pepper
1	cup sliced celery
1	6-ounce can tomato paste
⅓	cup thinly sliced green onions
2	cloves garlic, minced
1½	teaspoons paprika
½	teaspoon black pepper
¼	teaspoon salt
⅛	teaspoon bottled hot pepper sauce
1	bay leaf
1½	pounds peeled, deveined, cooked medium shrimp
3	cups hot cooked rice

PREP:
20 minutes

COOK:
5 to 6 hours (low) or 2½ to 3 hours (high)

MAKES:
6 to 8 servings

1 In a 3½-quart slow cooker combine undrained tomatoes, broth, onions, sweet pepper, celery, tomato paste, green onions, garlic, paprika, black pepper, salt, hot pepper sauce, and bay leaf.

2 Cover and cook on low-heat setting for 5 to 6 hours or on high-heat setting for 2½ to 3 hours.

3 Remove and discard bay leaf. Rinse shrimp; pat dry with paper towels. Stir shrimp into vegetable mixture. Serve over hot cooked rice.

Nutrition Facts per serving: 344 cal., 3 g total fat (1 g sat. fat), 227 mg chol., 673 mg sodium, 39 g carbo., 3 g fiber, 37 g pro.

This lively version of corn chowder uses the "three sisters" of Native American cooking: corn, beans, and squash.

THREE SISTERS CORN CHOWDER

PREP:

25 minutes

COOK:

*8 to 9 hours (low) or
4 to 4$\frac{1}{2}$ hours (high),
plus 30 minutes (high)*

MAKES:

6 to 8 servings

3　large red-skinned potatoes, peeled (if desired) and cut into $\frac{1}{2}$-inch cubes (about 1$\frac{1}{2}$ pounds)

1$\frac{1}{2}$　cups frozen whole kernel corn

1　cup frozen baby lima beans

$\frac{1}{2}$　cup chopped onion

$\frac{1}{2}$　cup chopped fresh Anaheim or poblano chile pepper* or green sweet pepper

$\frac{1}{2}$　cup chopped red sweet pepper

1　4-ounce can diced green chile peppers, drained

3　cloves garlic, minced

$\frac{1}{2}$　teaspoon salt

2　14-ounce cans vegetable broth or 3$\frac{1}{2}$ cups homemade vegetable broth

1　14$\frac{3}{4}$-ounce can cream-style corn

1　small zucchini, halved lengthwise and sliced

1　cup whipping cream

1 In a 4- to 6-quart slow cooker combine potatoes, frozen corn, frozen lima beans, onion, fresh chile pepper, sweet pepper, canned chile peppers, garlic, and salt. Pour broth over all.

2 Cover and cook on low-heat setting for 8 to 9 hours or on high-heat setting for 4 to 4$\frac{1}{2}$ hours.

3 If using low-heat setting, turn cooker to high-heat setting. Stir in cream-style corn and zucchini. Cover and cook for 30 minutes more. Stir in whipping cream.

*NOTE: When working with chile peppers, wear plastic or rubber gloves. If your bare hands do touch the chile peppers, wash your hands well with soap and water.

Nutrition Facts per serving: 383 cal., 17 g total fat (9 g sat. fat), 55 mg chol., 1,073 mg sodium, 54 g carbo., 6 g fiber, 10 g pro.

A saucy mix of garden vegetables and olives—ratatouille—makes this an extra satisfying soup. Serve with a green salad and buttered slices of crusty bread.

RATATOUILLE SOUP WITH BEANS

$^{1}/_{2}$ cup coarsely chopped onion

2 cups peeled eggplant cut into $^{3}/_{4}$-inch cubes

2 medium zucchini, halved lengthwise and cut into $^{1}/_{4}$-inch slices ($2^{1}/_{2}$ cups)

$^{3}/_{4}$ cup coarsely chopped red sweet pepper

$^{3}/_{4}$ cup coarsely chopped green sweet pepper

1 15- to 19-ounce can white kidney (cannellini) or Great Northern beans, rinsed and drained

1 cup hot-style vegetable juice or vegetable juice

1 $14^{1}/_{2}$-ounce can diced tomatoes with basil, oregano, and garlic; undrained

1 14-ounce can reduced-sodium chicken broth or $1^{3}/_{4}$ cups homemade chicken broth

1 $2^{1}/_{4}$-ounce can sliced pitted ripe olives, drained

6 tablespoons finely shredded Parmesan cheese

1 In a $3^{1}/_{2}$- or 4-quart slow cooker place onion, eggplant, zucchini, sweet peppers, and beans. Pour vegetable juice, undrained tomatoes, and broth over vegetable mixture.

2 Cover and cook on low-heat setting for 8 to 10 hours or on high-heat setting for 4 to 5 hours. Stir in olives before serving. Sprinkle each serving with Parmesan cheese.

Nutrition Facts per serving: 148 cal., 3 g total fat (1 g sat. fat), 6 mg chol., 945 mg sodium, 25 g carbo., 6 g fiber, 10 g pro.

PREP:

20 minutes

COOK:

8 to 10 hours (low) or 4 to 5 hours (high)

MAKES:

6 servings

As summer gives way to fall, bring home late-season vegetables at their freshest, in-season best, then simmer them slowly in this wonderfully varied soup.

FARMER'S MARKET VEGETABLE SOUP

PREP:

30 minutes

COOK:

*8 to 9 hours (low) or
4 to 4 1/2 hours (high),
plus 20 minutes (high)*

MAKES:

4 servings

1/2 of a small rutabaga, peeled and chopped (2 cups)

2 large Roma tomatoes, chopped

2 medium carrots or parsnips, chopped (1 1/2 to 2 cups)

1 large red-skinned potato, chopped

2 medium leeks (white parts only), chopped

3 14-ounce cans vegetable broth or 5 1/4 cups homemade vegetable broth

1 teaspoon fennel seeds, crushed

1/2 teaspoon dried sage, crushed

1/2 to 1/4 teaspoon black pepper

1/2 cup dried tiny bow ties

3 cups torn fresh spinach

1 recipe Garlic Toast (optional)

1 In a 3 1/2- or 4-quart slow cooker combine rutabaga, tomatoes, carrots, potato, and leeks. Add broth, fennel seeds, sage, and pepper.

2 Cover and cook on low-heat setting for 8 to 9 hours or on high-heat setting for 4 to 4 1/2 hours.

3 If using low-heat setting, turn cooker to high-heat setting. Stir in pasta. Cover and cook for 20 to 30 minutes more or until pasta is tender. Just before serving, stir in spinach. If desired, float a Garlic Toast on each serving.

Nutrition Facts per serving: 198 cal., 2 g total fat (0 g sat. fat), 0 mg chol., 1,313 mg sodium, 41 g carbo., 8 g fiber, 8 g pro.

GARLIC TOAST: Brush both sides of eight 1/2-inch baguette slices with 1 tablespoon garlic-flavor olive oil. Arrange on a baking sheet. Broil 3 to 4 inches from the heat for 1 minute. Turn; sprinkle with 2 teaspoons grated Parmesan cheese. Broil for 1 to 2 minutes more or until lightly toasted.

Grated fresh ginger, curry powder, and jalapeño chile pepper deftly season this hearty meatless soup.

CURRIED LENTIL SOUP

2	medium sweet potatoes (about 1 pound), peeled and coarsely chopped
1	cup dry brown or yellow lentils, rinsed
½	cup chopped onion
1	medium fresh jalapeño chile pepper, seeded and finely chopped*
3	cloves garlic, minced
1	14½-ounce can diced tomatoes, undrained
3	14-ounce cans vegetable broth or 5¼ cups homemade vegetable broth
1	tablespoon curry powder
1	teaspoon grated fresh ginger
	Plain yogurt or dairy sour cream (optional)
	Small fresh chile peppers and/or crushed red pepper (optional)

1 In a 4- to 5-quart slow cooker combine sweet potatoes, lentils, onion, jalapeño pepper, and garlic. Add undrained tomatoes, broth, curry powder, and ginger.

2 Cover and cook on low-heat setting for 8 to 10 hours or on high-heat setting for 4 to 5 hours. If desired, top each serving with yogurt and garnish with chile peppers.

*NOTE: **When working with chile peppers, wear plastic or rubber gloves. If your bare hands do touch the chile peppers, wash your hands well with soap and water.**

Nutrition Facts per serving: 316 cal., 2 g total fat (0 g sat. fat), 0 mg chol., 1,425 mg sodium, 60 g carbo., 18 g fiber, 18 g pro.

PREP:
20 minutes

COOK:
*8 to 10 hours (low) or
4 to 5 hours (high)*

MAKES:
4 to 6 servings

Need a new party stew? This one's festive and great for a group. Set the chowder on a buffet table next to bowls, spoons, and toppings. Round out the meal with cold beer.

CHEESE ENCHILADA CHOWDER

PREP:

25 minutes

COOK:

*6 to 8 hours (low) or
3 to 4 hours (high)*

MAKES:

6 servings

1	15-ounce can black beans, rinsed and drained
1	14½-ounce can diced tomatoes, drained
1	10-ounce package frozen whole kernel corn
½	cup chopped onion
½	cup chopped yellow, green, or red sweet pepper
1	small fresh jalapeño chile pepper, seeded, if desired, and finely chopped*
1	19-ounce can enchilada sauce
1	10¾-ounce can condensed cream of chicken soup
2	cups milk
1	cup shredded Monterey Jack cheese (4 ounces)
1	cup shredded cheddar cheese (4 ounces)
	Dairy sour cream (optional)
	Purchased guacamole (optional)
	Tortilla chips, coarsely broken (optional)

1 In a 3½- to 5-quart slow cooker combine beans, drained tomatoes, frozen corn, onion, sweet pepper, and jalapeño pepper. In a large bowl stir together enchilada sauce and soup. Gradually stir in milk until smooth; pour over bean mixture in cooker.

2 Cover and cook on low-heat setting for 6 to 8 hours or on high-heat setting for 3 to 4 hours. Stir in shredded cheese until melted. If desired, top each serving with sour cream, guacamole, and tortilla chips.

*NOTE: When working with chile peppers, wear plastic or rubber gloves. If your bare hands do touch the chile peppers, wash your hands well with soap and water.

Nutrition Facts per serving: 374 cal., 18 g total fat (10 g sat. fat), 47 mg chol., 1,536 mg sodium, 37 g carbo., 6 g fiber, 21 g pro.

Set out an assortment of toppings—sour cream, chopped avocado, sliced green onions, and/or chopped tomatoes—and warm corn bread to accompany this filling soup.

BLACK BEAN SOUP

1   pound dry black beans
6   cups water
1   cup coarsely chopped carrots
1   cup coarsely chopped onion
1   cup coarsely chopped celery
2   large* vegetable bouillon cubes
2   teaspoons ground cumin
2   teaspoons ground coriander
2   teaspoons dried savory, crushed
2   cloves garlic, minced
1   teaspoon chili powder
½   teaspoon black pepper
1   cup half-and-half or light cream

PREP:

1½ hours

COOK:

12 to 14 hours (low) or 6 to 7 hours (high)

MAKES:

6 to 8 servings

1 Rinse beans. In a large saucepan combine beans and enough water to cover them by 2 inches. Bring to boiling; reduce heat. Simmer, uncovered, for 10 minutes. Remove saucepan from heat. Cover; let stand for 1 hour. Drain and rinse beans.

2 In a 4- to 5½-quart slow cooker combine beans, the 6 cups water, the carrots, onion, celery, bouillon cubes, cumin, coriander, savory, garlic, chili powder, and pepper.

3 Cover and cook on low-heat setting for 12 to 14 hours or on high-heat setting for 6 to 7 hours. Mash beans slightly just before serving. Stir in half-and-half.

*NOTE: Each bouillon cube makes 2 cups broth.

Nutrition Facts per serving: 346 cal., 6 g total fat (3 g sat. fat), 15 mg chol., 706 mg sodium, 56 g carbo., 14 g fiber, 19 g pro.

Move over, chili powder! Jerk seasoning brings something new to the chili bowl.
Three colors of beans and the red sweet pepper add eye-catching appeal to the dish.

CARIBBEAN & SWEET PEPPER CHILI

PREP:

15 minutes

COOK:

6 to 8 hours (low) or
3 to 4 hours (high)

MAKES:

6 servings

1   15-ounce can black beans, rinsed and drained

1   15-ounce can red kidney beans, rinsed and drained

1   15-ounce can small white beans, rinsed and drained

2   7½-ounce cans chopped tomatoes with jalapeño peppers, undrained

1   14-ounce can vegetable or chicken broth or 1¾ cups homemade vegetable or chicken broth

1   12-ounce jar roasted red sweet peppers, drained and chopped

½   cup chopped onion

½   of a 6-ounce can (⅓ cup) tomato paste

1   to 3 teaspoons Jamaican jerk seasoning

4   cloves garlic, minced

1 In a 3½- or 4-quart slow cooker combine beans, undrained tomatoes, broth, roasted sweet peppers, onion, tomato paste, Jamaican jerk seasoning, and garlic.

2 Cover and cook on low-heat setting for 6 to 8 hours or on high-heat setting for 3 to 4 hours.

Nutrition Facts per serving: 183 cal., 1 g total fat (0 g sat. fat), 0 mg chol., 1,025 mg sodium, 41 g carbo., 12 g fiber, 15 g pro.

SALADS
& BREADS

7

Mesclun is a mixture of young, small salad greens and can include arugula, dandelion, frisée, mâche, mizuna, oak leaf lettuce, radicchio, and sorrel.

MESCLUN WITH ORANGES & OLIVES

START TO FINISH:

15 minutes

MAKES:

8 servings

3 tablespoons olive oil

2 tablespoons orange juice

2 tablespoons balsamic vinegar

12 cups mesclun or other mild salad greens

8 thin slices red onion, separated into rings

2 cups orange sections

²/₃ cup mixed country olives or kalamata olives

¹/₈ teaspoon salt

¹/₈ teaspoon black pepper

1 For dressing, in a small bowl whisk together oil, orange juice, and vinegar. Place greens in a large salad bowl. Drizzle with dressing; toss to coat.

2 To serve, divide greens mixture among 8 salad plates. Top each serving with onion rings, orange sections, and olives. Lightly sprinkle salads with salt and pepper.

Nutrition Facts per serving: 103 cal., 7 g total fat (1 g sat. fat), 0 mg chol., 151 mg sodium, 10 g carbo., 3 g fiber, 1 g pro.

This elegant salad is worthy of any special meal. The pear nectar dressing, toasted walnuts, and creamy blue cheese make a stellar combination.

MESCLUN WITH PEARS & BLUE CHEESE

1/4	cup pear nectar
2	tablespoons walnut oil or salad oil
2	tablespoons white wine vinegar
1	teaspoon Dijon-style mustard
1/8	teaspoon ground ginger
1/8	teaspoon black pepper
10	cups mesclun or torn romaine lettuce
3	medium red and/or green pears, cored and thinly sliced
1/2	cup broken walnuts, toasted
1/2	cup crumbled blue cheese or Gorgonzola cheese

START TO FINISH:

25 minutes

MAKES:

8 servings

1 For dressing, in a screw-top jar combine pear nectar, oil, vinegar, mustard, ginger, and pepper. Cover and shake well.

2 In a large salad bowl place mesclun and pears. Toss lightly. Drizzle with dressing; toss to coat.

3 To serve, divide salad among 8 salad plates. Sprinkle each serving with nuts and blue cheese.

Nutrition Facts per serving: 152 cal., 11 g total fat (2 g sat. fat), 5 mg chol., 110 mg sodium, 13 g carbo., 3 g fiber, 4 g pro.

Choose the herb you have on hand or like the best for the vinaigrette. This salad is perfect when fresh produce is not in peak season.

WINTER GREEN SALAD

PREP:
20 minutes
BAKE:
20 minutes
OVEN:
425°F
MAKES:
4 servings

4 Roma tomatoes, halved lengthwise and seeded
3 tablespoons balsamic vinegar
½ teaspoon salt
¼ teaspoon freshly ground black pepper
⅓ cup olive oil
1 teaspoon snipped fresh herb (basil, marjoram, oregano, rosemary, tarragon, or thyme)
⅛ teaspoon freshly ground black pepper
6 cups mesclun or torn mixed salad greens
1 cup sliced fresh cremini or button mushrooms
½ cup seedless red and/or green grapes, halved
¼ cup coarsely chopped walnuts, toasted

1 Line a small baking sheet with foil; lightly grease the foil. In a self-sealing plastic bag toss tomatoes with 1 tablespoon of the balsamic vinegar, ¼ teaspoon of the salt, and the ¼ teaspoon pepper. Seal bag; shake well to coat tomatoes.

2 Arrange tomatoes, cut sides down, on the prepared baking sheet. Bake in a 425° oven for 20 to 25 minutes or until tomato skins are bubbly and dark but not burned. Set aside.

3 For vinaigrette, in a screw-top jar combine oil, the remaining 2 tablespoons vinegar, desired herb, remaining ¼ teaspoon salt, and the ⅛ teaspoon pepper. Cover and shake well.

4 To serve, arrange the mesclun on 4 chilled salad plates. Top with mushrooms, grapes, and walnuts. Place tomatoes next to the salad mixture. Drizzle salads with dressing. Serve immediately.

Nutrition Facts per serving: 269 cal., 24 g total fat (3 g sat. fat), 0 mg chol., 308 mg sodium, 14 g carbo., 3 g fiber, 4 g pro.

Apple juice, basil, and onion add pizzazz to this fruit-and-spinach salad.

SPINACH-APPLE SALAD

2	tablespoons unsweetened apple juice
1	tablespoon salad oil
1½	teaspoons cider vinegar
½	teaspoon dried basil, crushed
¼	teaspoon onion powder
	Dash salt
	Dash black pepper
4	cups torn fresh spinach
2	medium apples, thinly sliced
2	medium oranges, peeled and sectioned

PREP:
20 minutes
CHILL:
30 minutes
MAKES:
6 servings

1 For dressing, in a screw-top jar combine apple juice, oil, vinegar, basil, onion powder, salt, and pepper. Cover and shake well. Chill for 30 minutes.

2 In a large salad bowl combine spinach, apples, and oranges. Shake dressing. Drizzle dressing over salad; toss gently to coat.

Nutrition Facts per serving: 62 cal., 3 g total fat (0 g sat. fat), 0 mg chol., 52 mg sodium, 10 g carbo., 2 g fiber, 1 g pro.

This spinach and beet salad is bursting with flavor. Sage, toasted walnuts, blue cheese, and a roasted shallot dressing are a mouth-watering combination.

SPINACH BEET SALAD

PREP:

20 minutes

BAKE:

25 minutes

COOL:

25 minutes

OVEN:

450°F

MAKES:

6 servings

2	shallots, peeled
3	small parsnips, peeled and sliced ½-inch thick
⅓	cup olive oil
2	small beets, trimmed, peeled, and quartered
2	tablespoons balsamic vinegar
2	teaspoons finely snipped fresh sage or ¼ teaspoon dried leaf sage, crushed
¼	teaspoon salt
¼	teaspoon black pepper
6	cups fresh baby spinach
¼	cup coarsely chopped walnuts, toasted
¼	cup crumbled blue cheese or feta cheese (1 ounce)

1 Tear off two 18×12-inch pieces of heavy-duty foil. Place shallots and parsnips in the center of 1 piece of foil. Drizzle with 1 tablespoon of the oil. Bring ends of foil together; seal to make a packet. Place beets in the center of the other piece of foil; drizzle with 1 tablespoon of the olive oil. Bring ends of foil together; seal to make a packet.

2 Place foil packets in a shallow baking pan. Bake in a 450° oven for 25 minutes, turning packets over once. Remove from oven. Let stand until vegetables are cool enough to handle, about 25 to 30 minutes. Chop shallots.

3 For dressing, in a screw-top jar combine shallots, remaining oil, the vinegar, sage, salt, and pepper. Cover and shake well.

4 Place spinach in a large salad bowl. Drizzle with half of the dressing; toss to coat. Divide spinach mixture among 6 salad plates.

5 Slice beets. Divide beets and parsnips among the salads. Drizzle with remaining dressing. Sprinkle with walnuts and cheese. Serve immediately.

Nutrition Facts per serving: 217 cal., 17 g total fat (3 g sat. fat), 4 mg chol., 221 mg sodium, 15 g carbo., 3 g fiber, 4 g pro.

Classic Caesar salad isn't a mystery to make, so you don't have to wait until you go out to have it. This version of the dressing uses refrigerated or frozen egg product, making it safer than those that use raw egg.

CAESAR SALAD

1	tablespoon chopped anchovies (4 or 5 fillets)
1/4	teaspoon dry mustard
	Dash Worcestershire sauce
1	clove garlic, minced
1/4	cup refrigerated or frozen egg product, thawed
1/3	cup olive oil or salad oil
2	tablespoons red wine vinegar
1	tablespoon lemon juice
8	cups torn romaine lettuce
1	cup croutons
	Few dashes black pepper
1/4	cup shaved or finely shredded Parmesan cheese (1 ounce)

START TO FINISH:
20 minutes
MAKES:
6 servings

1 For dressing, in a small bowl whisk together anchovies, dry mustard, Worcestershire sauce, and garlic. Add egg product; mix well. Slowly whisk in oil, vinegar, and lemon juice. Set aside.

2 In a large salad bowl combine romaine, croutons, and pepper. Drizzle with dressing; toss to coat. Top with Parmesan cheese.

Nutrition Facts per serving: 170 cal., 14 g total fat (3 g sat. fat), 6 mg chol., 239 mg sodium, 7 g carbo., 2 g fiber, 5 g pro.

Bold flavors—kalamata olives, feta cheese, and oregano—make this a delicious salad to serve alongside steaming bowls of stew.

GREEK SALAD

START TO FINISH:

15 minutes

MAKES:

4 servings

2   tablespoons olive oil or salad oil

2   tablespoons lemon juice

2   teaspoons snipped fresh oregano or $\frac{1}{2}$ teaspoon dried oregano, crushed

$\frac{1}{8}$ teaspoon salt

$\frac{1}{8}$ teaspoon black pepper

3   medium tomatoes, cut into wedges

1   medium cucumber, halved lengthwise and thinly sliced

1   small red onion, cut into thin wedges

8   to 10 pitted kalamata olives

$\frac{1}{2}$ cup crumbled feta cheese (2 ounces)

1 For vinaigrette, in a screw-top jar combine olive oil, lemon juice, oregano, salt, and pepper. Cover and shake well.

2 In a salad bowl combine tomatoes, cucumber, and red onion. Drizzle with vinaigrette; toss to coat. Sprinkle with olives and feta cheese.

Nutrition Facts per serving: 154 cal., 12 g total fat (4 g sat. fat), 17 mg chol., 369 mg sodium, 9 g carbo., 2 g fiber, 4 g pro.

So light, so cool, and so colorful, this fruit salad refreshes during even the hottest summer months. Picky youngsters will love it too, making it a perfect accompaniment for soup and a sandwich. (Recipe pictured on page 287.)

FRUIT CUPS WITH STRAWBERRY DRESSING

2	cups cut-up strawberries and/or whole raspberries
¼	cup frozen orange juice concentrate, thawed
2	teaspoons sugar
2	kiwifruits, peeled and thinly sliced
2	bananas, peeled and sliced
1	orange, peeled and sectioned
1	medium peach, plum, or nectarine; sliced
1	small apple or pear, cored and sliced

START TO FINISH:
25 minutes

MAKES:
6 servings

1 For dressing, in a blender or food processor combine half of the berries, the orange juice concentrate, and sugar. Cover and blend or process until smooth; set aside.

2 In a large bowl combine remaining berries, kiwifruits, bananas, orange, peach, and apple. To serve, place fruit mixture in small bowls; drizzle with dressing.

Nutrition Facts per serving: 120 cal., 1 g total fat (0 g sat. fat), 0 mg chol., 4 mg sodium, 29 g carbo., 4 g fiber, 2 g pro.

These biscuits are flaky and tender, as supreme as their name. Buttermilk adds a tanginess to their flavor, but milk works fine if you don't have buttermilk on hand.

BISCUITS SUPREME

PREP:
20 minutes
BAKE:
10 minutes
OVEN:
450°F
MAKES:
10 biscuits

3 cups all-purpose flour

4 teaspoons baking powder

1 tablespoon sugar

1 teaspoon salt

¾ teaspoon cream of tartar

¾ cup butter

1¼ cups buttermilk or 1 cup milk

1 In a large bowl combine the flour, baking powder, sugar, salt, and cream of tartar. Using a pastry blender, cut in butter until mixture resembles coarse crumbs. Make a well in the center of the flour mixture. Add buttermilk all at once. Using a fork, stir just until moistened.

2 Turn out dough onto a lightly floured surface. Knead dough for 4 to 6 strokes or just until dough holds together. Pat or lightly roll dough to ¾-inch thickness. Cut dough with a floured 2½-inch biscuit cutter.

3 Place biscuits 1 inch apart on an ungreased baking sheet. Bake in a 450° oven for 10 to 12 minutes or until golden. Remove biscuits from baking sheet and serve hot.

Nutrition Facts per biscuit: 273 cal., 15 g total fat (9 g sat. fat), 40 mg chol., 574 mg sodium, 29 g carbo., 1 g fiber, 5 g pro.

DROP BISCUITS SUPREME: Prepare as above, except add ¼ cup whipping cream with the buttermilk. Do not knead, roll, or cut dough. Drop dough by spoonfuls onto greased baking sheet. Bake as directed. Makes 12 biscuits.

Nutrition Facts per biscuit: 293 cal., 17 g total fat (11 g sat. fat), 49 mg chol., 576 mg sodium, 29 g carbo., 1 g dietary fiber, 5 g pro.

There's nothing better with soup or stew than hot biscuits. Cut this rich dough into handy sticks.

SAVORY BISCUIT STICKS

2	cups all-purpose flour
2	tablespoons sugar
2	teaspoons baking powder
¼	teaspoon baking soda
1¼	teaspoons cracked black pepper
¼	teaspoon garlic powder
6	tablespoons cold butter
½	cup shredded Asiago cheese (2 ounces)
1	egg, beaten
½	cup buttermilk or sour milk*
	Buttermilk or sour milk*
¾	teaspoon cumin seeds, crushed

PREP:
25 minutes
BAKE:
8 minutes
OVEN:
450°F
MAKES:
12 servings

1 In a large bowl combine flour, sugar, baking powder, baking soda, ¼ teaspoon of the pepper, and the garlic powder. Using a pastry blender, cut in butter until mixture resembles coarse crumbs. Stir in shredded cheese. Make a well in the center of the flour mixture; set aside.

2 In a small bowl combine egg and the ½ cup buttermilk. Add egg mixture all at once to flour mixture. Using a fork, stir just until moistened.

3 Turn out dough onto a lightly floured surface. Quickly knead dough for 4 to 6 strokes or just until dough holds together. Pat or lightly roll dough into a 12×6-inch rectangle. Brush lightly with additional buttermilk. Sprinkle dough evenly with remaining 1 teaspoon pepper and the cumin seeds; press lightly into dough. Cut dough into twenty-four 6-inch-long strips. Place strips 1 inch apart on ungreased baking sheets.

4 Bake in a 450° oven about 8 minutes or until golden. Serve warm or cool.

*NOTE: To make ½ cup sour milk, place 1½ teaspoons lemon juice or vinegar in a glass measuring cup. Add enough milk to make ½ cup total liquid; stir. Let mixture stand for 5 minutes before using.

TO MAKE AHEAD: Prepare and bake biscuit sticks as directed; cool completely. Place biscuits in a freezer container or bag and freeze for up to 3 months. To serve, unwrap biscuit sticks and place on baking sheets. Bake in a 350°F oven for 8 to 10 minutes or until heated through.

Nutrition Facts per biscuit stick: 164 cal., 9 g total fat (5 g sat. fat), 40 mg chol., 223 mg sodium, 18 g carbo., 1 g fiber, 4 g pro.

Sharp white cheddar cheese and spicy black pepper intensify the flavor of these biscuits.

PEPPERY WHITE CHEDDAR BISCUITS

PREP:

25 minutes

BAKE:

13 minutes

OVEN:

400°F

MAKES:

18 biscuits

4	cups all-purpose flour
2	tablespoons baking powder
½	teaspoon salt
½	cup shortening
¼	cup butter
1½	cups finely crumbled or shredded sharp white cheddar cheese (6 ounces)
2	to 3 teaspoons coarsely ground black pepper
1½	cups milk
1	egg
1	teaspoon water

1 Lightly grease a large baking sheet; set aside. In a large bowl combine flour, baking powder, and ½ teaspoon salt. Using a pastry blender cut in shortening and butter until mixture resembles coarse crumbs. Add cheese and pepper; mix well. Make a well in center of the flour mixture. Add milk all at once; stir until just moistened.

2 Turn out dough onto a lightly floured surface. Quickly knead dough for 10 to 12 strokes until almost smooth. Divide dough in half. Roll or pat each half into a 6-inch square, about 1 inch thick. Using a sharp knife, cut dough into 2-inch squares. Beat together egg and water; brush over biscuits. Place biscuits on prepared baking sheet.

3 Bake in a 400° oven for 13 to 15 minutes or until golden. Cool slightly on a wire rack. Serve warm.

TO MAKE AHEAD: Prepare and bake biscuits as directed; cool completely. Place biscuits in a freezer container or bag and freeze up to 3 months. To serve, wrap frozen biscuits in foil and bake in a 300°F oven about 20 to 25 minutes or until warm.

Nutrition Facts per biscuit: 247 cal., 14 g total fat (6 g sat. fat), 34 mg chol., 314 mg sodium, 24 g carbo., 1 g fiber, 7 g pro.

These popovers are pricked with a fork after baking to let the steam escape. Turn the oven off and return the popovers to the oven for a few extra minutes to make them nice and crisp.

OLD-FASHIONED POPOVERS

Nonstick cooking spray

2 eggs

1 cup milk

1 tablespoon cooking oil

¾ cup all-purpose flour

½ teaspoon salt

Butter (optional)

PREP:

15 minutes

BAKE:

35 minutes

STAND:

5 minutes

OVEN:

400°F

MAKES:

5 or 6 popovers

1 Generously coat the bottom and sides of 6 cups of a popover pan or five 6-ounce custard cups with nonstick cooking spray. Place the custard cups, if using, on a 15×10×1-inch baking pan. Set aside.

2 In a medium bowl beat eggs; beat in milk and oil. Add flour and salt; beat until combined but still slightly lumpy. Fill the prepared popover cups or custard cups half full.

3 Bake in a 400° oven about 35 minutes or until the crusts are very firm. Turn off oven. Using the tines of a fork, immediately prick each popover to let steam escape. Return the popovers to the oven for 5 to 10 minutes more or until of desired crispness. (Be sure the oven is turned off.) Remove popovers from cups and serve immediately. If desired, serve with butter.

CARAWAY RYE POPOVERS: Prepare as directed, except decrease all-purpose flour to ½ cup. Add ¼ cup rye flour or whole wheat flour and ½ teaspoon caraway seeds with the all-purpose flour.

Nutrition Facts per popover: 141 cal., 6 g total fat (2 g sat. fat), 89 mg chol., 282 mg sodium, 16 g carbo., 0 g fiber, 6 g pro.

Fresh chives add an appealing flavor spark to traditional corn bread. If you prefer the classic bread, simply omit the chives.

CORN BREAD WITH CHIVES

PREP:

20 minutes

BAKE:

15 minutes

OVEN:

425°F

MAKES:

8 servings

1¼	cups yellow cornmeal
¾	cup all-purpose flour
2	tablespoons sugar
2	teaspoons baking powder
1	teaspoon baking soda
½	teaspoon salt
2	eggs
⅔	cup milk
⅔	cup buttermilk or sour milk*
3	tablespoons butter, melted
3	tablespoons snipped fresh chives

1 Grease a 9×9×2-inch baking pan. Set aside.

2 In a large bowl combine cornmeal, flour, sugar, baking powder, baking soda, and salt. In a small bowl whisk together eggs, milk, buttermilk, melted butter, and chives. Add egg mixture all at once to flour mixture. Stir just until moistened. Pour batter into prepared pan.

3 Bake in a 425° oven for 15 to 18 minutes or until a wooden toothpick inserted in the center comes out clean. Serve warm or cooled.

*NOTE: To make ⅔ cup sour milk, place 2 teaspoons lemon juice or vinegar in a glass measuring cup. Add enough milk to make ⅔ cup total liquid; stir. Let stand for 5 minutes before using.

Nutrition Facts per serving: 207 cal., 7 g total fat (4 g sat. fat), 68 mg chol., 498 mg sodium, 30 g carbo., 2 g fiber, 6 g pro.

Jazz up a packaged biscuit mix with onion, cheese, and poppy seeds.
You'll want to serve this bread with a spicy chili or hearty stew.

CHEESY-ONION SUPPER BREAD

2	tablespoons butter
1	cup thinly sliced onion
1	egg
½	cup milk
1½	cups packaged biscuit mix
1	cup shredded sharp process American cheese or cheddar cheese (4 ounces)
1	tablespoon poppy seeds

PREP:
15 minutes
BAKE:
20 minutes
OVEN:
400°F
MAKES:
8 servings

1 Grease an 8×1½-inch round baking pan. Set aside.

2 In a medium skillet melt 1 tablespoon of the butter over medium heat. Add onion; cook and stir for 4 to 5 minutes or until onion is tender. Remove half of the onion slices and chop; set aside remaining onion slices.

3 In a small bowl whisk together egg and milk until combined. In a large bowl add milk mixture to biscuit mix; stir just until moistened. Add the chopped onion, half of the cheese, and half of the poppy seeds. Spread batter into prepared pan. Sprinkle with remaining cheese and poppy seeds. Arrange reserved cooked, sliced onion on top.

4 In the skillet melt remaining 1 tablespoon butter over medium heat; drizzle over onion mixture in baking pan. Bake in a 400° oven about 20 minutes or until a wooden toothpick inserted near the center comes out clean. Serve warm.

Nutrition Facts per serving: 207 cal., 12 g total fat (6 g sat. fat), 49 mg chol., 528 mg sodium, 17 g carbo., 1 g fiber, 7 g pro.

Refrigerated pizza dough makes these breadsticks easy to make. You'll love the dried tomato, Romano cheese, and rosemary mixture that nestles inside each stick. (Recipe pictured on page 288.)

TOMATO-CHEESE BREADSTICKS

PREP:

20 minutes

BAKE:

12 minutes

OVEN:

350°F

MAKES:

20 breadsticks

$\frac{1}{4}$	cup oil-packed dried tomatoes
$\frac{1}{4}$	cup grated Romano cheese
1	teaspoon snipped fresh rosemary or $\frac{3}{4}$ teaspoon dried rosemary, crushed
$\frac{1}{8}$	teaspoon cracked black pepper
2	teaspoons water
1	13.8-ounce package refrigerated pizza dough

1 Drain dried tomatoes, reserving 2 teaspoons of the oil. Finely snip tomatoes. In a bowl combine the reserved oil, tomatoes, cheese, rosemary, pepper, and water. Set aside.

2 Unroll pizza dough. On a lightly floured surface roll dough into a 10×8-inch rectangle. Spread tomato mixture crosswise over half of rectangle. Fold in half. Cut rectangle lengthwise into $\frac{1}{2}$-inch wide strips; twist each strip two or three times.

3 Place twisted dough strips 1 inch apart on an ungreased baking sheet. Bake in a 350° oven for 12 to 15 minutes or until golden brown. Cool completely on a wire rack.

TO MAKE AHEAD: Prepare and bake breadsticks as directed; cool completely. Place cooled breadsticks in a single layer in heavy foil. (Or place breadsticks in freezer container, separating layers with waxed paper.) Seal, label, and freeze for up to 3 months. To serve, wrap desired number of frozen breadsticks in foil. Heat in a 350°F oven about 15 minutes or until warm.

Nutrition Facts per breadstick: 84 cal., 2 g total fat (1 g sat. fat), 2 mg chol., 209 mg sodium, 14 g carbo., 1 g fiber, 3 g pro.

Have all of the ingredients for rolling ready before dipping the rolls into the melted butter because the butter will set up quickly.

CHECKERBOARD ROLLS

2 tablespoons poppy seeds

2 tablespoons sesame seeds

1 teaspoon lemon-pepper seasoning

2 tablespoons yellow cornmeal

2 tablespoons grated or finely shredded Parmesan cheese

3 tablespoons butter, melted

16 pieces (1.3 ounces each) frozen white roll dough

Butter (optional)

PREP:
20 minutes

CHILL:
overnight

STAND:
45 minutes

BAKE:
15 minutes

OVEN:
375°F

MAKES:
16 rolls

1 Grease a 9-inch square baking pan; set aside.

2 In a shallow dish combine poppy seeds, sesame seeds, and lemon pepper. In another shallow dish combine cornmeal and Parmesan cheese. Place butter in a third dish. Working quickly, roll frozen dough pieces in butter, then in one of the seasoning blends to lightly coat. (Coat half of the rolls with one seasoning blend and the remaining rolls with the other seasoning blend.) Alternate rolls in prepared pan. Cover rolls with greased plastic wrap. Place frozen rolls in refrigerator; let thaw overnight.

3 Uncover rolls; let stand at room temperature for 45 minutes.

4 Bake rolls in a 375° oven for 15 to 20 minutes or until golden. Cool slightly on a wire rack. If desired, serve warm with butter.

Nutrition Facts per roll: 137 cal., 5 g total fat (2 g sat. fat), 7 mg chol., 244 mg sodium, 19 g carbo., 1 g fiber, 4 g pro.

Ordinary frozen bread dough becomes something special when it's shaped into tiny balls and topped with crunchy seeds.

HAVE-A-BALL ROLLS

PREP:

20 minutes

RISE:

30 minutes

BAKE:

13 minutes

OVEN:

350°F

MAKES:

30 rolls

1 16-ounce loaf frozen white or whole wheat bread dough, thawed

1 egg white

1 tablespoon water

Fennel seeds, mustard seeds, and/or dill seeds

1 Lightly grease a baking sheet or thirty 1¾-inch muffin cups; set aside.

2 Divide dough into 30 pieces. Shape into small balls. Place rolls on prepared baking sheet or in prepared cups. Cover and let rise until nearly double (about 30 minutes).

3 Beat together egg white and water; brush over rolls. Sprinkle generously with desired seeds. Bake in a 350° oven for 13 to 15 minutes or until golden brown. Cool slightly on wire racks. Serve warm.

Nutrition Facts per roll: 37 cal., 0 g total fat (0 g sat. fat), 0 mg chol., 2 mg sodium, 7 g carbo., 0 g fiber, 1 g pro.

Cottage cheese is what makes this bread moist, tender, and a delight for the taste buds.

DILL BREAD

1	package active dry yeast
¼	cup lukewarm water (105°F to 115°F)
2	tablespoons sugar
1	cup cream-style cottage cheese
1	tablespoon dried minced onion
1	tablespoon butter
2½	teaspoons dill seeds
1	teaspoon salt
¼	teaspoon baking soda
1	egg, slightly beaten
2¼	to 2¾ cups bread flour or all-purpose flour
1	teaspoon butter, melted

PREP:
40 minutes

RISE:
1½ hours

BAKE:
35 minutes

OVEN:
350°F

MAKES:
16 servings (1 loaf)

1 In a large bowl combine yeast, warm water, and 1 tablespoon of the sugar. Set aside.

2 Meanwhile, in a small saucepan combine cottage cheese, the remaining 1 tablespoon sugar, the dried onion, the 1 tablespoon butter, 2 teaspoons of the dill seeds, the salt, and baking soda. Heat and stir just until mixture is warm (120°F to 130°F) and butter almost melts. Remove from heat.

3 Stir cottage cheese mixture and egg into dissolved yeast mixture. Using a wooden spoon, stir in as much of the flour as you can.

4 Turn out dough onto a lightly floured surface. Knead in enough of the remaining flour to make a moderately soft dough that is smooth and elastic (3 to 5 minutes); dough may be sticky. Shape dough into a ball; place in a lightly greased bowl, turning once to grease entire surface. Cover and let rise in a warm place until double in size (about 1 hour).

5 Grease a 1½-quart casserole. Punch dough down; turn out onto a lightly floured surface. Shape dough by patting or rolling it into a 7-inch round loaf; place in prepared casserole. Cover and let rise in a warm place until nearly double (30 to 40 minutes).

6 Brush dough with the 1 teaspoon melted butter. Sprinkle with the remaining ½ teaspoon dill seeds. Bake in a 350° oven for 35 to 40 minutes or until brown and bread sounds hollow when lightly tapped. If necessary to prevent overbrowning, cover loosely with foil for the last 10 to 15 minutes of baking. Immediately remove bread from casserole. Cool on a wire rack.

Nutrition Facts per serving: 106 cal., 2 g total fat (1 g sat. fat), 18 mg chol., 233 mg sodium, 16 g carbo., 1 g fiber, 5 g pro.

Split leftover wedges open and fill them with slices of ripe pears and smoked ham for spectacular sandwiches to serve with comforting soups.

SWISS CHEESE–WALNUT FOCACCIA

PREP:

45 minutes

RISE:

1 hour 20 minutes

BAKE:

25 minutes

OVEN:

375°F

MAKES:

24 servings (2 rounds)

3¼   to 3¾ cups bread flour or all-purpose flour

1   package active dry yeast

1¼   cups warm water (120°F to 130°F)

3   tablespoons olive oil

1   teaspoon salt

1   cup chopped walnuts

⅔   cup shredded Swiss cheese

½   teaspoon coarsely ground black pepper

1 In a large mixing bowl combine 1¼ cups of the flour and the yeast. Add warm water, 1 tablespoon of the olive oil, and the salt. Beat with an electric mixer on low to medium speed for 30 seconds, scraping sides of the bowl constantly. Beat on high speed for 3 minutes. Using a wooden spoon, stir in as much of the remaining flour as you can.

2 Turn out dough onto a lightly floured surface. Knead in enough of the remaining flour to make a stiff dough that is smooth and elastic (8 to 10 minutes). Shape dough into a ball; place in a lightly greased bowl, turning once to grease surface. Cover; let rise in a warm place until double in size (about 1 hour).

3 Punch dough down; turn out onto a lightly floured surface. Divide in half; shape each half into a ball. Place on lightly greased baking sheets. Cover and let rest for 10 minutes.

4 Flatten each ball into a circle about 9 inches in diameter. Using your fingers, press ½-inch-deep indentations about 2 inches apart into the surface. Brush with the remaining 2 tablespoons olive oil. Sprinkle with walnuts, Swiss cheese, and pepper. Cover and let rise in a warm place until nearly double (about 20 minutes).

5 Bake in a 375° oven about 25 minutes or until golden. Immediately remove from baking sheets. Cool on wire racks. Cut into wedges to serve.

Nutrition Facts per serving: 87 cal., 2 g total fat (0 g sat. fat), 0 mg chol., 90 mg sodium, 15 g carbo., 1 g fiber, 3 g pro.

Toasting the caraway seeds for this fragrant bread brings out their best and fullest flavor.

TOASTED CARAWAY & RYE SKILLET BREAD

1	teaspoon caraway seeds
1⅓	cups all-purpose flour
⅔	cup rye flour
1½	teaspoons baking powder
½	teaspoon salt
¼	teaspoon baking soda
2	tablespoons cold butter
1	cup buttermilk
	Nonstick cooking spray

PREP:
20 minutes
COOK:
20 minutes
MAKES:
8 servings

1 In a large heavy skillet heat caraway seeds over medium-low heat for 3 to 5 minutes or until toasted, shaking skillet occasionally to prevent seeds from burning. Remove seeds from skillet; set skillet aside to cool.

2 In a large bowl combine toasted seeds, all-purpose flour, rye flour, baking powder, salt, and baking soda. Using a pastry blender, cut butter into flour mixture until mixture resembles coarse crumbs. Make a well in the center of flour mixture. Using a fork, stir in buttermilk just until moistened. Turn out dough onto a well-floured surface. Quickly knead dough for 10 to 12 strokes until dough is nearly smooth. Roll or pat dough into a circle about 7 inches in diameter and ¾ inch thick. Cut into 8 wedges.

3 Coat the cool skillet with nonstick cooking spray. Heat skillet over medium-low heat for 1 to 3 minutes or until a drop of water sizzles. Carefully place the dough wedges in the pan.

4 Cook, covered, about 20 minutes or until golden brown and a wooden toothpick inserted into the side of a wedge comes out clean, turning wedges several times to brown both sides. (Sides may still look moist.) Check bottoms occasionally during cooking and decrease heat, if necessary, to prevent overbrowning. Serve bread warm or at room temperature.

Nutrition Facts per serving: 140 cal., 4 g total fat (2 g sat. fat), 9 mg chol., 323 mg sodium, 23 g carbo., 2 g fiber, 4 g pro.

This dough is sticky, so be sure to coat your hands well with flour before and during shaping. (Recipe pictured on page 288.)

CORNMEAL SKILLET ROLLS

PREP:

30 minutes

RISE:

40 minutes

BAKE:

30 minutes

OVEN:

375°F

MAKES:

16 rolls

½ cup yellow cornmeal

1 cup boiling water

¼ cup molasses

1 tablespoon butter or margarine

1 teaspoon salt

1 egg

1 package active dry yeast

¼ cup lukewarm water (105°F to 115°F)

3 cups all-purpose flour

Yellow cornmeal

1 Grease a 9-inch cast-iron skillet or 9-inch round baking pan.

2 In a small bowl combine cornmeal and boiling water; stir until combined. Add molasses, butter, and salt, stirring until butter melts. Stir in egg until combined; set aside.

3 In a small bowl dissolve yeast in the lukewarm water. Let stand until foamy, about 5 minutes.

4 In a large bowl combine the flour, cornmeal mixture, and yeast mixture. Beat with a wooden spoon until a dough forms (dough will be soft and sticky).

5 With well-floured hands, pinch off sixteen 2-inch pieces of dough. Shape each piece into a ball. Place balls, touching each other, in the prepared skillet or baking pan, flouring hands as necessary. Cover and let rise in a warm place until double (about 40 to 45 minutes). Sprinkle with additional cornmeal.

6 Bake in a 375° oven for 30 to 35 minutes or until golden brown and rolls sound hollow when lightly tapped. Cool slightly. Serve warm from the skillet or, to serve at room temperature, remove rolls from skillet and cool on a wire rack.

Nutrition Facts per roll: 129 cal., 1 g total fat (1 g sat. fat), 15 mg chol., 158 mg sodium, 25 g carbo., 1 g fiber, 3 g pro.

The pungent flavor of sage partners well with meaty olives in this delicious and crusty European-style baguette.

SAGE-OLIVE BAGUETTES

3½   to 4 cups bread flour or unbleached all-purpose flour

1   package active dry yeast

½   teaspoon salt

1¼   cups warm water (120°F to 130°F)

½   cup coarsely chopped, pitted kalamata olives

2   to 3 tablespoons snipped fresh sage or 2 to 3 teaspoons dried sage, crushed

1   egg white, slightly beaten

1   tablespoon water

PREP:

20 minutes

RISE:

1 hour 35 minutes

BAKE:

30 minutes

OVEN:

375°F

MAKES:

14 servings (2 baguettes)

1 In a large mixing bowl stir together 1 cup of the flour, the yeast, and salt; add warm water. Beat with an electric mixer on low to medium speed for 30 seconds, scraping sides of bowl constantly. Beat on high speed for 3 minutes. Stir in the olives and sage. Using a wooden spoon, stir in as much of the remaining flour as you can.

2 Turn out dough onto a lightly floured surface. Knead in enough of the remaining flour to make a stiff dough that is smooth and elastic (8 to 10 minutes). Shape dough into a ball; place in a lightly greased bowl, turning once to grease surface. Cover and let rise in a warm place until double (about 1 hour).

3 Punch dough down; turn out onto a lightly floured surface. Divide in half; shape into balls. Cover and let rest 10 minutes. Meanwhile, lightly grease 2 baking sheets or 2 baguette pans; sprinkle with flour.

4 Roll each portion of dough into a 14×5-inch rectangle. Starting from a long side, roll up into a spiral; seal well. Pinch ends and pull slightly to taper. Place loaves, seam sides down, on prepared baking sheets or in baguette pans. Beat together egg white and water; brush over loaves. Cover and let rise until nearly double (35 to 45 minutes).

5 With a sharp knife, make 3 or 4 diagonal cuts about ¼ inch deep across tops of loaves. Bake in a 375° oven for 20 minutes. Brush again with egg white mixture. Continue baking for 10 to 15 minutes more or until bread sounds hollow when lightly tapped. Immediately remove bread from baking sheets or pans. Cool on a wire rack.

Nutrition Facts per serving: 132 cal., 1 g total fat (0 g sat. fat), 0 mg chol., 103 mg sodium, 25 g carbo., 1 g fiber, 5 g pro.

Sesame oil and toasted sesame seeds give this bread a wonderful flavor.
Serve it with an Asian-style soup or mild broth-based soup to allow the flavor to shine.

SESAME BÂTON

PREP:

30 minutes

RISE:

1 hour 35 minutes

BAKE:

30 minutes

OVEN:

375°F

MAKES:

15 servings

2½   to 3 cups all-purpose flour

1   package active dry yeast

1   teaspoon salt

1   cup warm water (120°F to 130°F)

1   teaspoon toasted sesame oil

¼   cup sesame seeds, toasted

1   egg white, beaten

1 In a large mixing bowl stir together 1 cup of the flour, yeast, and salt. Add the warm water and the oil; beat with an electric mixer on low to medium speed for 30 seconds, scraping bottom and sides of bowl. Beat on high speed for 3 minutes. Using a wooden spoon, stir in half of the sesame seeds and as much of the remaining flour as you can.

2 Turn out dough onto a lightly floured surface. Knead in enough of the remaining flour to make a stiff dough that is smooth and elastic (8 to 10 minutes). Shape the dough into a ball; place in a lightly greased bowl, turning once to grease surface. Cover and let rise in a warm place until double (about 1 hour).

3 Punch down dough; turn out onto a lightly floured surface. Cover and let rest for 10 minutes. Lightly grease a large baking sheet; set aside.

4 On a lightly floured surface roll dough into a 15×10-inch rectangle. Starting from a long side, roll up into a spiral; seal well. Pinch ends and pull slightly to taper. Place loaf, seam side down, on prepared baking sheet. Brush with egg white. Sprinkle with remaining sesame seeds. Cover and let rise until nearly double (35 to 45 minutes).

5 Bake in a 375° oven for 30 to 35 minutes or until bread sounds hollow when lightly tapped. Immediately remove bread from baking sheet. Cool completely on a wire rack.

Nutrition Facts per serving: 89 cal., 2 g total fat (0 g sat. fat), 0 mg chol., 160 mg sodium, 15 g carbo., 1 g fiber, 3 g pro.

One bite leads to several more when you sample these rich, cheesy crackers. To save last-minute hassle, bake them ahead and freeze for up to 2 weeks.

CHEDDAR-PECAN CRACKERS

1   cup sharp cheddar cheese, shredded (4 ounces)

¼   cup butter

¼   teaspoon dried thyme leaves, crushed

⅛   teaspoon cayenne pepper

¾   cup all-purpose flour

½   cup finely chopped pecans

     Nonstick cooking spray

1 In a medium mixing bowl bring cheese and butter to room temperature (about 30 minutes).

2 With an electric mixer beat cheese and butter until combined. Add thyme and cayenne pepper. Beat until combined. Using a wooden spoon, stir in flour and pecans until combined. Form into a ball. Shape into an 8-inch log. Wrap with plastic wrap and chill for at least 4 hours or until the mixture is firm.

3 Lightly coat a baking sheet with cooking spray. With a sharp knife, cut dough into ⅛-inch slices. Place on prepared baking sheet. Bake in a 350° oven about 10 minutes or until lightly browned. Cool on wire racks.

Nutrition Facts per cracker: 26 cal., 2 g total fat (1 g sat. fat), 4 mg chol., 20 mg sodium, 1 g carbo., 0 g fiber, 1 g pro.

PREP:
20 minutes

STAND:
30 minutes

CHILL:
4 hours

BAKE:
10 minutes per batch

OVEN:
350°F

MAKES:
about 60 crackers

INDEX

METRIC INFORMATION

The charts on this page provide a guide for converting measurements from the U.S. customary system, which is used throughout this book, to the metric system.

Product Differences

Most of the ingredients called for in the recipes in this book are available in most countries. However, some are known by different names. Here are some common American ingredients and their possible counterparts:

- **All-purpose flour** is enriched, bleached or unbleached white household flour. When self-rising flour is used in place of all-purpose flour in a recipe that calls for leavening, omit the leavening agent (baking soda or baking powder) and salt.
- **Baking soda** is bicarbonate of soda.
- **Cornstarch** is cornflour.
- **Golden raisins** are sultanas.
- **Green, red, or yellow sweet peppers** are capsicums or bell peppers.
- **Light-colored corn syrup** is golden syrup.
- **Powdered sugar** is icing sugar.
- **Sugar** (white) is granulated, fine granulated, or castor sugar.
- **Vanilla** or vanilla extract is vanilla essence.

Volume and Weight

The United States traditionally uses cup measures for liquid and solid ingredients. The chart below shows the approximate imperial and metric equivalents. If you are accustomed to weighing solid ingredients, the following approximate equivalents will be helpful.

- 1 cup butter, castor sugar, or rice = 8 ounces = $^1/_2$ pound = 250 grams
- 1 cup flour = 4 ounces = $^1/_4$ pound = 125 grams
- 1 cup icing sugar = 5 ounces = 150 grams

Canadian and U.S. volume for a cup measure is 8 fluid ounces (237 ml), but the standard metric equivalent is 250 ml.

1 British imperial cup is 10 fluid ounces.

In Australia, 1 tablespoon equals 20 ml, and there are 4 teaspoons in the Australian tablespoon.

Spoon measures are used for smaller amounts of ingredients. Although the size of the tablespoon varies slightly in different countries, for practical purposes and for recipes in this book, a straight substitution is all that's necessary. Measurements made using cups or spoons always should be level unless stated otherwise.

Common Weight Range Replacements

Imperial / U.S.	Metric
$^1/_2$ ounce	15 g
1 ounce	25 g or 30 g
4 ounces ($^1/_4$ pound)	115 g or 125 g
8 ounces ($^1/_2$ pound)	225 g or 250 g
16 ounces (1 pound)	450 g or 500 g
$1^1/_4$ pounds	625 g
$1^1/_2$ pounds	750 g
2 pounds or $2^1/_4$ pounds	1,000 g or 1 Kg

Oven Temperature Equivalents

Fahrenheit Setting	Celsius Setting*	Gas Setting
300°F	150°C	Gas Mark 2 (very low)
325°F	160°C	Gas Mark 3 (low)
350°F	180°C	Gas Mark 4 (moderate)
375°F	190°C	Gas Mark 5 (moderate)
400°F	200°C	Gas Mark 6 (hot)
425°F	220°C	Gas Mark 7 (hot)
450°F	230°C	Gas Mark 8 (very hot)
475°F	240°C	Gas Mark 9 (very hot)
500°F	260°C	Gas Mark 10 (extremely hot)
Broil	Broil	Grill

*Electric and gas ovens may be calibrated using Celsius. However, for an electric oven, increase Celsius setting 10 to 20 degrees when cooking above 160°C. For convection or forced air ovens (gas or electric), lower the temperature setting 25°F/10°C when cooking at all heat levels.

Baking Pan Sizes

Imperial / U.S.	Metric
9×1$^1/_2$-inch round cake pan	22- or 23×4-cm (1.5 L)
9×1$^1/_2$-inch pie plate	22- or 23×4-cm (1 L)
8×8×2-inch square cake pan	20×5-cm (2 L)
9×9×2-inch square cake pan	22- or 23×4.5-cm (2.5 L)
11×7×1$^1/_2$-inch baking pan	28×17×4-cm (2 L)
2-quart rectangular baking pan	30×19×4.5-cm (3 L)
13×9×2-inch baking pan	34×22×4.5-cm (3.5 L)
15×10×1-inch jelly roll pan	40×25×2-cm
9×5×3-inch loaf pan	23×13×8-cm (2 L)
2-quart casserole	2 L

U.S. / Standard Metric Equivalents

$^1/_8$ teaspoon = 0.5 ml	
$^1/_4$ teaspoon = 1 ml	
$^1/_2$ teaspoon = 2 ml	
1 teaspoon = 5 ml	
1 tablespoon = 15 ml	
2 tablespoons = 25 ml	
$^1/_4$ cup = 2 fluid ounces = 50 ml	
$^1/_3$ cup = 3 fluid ounces = 75 ml	
$^1/_2$ cup = 4 fluid ounces = 125 ml	
$^2/_3$ cup = 5 fluid ounces = 150 ml	
$^3/_4$ cup = 6 fluid ounces = 175 ml	
1 cup = 8 fluid ounces = 250 ml	
2 cups = 1 pint = 500 ml	
1 quart = 1 litre	

What's for Dinner? **FIND THE ANSWER HERE**

Better Homes and Gardens.
BIGGEST BOOK OF EASY CANNED SOUP RECIPES
Skillet Dinners • Casseroles
Slow Cooker Meals

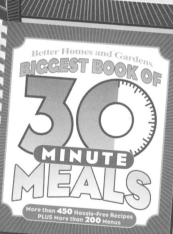

THE NUMBER ONE **#1** NATIONAL BEST SELLER
Better Homes and Gardens
BIGGEST BOOK OF SLOW COOKER RECIPES
CHAPTERS: 5-Ingredient Recipes & One-Dish Dinners

Better Homes and Gardens.
BIGGEST BOOK OF GRILLING
Hundreds of Sizzlin' Recipes for Charcoal and Gas
PLUS: Sassy Sauces, Rubs, and Marinades

Better Homes and Gardens.
BIGGEST BOOK OF CASSEROLES
MORE THAN **380** Delicious Comfort Food Favorites

Better Homes and Gardens
BIGGEST BOOK OF 30 MINUTE MEALS
More than **450** Hassle-Free Recipes
PLUS More than **200** Menus

Get dinner to the table fast
with delicious recipes the whole family will enjoy!

Meredith® BOOKS